TV a-Go-Go

Rock on TV from American Bandstand to American Idol

Jake Austen

CHICAGO
REVIEW
PRESS

An A Cappella Book

Library of Congress Cataloging-in-Publication Data
Austen, Jake.
TV-a-go-go: rock on TV from American Bandstand to American Idol / Jake
Austen.— 1st ed.
p. cm.
Includes bibliographical references and index.
ISBN 1-55652-572-9
1. Rock music on television. 2. Music television—United States—History
and criticism. I. Title.
PN1992.8.M87A88 2005
791.43'657—dc22
2005000514

Cover design: Rachel McClain

Cover images: Front cover photographs: *American Bandstand* and
Hullabaloo images copyright © Michael Ochs Archive.com; *American Idol*
image copyright © FremantleMedia Ltd.; televisions comks13413\Getty
Archives, LS015008\Getty Archives, LS018346\Getty Archives,
LS016154\Getty Archives, AA053793\Getty Archives

Interior design: Pamela Juárez

© 2005 by Jake Austen
All rights reserved
First edition
Published by Chicago Review Press, Incorporated
814 North Franklin Street
Chicago, Illinois 60610
ISBN 1-55652-572-9
Printed in the United States of America
5 4 3 2 1

*To my daughter Maiya, the most musical and
telegenic person I know; to my wife Jacqueline,
whose love and support makes all my work
possible; and to my parents, who obviously let me
watch too much TV growing up*

Contents

Acknowledgments

I would like to especially acknowledge Jack and Elaine Mulqueen, who have inspired me profoundly, and also offer gratitude to the following folks whose generosity of time, talent, and resources made this book possible: Bob Abrahamian, Chase Adams, Ben Austen, John Battles, Ken Burke, Art Fein, Gary Pig Gold, Barbara Holt, Phil Milstein, Jim Newberry, James Porter, Domenic Priore, Jacqueline Stewart, Nikki Stewart, Yuval Taylor, and the movers and shakers in the *Soul Train* Yahoo group.

Introduction

Ten years ago I found myself sitting in the Bartlett Hills Golf Club restaurant in Bartlett, Illinois, a quaint suburban village forty-five minutes from Chicago. Jack Mulqueen, a polite, soft-spoken, devoutly religious sexagenarian, was treating me to the blandest meal I'd ever tasted. A friend of mine was writing an article about Mulqueen and had asked me to go to his home to pick up some archival photographs. It seems that in the 1960s Mulqueen had produced a local dance show called *Kiddie-a-Go-Go* that featured preteens frugging, swimming, and ponying to the hits of the day. After a pleasant afternoon enjoying Mulqueen and his wife Elaine's hospitality I headed home to the South Side of Chicago, my mission accomplished. The photos were in hand, and to make my journey worthwhile Mulqueen had thrown in a videotape of *Kiddie-a-Go-Go*.

At some time during the next week my wife and I popped the tape into the VCR. My jaw dropped. Though the concept seemed simple—kids dance around—the show was mind-blowing. Elaine (as "Pandora," the mod harlequin) led a hootenanny that was raw, ridiculous, and sublimely surreal. The dancers displayed both the awkward self-consciousness and the total abandon that mark the start and finish lines of the pursuit of cool. The editing and camerawork were as instinctual, imperfect, and dynamic as the best garage rock. The wide shots of the pint-size terpsichoreans evoked a sense of both modernist kinetic artwork and stylized ethnographic ritual. While the rigid formal aspects of television were all in place, the energy of this show somehow fulfilled rock 'n' roll's promise of actual chaos and, to a degree, danger (those children were swept up in hypnotic rites!).

This was possibly the best music-themed television show I had ever seen, which meant that Mulqueen—that mild-mannered gentleman, a bespectacled Bob Newhart look-alike—was one of the greatest rock 'n' roll TV producers of all time!

But that didn't make any sense. This man was no rock 'n' roller. Mulqueen isn't in Howard Stern's demographic; he's in Paul Harvey's. So how could he be so good at capturing the elusive spirit of American teenage music on the boob tube?

Courtesy Jack Mulqueen

Rock critics and the pop music intelligentsia have long viewed authenticity as one of the most crucial elements of rock music. The Alan Lomax field recordings of rock's raw, rural predecessors; Elvis' teenage sexual fury; *Sgt. Pepper's* uncompromised artistic statements; and the rappers who rhyme about gunplay and then die in a hail of bullets have all become icons of legitimacy, spawning reams of celebratory or analytical rock journalism.

But television, print media's usurping sibling, has always demonstrated either disinterest in or disrespect for "realness" by presenting to the kids of America their own music only after coloring it with a tint of artifice darker than Dick Clark's hair dye. Despite rock 'n' roll's King being forced to sing to a dog (in matching tuxedos), despite make-believe bands made of figurative (and literal) puppets, and despite the proliferation of elaborate music videos often designed to hide the shortcomings of "artists," something amazing happened. Was it because the kids didn't notice everything was counterfeit? Or was it perhaps because something real (or, at least, really entertaining) emerged from the falseness? Somehow the fake Monkees shared the charts with the real Beatles. Somehow rebellious Tupac and Slayer fans found themselves voting for corny, wholesome American Idols. And somehow the contrived creations of pleasant squares like Mulqueen captured the unhinged energy of rock 'n' roll with far greater clarity than most long-haired, hotel-trashing, guitar-smashing hooligans ever could.

Maybe having acts lip-synch to their recordings delivered exactly what the audience wanted—a moving image to go with a perfect-sounding record. Maybe the power of the Beatles on *The Ed Sullivan Show* was enhanced because they stood where the producers told them (as opposed to hundreds of other bands' free, loose, and unmemorable *Saturday Night Live* performances). And perhaps it's more fun to see a marginally talented teen such as Avril Lavigne deliver pop perfection in a slick music video than to watch her struggle through a live performance. The soul of rock 'n' roll is certainly wild, raw, and dangerous. But as television has proven over and over again in the last half-century, one of the best ways to present this energy is to impose structure, make it adhere to the laws of entertainment passed down from vaudeville stage to vaudeville stage, and, ultimately, constrain it to fit within a box situated right in your living room.

The idiosyncratic history of rock on TV as presented in this book serves two missions. In the essays contained herein I will offer opinionated histories of underdocumented aspects of rock on TV (cartoon rock bands, black-audience music programming, punk on television). For the overdocumented subjects (the Monkees, Dick Clark, 1956 Elvis Presley on TV), I will try to examine why the artifice of rock 'n' roll on TV feels so good to me.

When I watch rock music on TV I want to be profoundly entertained. To ensure this experience I put my trust in craftsmen, visionaries, and hacks alike, everyone responsible for making rock 'n' roll rebellion fit onto the family-friendly stage. I don't expect watching a TV show to give me the palpable energy of a live concert or to be as intimate and profound as a meditative late-night listen to an album via headphones. But in some ways what I expect—and often get—is better, more direct, and less pretentious than any other presentation of rock 'n' roll. *Nothing* makes me feel like a crazed fourteen-year-old girl in 1964 the way watching the Beatles on *Ed Sullivan* can. *Nothing* makes me feel funkier than watching a 1973 *Soul Train* line. These are transformative, visceral experiences, possible only because the makers of television rarely consider rock 'n' roll a sacred art form. The efficiency and impact of lip-synching, "fake" bands, image over talent, and scripted interviews makes perfect sense to them.

In this book I want to present both a big picture and a celebration of these usually overlooked, oft-ridiculed moments. Obviously a comprehensive overview of all rock on TV is impossible. In the 1950s and 1960s it was feasible to catch every nationally televised moment of rock-oriented programming and still be a functioning human. But today, between cable music channels, syndicated entertainment programs, network musical reality shows, and the endless coverage on gossip and news shows of pop stars' shenanigans and legal woes, there are several hundred hours of new music-related programming every week. No one writer could cover everything and nobody would want to read a book that did. But this book is absurdly broad anyway. I'm asking baby boomers to give my musings on *Making the Band II* a chance and Generation Z kids to give my ramblings on Bo Diddley a whirl.

This book features ten freestanding but interlocking essays on various facets of TV rock history. Though the book is arranged more or less chronologically (*Ed Sullivan* toward the beginning, reality TV toward the end), many chapters span decades. The section on dance shows, for example, covers more than half a century.

As an oasis of relief after ten hefty chapters I offer a couple of appendixes that provide dozens of small, tasty chunks of TV rock highlights from around the world and across history. Whether you approach this book as a fun, nostalgic romp or as a somewhat scholarly defense of an art form that is widely considered "low," *TV-a-Go-Go* strives to be as satisfying as lying on the couch and bopping your head to your favorite band on TV.

Meeting Mulqueen profoundly changed my life. After multiple viewings of the *Kiddie-a-Go-Go* tape, my wife and I went down to Chicago's cable access network and signed up to produce our own dance show for kids, *Chic-a-Go-Go*. After almost a decade on the tube we have made hundreds of episodes featuring children dancing to weird music and rock stars being harassed by Ratso, our puppet host. I've done many things in my life, but few have been as satisfying as getting Robo from Black Flag to tell the kids, "School is cool," having the Shirelles sing "Happy Birthday" to my puppet, or watching the members of Cheap Trick flirt with a rat made from an old sock. Of course, our goofy noncommercial endeavor in no way gives me a feel for what it is really like to claw and hustle to create professional rock 'n' roll TV. But the production experience has given me a pretty good eye for watching old (and new) music shows, which I do with great frequency these days.

And that's another result of meeting the Mulqueens. After their video proved so inspirational, I went deep into the world of obscure-TV-show video swapping, where treasures are there for the taking if you have two VCRs, some good stuff to trade, and a hunch that the Romanian Michael Jackson fanatic who claims to have that elusive *Soul Train* episode is operating in good faith. With the advent of DVD complete-season box sets, this weird world has become more mainstream; obsessive TV collecting has now shifted from the underground to K-Mart. And that's a good thing.

So all you TV rock fans out there—and that includes anyone who ever danced along with *Bandstand*, stayed up late to see your favorite artist on *Saturday Night Live*, or voted on *American Idol*—check out what I have to say here. I hope you groove to it, and if you disagree with something, I'd love to talk about it . . . right after I watch this Romanian bootleg of a Japanese-subtitled *Soul Train* episode.

> "We gathered round to hear the sound comin' on the little screen / The grief had passed, the old men laughed, and all the girls screamed"
> —John Fogerty ("I Saw It on TV")

Rock Around the Box

Proto TV Rock and the Order of St. Sullivan

"Ladies and gentlemen," the gargoyle of an emcee announced to his rapt studio and vast TV audiences, "as everybody knows, whenever any new musical trend has evinced itself in the popular field, the first area to find out about it in advance is Harlem." His audiences had to wait a bit longer to learn the name of the Next Big Thing as the host's tongue got tangled in a string of his signature mala-propisms. "Roll . . . rhythm and, uh . . . rhythm and roll . . . rhythm and color. . . ." Finally, he managed to locate his desired phrase: *"Rhythm and blues!"*

The appellation Ed Sullivan stumbled upon with such difficulty that night—Sunday, November 20, 1955—was incorrect. When that "wonderful folk-blues singer" Bo Diddley kicked off Sullivan's presentation of Dr. Jive's Apollo The-ater–based musical revue, what he was playing was *not* R&B. Instead, Diddley was introducing *rock 'n' roll* to America's living rooms.

1

At its best, rock 'n' roll boils down the cultural miscegenation of American music to its most potent concentration. This perfectly describes the hypnotizing, pounding, rhythm-driven music that guitarist Diddley—along with drummer Clifton James, tuba-player-turned-maracas-genius Jerome Green, and second guitarist Bobby Parker—unleashed that night. During the 1950s many R&B artists had met the musical criteria for rock 'n' roll, but only a few grasped the intangible elements that marked its cross-pollination of R&B, hillbilly, blues, country, jazz, Irish music, boogie-woogie, and other folk sounds. Saturated with super-cool attitude, doing a sly, funky dance across the TV screen, and singing "Bo Diddley"—a theme song that balanced nursery rhyme innocence with dirty-joke naughtiness—Diddley on *Sullivan* made these intangibles downright tangible.

Honoring the ancestors more overtly than his peers, Bo's chanting praise songs incorporated a distinctly African beat. But he also sent a message to future long-haired metal guitarists, uncouth punks, and suburban garage rockers, announcing a new religion that involved the stroking worship of a phallic idol.

Bo Diddley. Courtesy Jake Austen

Diddley spent the last fifty-five seconds of a performance that clocked in at less than two minutes intimately engaged with his guitar—a guitar with a distorted, damaged tone that sang like a human being in a voice simultaneously joyous and mournful. Diddley was rock 'n' roll's first guitar hero. He was no shredding Eddie Van Halen; his playing was minimalist and rudimentary. But that simplicity is part of rock's invitation to untrained teenagers, and when Diddley took his bow before giving up the stage to the purer R&B of Lavern Baker and the rest of Dr. Jive's all-stars, he had baptized network TV with rock 'n' roll. He wasn't the TV rock messiah; his appearance didn't cause the world to move. But his big beat presaged something grand on the horizon. In less than a year, everyone would understand.

Experimental TV stations were set up around the United States and TV sets were commercially available by the late 1930s. After a half-decade break in the 1940s when broadcasting was suspended during World War II, America was ready to suckle at the boob tube. In 1947 there were more than 100,000 TV sets in the United States, representing about 0.5 percent of the nation's homes. But within the next five years more than half of all American families adopted an idiot box. TV launched some of its most enduring shows immediately, and before the 1950s dawned viewers were chuckling with *Howdy Doody* (NBC, 1947–1960; syndicated, 1976), nodding along to *Meet the Press* (NBC, 1947–present), and wondering why a tongue-tied, stone-faced gnome was hosting his own variety show, *Toast of the Town*, later called *The Ed Sullivan Show* (CBS, 1948–1971).

Music-themed shows were an important part of TV programming from the start. TV has always existed primarily to sell things (initially to sell TV sets themselves, as the first licensed network, Dumont, was owned by a TV manufacturer). But early TV cast itself as more than a tool for commerce. Bringing opera and classical music to the airwaves demonstrated that the medium could deliver high culture to the masses, and early viewers tuned in to shows like *Chicago Symphony Chamber Orchestra* (NBC, 1951–1952), *Television Recital Hall* (NBC, 1951–1954), *Opera Cameos* (Dumont, 1953–1955), *Mantovani* (NBC, 1958–1959), and even *Opera vs. Jazz* (ABC, 1953), which wasn't nearly as confrontational as it sounds. Even lowbrow music was packaged as culturally relevant, with semi-naughty entertainment presented in a historical context on *Gay Nineties Review* (ABC, 1948–1949), a vaudeville revival hosted by an octogenarian stage veteran, and *Captain Billy's Mississippi Music Hall* (CBS, 1948), another re-creation of nineteenth-century entertainment.

But these shows were not hits. The mainstream didn't want high culture. Early TV audiences reacted more positively to wrestling, boxing, roller derby, and cowboy movies than to operas, symphonies, plays, and orations. And when it came to music, Americans were strictly middlebrow. With the exception of Dumont, the TV networks had previously been radio networks, and many of the singing stars and musical shows they brought to the early airwaves had established themselves already as the bland, reliable favorites of America's housewives.

The Perry Como Show (NBC, 1948–1950, 1955–1963; CBS, 1950–1955) was a variety program hosted by barber-turned-singer Como, one of the most laid-back singers in pop history (on *SCTV* Eugene Levy parodied Como's undemonstrative style by presenting a faux Como TV special where the singer didn't get out of bed). Como had a pleasant voice that showed no grit and little emotion, and his program was as vanilla as his singing. But vanilla is a popular flavor, and America gladly traveled down the middle of the road with him. Though occasionally he would have some rocking guests (Hank Williams, Fats Domino, the Everly Brothers), the sublimely serene Como wasn't fond of rock 'n' roll (he seemed disgusted by Carl Perkins when Perkins performed "Blue Suede Shoes" on the show). But unlike some of his peers, he was unscathed by rock's onslaught and stayed his bland course, making TV specials until 1994.

Ted Mack's *Original Amateur Hour* (Dumont, 1947–1949; NBC, 1949–1954, 1957–1958; ABC, 1955–1957, 1960; CBS, 1959, 1960–1970; Family Channel, 1992) was not unlike today's *American Idol*, presenting up-and-coming performers and letting home viewers vote to determine a winner (albeit with postcards, not text messaging). Like *American Idol*, it showcased youngsters making dull, adult music that suppressed the combination of energy and innocence that makes teens interesting. One notable exception took place on September 9, 1956. Immediately following Elvis Presley's *Ed Sullivan* debut, the *Amateur Hour* welcomed the Rock 'n' Roll Trio. Johnny Burnette, Dorsey Burnette, and Paul Burlison were three of Memphis's most talented musicians and this TV exposure led to a record deal and an excellent (though poor-selling) album. But to neutralize the trio's driving rhythms, the episode also featured a number of typical *Amateur Hour* acts: a harpist, two classically trained vocalists, four vanilla pop acts, a yodeler, and a mime.

The show that best exemplified pre–rock 'n' roll music programming was *Your Hit Parade* (NBC, 1950–1958; CBS, 1958–1959, 1974). Each week the show's cast sang its interpretations of the country's seven top tunes (determined by a mysterious survey), plus a few familiar chestnuts. Eileen Wilson, Snooky Lanson, Dorothy Collins, and other well-scrubbed songbirds sang the compositions accom-

panied by an orchestra led by Raymond Scott (decades after his eccentric, visionary compositions with the Raymond Scott Quintette that Warner Brothers drew
from to create the soundtracks to its most outrageous cartoons). *Your Hit Parade*
was known for its army of dancers (including a young Bob Fosse), gaudy sets, and
ornate costumes. Its elaborate production numbers created literal and fantasy
interpretations of pleasant piffle like "Peter Cottontail," "Come On-A My House,"
"Glow Worm," "How Much Is That Doggy in the Window," and "The Ballad of
Davy Crocket." If a song was on the charts week after week a new visual interpretation was required each time, leading to numerous incarnations of lushly choreographed hokum.

Your Hit Parade had been popular on radio since 1935, but by the mid-1950s
popular music was taking a new direction. Fans were beginning to define "hits" as
specific to certain artists, rather than as catchy song crafting. "In the record industry," NBC producer Parker Gibbs lamented to *Billboard* in 1957, "it is becoming
more apparent that the interpretation of a song or the 'sound' of a record is the
selling factor." So when it came time to give LaVern Baker's "Tweedlee Dee" and
Elvis Presley's songs the *Your Hit Parade* treatment, the prim, pretty women in ball
gowns and handsome Snookys in ties would no longer cut it.

By the mid-1950s the first wave of TV children, weaned on Howdy Doody's
doings, were hitting their teen years. The spectacle of *All Star Wrestling* and the
gut appeal of TV cowboys (and wild Indians) had primed them perfectly for the
rock 'n' roll bands that began to get TV exposure. On the fateful Sunday when
Bo beat on his musical phallus, a Pandora's box was opened and TV rock 'n' roll
was born.

Critics, fans, and cultural scholars have cited all sorts of dates as the birth of
rock 'n' roll, including the 1947 recording of Roy Brown's "Good Rockin' Tonight,"
Jackie Brenston and Ike Turner's 1951 "Rocket 88" recording session, and disk
jockey Alan Freed's March 21, 1952, Moondog's Coronation Ball. That massive
concert, featuring Paul "Hucklebuck" Williams, Screaming Jay Hawkins, and the
Dominoes, was shut down by the fire marshals shortly after it began because thousands of young revelers nearly started a riot. The idea that rock 'n' roll was born
out of a moment when upbeat R&B promoted by a jive-talking huckster moved
a mighty mass of people to congregate and unleash the savage fury of youth is an
appealing creation myth because it involves audience reception instead of artistic endeavor.

Frequently Elvis Presley is credited as the father of the movement (as in a recent *Rolling Stone* story entitled "Truck Driver Invents Rock & Roll"). Recognizing Presley's role as the beautiful white messenger who recontextualizes R&B as rock 'n' roll is legitimate (he really did do that), but certainly Presley's predecessors, black and white, made songs and records that sounded like rock 'n' roll. However, the phenomenon isn't just about the music. It is about kids exerting their wills in emotional and economic ways, leading America to become the youth-centered culture it remains today. For rock 'n' roll to be more than a cross-cultural musical footnote, there has to be the frenzy, and it has to be white girls with spending cash doing the frenzying. Marking rock 'n' roll's birth is not only about using aesthetic criteria to determine the sonic attributes of the genre, but, more importantly, it's also about recognizing the moments when certain audiences—those with access to money—*embrace* the music. Numerous factors (including postwar economics, the introduction of the 45-rpm record, and Moondog and his ilk spinning R&B records for white listeners) culminated in the mania that developed around Presley. Even when Presley's earliest records were released on the country music charts, the audience reaction indicated that something new was happening. Even on tour with Hank Snow, if you made blond girls in saddle shoes shake, rattle, and roll, you might be a rock 'n' roller.

It is this shift in reception that marks the beginning of rock 'n' roll. History can't consider even the rockingest, wildest R&B, honky-tonk, boogie-woogie, jump-blues, hillbilly, hot jazz, and backwoods musical messes anything but proto-rock leading up to the real thing. It is not simply a matter of race. Bill Haley and the Comets were a white jump-blues band that rocked. Bo Diddley is black, but the *Ed Sullivan* performance of "Bo Diddley," his breakthrough hit that cast a spell over black and white concertgoers around the country, was rock 'n' roll. Despite similarities, it wasn't quite jump blues or R&B. Five minutes after Bo left the stage Willis "Gator Tail" Jackson unleashed an insane performance that dwarfed Diddley's in terms of wildness. Jackson went totally ape-shit, playing breakneck-speed, honking, skronking saxophone while falling on the ground, jumping like a maniac, and making his horn sound like it was having a heart attack. But despite its fierceness and absurdity, Jackson's performance wasn't rock 'n' roll. It was manic hard bop with a coarse R&B twist, the kind of music that spent the late 1940s and early 1950s helping to lay a foundation for the rock to come.

The many variety shows on the air in the 1950s made wild R&B familiar to Middle America. African American proto-rock 'n' rollers were no strangers to TV. As early as 1949 Ed Sullivan welcomed R&B pioneers such as the Ravens, with their brilliant bass vocalist Jimmy Ricks, to his show. Louis Jordan, the man synonymous with jump blues (the rocking marriage of big band swing and R&B drive), appeared on TV several times, including dynamic performances on *The Steve Allen Show* (CBS, 1950–1952, 1967–1969; NBC, 1956–1960; ABC 1961; syndicated, 1962–1964, 1967–1969, 1976). Big Joe Turner, perhaps rock 'n' roll's most direct ancestor, did a spot on *Showtime at the Apollo* (syndicated, 1954), tearing up a wild version of "Shake, Rattle and Roll." And, with apologies to he of the Gator Tail, the wildest black act to make waves over the airwaves was the underrated proto-rock act known as the Treniers.

Formed at Alabama State University in 1939, the band was fronted by identical twins Claude and Cliff Trenier and anchored by the great saxophonist Don Hill. Claude and Cliff performed and recorded with Jimmie Lunceford and Charlie Mingus before establishing their own band as a popular nightclub act in the late 1940s. They gained a reputation as exciting performers, on par with Louis Jordan (as a stage act, if not musically), and when TV came calling they were ready. Throughout the 1950s and 1960s the Treniers appeared on more TV shows than any pre-Motown black group, including *The Ed Sullivan Show*, *The Steve Allen Show*, *The Jackie Gleason Show* (CBS, 1952–1959, 1961–1970), *The Perry Como Show*, *The Colgate Comedy Hour* (NBC, 1950–1955), *The Jack Paar Show* (CBS, 1953–1956; NBC, 1962–1965), *The Tonight Show* (NBC, 1954–present), *Ernie Kovacs* (NBC, 1951–1952, 1955–1956; CBS, 1952–1953), *The Red Skelton Show* (NBC, 1951–1953, 1970–1971; CBS, 1953–1970), *The Mike Douglas Show* (syndicated, 1963–1982), *The Dean Martin Show* (NBC, 1965–1974), *The Merv Griffin Show* (NBC, 1962–1963; syndicated, 1965–1969, 1972–1986; CBS, 1969–1972), *The Joey Bishop Show* (ABC, 1967–1969), and numerous specials hosted by the likes of the Dorsey Brothers, Bing Crosby, and Paul Whiteman (on Whiteman's special they performed an outrageous fifteen-minute set).

The Treniers were in demand on TV for two reasons. They were well liked in the industry (Bill Cosby named the character Cliff Huxtable on *The Cosby Show* after Cliff Trenier) and, more importantly, they were incredibly entertaining. They were a flash act that specialized in dynamic, dazzling stage moves (both choreographed and improvised) and intensely energetic performances. The Treniers were models for both the cool choreography of the Temptations and the acrobatic dynamism of acts like James Brown and Jackie Wilson.

But they were *acceptable* on TV for a whole different reason. One key to differentiating proto-rock 'n' roll from rock 'n' roll is to gauge the public's reaction. The Treniers were handsome, especially the twins' dashing brother (and occasional lead singer) Milt. And though they kept their gyrations to a minimum on TV, their wild action-packed performances were full of the kind of virile, ener-

The Treniers. Courtesy Jake Austen

getic abandon that so terrified parents when Elvis Presley came along. They wore their conked hair long (so it would come loose during jumps and leaps, a la Cab Calloway), and if there was any doubt about where they were coming from, one only had to look at their song titles: "It Rocks, It Rolls, It Swings," "Rockin' On Sunday Night," "Rock 'n' Roll Call," "Good Rockin' Tonight." When they performed their raucous "Rockin' Is Our Bizness" on a 1954 episode of Martin and Lewis's *Colgate Comedy Hour*, the ultra-kinetic seven-person act made their presence more intense by squeezing into a tight configuration as if they were being forced to play in a closet. Before breaking down into some nuttiness involving Dino and Jerry dancing with the boys, the highlight of the segment involved the Treniers' famous "bug dance." A harbinger of pop locking, the bug dance featured each member pretending to be attacked by an itchy bug, exploding into a spastic, staccato dance solo, complete with limbs whirling, hair flying, hips swiveling, and face convulsing. This was *not* Perry Como! The Treniers were a wild, sexy, crazed band that rocked and rolled!

So why was there no parental outrage when the Treniers, the Ravens, Jordan, and Turner shook and rattled their way into America's living rooms?

Perhaps it was because of the prevailing perception that these performances were simply a continuation of a long tradition of blacks entertaining whites. A stereotype that had held since slavery was that blacks were inherently gifted singers and dancers. Historically this resulted in African Americans being put in demeaning performative situations (represented, for example, in the 1915 film *Birth of a Nation* in a segment that shows black slaves dancing for white visitors). But the first half of the twentieth century provided some exceptions to this dehumanizing dynamic; some performers were able to transcend the stereotype. Comedian Bert Williams became one of America's most popular entertainers in the early twentieth century, starring in the Ziegfeld Follies, bringing dignity to racist minstrel-show conventions. In 1921 composers Eubie Blake and Noble Sissle, along with black vaudevillians Fluornoy Miller and Aubrey Lyles, brought the show *Shuffle Along* to Broadway, drawing in droves of sophisticated Manhattan theatergoers before hitting the road and breaking the color line at white theaters around the country. This show is partially credited with launching the Harlem Renaissance, the black arts movement of the 1920s and 1930s during which whites gave financial support to black creativity. Harlem became a trendy destination for whites, and while the Cotton Club and its uptown neighbors certainly played up racist themes (wild jungle motifs, in particular) they also presented brilliant black performers such as Duke Ellington. It was precedents like these that made African American artists suitable for white mainstream TV viewers, even if their talents/innovations were not fully recognized. The reason white viewers didn't feel threatened was that they considered these performers acceptable family entertainment. Because the teenage girls weren't clamoring for Cliff Trenier, his wildness could be read as peppy instead of virile. That would change when the kids started choosing the channel.

Elvis Presley was a truck driver from Memphis with a thick lower lip that made him an adorable mama's boy and a sneering upper lip that made him a desirable bad boy. His clear, rich voice set the standard for rockabilly (an R&B/hillbilly hybrid, the compound word revealing that *rock* meant black music in the 1950s) and his dynamic swiveling hips and spasmodic dance moves turned young girls into swooning, screaming hormone factories. When RCA bought his contract from the visionary Sun label in 1955 they wanted to do to all the girls in America what Presley's concerts were doing to girls in the South.

Between January 28, 1956, and January 6, 1957, the twenty-one-year-old Presley performed on TV ten times on four different programs. A tenacious manager, a hardworking RCA record executive, and powerful William Morris agents secured the first gigs, but by midyear everyone wanted Presley. The hosts and producers of the shows he appeared on were indifferent or hostile toward rock 'n' roll, but that didn't matter. They very likely didn't like plate spinners or chimps on bicycles either, but they booked them just the same. What was important was that the early variety shows had filmed every kind of entertainment in the world, from opera to ventriloquists, from acrobats to dancing bears. Presley, with his wild wiggles and driving rhythms, was visual, compelling, potentially good TV.

When Presley and the TV crews collaborated the results were spectacular. However, TV was sometimes inept when it came to showing the always-cooperative Presley in his best light. Presley's first TV appearance was his best. *Stage Show* (CBS, 1954–1956) was a variety show starring bandleaders Jimmy and Tommy Dorsey. Produced by Jackie Gleason as a half-hour lead-in to his show, *Stage Show* was well named, as its most interesting aspect was its tremendous stage. Because of its size the show's directors were creative with the lighting design and on January 28, 1956, Presley reaped the benefit. In a tight composition that perfectly fit the TV screen, he was flanked by his guitarist Scotty Moore, leaning a little to the right, and his bassist Bill Black, whose upright bass was angled to the left. The result was a perfect V framing the young singer. A series of spotlights pooled around each musician, with a pitch-black background creating a dramatic ambience. As Presley ripped through a medley of "Shake, Rattle and Roll" and "Flip, Flop and Fly" his bubbling energy was apparent, but his already infamous gyrations were lost due to the tight shot. However, as soon as Presley erupted into a frenzy of spectacular spasms the director cut to an aerial shot, fully capturing the King in all his glory. Clearly the performers were completely complicit with their instructions on where to stand and when to move, and clearly the producers understood what made Presley special. The result was a TV segment that perfectly captured the dynamism of the act. Presley was electric; as he did the suggestive "Baby, Let's Play House" (neutered only slightly by the lyric change "be with another man" to "wed another man") the screaming girls reacted and he fed off them. When "you may have a pink Cadillac" bubbled from his vibrating body, Elvis swaggered like a cocky rookie boxer convinced his championship is inevitable.

On the return visit to the show Presley was positioned a full five feet in front of his band; they stood in dim shadows. Presley had gained a national reputation, which meant that he now deserved to have the spotlight all to himself. The ratings were strong for his four appearances but not spectacular. Had the ratings been to the moon Gleason might have given Presley more leeway, but since Gleason didn't like Presley's music in the first place, the smattering of complaints from viewers outraged at the singer's suggestive moves was enough to pull the plug. The option for the fifth and sixth appearances was declined.

Presley's appearances on *The Milton Berle Show* (NBC, 1948–1956; ABC, 1966–1967) were less visually impressive but more culturally relevant. His first visit to the program took place on an aircraft carrier where Presley and Uncle Milty (a TV god in the 1940s but fading fast in the 1950s) entertained the troops and screaming girls (who were bussed in from a high school). The episode did not look good (when it comes to shows shot on aircraft carriers Cher and George W. Bush could teach NBC a few things). The most notable thing was a skit in which Berle comes out in a clown suit that approximates Presley's cat clothes and introduces himself as Melvin Presley, Elvis's twin. While Berle's manic impersonation was kind of funny, and while seeing beautiful Elvis and grotesque Milty side by side was interesting, the notable thing here is that Presley had actually had a real twin, a stillborn brother.

Presley's next *Milton Berle* appearance proved more auspicious. Shot in a studio this time the production was rudimentary and featured boring lighting and cable access–level editing. However, the performance was far from average. A lame duck certain to be canceled soon, Berle had no fears about showcasing the young man's percolating and vibrating—and Presley took full advantage. At the end of "Hound Dog" he signaled the band to follow him on an extended ad-lib reprising the song as a slow, bawdy burlesque number, with the crowd erupting with every staccato flourish. Presley seemed wicked and crafty as he flirted with the camera and contorted his body, but at the same time he was not serious at all. It is this balance of savagery and silliness that made his youthful image so intriguing. The pundits, however, were not amused.

The *Milton Berle* performance set off a firestorm of criticism that accused Presley of everything from inciting juvenile delinquency to causing teenage idiocy. The idea that he posed a danger to America's youth led to a judge barring him from gyrating at a local concert and the *New York Times* suggesting that schools add sex education classes to temper the damage Presley had likely done to teenage morals. NBC wanted no part of this controversy, and promised the public that

Presley would not bump or grind during his scheduled appearance on *The Steve Allen Show*. But it was Allen himself who decided that a mere ban on pelvis-wiggling was insufficient.

Steve Allen was a TV pioneer, helping to launch the *Tonight Show*, and bringing a smart, anarchic sense of humor to the medium that inspired such future icons as David Letterman. Allen created some of TV's most unusual moments, like *Meeting of the Minds* (PBS, 1977–1981), a talk show on which he interviewed historical figures (played by actors). He was one of the funniest men on early TV and his wry wit was a pleasant contrast to TV's rampant low humor (Allen's soft-spoken ad-libs yielded a comparable laugh count to Uncle Milty's howling buffoonery). However, Allen is not a universally beloved figure, as his legacy includes a reputation among rock 'n' roll fans as an enemy of the music.

Steve Allen had no obligation to like rock' n' roll. And he didn't. Though he occasionally had a left-handed compliment for Presley or Jerry Lee Lewis, or whimsical praise for the music ("I love rock, I don't care for roll that much . . ."), his genuine attitude was summed up in his 1994 book, *Reflections*. In that tome Allen assured youngsters who thought his dismissal of rock music was just a curmudgeon's reaction to the replacement of the old by the new that they were wrong. It was, he assured, "[a] fact that something superior has been replaced with something inferior," adding that "Rap 'music' is the reduction ad absurdum of a general trend since the mid-1950s away from the glorious, soaring, harmonically rich melodies characteristic of the Golden Age."

Allen was a genuine curmudgeon, and at times a hypocritical one. In 1999 he lent his face to the Parents Television Council, appearing in full-page newspaper ads declaring, "TV Is Leading Children Down a Moral Sewer." That was after appearing in an episode of *Homicide: Life on the Street* (NBC, 1993–2000) where he played a violent, foul-mouthed husband who kills a man in a failed attempt to murder his wife with a shotgun. He wrote several books of cultural criticism late in life accusing American culture of regressing and dumbing down, but Allen's literary contributions, particularly his later ones, were examples of, rather than exceptions to, this trend. Anyone who put aside a good book to read his 2001 work *Vulgarians at the Gate*, a large print, loosely researched, semi-coherent rant against the immorality of Tupac, *Shasta McNasty*, and everyone else, almost certainly became markedly dumber for the effort.

Rock fans had been peeved at Allen for decades by the time he wrote that book. One reason for this was Allen's signature routine in which he read lyrics from rock 'n' roll classics such as "Be Bop A Lula" as if they were erudite poetry. His dramatic oration meant to point out the lyrics' insipidness. While this can be funny (it was revived in the 1990s by the African American comedy show *In Living Color* with rap lyrics), it also points out Allen's misunderstanding of rock 'n' roll. Steve Allen came from the sheet music era, where songwriters crafted compositions that anyone could play around the piano at home. But rock 'n' roll has always been a performance medium, and the nonsense lyrics of Gene Vincent (or, especially, Little Richard) weren't meant to stand alone, but instead were expressions of the semi-coherent sexual frenzy barely contained within the recordings and live performances. Rock 'n' roll was about the excitement the artists pitched and the kids caught; it wasn't supposed to hold up when lyrics were amputated from the big beat.

But that comic bit was just one of Allen's misdemeanors. To (oversensitive) rock fans, the way Steve Allen treated Elvis Presley was his federal crime.

Allen thought Presley was talentless and absurd, and so he decided to goof on him. Allen set things up so that Presley would show his contrition by appearing in a tuxedo and singing his new song "Hound Dog" to an elderly basset hound in a matching tux. Always respectful, Presley did as good a job as anyone can be expected to do when dog-serenading. The dog was a little startled when Presley first started to sing, but for the most part it seemed bored. Presley was later featured in a mediocre cowboy sketch with Allen, Andy Griffith, and Imogene Coca. As "Tumbleweed Presley" his big joke was "I'm warning you galoots, don't step on my blue suede boots."

Prior to this show, there had been a huge buzz around Presley, and his controversial reputation should have been reason enough to write the funniest, sharpest material for this highly anticipated episode. Instead it was just average. More importantly, having seen Presley's spectacular performances on the preceding shows, Allen should have been excited to have him on. That was far from the case. Allen's misunderstanding of Presley was deep to the point of being almost pathological.

Appearing on the L.A. cable program *Art Fein's Poker Party* in 1992, Allen dismissed Presley's talent, comparing his voice to a nail's rasp and a buzz saw. "A beautiful sound he never had . . . it was chiefly his face, a cuteness, a likability." Ultimately Allen misunderstood not only Presley, but also his role in cultural history. "I made Elvis funny [on my show], he's not funny." Actually, Presley was relatively funny. He was constantly making jokes, his droll delivery was usually on beat, and he had a decent sense of humor (his video collection had Monty Python tapes among the NFL games and porn). More importantly, making Presley funny was not the most prudent use of a musical artist at the apex of his popularity. Allen had an opportunity to allow spectacular TV to happen. He didn't take it.

That didn't matter in the short run. Presley was so hot at the time that no hokey sketch was going to keep the kids away. Allen's ratings were spectacular and he clobbered his competitor Ed Sullivan, an extremely rare victory. Sullivan, though just as ego-driven as Allen, wouldn't make the same mistakes Steverino made.

As usual, when TV rock 'n' roll history was being made, Sullivan was presiding over it. The crown Sullivan wore as the king of TV rock 'n' roll, however, sat uncomfortably on his big head. Bo Diddley's pioneer 1955 appearance on his show went down in spite of, not because of, Sullivan. As legend tells it, some of Sullivan's people overheard Diddley casually singing Tennessee Ernie Ford's "Sixteen Tons" in the dressing room as Dr. Jive's Rhythm and Blues Review collectively prepared for its appearance. They asked Diddley to perform the song on the show that night. When the curtain parted Diddley instead unleashed his rocking theme song. Bo himself has told the story of his *Ed Sullivan* misadventure countless times, and like the children's game "telephone," the words transmogrify a bit with each telling. Diddley's alternate explanations include not being able to read the cue card lyrics for "Sixteen Tons" because of poor eyesight and misunderstanding the instructions and thinking he was supposed to do "Sixteen Tons" in addition to the song he had planned. He has even chalked it up to a typographical error ("They printed the program wrong with my name ["Bo Diddley"] followed by 'Sixteen Tons,' I just read the program and did what it said on there"). Bo offered a more likely explanation in his biography, *Living Legend*. "Chess [Diddley's recording label] tol' me that if I'da did 'Sixteen Tons' an' *not* 'Bo Diddley,' that would have been the end of my career right there—which, they were *right*, 'cause they were pushin', tryin' to sell my record." (Diddley later would record a version of "Sixteen Tons.")

Diddley continues, "So, Ed Sullivan says to me in plain words: 'You're the first black boy—quote—that ever double crossed me!' I was ready to *fight*, because I was a little young dude off the streets of Chicago, an' him callin' me 'black' in them days was as bad as sayin' 'nigger.' My manager says to me 'That's Mr. Sullivan!' I says: 'I don't give a shit about Mr. Sullivan, [h]e don't talk to *me* like that!' An' so he told me, he says: 'I'll see that you never work no more in show business. You'll never get another TV show *in your life!*'"

Diddley's perennial revisions make it difficult to determine exactly what happened, but the guitarist never did appear on the *The Ed Sullivan Show* again, and he didn't make it back to TV until well into the 1960s. As for Sullivan's racism, it's hard to say what he really felt about African Americans. A workaholic with many acquaintances but few friends, Sullivan was an enigma. He reportedly expressed harsh opinions of gays, communists, and competing columnists. But he always seemed supportive of blacks, not only as entertainers (he produced a black vaudeville revival show early in his career) but also for their church-bred conservative beliefs that conformed to the values he wanted his show to reflect. In *Living Legend* Diddley boasts of being, "the first black dude to be on *The Ed Sullivan Show*," but in fact Sullivan had black guests as early as 1949, when the Ravens performed "My Sugar Is So Refined." Other black celebrities who appeared prior to Diddley include Fletcher Henderson, Ethel Waters, Billy Eckstine, Pearl Bailey, the Ink Spots, Sarah Vaughan, Sammy Davis, Jr., Katherine Dunham, Jackie Robinson, Lena Horne, Joe Louis, Eartha Kitt, Sugar Ray Robinson, and the Harlem Globetrotters. Nat King Cole was a frequent guest who had appeared a few weeks prior to Diddley. In the 1960s, when Motown acts appeared on the show, Sullivan displayed a rare generosity with his smile. He was seemingly charmed, even enchanted, by Diana Ross.

But Presley was another story. Though he eventually called him a "real decent, fine boy" on the air, Sullivan was not initially impressed with the man who would be King, calling him "not my cup of tea," and publicly vowing that Presley wouldn't grace *The Ed Sullivan Show* stage. But he was not happy about being bested in the ratings by Allen. When recanting his vow (upon booking Presley for a mammoth $50,000 for three appearances) Sullivan offered only left-handed compliments, calling Presley a "pale replica" of Johnnie Ray. Of the infamous *Milton Berle* performance Sullivan offered, "I don't know why everybody picked on Presley. I thought the whole show was dirty and vulgar."

On the night of September 9, 1956, Presley's debut on his show, Sullivan was convalescing from a car accident so he watched at home—along with a spectacular 82.7 percent of TV viewers in America. Because important *Ed Sullivan* shows commanded larger audiences than his competitors could hope for, and because the media was complicit in hyping these shows as groundbreaking, everyone tuned in. And Presley's *Ed Sullivan* appearances were built up so mythically that everyone also felt obligated to be affected—either swept up in the excitement, outraged, disgusted, or disappointed. With this much attention and impact, Presley's *Ed Sullivan* debut stands as the first earthshaking TV rock moment. Elvis mythology says that Sullivan censored Presley by only shooting from the waist up, and Sullivan helped propagate this by telling *TV Guide*, "as for his gyrations, the whole thing can be controlled with camera shots." In truth Presley's whole body is in full view during his first visit, though the tame material he opened with made it clear that his manager, Colonel Parker, and he were using this show to try to convince adults that the singer didn't represent evil. Opening with the relatively mellow "Don't Be Cruel," Presley then introduced his new slow jam, "Love Me Tender," shot in loving close-ups of his pouting lips and sleepy-eyed face. Like the rockers to follow, from KISS to Poison to L.L. Cool J, Elvis would be blessed by the power of the mushy, hokey ballad. One million advance orders for the song poured into RCA over the next week. Not only were all the hypnotized girls screaming and swooning, they were also spending—a powerful demonstration to the music industry of TV's potential as a promotional tool.

For his second set Presley cut loose with a campy take on Little Richard's "Ready Teddy." Presley was shown head to toe, and numerous gyrations made the cut, but as promised, Sullivan had done some deft camera work, and with various zooms and odd angles (one shot from behind has Presley's shaking hips blocked by drums) nothing too salacious got out over the airwaves. Overall, Presley's *Ed Sullivan* performances didn't look as good as his *Stage Show* appearances, but wisely Sullivan made sure the microphones were positioned to catch all the screeches and squeals of the girls in the crowd, and their presence amply demonstrated what the rock 'n' roll phenomenon was all about. Unfortunately there are no prepared shots of screaming girls in the audience, and when the crowd is shown we see why. Most of the audience is made up of the same Eisenhower-era company men and their wives that were always in the Sullivan studio. To visually convey teenage-girl energy the young ladies need to be bunched together, an arrangement that Sullivan wouldn't overlook the next time rock 'n' roll went through a revolution on his stage.

Presley made two more appearances on *The Ed Sullivan Show*. It was less than four months between his first and third shows, but in that time Elvis had grown from a kid to a man. He'd completed his first movie and had a dozen hit singles (five number ones) under his belt. Twenty-two million dollars' worth of chintzy Elvis merchandise had been sold. Presley was a confident, happy, playful, almost giddy screen presence. Wearing an absurd gold lamé vest, and with his hair died midnight black, he looked somewhat silly, and not particularly dangerous. Oddly, this was the show that CBS decided to censor, and the cameras shot Presley only above the waist, a situation he countered by bringing "Don't Be Cruel" home with some odd flamenco arm flourishes. For his last number Elvis sang the gospel standard "Peace in the Valley" in a rich, deep, clear voice, his eyes turned toward heaven. His prayers were soon answered as the show ended with Sullivan, as he always did, saying what an outstanding guy his guest was. But (perhaps moved by the hymn) Sullivan may have actually meant it this time, as he sounded almost human and even came close to making eye contact.

Presley's exit from the Sullivan stage that night marked the beginning of the end of his tenure as a mortal. Colonel Parker feared overexposure so he decided to keep Presley off TV, and no shows were able to offer a fee large enough to sway that opinion. Presley's raging popularity also made concert tours increasingly chaotic and beyond the scope of what 1957 could handle. He was too big for TV, and too big for concerts. He purchased a huge, gated mansion and locked himself away from normality. His respite from this would come in early 1959 when he was drafted and shipped out to a German army base.

Presley would appear on TV only a few more times during his life. In 1959 his disembodied voice traveled across the ocean via phone line to a local L.A. teen show, *Wink Martindale's Dance Party*, to (falsely) deny a rumor that he was engaged. In late 1960 the tuxedo contingent officially welcomed Presley back from the army when he appeared on the *Frank Sinatra Timex Show* (ABC, 1959–1960). In 1968 he made a powerful return to TV in the spectacular *Singer Presents Elvis* (now known as the *'68 Comeback Special*). A ratings and artistic triumph, it featured a beautiful thirty-three-year-old Elvis looking equally comfortable in tight black leather and bluesy rock 'n' roll. In 1973 Colonel Parker arranged for NBC, and TV stations around the world, to broadcast *Elvis: Aloha from Hawaii via Satellite*. The show, which introduced the world to Elvis in his Captain Marvel white jumpsuit mode, was a global sensation (95 percent of Japanese TVs that were on that night were tuned to it) and spawned a number-one soundtrack LP (despite being released only for quadraphonic record players, a technical innovation that never caught on).

The King has enjoyed a far greater TV presence since his death, starting with *Elvis In Concert*, an elaborate concert special he taped the summer he died, which was ghoulishly broadcast on CBS in October 1977 two months after his demise. Over the ensuing decades there were a number of biographical made-for-TV movies and miniseries (one starring *Miami Vice*'s Don Johnson as Presley) as well as specials, documentaries, and even an ambitious but short-lived dramatic series about his early career called, simply, *Elvis* (ABC, 1990). But of the dozens of hours of televised Presley necrophilia, one show stands tall above the rest. It is a 1987 documentary that is a deftly crafted, smartly narrated (by Levon Helm) compilation of TV appearances from a magical year that stands as TV rock's Book of Genesis. It is called *Elvis '56*.

Presley didn't launch a rock 'n' roll offensive to liberate TV from the squares. In fact, he abandoned TV when he was at his hottest. By staying off the air, then leaving the country to be part of the U.S. Army, he perhaps protected his career from overexposure, but he certainly let TV rock calm down more than his initial promise had foretold.

One of the great myths of rock 'n' roll history is that as the 1950s turned into the 1960s rock 'n' roll disappeared until the Beatles raised it from the dead. This supposedly occurred because all the icons were abruptly lost: Elvis went into the army, Little Richard went into the ministry, Buddy Holly went to rock 'n' roll heaven, and both Jerry Lee Lewis and Chuck Berry went into little girls' personal space. They were replaced with safe, wussy teen idols cast by Dick Clark, and America lost rock 'n' roll until 1964 when the mop tops came over to remind us what it's all about.

But the idea of the dead rock 'n' roll period is bogus, as rock was being revitalized on two fronts during those years. A new breed of black artists such as James Brown and Stevie Wonder emerged to create not only unbelievable records but also a whole new wave of moves and sounds to be appropriated by non-innovators on both the white and black charts. Also, the American garage rock movement, which would absolutely explode after the Beatles' arrival, was off to a very healthy start, with the raw, powerful Northwest rock scene establishing itself with the Wailers (the greatest house party band of all time) and with the release of the ultimate garage single, "Surfin' Bird," by Minnesota's Trashmen.

But as far as national TV went, the myth holds up. Safe, smooth music was the new pop (actually, it was the old pre-rock pop back on top again) as Paul Anka, Neil Sedaka, and Barbra Streisand took to the airwaves. Though rock 'n' roll changed pop music by making it primarily youth oriented, the teen idols and early 1960s pop-oriented vocalists made records for kids that also met with parents' approval. Even the best acts that made prominent TV appearances, like the Everly Brothers and the Beach Boys, weren't exactly pelvis swiveling threats. Only the emergence of Jackie Wilson, who combined Rat Pack smoothness with James Brown dynamism, brought any real fire to prime-time music programming in those years.

But that would change on February 9, 1964, when Ed Sullivan once again emerged as the patron saint of TV rock, despite not being particularly fond of the music.

The Beatles were Sullivan's new superstars. Always on the lookout for overseas talent and impressed by their good manners (though not necessarily by their songs) he had signed them up early. His timing was impeccable, and he secured them for a pittance ($3,500 per show as opposed to more than $16,000 per show for Presley eight years prior) just before America succumbed to Beatlemania. The Beatles began as a group of leather-clad English lads honing their craft in the decadent German beat scene (their name a variation on the genre, like calling a band the Punkles or the Rapples). Cleaned up by manager Brian Epstein, they soon enraptured the world with their combination of catchy pop, cute looks, funny haircuts, witty charm, and distinct personalities (a rarity among groups in those days). Beatlemania caused young women to go into hysterics and young boys to buy guitars.

The show opened with Sullivan announcing that the Beatles had received a congratulatory telegram from Presley and Colonel Parker. He followed this with a boast that he believed the Beatles would be as big as his other discoveries, Topo Gigio the puppet mouse and the Singing Nun. With a minimum of mumbling he introduced the band and before they hit the first note the segment opened with the shots that had been missing from all of Presley's *Ed Sullivan* performances; finally the TV audience could *see* the screaming girls. The element that makes rock 'n' roll relevant, the receptive fan, was given screen time, and the result absolutely energized the show.

The Beatles opened with "All My Loving" and in their suits, ties, and Beatle boots they look like giddy kids playing dress-up. In case there was any question of where to look, the fantastic pop art set, a series of low-relief traffic-sign arrows, dramatically pointed toward the Beatles. The band is framed beautifully, their spacing and composition absolutely perfect for the screen, with Ringo's drum riser placing him at the perfect height so that every Beatle is of equal stature. Knowing this show was perhaps the most important he would ever do, director Tim Kiley created a meticulously shot sequence synchronized not only to the music but also to the band's movements. The cooperative Beatles stood on their marks and moved where they were supposed to—a fact that was made clear by George Harrison's journeys to and from Paul McCartney's microphone. Perfectly composed side views of the three singing Beatles were never compromised by Harrison's taking a step to his left or right. This may be the ultimate TV rock segment, not simply because of its popularity and its place in history (it emerged as the highest rated show in TV history to that point) but also because it was staged perfectly for the visual medium. It looked absolutely fantastic.

This triumph is in spite of the Beatles performance not being spectacular, in many ways less impressive than Presley's *Ed Sullivan* jaunt, and certainly far inferior to Presley's *Stage Show* appearance. Though they were world-beaters in England, were in the midst of conquering the United States, and were veterans of the German beat scene where bands became perfect performers by playing live shows forty hours a week, the boys seemed a little nervous and imperfect. McCartney's voice wasn't as clear as on record; John Lennon's harmonies were pretty bad, and they never bubbled with excitement or energy. But all of this was tempered by the enthusiastic screams of the enthralled audience composed almost completely of young girls. Lennon may not have sung all that well, but tell that to those two girls licking their lips or that girl in the nerdy glasses who almost cries.

With all the technical successes of the show there is one fun, but ultimately silly innovation: a sequence of superimposed names over each Beatle so the girls at home know who they are. With the perfect shot choreography and the elaborate set it is pretty amazing that they managed to miss a typo. But maybe it was intentional. After Lennon's fans are let down by the information "John: Sorry Girls, He's Married:" they can still imagine that the information beyond that second colon might keep hope alive. (as in ": He's getting divorced" or ": She has two weeks to live").

The Beatles did three songs, ending their first set with "She Loves You," followed by forty minutes of Beatle-free impressions, card tricks, comedy, and song and dance. Sullivan loved to book international performers and stacked the Beatles shows with British acts. Ironically, one of these performers would one day knock the Beatles off their pop chart perch. The London cast of *Oliver!* was on Broadway at the time, and starring as the Artful Dodger was little David Jones, who would a year later successfully audition to become one of the Monkees. On *The Ed Sullivan Show* tiny teenage Davy sang with confidence (and shrillness) and managed to roll his top hat down his arm and catch it. In 1967 he would do an even more impressive trick and outsell the Beatles.

Toward the end of the show the Beatles returned for two more songs on a new mod set. McCartney's voice sounded better, and there was some impressive swooping camera work. Sullivan was very pleased with the crowd, praising the kids for not rioting ("You've been a fine audience despite severe provocation"), and he made a point of shaking hands with the Beatles and calling them nice lads. The only real black mark on the show was that Sullivan didn't trust the Beatles to bring the show home. After "I Want to Hold Your Hold" he brought on the acrobatic, contortionist/puppet dance act Wells and the Four Fays.

The Beatles returned to *The Ed Sullivan Show* three times. The next week the show was shot at a Florida hotel. The set and sound were worse, but the Beatles' performance was much better; a week in the United States had boosted their self-confidence. The humidity had the boys covered in sweat (not too appealing on them, but pretty interesting later in the show when Mitzi Gaynor sang "Too Darn Hot" with her cleavage glistening with perspiration), and the crowd, perhaps drained from the weather, seems more dreamily enchanted than hysterical.

The show the next week was not live. It was taped in New York. The program was again exquisitely shot and the Beatles did fine during their three songs. But most interesting this time are some variations on the crowd shots. At one point a gaggle of teenage *boys* are shown coolly talking among themselves, ignoring the Beatles. And one screaming girl shows her intense, howling love for the Beatles then notices that she is on TV. As she stares at herself on a monitor her excitement and screaming intensify. Her reaction is a perfect reminder that part of the excitement of TV rock' n' roll is the thrill of TV.

The Beatles returned to Sullivan's stage one more time in late 1965, but by then they were another species. As a handsomer John led them through some of the tunes from their movie *Help!* it was very obvious that the cute boys were now confident genius men. The show had also gained technical sophistication, superimposing pre-filmed images of the Beatles over the performance, using innovative camera tricks, and creating a stunning set.

But one element remained constant. Sullivan was always a strange, awkward man who demonstrated no affection for or understanding of the music that made the little girls go wild. At the same time, he was a man whose ego made him glow with pride at roping in each generation's phenomenon, be it Elvis Presley, the Rolling Stones, Topo Gigio, the Supremes, the Singing Nun, Dr. Jive's Rhythm and Blues Revue, or even the Beatles. Reviewing the Beatles on *The Ed Sullivan Show* the *New York Times'* wet blanket Jack Gould couldn't get past their suits, calling the boys "conservative conformists." While they were polite, well-dressed, and musically mild, the Beatles ultimately were leaders, not followers. But Gould's confusion is understandable. Early TV rock producers had to perform a juggling act in which the rockers remained pleasing for the powerful, screeching audience, yet palatable to that audience's parents who still believed they were in charge. But as Sullivan proved time and time again, when a square guy puts something on a square screen even the roundest peg can fit perfectly.

2

Lip-Synch Traces

Dick Clark, Jack Good, and TV Dance Shows

E ven though it's one of soul great Joe Tex's most obscure and silliest songs, I've always liked "Grannie Stole the Show," and certainly not because I find the funky-grandma cliché funny (I left to get popcorn when that old lady did "Rapper's Delight" in *The Wedding Singer*). What I love about the song is its celebration of the participatory nature of dance shows. As far as I'm concerned the dance show is TV at its best. On the simplest level, it is just fun to watch people dance, and I always find the kinetic energy of a mass of people moving to a groovy beat exhilarating. Factor in the ethnography—urban kids proudly disseminating "new" dance moves that can often be traced back centuries to Africa—and you have some of the most fascinating programming on television. Plus the guys look cool and the girls are pretty.

But more importantly, the kids (no matter how fly or sexy or athletic) are not movie stars or millionaires or untouchables. They are not Hollywood creations but civilians like the rest of us, a fact that puts viewers squarely inside the TV screen. And more amazingly, the TV screen opens up into our homes, and as we (and Grannie) dance along, our living rooms become an extension of the TV studio. It is the ultimate interactive media.

"I used to go after school to see the girls across the street," recalled musician Eddie Shaw of the Monks, "and we would dance to Dick Clark. . . . It was the fifties, we were sexually repressed, so all we could do was dance." And dance they did. For more than fifty years dance shows have kept America's hearts pumping, have kept the record executives jogging to the bank, and have turned wild-eyed rebel rockers into harmless mimes through the magic of lip-synching. And the man most responsible for these lofty triumphs didn't even dig the music.

One of comedian Bill Hicks's most famous routines posits that Dick Clark is the Anti-Christ. The late cult-hero comic imagines Clark unzipping his human skin to reveal a "cloven-hoofed, horned wolverine" who sodomizes John Davidson with a massive, grotesque, spiked penis, impregnating the pop singer so that he spawns a brood of Tiffanys and Whams—bland pop stars who spread his evil through their music. Though certainly the most graphic, this isn't the only representation of Clark as Satan. The theme recurs in the 1999 movie *Lush*, on the "Ask Satan" Web site, and in numerous stand-up routines. Usually this is in reference to his mysterious perpetual youthfulness, or mighty powers as a media giant. But Hicks explained that his beef with Clark "is just about mediocrity and lowering the standards of the world."

Perhaps Hicks lets Clark off easy. In his film *Bowling for Columbine* Michael Moore manages to blame Clark for high school gun violence (by drawing a crooked line from the obscenely poor wages Clark's chain of rock 'n' roll theme restaurants pays to an impoverished employee involved in such bloodshed). And David Pichaske, in his book *A Generation in Motion*, called Clark "the biggest single pollutant of rock music."

I don't think Dick Clark is Satan. I'm also uncomfortable with the idea of Clark as a villain. The problem is that Clark is not a rock 'n' roll hero. An admittedly opportunistic businessman who has been very candid about his motives (quotes over the years include "I don't make culture, I sell it," "I was an entrepreneur, I used every single opportunity I could to make money," and "I am the fastest follower in the business"), Clark never claimed to be a rock pioneer. I would love it if the most important man in TV rock history were an obsessive devotee of the music—Clark didn't listen to rock until he got the job—but my preference

American Bandstand®

Dick Clark

Courtesy Jake Austen

is not Clark's fault. If Clark is guilty of anything it's being a serial capitalist. It just so happened that the tool that best suited his dollar-bills-in-the-eyes ambitions also happened to be the show that got America dancing.

Though it would be the domino that made the rest of the country tumble into teen dance-show mania, *American Bandstand* was hardly the first program to play records and was certainly not the first dance show on TV. Around the country a number of DJs did versions of their radio shows on TV, including Los Angeles DJ Al Jarvis, who spun discs and had teens dance on some of his TV outings. Several early TV programs featured professional dancers instructing and demonstrating their moves, including *Let's Rhumba* (NBC, 1946–1947) and the ballroom dance shows *Let's Dance* (ABC, 1954) and *Arthur Murray* (ABC, 1950, 1951–1952; Dumont, 1950–1951, 1952–1953; CBS, 1952, 1953, 1956; NBC, 1953–1954, 1955, 1957, 1958–1960). In Minneapolis *Jack's Corner Drug* (WTCN-TV, 1952), a show very similar to the original *Bandstand*, debuted just before the Philadelphia powerhouse. And most importantly, Philadelphia produced *Paul*

Whiteman's TV-Teen Club (ABC, 1949–1954), a dance and talent show starring the tepid jazz legend that was the first national show to feature youngsters dancing to pop music. Dick Clark appeared on that show to help advertise candy.

The development of *American Bandstand* starts with Bob Horn, a hard-living DJ with attitude, who became a favorite with Philly's teens on account of his rockin' radio program, *Bandstand*. The show's success got Horn hired at the powerful WFIL radio station, where he got the opportunity to host a show on the TV outlet presenting Snader Telescriptions (short films of jazz, blues, and country artists). The outdated music video precursors were not too popular (although one dubious legend has it that bored teenage girls started dancing to the movies in the studio and a camera turned toward them, instantly inventing the dance-show genre). The show was quickly revamped as the more rocking TV version of the radio show, and *Bandstand* (WFIL, 1952–1957) was born.

The idea of a show with dancing was not new to the City of Brotherly Love (in addition to Whiteman's show a popular local radio show called *950 Club* had guests in the studio dance to recorded easy-listening music as early as 1945), but the brash Horn made the kids feel empowered. It was under Horn's reign that most of *Bandstand*'s signatures developed, including a dancer's club; a rate-a-record segment; a programming slate of rock 'n' roll, pop, and mild R&B records; membership cards; an age window (dancers had to be between thirteen and seventeen); a committee of elite teens who felt like big shots (and were obligated to show up in rain or snow); and a dress code that required ties for the boys and skirts or dresses for the girls. It also became massively popular, with more than 1,500 kids (excited by the radio hype) turning up the first day for 200 dance spots. The show aired weekday afternoons for seventy-five minutes (it would soon increase to two hours and then to two and a half).

Horn had created something wonderful, but fate would soon step in to hand the golden reins of *Bandstand* to a better horseman.

Dick Clark was born in Bronxville, New York, on November 30, 1929. As a kid he became enamored with radio, and thanks to a mellifluous voice and an uncle who owned a radio station he became an on-air weather reader as a teenager. When he went to college at Syracuse he worked at the university radio station and also spun country records on a local AM station. After school he got a job reading news (as Dick Clay) and spinning hillbilly music (as Cactus Jack) on a midsize station until his father and uncle, a radio big shot, arranged a job for him at WFIL in Philadelphia. There he began spinning vanilla pop under his own name. To help boost Clark's lackluster ratings Bob Horn stopped in twice during each show to holler at his fans. In return Clark helmed Horn's television show when Horn took vacations. Charmed by TV's magic, Clark considered moving to another market to emcee his own show (*Bandstand* was such a local ratings success that many teen dance shows began popping up around the country). In the end, a move out of town would not be necessary.

It has never been proven in court that Bob Horn slept with underage dancers from the show because the case was dropped on a technicality. Put on "vacation" soon after the charges were made, Horn subsequently was involved in two drunk-driving incidents, one very serious, and was then charged with the double whammy of not paying taxes for payola he'd received. After settling his legal matters he left Philadelphia for Texas and never returned.

On July 9, 1956, Clark took over *Bandstand* (crossing a picket line of dancers protesting Horn's dismissal). He instantly tried to win the kids over with a disposition that was far warmer than Horn's. Unlike the crazed rock 'n' roll personalities who breathed the music—madmen like New York's Alan Freed, Cleveland's Mad Daddy, and Memphis's Dewey Phillips—Clark's style was reserved and professional. He wasn't hip enough to offend parents and he wasn't square enough to turn off kids. The show continued to be tremendously popular and in 1957 Clark's ambition and persistence led the national ABC network to give *Bandstand* a trial run. ABC was the smallest and weakest of the networks at the time, with the fewest affiliates and the fewest programming hours; it would remain the last black-and-white network, long after its rivals went to color. *Bandstand* was its very first afternoon program. Having little to lose (WFIL agreed to continue to pay for the show if ABC paid for the cable hookup from Philadelphia to New York), the alphabet network had few fears about programming rock 'n' roll. In fact, it was launching a nighttime show starring the most infamous DJ in the world—the man who gave rock 'n' roll its name.

The Big Beat (ABC, 1957) starred Alan Freed, the "Moondog," whose love of wild R&B had gained him a huge black following. He had introduced the music to white teens in Cleveland in 1951, and had caused the first rock 'n' roll riot at his oversold Moondog's Coronation Ball in 1952. He moved to New York in 1954; there he took advantage of his proximity to the media world by starring in rock 'n' roll movies, and eventually landed this TV program. His guests included the Everly Brothers, Fats Domino, Clyde McPhatter, Dale Hawkins, Chuck Berry, Jerry Lee Lewis, Mickey and Sylvia, Bobby Darin, and, unfortunately for Freed, Frankie Lymon and the Teenagers. After his performance, Lymon (a cute African American teen pop star) went into the crowd and danced with a white girl. This enraged some Southern affiliates and the show was canceled. Remarkably, this did not kill the *Bandstand* deal, and on August 5, 1957, the show, retitled *American*

Bandstand (ABC, 1957–1987; syndicated, 1987–1989; USA, 1989), debuted and was quickly a nationwide smash.

Certainly the network must have demanded that an incident like the Lymon one never be allowed to occur on the new show. To avoid such a problem all guests went to sign autographs after they performed and never danced with the kids. *Bandstand*'s history of race relations is somewhat confusing. In the past Clark implied that blacks (a significant portion of the Philly teen population) simply had not wanted to come to the show and dance with a bunch of white kids. However, in a recent *Onion* interview he implied that the show was officially segregated in its early days (and slow to integrate after that). It's possible the segregation happened through sly Jim Crow tactics. Dancers needed membership cards, which could be distributed at the producer's discretion, and the few black couples who showed up to dance were usually kept off camera, which discouraged them from returning. The show would not feature blacks prominently until it left Philadelphia for Los Angeles in 1964.

These segregationist policies were likely the show's and not that of the urban Italian-American dancers who attended integrated schools and loved black music (they forced Horn to play the real "Sh-Boom" by the Chords and not the white cover version by the Crew-Cuts). Even the blond super-couple on the show, Bob Clayton and Justine Carelli (who collectively received thousands of fan letters a week), were far from WASPish surfers—they were swarthy, ethnic-looking kids with dark eyebrows. Two of the most popular dancers were Puerto Rican sisters Ivette and Carmen Jimenez, and they, along with the rest of the olive-skinned and dark-haired kids, hardly constituted a white-bread crowd.

Musically the show embraced black artists, hosting the national TV debuts of the Miracles, Four Tops, Jackie Wilson, and James Brown (who practically lived on the show in the 1960s). By 1965 (the year that Famous Hooks, a dance-show addict who appeared on practically every L.A.-based dance program, became the first African American dancer featured prominently on *American Bandstand*), 35 percent of musical guests were black. But despite making money for black artists and labels, the show certainly was guilty of under-representing the Philadelphia population that was responsible for developing many of the best dances.

There were two things, though, that Dick Clark was not guilty of: being unambitious and accepting payola (at least not by his definition). As the show became more successful (and a song's exposure on *American Bandstand* became crucial to its success as a record) Clark and a network of Philadelphia friends, songwriters, record label owners, and talent scouts worked together to create a system of cronyism and influence that always resulted in generous rewards for

Bob Clayton and Justine Carelli. Courtesy Jake Austen

Clark. He owned or co-owned dozens of companies: music publishers, record labels, management companies, record distributors, and a record manufacturing plant (some labels reportedly believed they would get favorable airplay on *American Bandstand* if they used that pressing plant). Clark played records he released himself, sometimes over forty times in a matter of months. Worse yet, he made agreements with other labels that he would play their records regularly if they gave him a portion of the song publishing rights (making him a co-owner of the song in perpetuity, and earning him a portion of all future song royalties). Occasionally these would become monster hits because of the exposure, and some of these were even pretty great records like Huey "Piano" Smith's "Don't You Just Know It" and Danny and the Juniors' "At The Hop."

But to the Bill Hickses of the world his worst crime was promoting mediocre records by handsome local boys whose careers were crafted, in part, to capitalize on the national exposure *American Bandstand* afforded them. Some of these "teen idols" didn't even want to become pop singers. Frankie Avalon was a horn player and Fabian was just a hunky kid trying to get his dad to the hospital when he was tagged to be the next Elvis Presley (minus the talent of course). These boys, whose records were merely pleasant, and who were only fair singers (though Avalon became a pretty good comic actor in the sly *Beach Party* movies), became stars because of their appearances on a national TV show. This fact made them bogus in the eyes of many rock purists.

Fabian. Courtesy Jake Austen

Clark-as-Satan theorists view the late 1950s and early 1960s, when the best rockers were replaced by vanilla pop singers in the chart listings, as Clark's greatest evil triumph. That's unfair for several reasons. *American Bandstand* had a good relationship with real rocker Jerry Lee Lewis (one of the rare artists who always, at his insistence and Clark's indulgence, performed live on the show), and would have certainly continued to support him if he hadn't become a child molester in the eyes of the public (Lewis reportedly wanted to introduce his child-bride on Clark's show just before his disastrous English tour, but Clark declined). *American Bandstand* would have had Presley on every week if Colonel Parker, who demanded huge fees far beyond the scale payments all guests received, had allowed it. *American Bandstand* also did play good black artists and Northwest garage bands and anything interesting that charted. But Clark was most inclined to play records he and his Philadelphia associates had interests in, and many of these records were by the teen idols.

It's worth mentioning that while Presley's sneer revolutionized the music industry, it didn't wipe the slate clean. Young girls have always swooned over clean-cut, dreamy schmaltz singers, and the pop that preceded the original rock 'n' roll boom has never totally left the charts. Avalon's unchallenging but easy-on-the-ears "Venus" wasn't something Clark concocted in order to neuter rock. It was already out there and he capitalized on it. And he may have personally dug it more than he did Gene Vincent, which was a nice bonus to the ton of money he made for his web of business concerns by helping turn Philly hunks into national superstars.

Despite the blatant transparency of these dealings, Clark was certain he had done nothing illegal—and he may have been right about that. Airplay of unmeritorious material was a fact of rock 'n' roll life at the time, as payola (compensating a DJ to play a specific record) was common and seemingly legal, and the "gifts" of song publishing Clark received were fairly standard business practice (Alan Freed helped make Chuck Berry's "Maybeline" a hit after being given a piece of it, and Elvis Presley was sometimes granted songwriting credit on tunes he agreed to record). But the game-show scandals in the 1950s had made congressmen wary of dishonest media and aware of the national exposure a good hearing afforded politicians (in an election year), so lawyers scoured the books for existing laws that rendered these odious practices illegal. DJs from coast to coast were investigated, and anyone stigmatized with a scarlet "P" (for payola) could virtually say good-bye to his career.

All this explains why ABC took Clark to the woodshed. The network brass told him he could either give up his television job or give up all his music industry interests. He agreed to do the latter and sold off his numerous companies. Stripped of his music holdings over the ensuing years he only had his television production companies, real estate, a booking agency, a cosmetics line, lucrative tours for his Dick Clark Caravan of Stars, some Arby's franchises, radio stations, a Dr. Pepper distributorship, a film production company, and oil wells to comfort him.

Clark was called before the House of Representatives to testify, and some thought that he sold out the Alan Freeds of the industry to keep his own hands clean. (Actually, Freed angrily told the panel to go after Clark.) Clark, though not totally forthcoming, boldly stated that he took publishing rights in exchange for airplay, his record companies actually doled out payola to DJs, and it was all legal. Certainly his clean-cut looks and calm manner made him a more sympathetic figure than the wild-eyed, race-mixing Freed. But the real reason he got away with everything was that he presented himself as a shrewd American capitalist. Other DJs took concealed cash like drug dealers making a score, but Clark took over contracts like a CEO making a business deal. One thing these wealthy congressmen understood was big business. Clark was one of their own.

Despite losing his financial interests in the music, Clark kicked off the 1960s by helping to launch a schoolmate of Fabian's and Avalon's into superstardom. Clark's wife renamed Ernest Evans as Chubby Checker and Clark got him to record a sound-alike version of "The Twist," a promising record by Hank Ballard (who was never justly compensated for his work). The twist craze became one of

Chubby Checker. Courtesy Jake Austen

the nation's biggest fads and Clark, just off the hot seat, became America's hero for introducing it.

Perhaps Clark wasn't great for 1950s music. He did use his influence to promote the tamer side of rock 'n' roll. But in the early 1960s, he added a segment in which local DJs would call the show and recommend regional garage rock songs, which then broke nationally. As album-oriented progressive rock took hold in the late 1960s, though, Clark was no longer as valuable a player. When his well-scrubbed dancers in tailored faux–hippie couture attempted to do simple dances to complex music, it was clear that the show had become an awkward follower and not a powerful leader. It didn't help that the network had decided that the afternoon was valuable TV real estate, reducing Clark's daily show to sixty minutes in 1961, then to thirty minutes in 1962. By the end of 1963 he was scaled back from five weekday shows to a single hour on Saturday afternoons.

Clark kept his flagship going but began to concern himself with other interests, most notably his non-dance-show TV productions (game shows, cartoons, made-for-TV movies, award shows, and music specials). He also became a TV presence beyond *American Bandstand*. Over the decades Clark has also helmed the musical shows *Dick Clark's World of Talent* (ABC, 1959), *Dick Clark Presents the Rock and Roll Years* (ABC, 1973–1974), *Dick Clark's Live Wednesday* (ABC, 1978), *Dick Clark's Nitetime* (syndicated, 1985), and *Live! Dick Clark Presents* (CBS, 1988). The nonmusical shows he has emceed include *The Object Is* (ABC, 1963–1964), *Missing Links* (NBC, 1963–1964; ABC, 1964), *$10,000 Pyramid* (CBS, 1973–1974; ABC, 1974–1980; syndicated, 1974–1979, 1981–1989, 1991, 2002–2004 [note: the show eventually inflated to *$100,000 Pyramid*, and its most recent incarnation featured Donny Osmond hosting instead of the behind-the-scenes Clark]), *Krypton Factor* (ABC, 1981), *Inside America* (ABC, 1982), *TV's Bloopers and Practical Jokes* (NBC, 1984–1986, 1988), *The Challengers* (syndicated, 1990–1991), *Scattergories* (NBC, 1993), and *The Other Half* (syndicated, 2001–2003). Clark has even appeared as an actor on such shows as *Perry Mason* (CBS, 1957–1966), *Coronet Blue* (CBS, 1967), *The People Next Door* (CBS, 1989), and *Dharma and Greg* (ABC, 1997–2002). Add to this his American Music Awards broadcasts and his annual *Dick Clark's Rockin' New Year's Eve* and you have a full plate (and wallet). When *American Bandstand* finally came to a gasping halt at the end of the 1980s (with a young replacement host stepping in for the final slate of shows), Clark was a man with well over $100 million in the bank and plenty to keep himself busy.

It's hard to call a man who so honestly follows his nature a rogue. I always liked *American Bandstand*, and even though I never felt Clark was particularly invested in rock 'n' roll (he never got as excited on *American Bandstand* as he did when something really cool happened on *Pyramid*—I believe he loved *that* show), he was all right by me. If there's one thing that marks him as a cad in my eyes it is his cavalier treatment of his own legacy. *American Bandstand* has such an important place in history, yet Clark hoards the tapes and when he does release bits and pieces, he creatively rewrites his own history. One *Best of Bandstand* tape featured no actual *American Bandstand* performances, but rather clips from *The Dick Clark Show* (ABC, 1958–1960), a nighttime program that had better production values than the live, bare-bones daily show. A recent fiftieth anniversary special had Clark presenting footage from the American Music Awards as if it had been on *American Bandstand*. One funny criticism I have heard is that whenever Clark does a nostalgic *American Bandstand* special he has the kids dress in jeans and leather jackets—fashion that was banned from the show during the 1950s. Unfortunately, if the kids today never get to see the historic original footage they are going to believe that this *Happy Days* version was the real thing.

Jack Good was the Anti-Clark. Unlike Clark, who deftly mastered the rock 'n' roll business because he was interested in the business rather than the rock 'n' roll, Good was an intellectual (an Oxford grad), a dandy, and an artist who loved and respected rock and R&B. He once wrote an essay comparing Gary "U.S." Bonds's recordings to French Impressionist painting. While Clark focused on making his show, record sales, and every element of the industry work smoothly and efficiently, Good was interested in making rock 'n' roll *rock* and *roll*.

As a rookie TV producer Good quickly established himself as the hero of British TV rock. His first success was *6.5 Special* (BBC, 1957–1958), named after its starting time, 6:05 P.M., a historically significant scheduling because prior to this show the BBC had gone black from 6 P.M. to 7 P.M. to allow parents to put their kids to bed. Good's *6.5 Special* was a frenetic triumph that combined rock 'n' roll, Lonnie Donnegan skiffle, and novelty numbers in a live action-packed Saturday night jamboree. The show was successful, but the BBC and Good didn't see eye to eye, so Good moved on to *Oh Boy!* (ITV, 1958–1959), featuring dual Elvis Presley apers Billy Fury and Cliff Richard. The show was faster, more furious, and harder rocking than *6.5 Special*, and its reputation led ABC (always looking for a bargain) to air four episodes as a summer replacement series in the United States. The show was poorly received. Good continued to produce British rock shows, but possibly fueled by his American failure and possibly by wanderlust—

he told *Melody Maker* "I'm a bit of a rover"—he traveled to the United States and produced a pilot of a Jack Good–style American rock 'n' roll TV show.

The pilot didn't set Hollywood on fire, but after a few rounds it made it back to ABC, and the network agreed to give it a try. What Good delivered may have looked like just another show on paper (it was hosted by a DJ, it had dancers, it had a "pick of the week"), but on the screen it was like nothing else.

Yes, host Jimmy O'Neill was a DJ, and he was as handsome and clean-cut as Clark, but he had a little bit of Moondog in him as well. Bouncy platter patter punctuated his plugs and introductions—what few introductions there were. Once an episode of *Shindig* (ABC, 1964–1966) took off, it was *gone*. One song segued into another; the camera would cut from one performer to another just as the first performer's song was finishing; one, two, or three other artists might join the singing star; one tiny Neil Sedaka piano would sit atop one grand Jerry Lee Lewis piano as both artists pounded out a duet.

Yes, *Shindig* had dancers, but instead of some regular kids doing their thing, it featured a unit of highly trained go-go dancing girls. And what girls! Though their dancing never evoked a stripper pole or a girl jumping out of a cake, their sexiness was undeniable. Sure they wore long skirts, high socks, and headbands, but they still managed to pile that hair high and shake it with abandon until the chaste clothing brought to mind naughty Catholic schoolgirls.

Jimmy O'Neill and Jack Good on *Shindig*.

But what really differentiated *Shindig* from *American Bandstand* (and the *Big Beat* and *Your Hit Parade* and everything else that preceded it) was its attitude. "America had not seen pop TV like Britain knows them," Good told a writer at *Melody Maker*. "The idea that pop music can be presented visually and artistically, with live music, was entirely new [to them]."

Shindig really was an artistic triumph. While there was a sense of liveliness and energy, this was also the most controlled and planned presentation of rock ever shot for TV. Performers, while encouraged to give their all with a loose and free vibe, were also instructed to do so in exactly the right spot, and to move at exactly the right time. Good would choreograph the singer to fit the camera's movements (he told one performer, "If the camera is on a long shot, let's have plenty of action. When it is on your face a sneer will get a scream").

And the camera movements were intense, with dynamic super-tight close-ups, swooping aerial shots, intense angle after intense angle, precise edits on the beat, and dramatic zooms. Most important to the photography was the composition. While the set seemed simple and spare, it was actually a brilliant design, as it contained several levels at varying depths that allowed the producers to compose shots that balanced the performer against the house band (the Shindogs, featuring L.A. session genius James Burton on guitar), the backup singers (the Blossoms, featuring Darlene Love), and the Shindig dancers. The deftly placed dancers, always moving in seductive unison, became the set's main design element, with sculptural lighting a close second. As the room was filled (lushly, not densely) with layer upon layer of moving, grooving humanity, a wide shot that almost ignored the star was as exciting as a close-up of his or her face or feet or fingers pounding on a keyboard or playing a guitar. Such shots tend to seem overdone today, but as *Crawdaddy* said in the 1970s, "Good single-handedly created the broadcasting clichés that still dominate televised rock."

With all this excitement on stage Good did not forget the most critical element of rock 'n' roll excitement—the audience. Though the show hired only professional dancers, kids in the audience would jump up and dance, and the camera made their presence known. While it didn't feature the broken fourth wall of *American Bandstand* and other teen dance shows, *Shindig*'s focus on the crowd's palpable excitement made TV viewers feel like they were part of the action.

With a setup as amazing as this even a dull act like Billy Kramer was exciting. But *Shindig* rarely featured dull acts; Jackie Wilson, the Righteous Brothers, Marvin Gaye, Tina Turner, James Brown, The Kingsmen, the Isleys, the Rolling Stones, and even Howling Wolf appeared on the show. While shows like *Ed Sullivan* were manned by true professionals who eventually figured out how to shoot the excitement of the crowd and how to compose the acts for maximum effect, they never understood what the music was about well enough to capture it lovingly. Good, on the other hand, understood and cherished rock 'n' roll, and he wielded his mastery of TV's seductive powers as a patron of the arts, furthering a form of music that he considered culturally vital. This manifested itself in moments of dynamic alchemy, as when dozens of go-go dancers did the monkey in unison while Jerry Lee Lewis screamed "Great Balls of Fire," and the stage lights flickered like flames on the back wall. There was nothing on TV that could match *Shindig*.

Shindig was a ratings success, but Good was a temperamental artist who did not take kindly to network interference (he reportedly was booking too many black acts for some affiliates' tastes), and he walked off the show during the second season. Without him the show became average and the network soon canceled it—but not before it welcomed a rival intent on equaling *Shindig*'s prime-time dynamism.

Hullabaloo (NBC, 1965–1966) also featured rock music presented in tightly designed, intensely planned production numbers (in full color, as opposed to *Shindig*'s black and white). But it had a mission: to appeal to American parents as well as American kids. So acts like Marianne Faithfull, the Supremes, the Zombies, the Shangri-Las, the Astronauts, Joe Tex, Dusty Springfield, the Impressions, and Sam the Sham were introduced by (and often paired with) old-time showbiz standard bearers like Steve Lawrence, Jerry Lewis, Alan King, Pat Boone, Joey Heatherton, George Hamilton, and the always-anxious-to-act-hip Sammy Davis, Jr. The host, whether a singer or not, would do a medley of the week's top hits, so if you ever wanted to hear Jerry Lewis cover the Beatles, *Hullabaloo* was your place. Compared to *Shindig* it was pathetic—the go-go girls weren't as sexy, the camerawork wasn't as exciting, and the absurd incongruity of Vegas lounge and rock club performers tempered the excitement of the music.

As flawed as it was, however, the show was good for some of the same reasons that made *Shindig* so successful. It used the manipulative, evocative, dynamic powers of television to make contemporary music acts extremely visually entertaining. *Hullabaloo* was good television; it just wasn't good rock 'n' roll television, because the producers had no real respect for the music. This was clear from the show's amusing but absurdly inappropriate production numbers.

When Cannibal and the Headhunters performed they were placed on a jungle set—relatively fitting for cannibals, but certainly dumb. When Barry McGuire performed his protest song "Eve of Destruction" he sang in the middle of a demolition derby—a brazen dismissal of the song's message (though some would say he was an insincere opportunist who deserved it). But when, in a tropical setting, the Byrds' earnest country-rock was upstaged by go-go dancers with guns who were apparently "byrd"-hunters, it just seemed so disconnected from the point of the music that there was no reason for rock fans to watch it . . . unless they just wanted to be entertained. It might be smarmy, it might be insincere, but *Hullabaloo* was definitely entertaining when performers like Sammy Davis, Jr., walked onto the set.

Though *Hullabaloo* and *Shindig* only lasted two seasons each, they represented a high point for TV rock—especially *Shindig*. Its early episodes contain some of the best filmed performances of the new generation's heroes. While their ultimate ratings failures told TV programmers to forget about prime-time rock, their innovations also told TV rock people to raise the bar. Dick Clark answered this new challenge with his own innovation. His new daily weekday dance show, *Where the Action Is* (ABC, 1965–1967), was a more ambitious, dynamic show than *American Bandstand*.

Here Clark appeared as a disembodied voice announcing the guests, with an awesome house band (the Revolutionary War–garbed Paul Revere and the Raiders, who became huge stars thanks to this exposure) leading the action to where it was. And where was it? Everywhere! Unlike his studio-bound flagship show, *Action* was shot outside at a number of locations (beaches, bridges, boardwalks). Informed more by Frankie and Annette movies than by *American Bandstand*, *Where the Action Is* featured bands lip-synching hits while surrounded not by amateur teenage dancers, but rather by faux-swooning, faux-grooving, carefully positioned extras. Some of these segments had a touch of silly cleverness (as the Outsiders play on a boardwalk, the home viewers notice that there are "dancers" inside the coffin-like wooden sheds, dancing with their eyes, the only body part visible). Some segments were a bit dreary. Since there was no master set a crew could shoot a band miming across the Atlantic, but the inferior camerawork of the English segments (and in one case, a depressed looking Van Morrison) made those clips fall flat.

As a rule I don't like music shows that are shot outdoors. The loss of control of light and atmosphere usually hurts the program, as on an episode of *Where the Action Is* when the bright sunshine washed out Question Mark and the Mysterians, a nocturnal band that shouldn't have been singing their creepy song "96 Tears" in anything even approaching daylight. One of the most visually corrupt dance shows ever was *The Grind* (MTV, 1995–1999), which featured attractive dancers in bathing suits suggestively gyrating by a pool. With no walls or consistent depth to the environment the show just felt untethered. The only good outdoor dance show is the Latin program *Caliente* (Univision, 1995–present), which is so focused on ogling the pretty girls, and is so dismissive of the lip-synching bands (cutting to their videos during their performances), that it somehow works. It also helps that salsa dancing looks natural outdoors, while the club dancing on *The Grind* seemed out of place. When Clark finally ended *American Bandstand* in the late 1980s he did so after moving it outside. In a 1994 interview with *American Bandstand* biographer John Jackson, Clark recalled what he thought when he viewed the footage of the final shows: "It had no lighting and no production value and it really hurt!"

Clark inspired hundreds of copycats to get their local kids' feet moving. Between *Bandstand*'s national debut in 1957 and its semiofficial name change to *American Bandstand '70* thirteen years later, cities all around the country launched their own local teen dance shows, and since breaking a record regionally was important to an artist's success, recording stars were more than willing to visit dinky TV studios in the Midwest, Texas, and along the coasts. A local Cleveland broadcast may not have compared to doing a national show in New York or L.A., but as far as getting exposure for your record, it was the equivalent of doing several dozen record hops and one-nighters in small Ohio towns.

It would take a book twice this size to describe the hundreds of local dance shows that were produced in North America in the 1950s and 1960s, so I will list only a few, but in nearly every case the product was similar. A popular local DJ emceed a televised record hop sponsored by a local business, which he plugged ad infinitum. The kids mostly danced, and occasionally they got to express inarticulate opinions about the merits of a song or their high school. Local and a few national acts lip-synched to their current record. The execution was almost always clumsy (most shows were live) and it didn't really matter because most viewers just wanted to learn the new dances and see their friends (or their fantasy friends or their favorite singers).

Baltimore's *The Buddy Deane Show* (WJZ, 1957–1964) became one of the highest rated local TV shows in America because *American Bandstand* was not picked up by the Baltimore ABC affiliate. John Waters's movie and subsequent Broadway musical *Hairspray* was inspired by this legendary dance show. *The Buddy Deane Show*, just like Waters's fictional *Corny Collins Show*, had a "Negro Day" once a month in lieu of integrating the dance floor. When the civil rights movement forced the show to choose between integration and cancellation, the producers chose the latter. They canceled the show rather than allowing blacks and whites to dance near each other.

Cleveland was one of the great TV rock towns. According to his memoir, a then unknown Dick Clark, bitten by the *Bandstand* bug after briefly substituting for Bob Horn, told a Cleveland TV station that he wanted to come out and launch a show in Ohio. Horn's scandal made the move unnecessary for Clark, but the idea stuck, and soon *Cleveland Bandstand* (WJW, 1955–1960) was born. Popular DJ Phil McClean hosted the show, and in its final year it was briefly emceed by up-and-coming DJ Casey Kasem (who would eventually move on to L.A. to host another teen dance show for Clark).

After *Cleveland Bandstand*'s demise kids were entertained by a long-running local TV talent show that embraced rock 'n' roll and R&B acts in the 1960s. *The Gene Carroll Show* (WEWS, 1948–1979) showcased the teenage debut of Bobby Womack and his brothers, as well as hundreds of other rock and soul wannabes.

Cleveland eventually was home to one of the great rock TV shows of the 1960s. Herman Spero was no stranger to dance shows, having produced *Polka Varieties* (WEWS, 1956–1971). Seeing an opportunity he launched a new, ambitious program locally as *The Big 5 Show* (WEWS, 1964) and quickly expanded it to national syndication as *Upbeat* (WEWS, 1964; syndicated, 1964–1971). Shot in color (which Clark's ABC network was slow to embrace), *Upbeat* was quickly picked up in a hundred cities and boasted such guests as Simon and Garfunkel, the Lovin' Spoonful, Terry Knight and the Pack, Stevie Wonder, Wayne Cochran, and James Brown (as well as local acts like The Damnation of Adam Blessing). *Upbeat* is best remembered as the show Otis Redding played the day his plane crashed, but it should be remembered for being ahead of its time. Its format (with loosely choreographed, hand-clapping Upbeat Girls positioned around the band) preceded *Shindig* and *Hullabaloo*, and its eclectic booking policy (Dizzy Gillespie, Iron Butterfly, and Jimmy Smith all played the show) preceded *Midnight Special*. Bands became harder to book as the 1970s dawned and *Upbeat* folded up its tent, correctly predicting that the early 1970s would not be a great time for local rock 'n' roll dance shows.

In Chicago Jack Mulqueen, who had honed his chops as an entertainer in the military, began doing puppets on *Bozo's Circus* and his own children's show, but his ratings started to drop due to competition from big-budget network shows. "A lot of them had original cartoons, which I just couldn't compete with. Then I discovered a great combination: what is another thing that kids like to watch? They like to watch kids! Themselves! And right about that time Sam the Sham was doing 'Little Red Riding Hood,' and the dances were the monkey, the swim, the Popeye, and the pony . . . it was perfect for kids."

The next thing you know Mulqueen reinvented his wife Elaine as Pandora the go-go harlequin, and *Kiddie-a-Go-Go* (WBKB, 1965–1966; WCIU, 1966–1970) was born. Like all other dance shows, the program played popular songs and musical guests (including the Left Banke, Jerry Butler, the Shadows of Knight, and Lesley Gore) visited the set and lip-synched. But all the dancers were preteens, and some were even toddlers. Boy Scout troops, kids who took dance classes, and babies with rhythm grooved on the show, making it one of the most exceptional in the country. One time Pandora even charmed her guest Dick Clark into doing the monkey on the show. In a letter to Jack Mulqueen, Clark exclaimed, "Believe me, it was the first time I've danced on television."

Not surprisingly, the Mecca of local dance shows (with a few syndicated ones thrown in for good measure) was L.A., where TV production is the heartbeat of the city and attractive, outgoing teens propagate like weeds.

While numerous excellent dance shows pulsated in Hollywood in the 1960s, there was only one you really needed to see to realize how fertile the dance-show soil was—a continuous show that changed names and hosts every few years. As the 1950s waned, Angelenos were able to enjoy their own bandstand when Wink Martindale relocated his Memphis teen dance show (which had boasted a hotline to Elvis) to the City of Angels. *Wink Martindale's Dance Party* (KHJ-Channel 9, 1958–1962), filmed outside on the Pacific Ocean Park pier, drew the top talent and was one of the most popular local shows. When Wink moved on, his future game-show colleague Bob Eubanks took over the show, which was renamed *Pickwick Dance Party* (KHJ-Channel 9, 1962–1964). And when Eubanks stepped aside the daily dance duties were passed on to Sam Riddle, who called his version of the program *Ninth Street West* (KHJ-Channel 9, 1964–1966). Riddle proved so popular that a *Shindig*-inspired Saturday-night spinoff quickly appeared called *Ninth Street-a-Go-Go* (KHJ-Channel 9, 1964), which proved to be such an awesome force that it morphed into the nationally syndicated *Hollywood-a-Go-Go* (syndicated, 1965), one of the most exciting dance shows of the era, as it added a lurid Sunset Strip vibe to the fundamentally wholesome dance-show model.

As his national nighttime show danced on and eventually out, Riddle's daytime local magic continued, under the new name *Boss City* (KHJ-Channel 9, 1966–1969). Riddle's reign of boogie-mongering finally came to an end in 1967 when he passed the crown to popular DJ Don Steele, who eventually renamed the program *The Real Don Steele Show* (KHJ-Channel 9, 1969–1975), and rode that horse well into the Ford administration to the beat of the Sweet's glam rock, Shango's Latin grooves, the best funk of the day, and an occasional Led Zeppelin cut. That single amorphous franchise alone would qualify L.A. as Dance City, but the channel nine juggernaut is only half the story, as L.A. was home to many more memorable dance shows.

Lloyd Thaxton left his popular *Leave It to Lloyd* show in Toledo, Ohio, to chase his Hollywood dreams. Soon he was hosting the local *Lloyd Thaxton's Record Shop* (KCOP, 1959–1961), which became the teen dance hit *Lloyd Thaxton* (syndicated, 1961–1968). Thaxton didn't try to be a cool teenager but rather acted nutty a la Soupy Sales, creating a unique show through his embrace of folk and country as well as pop acts like the Monkees, the Turtles, and Jan and Dean.

Another popular L.A. show that was syndicated nationally was *Shivaree* (syndicated, 1965–1966) starring DJ Gene Weed. A busy and exciting production that played up the audience's screams and shrieks, *Shivaree* welcomed the Rolling Stones, the Supremes, the Byrds, the Ronettes, James Brown, and even Allan Sherman to its stage in the KABC studio.

Shebang (KTOA, 1965–1967) was a full-color Hollywood romp produced by Dick Clark and starring former *Cleveland Bandstand* host (and future voice of Shaggy and Robin the Boy Wonder in Hanna-Barbera cartoons) Casey Kasem. Most notable about this production was the "Sweetheart Tree," a segment where Kasem read schmaltzy letters and dedications sent in by young viewers in a voice as tender as one can possibly be while still sounding like a 1960s AM radio robot. This shtick would become his signature when he began hosting the syndicated radio show *America's Top Forty* in 1970.

The best of them all was the consummate L.A. teen party show, *Groovy* (KHJ-Channel 9, 1967–1970). Though it would eventually move inside and have other hosts (including Sam Riddle and extremely popular perky surfer girl Cam Nelson), when it was launched *Groovy* lived up to its name by taking place on a beach presided over by shirtless, blond surfer hunk Michael Blodgett (an aspiring actor who is most famous for losing his head in *Beyond the Valley of the Dolls* and is not as well known for helping write the screenplay for *Turner and Hooch*). *Groovy* featured bikini contests, pie fights, and lots of sand getting in the gear of acts like Steppenwolf, Tommy James and the Shondells, and Bobby Vee. Though I normally don't like outdoor dance shows, dancing was an afterthought on *Groovy*; it came right after splashing, laughing, and bikini-watching. But it wasn't all playing around—on one show Blodgett wrote the word *prejudice* on a little wooden tombstone, stuck it in the sand, and cheerfully declared, "Today we're burying prejudice on *Groovy*!"

One prejudice that's not so easy to bury is the disdain many rock fans have for lip-synching. Even if one considers the practice of miming to one's own record to be a heinous crime there are two very practical reasons to support it. From the perspective of the television producers, it is impossible on some shows for a band to do a sound check and move their equipment in and move their equipment out. On a live daily program such as the original *Bandstand*, there wasn't sufficient time or resources for rehearsals, sound men, or roadies. If no one had lip-synched there would have been no guests on those shows.

From a music fan's perspective there is a matter of history to contend with. If you are unwilling to dig a lip-synched performance you are dismissing decades of important documentation. "There's so few pieces of live footage out there," rock historian Domenic Priore noted, "and you have to just say, 'You know what? You almost never see Louis Jordan on a live tape.' There's, like, thirty Louis Jordan songs in his films that are lip-synched. To see Chuck Berry in his prime you have to look at footage of him lip-synching. In a lip-synched performance you can get a feeling from the way the performer moves, the way the performer dances or affects the audience. You get an idea of what the performer was really like from looking at those things. Ultimately, if you hate lip-synching, you're not gonna be able to see some of the best performers of the twentieth century."

There is an art to lip-synching, and a great artist, even the best live artist, can take advantage of it. On *Shindig*, the most aesthetically successful of the TV rock programs, James Brown did two of my favorite televised rock performances. For "Please, Please, Please" he sang live and commanded the camera's eye as he went into his classic cape routine, in which he falls to his knees, has a valet drape a cape over his shoulders and assist him off the stage, only to reignite in a burst of surprise energy. That is Brown's most classic shtick, and it felt intensely vital and fresh because of the directness and grit of his live voice.

However, in his other great *Shindig* number Brown lip-synched to "Papa's Got a Brand New Bag." Brown was up on a pedestal, unencumbered by a microphone—or by the responsibility of really singing—and he gave a clinic to the *Shindig* go-go girls on dancing; he busted signature move after signature move, especially concentrating on his shuffling, scrambling footwork. Not only did the lip-synching allow this moment to be more about movement than singing, but it also liberated the *Shindig* producers to create a powerful, original visual statement instead of focusing on being ethnographic rockumentarians capturing a "real" live performance. Perhaps Brown's live number was better than his lip-synch number, but the lip-synch number was awesome and would not have been as amazing if Brown had sung it live.

The best rock 'n' roll TV performers (an admittedly small group) look at lip-synch shows as an opportunity to perform in ways that the mechanics of live music make difficult or impossible, and TV lip-synching should be appreciated as its own special form, not as an inferior compromise. And even the more ubiquitous uninspired lip-synch performers have something to offer, as the artists often reveal something about themselves by the playfulness or the posturing that such performances allow. And, of course, unintentionally bad lip-synch performances, with mouths and singing out of synch like a kung fu movie, are pretty funny.

Intentionally bad lip-synching can be pretty amusing as well. When Pink Floyd appeared on *American Bandstand* their enigmatic singer Syd Barrett (likely in a move of defiance rather than as a sign of the drug damage that would soon oust him from the band) never moved his lips during the song. More obviously intentional were the antics of Johnny Lydon (known as Johnny Rotten during his reign of terror in the Sex Pistols). Lydon's post-Pistols band Public Image Limited appeared on *American Bandstand* and, lip-synching for the notoriously preppy and straight-laced 1980s *Bandstand* dancers, Lydon decided to give up on television convention and started running helter-skelter around the studio (the cameras valiantly kept him relatively in frame most of the time), sticking the microphone in the faces of the young Republicans in the crowd, who (getting a liberating taste of punk spirit) began to lip-synch Lydon's lyrics—to a song they had obviously never heard before. This was not a live show, so clearly booking Lydon, letting him do whatever he wanted, and airing it was a bold, funny move—give Dick Clark credit! But give more credit to Lydon who not only gave a taste of freedom to Izod-wearing studio members that day but also liberated the art of lip-synching.

While many performers hate to do it ("I don't like it. It's a few steps away from reality for sure," Jim Peterik of the Ides of March/Survivor told me), others, like Michael and Janet Jackson, consider their recorded versions the masterpieces, and they want to be free during concerts and TV appearances to concentrate on the choreography. Most of their fans seem content with that. In fact, since the 1950s, when Clark's *Bandstand* swept the nation, the kids never seem to have felt ripped off by lip-synching. (When Ashlee Simpson was revealed to be using vocal tracks on *Saturday Night Live* in 2004, most of the harsh teenage criticism came from kids who already disliked her. Her fans were quick to come to her defense.) When the DJ replaced the live singer on radio the masses began to think of the recording, not the sheet music, as the "song." Singers and bands became stars, their talent at interpretation usurping songwriting ability in the eyes of the fans. A favorite record deserved multiple spins and part of the appeal was its familiarity. To have an artist come before you and sound different than what you are familiar with may appeal to Deadheads, Phish fans, and jazz aficionados, but to the fourteen-year-old watching *American Bandstand* it would have been a heinous crime. When the Beatles and Dylan championed the rocker as *artiste*, chucking a tradition of generations of recording artists who were rarely expected to compose their own music, that didn't change the opinion of the youngest, purest pop fans. In a music video today the artist always sounds as perfect as the CD, and when Britney Spears or Avril Lavigne or Pink decides to sing live at a televised awards show and sounds hoarse or flat or thin-voiced, she's doing nobody any favors.

While many serious rock fans would disagree, I believe that appearance, performance, fashion, and stage presence can be equally important or sometimes more important than the ability to sing. (And for rock fans who disagree, let me ask how come you don't see many fat rock stars?) To me Milli Vanilli is totally legitimate even though studio singers, not the members of the band, recorded all their songs. In fact, their music was awful, and they should be proud not to have been on that record. It was their big muscles, absurd outfits, silly posturing, awkward dance moves, weird beauty, and odd German accents that made them appealing. Even for people who liked their songs, clearly it was the boys' looks that made

Courtesy Jake Austen

them as big as they were. Despite not singing live or on the record, Milli Vanilli was a "real" act because doing pushups and practicing dance moves were more important to their success than singing.

In their *Behind the Music* episode, the moment when their CD skips during a concert is identified as the beginning of the end for the act. But that is bullshit; watching the footage there is no outrage from the fans, who all knew that the boys were lip-synching. And in the days of Dick Clark's Caravan of Stars and endless record hops, performers would lip-synch to a vinyl 45 in a gymnasium full of stomping teens, causing thousands of mildly embarrassing moments instantly forgiven by loyal fans. What ruined Milli Vanilli was the Grammy Awards, which gave the pair a ridiculous honor of Best New Artist and then acted outraged and surprised to discover that a Euro-dance act was prefabricated.

Lip-synching is an art form and a convenience and has been an integral part of pop music—especially on TV—for more than half a century. For any elitists who can't dig this, read my lips: "Get over it."

The outrageous example of Milli Vanilli aside, the issue of lip-synching became somewhat meaningless in the video age. No one sings live in a music video. But the advent of video was also supposed to kill the dance show, and though it certainly injured it, the old bird keeps breathing.

Shows with professional dancers, like *Hullabaloo* and *Shindig*, were the first to revive, in the form of the disco-centric top-forty countdown show *Solid Gold* (syndicated, 1980–1988) and later as its copycat *Dancin' to the Hits* (syndicated, 1986). Jim Peterik, one of the few performers who had chart hits that had him courted by Dick Clark in the 1960s (when he was with the Ides of March) and by the new shows in the 1980s (when he wrote and performed "Eye of the Tiger" with Survivor) was on Clark's *Get It Together* (ABC, 1970), hosted by Mama Cass Elliot, as well as on *Solid Gold*. "There's really not much difference between the two," Peterik laments. "*Solid Gold* came very much from the same machine, the same prepackaged, preprogrammed machine as all the sixties and early seventies shows did."

The next wave of dance shows was more true to the first wave of TV teen parties. *Dance Party USA* (USA, 1986–1991) was originally launched as a local show called *Dancin' on Air* before it became a cable hit that mirrored (on a small scale) the original *Bandstand* phenomenon. Like Clark's show, *Dance Party* originated in Philly, and it also had cool dancers who received lots of fan mail (like

Bobby with the sunglasses, Kelly Ripa, who went on to talk-show fame, and "Princess," who dressed all in purple like her hero, Prince). Kids would watch all over the country after school and dance along, and all the big pop stars—Debbie Gibson, the Jets, Paula Abdul—would visit the set and lip-synch. I had friends who would watch every day just to laugh at the kids' awkward dancing, but since they watched every day I'm sure the cable channel and sponsors didn't mind. More "mature" was *Club MTV* (MTV, 1987–1992), the music channel's re-creation of a dance club, with older teens wearing revealing outfits and terrible hair. Hosted by Downtown Julie Brown, this was one of the network's early forays into developing original programming (after only playing videos for their first few years), and it was fitting that they chose this tried-and-true format. In the 1990s *Party Machine with Nia Peeples* (syndicated, 1991) was a dance show that aired after Arsenio Hall's talk show. Though it was a decent show, the fact that it broke the established formula by playing late at night instead of late in the afternoon was a problem, and the show didn't last a year (though it did introduce America to Another Bad Creation, the best all-toddler hip-hop group ever).

Another wave of dance revival came on public access and leased-time airwaves, as young adults who grew up with dance shows realized that it was in their power to revive the genre. Without commercial considerations independent producers could treat the genre as an art form and a public service rather than as a product. In L.A. Domenic Priore and the lovely emcee Audrey Moorehead painstakingly brought back to life the glory days of L.A. dance shows. *It's Happening* (L.A. Cable Access, 1989–1994) was a labor of love, a modern show with high production values that re-created the vibe of a 1960s dance show in elaborate detail (although, unlike their 1960s garage counterparts, guest bands like the Untamed Youth and the Tell Tale Hearts played live on this show). The secret to *It's Happening*'s aesthetic success was its access to the intense mod, rockabilly, and garage scenes in Southern California. "We didn't have to provide costumes," Priore explains. "Everyone wore their own clothes."

In Fairfax, Virginia, Greg Milewski, an obsessed doo-wop fan, created *Platter Party* (FCAC, 1993) which had original 1950s doo-wop acts perform for 1990s junior high kids. In Chicago, producer Elma Lucas was teaching dance to children in the infamous Cabrini-Green housing project when a Chicago Access Network producer asked her to bring some of her students onto the channel. Inspired by the facility Ms. Lucas began producing her own show, *Elma and Company* (CAN-TV, 1993–present), inviting underprivileged children to come enjoy themselves and be inspired by uplifting messages from Chicago's best R&B and hip-hop acts. Opting to inspire little more than giddy fear, New York's *Ghoul-a-Go-Go* (various cable channels, 2001–present) combines the can't-miss formula of goofy, comedic monsters and enthusiastic preteen dancers.

But noncommercial TV is of little interest to the man who helped launch this phenomenon. So over a decade after *American Bandstand* left the airwaves, the serial capitalist got right back in the fray. In 2002 he returned *American Bandstand* to the air in the form of a nighttime drama called *American Dreams* (NBC, 2002–present). On this show we get to see that the Justines and Ivettes who danced on the show were sensitive protagonists who, rather than learning about nepotism, segregation, ruthless opportunism, and the championing of mediocrity while in the presence of Clark and the show's staff, instead learned about racial tolerance, the moral complexities of protest music, and the virtues of good spelling. The show is pretty schmaltzy and not my cup of tea, but as a new page in the thick book of the revisionist history of *American Bandstand* I think it is one of the most readable. Plus, it's got a good beat, you can dance to it. I'd give it an 81.

3

Faking the Band

Keeping It Unreal with Monkees, Partridges, and Their Play Pals

When *Behind the Music* asked Micky Dolenz about the Monkees developing into a functioning band, he replied, "I've often equated it to Leonard Nimoy really becoming a Vulcan."

"This Vulcan line, Micky," an exasperated Peter Tork retorted, "give it up, for God's sake."

The fact that the Monkees themselves were dismissive, defensive, and at times confrontational about whether they were a "real" band isn't surprising. They were four kids thrust into a situation that yielded intense adulation tempered by harsh denigration. Many critics dug what they were doing and the young masses went ape-shit. But the rock intelligentsia told the world—and the Monkees— that they were as bogus as a Beverly Hills boob job.

But in fact the Monkees were completely *real*. They didn't write most of their music, but Elvis didn't write *any* of his. They didn't play the instruments on their recordings, but neither did most Motown artists. Svengalis dressed and directed them, much like Brian Epstein did the Beatles. They were cast through a newspaper announcement and auditions . . . not unlike KISS or the hundreds of other bands assembled through music classifieds every day. And the main thing is that millions of people saw them, heard them, and were moved by them. If those reactions were real (and they *were*) how could the band be fake?

As far as I'm concerned, any documented band, even a fictional group that makes a stupid cartoon cameo in a *Jetsons* episode, is far more real than a gritty, brilliant band that rehearses in a garage but never records or plays a show. Hundreds of thousands of kids watched Jet Screamer woo Judy Jetson singing, "Eep Op Ork Aha," and that song, along with Jet's good looks and cool moves, were burned into their consciousnesses. Mr. Screamer is a real and vital musician as far as that audience is concerned, and those kids aren't stupid; they just are more invested in digging the tune than in snobbish imaginings of conceptual authenticity. Audience reception is a powerful force and credibility is an intangible haint, so in my opinion every band that has ever appeared on a record or a TV show or in a movie is *real*. Even if they are just studio hacks slapping a random name on a record label, even if they are actors lip-synching to someone else's track, and even if they are completely fictional. Electric Mayhem (the *Muppet Show* band) is a real band, the Chipmunks are a real band, Milli Vanilli is a real band, Da Band is a real band, Spinal Tap is a real band, those capuchin monkeys playing instruments at the beginning of *Son of Kong* are a real band, the Blues Brothers are a real band, the Fabulous Stains are a real band, the heavy metal band in the 1986 *TV Guide* commercial that sings, "We're screaming at the top of our lungs . . ." is a real band.

And I'm supposed to think the Monkees, a touring band that played their own instruments in concert, that was popular in part because of the distinctive quality of its members' singing voices, and that outsold the Beatles and the Stones combined for a year are bogus?

The main reason that many people, some Monkees included, view the Monkees as less than legit is that they were, on some level, actors hired to play a band on TV. But two of them weren't even actors. There had never been anything exactly like the Monkees before. They were the greatest made-for-TV band of all time, perfectly balancing an excellent show with excellent records, each medium enhancing their success in the other. Those four manic Monkees, and their clever, complicit zookeepers, combined some of the best new ideas hatched in the youth-centric 1960s with some of the oldest, crassest showbiz practices, and the results shone iridescent before the inevitable burnout. If the Monkees are a fake band, then an army of millions (with which I proudly march) has loudly declared, "*We love fake bands!*"

Of course, *The Monkees* wasn't the first TV show about making it (or faking it) in the music biz. *I Love Lucy* (CBS, 1951–1961), the grand dame of sitcoms, was about a struggling Latin bandleader and his kooky wife's attempts to participate in his shows. *It's Always Jan* (CBS, 1955–1956) featured real-life movie star Janis Paige as a make-believe nightclub singer. But the key program that married rock 'n' roll and chuckles, and subsequently demonstrated the broad "you rub my back, I'll rub yours" possibilities of the TV and record industries, was *The Adventures of Ozzie and Harriet* (ABC 1952–1966), in which Ricky Nelson—unlike Elvis, Perry Como, or Desi Arnaz, who were all known musicians before TV made them huge stars—created a music career from scratch under the TV camera's watchful eye.

The patriarch of the Nelson clan, Ozzie Nelson, was a savvy showbiz veteran by the time rock 'n' roll reared its pompadoured head. He helmed a fairly popular big band in the 1930s, and became a radio fixture as Red Skelton's on-air bandleader. When Skelton was drafted in 1944, Nelson remained on radio, eschewing music for a sitcom about his home life that costarred his wife, singer Harriet Nelson, and two actors playing their sons. Eventually his real sons took over the roles and the show moved to TV, where it became the prototypical domestic sitcom.

Despite being held up as a symbol of unrealistic, white-bread family life (especially in endless comparisons between the similarly nicknamed Ozzie Nelson and Ozzy Osbourne, both aging musicians who cast their real-life wives and kids as TV comedy stars), the show was groundbreaking. It established the family sitcom clichés (ineffective dad, practical mom, wisecracking kid, wacky neighbor) that would be perennially recycled and riffed upon. Thanks to Ozzie and Harriet's bland prototype, sitcoms like *The Munsters* (CBS, 1964–1966), *The Addams Family* (ABC, 1964–1966), *Bewitched* (ABC, 1964–1972), and *I Dream of Jeannie* (NBC, 1965–1970) could (indirectly) address integration, racism, and intermarriage; seemingly middle-of-the-road sitcoms like *Leave It to Beaver* (CBS, 1957–1958; ABC, 1958–1963) could explore middle America's hypocrisy (the Cleavers are an island of functionality surrounded by liars, abused children, and assholes).

Because *Ozzie and Harriet* was so square, it might have been expected that pop records released by the cute kid on the show would be dismissed as novelty records like discs released by Shelley Fabares from the *Donna Reed Show* (ABC,

1958–1966) or Kim Fields from *Facts of Life* (NBC, 1979–1988). But Ricky Nelson was special. He developed his interest in rock 'n' roll himself, rather than having it thrust upon him by handlers, and most importantly he knew good music. "He didn't have the most passionate vocal style," explains rockabilly writer Ken Burke, "but he was sincere, and he had remarkably good taste; he knew how to pick songs and musicians and producers. He is responsible for keeping rockabilly alive long after the craze died down."

Like the great Eddie Cochran, Nelson was a suburban rockabilly rather than a genuine southern musician, but his approach to pop with a southern flavor was original. One of the keys to his success (in addition to his Elvis-but-handsomer looks) was that unlike his father, who was always more of a businessman than a musician, and unlike his sons, who formed the bland duo Nelson in the 1990s (and currently are managed by *NSYNC guru Lou Pearlman), Nelson's soul was completely into his music, even if his chops weren't the tops.

Ricky Nelson. Courtesy Jake Austen

When Nelson first became enamored with Elvis, his father set him up with the best studio musicians (Richie Frost and Earl Palmer on drums, Barney Kessel and Joe Maphis on guitar). Nelson's competent R&B covers, like Fats Domino's "I'm Walking," were far more spirited than Pat Boone's infamous versions. But Nelson reached his apex when he took initiative, assembling his own band (led by guitar genius James Burton), choosing his songwriters (including the Burnette Brothers and Gene Pitney), and creating records as giddily fun as "Hello Mary Lou" and as stark and eerie as "Lonesome Town." By respecting rockabilly Nelson earned the respect of such genuine talents as Sonny Burgess, Faron Young, and Carl Perkins. And he did this all while singing the songs each week at the end of a corny sitcom.

Calling Ricky Nelson and his group, as seen on *The Adventures of Ozzie and Harriet,* a fake band is far more complicated than calling the Monkees or the Partridge Family fake. Ostensibly Rick Nelson played himself on the show, surrounded by his real-life family. Indeed when the boys got married their real wives appeared onscreen as "characters." But the TV Nelsons were not the real family. Harriet was not the domestic goddess she portrayed on the tube (she had cooks and maids for that), and Ozzie Nelson was no bumbling buffoon. He was one of the shrewdest guys in the business, exerting complete creative control over the show he wrote, directed, and starred in. When he discovered his son's rockabilly talents, he deftly guided Ricky's career and wove the songs into the show (originally as part of the narrative but eventually as a separate performance that ended each episode), leading to increased TV ratings and phenomenal record sales. Ricky Nelson's first concerts, first exposure as an artist, and first broadcasted music were all in the context of this make-believe show, creating the template for future fake-band shows to follow. The real Rick Nelson was playing music he really liked, but he was playing it in his role as the fictional Ricky. This confusing situation would haunt him later in life, and his adult country-rock (without the hypnotizing power of TV to promote it) never drew the thunderous applause of his teen hits. He was on the way to play an "oldies" concert when his plane crashed on New Year's Eve, 1985.

That tragedy was generations of teenagers away in the summer of 1965 when a *Variety* ad declared, "MADNESS!! AUDITIONS—Folk & Roll Musicians-Singers for acting roles in new TV series." That blurb led to a cattle call drawing 473

wannabe stars to Columbia-Screen Gems offices, including Mickey Rooney, Jr., Rodney Bingenheimer, and future members of Three Dog Night, Love, and Buffalo Springfield.

The project these kids were auditioning for was *The Monkees* (NBC, 1966–1968), a show that on one hand was designed to be a product of the new Hollywood—a maverick, youth-driven endeavor that would combine the spirit and innovation of independent experimental cinema with genuine respect and regard for the perspective of the youth audience. On the other hand, it could be read as pure old-school Tinseltown—a cynical, crass attempt to co-opt another million-dollar idea, dumbed-down for American kids who didn't know the difference.

The source was Richard Lester's 1964 Beatles movie *A Hard Day's Night*. American-born Lester was a TV director who relocated to England in his early twenties and forged a relationship with comedy genius Peter Sellers. Marrying the comic sensibilities developed during that collaboration with his interests in teenage music, Lester directed a series of rock 'n' roll movies that used a wacky collage of camera tricks and special effects to create visuals that captured the energy of the music.

The Monkees intended to re-create the Beatles' sped up, jump-cut, kaleidoscopic visual frenzy, with the boys being pursued by female fans or playing their popular songs. But it also set out to mimic the way the Beatles' personalities translated to the screen. Although individual stars like Elvis and Sinatra had made easy transitions to the movies, an entire band becoming "characters" was another matter. Historically only a band's lead singer and, less frequently, a charismatic instrumentalist were known to the public. But in *A Hard Day's Night*—as in *The Fantastic Four* comic book that had debuted three years earlier—each Beatle had his own distinct powers, personality, and lovable quirks. The ease with which these came across on celluloid inspired the men behind *The Monkees*.

Bob Rafelson and Bert Schneider developed the idea of turning the whimsical rock 'n' roll anarchy of *A Hard Day's Night* into a TV series. Rafelson, just thirty in 1965, had a résumé that included stints as a rodeo rider, jazz drummer, movie producer, and—as the creator of the folk music show *Hootenanny* (ABC, 1963–1964)—music TV pioneer. Schneider, another youthful TV producer, had used the all-American combination of drive and nepotism (his dad was president of Columbia Pictures) to become a vice president at Screen Gems Television. After an audition process that was both exhaustive and innovative (they played mind games with potential Monkees to test their improv skills), Bob and Bert settled on a quartet that had both great energy and four distinct personalities; they were also obvious stand-ins for the Liverpool superstars.

The Monkees' cute Paul McCartney type (though he was more of a Ringo Starr in terms of his creative contribution) was tiny Englishman Davy Jones, who had trained to be a jockey before his good looks led him to musical theater. Cast as the introspective George Harrison of the band (despite having more the vision and drive of John) was Texas-bred guitarist Michael Nesmith, who had moved to California to make it on the music scene after the Air Force and college didn't work out. The group's charismatic John Lennon (though he was a cheerier personality, a la McCartney, with some wacky Ringo thrown in) was Micky Dolenz, a former child actor who had costarred with legendary little person Billy Barty and Bimbo the baby elephant when he played Corky in *Circus Boy* (NBC, 1956–1958). And the goofy Ringo Starr role (though his outstanding musicianship and meditative nature was more that of George Harrison) was filled by Peter Tork, who had deftly negotiated the Greenwich Village folk scene before becoming a singing dishwasher in Los Angeles.

Their primates in place, the producers went about making arrangements for the Monkees' music. Record guru Don Kirshner, already a bigwig at Screen Gems, specialized in making hits by fostering a rock 'n' roll Tin Pan Alley, where genius songwriters like Neil Diamond, Carole King, and Gerry Goffin churned out AM radio gold for various acts. He had complete creative control over the music for the project and assembled the best songwriters (including Tommy Boyce and Bobby Hart, who had both auditioned to be Monkees) and top studio musicians to create sweet rock candy for the Monkees to lay vocals over. The first Monkees single, "Last Train to Clarksville," was a magnificently crafted record, perfect for Micky's voice, with hooks around every bend and the drums masterfully simulating chugging train sounds. It was released before the show debuted, and by the time the Monkees were on TV they already had a hit record.

The Monkees, a fantasy about cool, wholesome rockers living together in a beach house and going on bizarre mock adventures, felt like nothing else on TV at the time. It was a youthful, nutty triumph, giving nods not only to Lester's new cinema and the visual vibes of the emerging counterculture, but also to black-and-white Hollywood's screwball comedies and madcap silent movies. The musical vignettes, often cited as a clear prototype for MTV videos, featured the boys doing zany visual non sequiturs. The comedy on the show was scripted but loose; an improv vibe balanced with borscht belt one-liners. The Monkees were funny guys, though not funnier than the Beatles (the Fab Four's first U.S. press conference was a comedic knockout, whereas most jokes at the Prefab Four's English press conference bombed). Both groups featured young men with impeccable comic timing. However, whereas the Beatles were masters of the deadpan (an effective comic technique that makes silly jokes seem profound), the Monkees shamelessly mugged, turning themselves into living cartoons by means of their broad, goofy humor.

But they weren't just cartoons. There were several indicators that the producers of the show had purposefully promoted the band's authenticity as a selling point. For one, the Monkees used their real names on the show, particularly significant when one considers that two Monkees (Dolenz and Nesmith) had previously used stage names (early press material even bills "Michael Blessing," the name Nesmith had used as an obscure recording artist). Also, the Monkees' screen tests, bloopers, and casual interview segments were included in the body of the episodes to emphasize that the wacky personas seen on screen were not some scriptwriter's invention, but in fact the genuine personalities of the show's stars.

Monkeemania rivaled the Beatles frenzy, as tens of millions of Monkees records were sold in 1967. Every day 14,000 Monkees fan letters arrived at *16 Magazine*, indicating that though the show wasn't top rated it was a smash with its target demographic. The Monkees traveled the United States and England playing to massive crowds at sold-out concerts (an impressive feat considering Micky had just learned drums, and Davy was a tambourine neophyte). The show won the 1967 Emmy for best comedy.

But all was not well in Monkee land. On the positive side, critics and media watchers had some good things to say about the show, though praise was often tempered with jabs (*TV Guide*, in a generally positive review, attributed to the Monkees "comedy you outgrew in kindergarten"). Yet the reactions of the elitist gatekeepers of the "serious" rock world, aghast that the Monkees used studio musicians and songwriters, irked the Monkees—particularly Nesmith, who took criticism poorly.

Jimi Hendrix, who briefly crashed at Peter Tork's pad and opened for the Monkees for a few incongruous concerts, told *Melody Maker* in 1967, "Oh God, I hate them! Dishwater." That same year the *London Sunday Mirror* amazingly called them "a disgrace to the Pop World" (in Britain the pop world they were supposedly disgracing was at the time highlighted by Freddie and the Dreamers leading an inane, juvenile dance, Screaming Lord Sutch wearing a Halloween costume, and comedian Ken Dodd crying schmaltzy crocodile tears). According to David Pichaske's book *A Generation in Motion*, the Monkees were "so crass as to congeal the blood of every struggling sixties rock group and all of their fans."

Of course, if they were a dishwater disgrace hated by every true rock advocate then the millions of fans who dug the Monkees were chumps—enemies of real rock who were complicit in this heinous fraud. A more sober and just analysis was offered by Jim Curtis in his book *Rock Eras*. "The Monkees offer a test case for one's allegiance to democracy or elitism. In the sixties, a lot of critics showed their nascent elitism by giving the Monkees a lot of abuse. . . . [A]s usual, such criticism misses the point, and expresses the same elitism and snobbishness which characterizes those people who won't listen to anything but Beethoven. The crucial point is that no one bribed all those kids who bought Monkees records."

Off TV the Monkees members had rock credibility, hanging with counterculture heroes who may not have dug the program but definitely enjoyed their company. David Crosby called them "four dynamite, bright, aware, grooving, creative cats." Derek Taylor, the former Beatles publicity man who booked the Monterey Pop festival, admired the boys, years later lamenting his cowardice for not booking them. But hanging out with the Beatles in England, and befriending the Jefferson Airplane and Buffalo Springfield in California, didn't make the Monkees feel better—it actually made them agree with their critics.

Michael Nesmith had special reasons to resent not playing on Monkees records. An ambitious songwriter, he wanted to record his own music. He also hated most of the Monkees tunes, for though the hits were mostly high-quality pop, the early LPs also included toothless ballads for Davy and second-rate Beatles knockoffs. Most importantly, since Nesmith didn't sing lead on the singles, he literally had nothing to do with them. The Monkees might have been as real as Elvis or Sinatra because their distinct voices were crucial to their recording successes. But that logic means nothing to the members of the group who have to play live versions of records they had taken no part in.

Peter Tork was also frustrated, but Mike was an angrier, more vocal and demonstrative Monkee. In a meeting with Kirshner, Nesmith exploded, violently demanding that the Monkees be let out of their cages, given guitars, and allowed to make their own music. Soon Kirshner was fired, taking with him his next Monkees hit, "Sugar Sugar." Rafelson and Schneider got credit for being loyal to youth and freedom; they also no longer had to turn over a huge portion of Monkees profits to the man whose contributions had certainly helped make the Monkees the biggest band in the world.

In *Behind the Music: The Monkees* (VH1, 2000), Kirshner was still indignant. From an outsider's perspective it seems obvious that only Peter and Michael, both competent musicians, wanted to play on records. If Kirshner had let them play with the studio musicians and maybe let Mike write one more song a record (he already got to do two) the golden goose could have lived on. But Don Kirshner's huge ego was likely what made him so successful, and to this day he can't believe he was fired.

Kirshner took his potential hit to another band that was far more pliable. The Archies were an animated rock band that despite being drawings rode "Sugar Sugar" to the top of the charts, sparking the cartoon-band TV rock revolution (which has its own chapter in this book) and taking the concepts of fake bands and rock authenticity to another level. To fill the Kirshner gap the Monkees brought in Chip Douglas (not to be confused with the character from *My Three Sons*) to lead the production of *Headquarters*, on which the band played their own instruments and did a substantial amount of writing. The album was excellent—perhaps not as slick as the previous two, but certainly less schmaltzy (even the misty "Shades of Gray" had more substance than some of the puffier early Davy songs). *Headquarters* didn't match its predecessors' unbelievable sales, nor yield hit singles, but it went platinum, a satisfying victory for the Monkees. That victory, however, was largely symbolic.

Making a hit album is hard work, and with their TV production schedules it was impossible for the band to devote the same time to *Headquarters'* follow-up LPs. So they returned to the Kirshner model with studio musicians and less of their own songwriting. As the hot Monkees fad cooled, record sales got slower. Continuing that trend, the second season's TV ratings were softer despite (or perhaps because of) the Monkees' fresh autonomy, which made the programs weirder and wilder than earlier episodes.

When the series was canceled the band, Rafelson, and Schneider, believing that the Monkees concept was bigger than the show, prepared a series of movies and TV specials (a proposed variety show was rebuffed by the network). The first order of Monkee business was for the band, their producers, and an up-and-coming icon of cool, Jack Nicholson, to go on a retreat, get super-stoned, and map out *Head*, a swirling anti–Viet Nam, anti–corporate rock, anti-advertising art-house movie that featured the Monkees committing suicide in one scene and portraying dandruff in another. Written by Nicholson and costarring Frank Zappa, Sonny Liston, and Victor Mature, this R-rated movie starring a band with teenybopper fans was an inevitable financial failure. Some have speculated that Rafelson and Schneider calculated this flop so they could wash their hands of Monkee shit and move on to genuine hip projects (with Monkees money and Jack Nicholson in tow Schneider next made *Easy Rider,* and Rafelson made *Five Easy Pieces*). I don't believe that to be the case, because *Head*, though certainly a mess, is an amazing movie. Part of the concept of this psychedelic, partly linear project was to be completely unlike the Monkees' sitcom, but actually its greatest strength was the visual language it shared with the TV show. Though the photography is far more beautiful, and at times infinitely grimmer, its eclectic, chaotic, instinctual, vibrant imagery invokes the show's best moments.

After the unpopular but artistically sound *Head* the Monkees killed their multimedia career by making the unpopular and artistically dreadful TV special *33 1/3 Revolutions per Monkee*. This should have been a masterpiece, as it was crafted by one of the best TV rock producers of all time, Jack Good. But it looks cheap (not unlike the low-budget British sci-fi show *Dr. Who*); the musical numbers, including a segment that squanders Jerry Lee Lewis, Fats Domino, and Little Richard, are filmed atrociously; and the entire thing is one long ham-fisted whine about being prefabricated (Davy as a wind-up doll, get it?). The remaining TV specials the Monkees were contracted for were squelched. After entering TV with a rocking bang the Monkees exited with a sorry whimper.

Eager for his own trip, Tork quit the Monkees after the TV special. Over the next few years the band would continue to record and perform new material of varying quality as a trio, then after Nesmith quit as a duo (the ever popular drum and tambourine configuration), and eventually as a bastardized quartet with Monkees songwriters Boyce and Hart filling in for Tork and Nesmith. As each reconfiguration met with diminishing public interest the individual members pursued their own interests. Jones embarked on a less than spectacular solo career, which was subsidized by late-breaking Japanese Monkeemania. Dolenz went down contradictory paths, becoming both a decadent dilettante who jammed with rock 'n' roll luminaries in his home studio while hosting endless parties, and a hardworking jack-of-all-trades who played music, acted (he auditioned to be Fonzie on *Happy Days*), did cartoon voice work, directed, and produced. Tork's commitment to the hippie ideals of self-exploration, communal living, mind-expansion, and altruism led to the quick dissipation of his Monkee money. He taught school, worked in restaurants, did a brief prison stint for drug possession, and played with a parade of bands, none particularly focused.

Nesmith had the most successful post-Monkees career due to talent (he made a series of critically lauded country-rock albums), fortune (the Nesmiths became multimillionaires, as Mike's mom had invented Liquid Paper), and vision. Despite his gripes, Nesmith apparently was the Monkee paying the most attention during their TV days, leading him to explore music video as an art form and an industry. He produced elaborate promotional videos for his own music, a freestanding video album called *Elephant Parts* (sold to home viewers on videotape and laser disc, earning the first video Grammy), and eventually produced a feature film that cast video directors as the new rock stars (*Tapeheads*, with John Cusack and *Soul Train*'s Don Cornelius in a rare acting role). Most significantly, he produced the cable TV show *Pop Clips* (Nickelodeon, 1980), America's first music video show. That proved to be a pilot, as Warner Communications (who owned Nickelodeon) subsequently launched MTV based on the *Pop Clips* model. The *Monkees*-inspired, whimsical, chock-full-of-video-tricks style that Nesmith perfected in his own productions became the look of MTV in its early days.

The video channel would eventually make a significant gesture of gratitude, launching an all-day marathon of *Monkees* episodes in 1986 to celebrate the show's twentieth anniversary. The marathon was a huge hit. Though the sitcom had never disappeared (reruns had run in local syndication), this recontextualization on the hip music channel was a revelation. Not simply a nostalgia trip, a whole new generation of kids flipped over the timeless music, unique visuals, funny jokes, and charming personalities. The Monkees were all over MTV, as interviewees, guest VJs, and eventually as video stars, when fresh interest led to a new album, hit single, video, and ridiculously successful stadium tour (though Nesmith's participation with the new material and tour was limited to a guest appearance during an L.A. concert). The frenzy eventually cooled, but the revitalized Monkees were able to tour with some regularity on the oldies circuit to enthusiastic crowds.

Then for their thirtieth anniversary the band recorded a new album, *Justus*, as a quartet again, and returned to TV with the special *Hey Hey It's The Monkees* (ABC, 1997), directed by Nesmith. Although the program looked a little dated, due to the overexposure of Nesmith's signature style by imitators, it drew respectable ratings (more than ten million viewers).

All the *Monkees* episodes have been available on video for twenty years (before the DVD craze, the Monkees initiated the complete-season phenomenon with suitcase-size VHS sets). Virtually every note they ever recorded is available on CD, including series of bootlegs that collect the most absurd rarities. Monkees fans have even published exhaustive documentation of every recording session, something Beatles fans have always done—but the Monkees weren't even at many of those sessions! Obviously the Monkees are very important and very real to an army of fans, and their legacy is powerful—too powerful for them to have ever been contrived, illegitimate "dishwater."

"There was kind of willingness on the part of the press to believe that a Monkees phenomenon of that magnitude could be manufactured," Michael Nesmith told Eric Lefcowitz in an interview that appeared in *Monkees Business Fanzine*. "If you can do that, if you can manufacture that, then they should have manufactured another one right away. Easy. Do it again. But they can't."

It seems that Mike is likely correct. A number of shows have been designed to re-create Monkees-like magic, but successes have been elusive. Handsome Bobby Sherman became a hot pop music star based on his nonmusical show, *Here Come the Brides* (ABC, 1968–1970), but when they tried to make him Monkees-big by casting him in a fake band show, *Getting Together* (ABC, 1971–1972), the public wasn't buying it, and the program barely lasted four months. In *A Year at the Top* (CBS, 1977), Paul Shaffer and Greg Evigan negotiate a deal with the devil to make it as rock stars, but even a deal with Don Kirshner (who made the music for the series) didn't help. The show lasted five episodes and the LP sold about five copies. That same year *Sugar Time!* (ABC, 1977–1978), with Barbi Benton leading a trio of female rock-star wannabes, also failed to make any musical magic. *The Righteous Apples* (PBS, 1980) was African American producer Topper Carew's *heavy* show about a famous young band (they have their own TV show on this TV show) righting injustices. But instead of investigating silly mysteries like Hanna-Barbera's cartoon bands, they take on hate crimes, including a racist South African abortion doctor who intentionally sterilizes black women. Needless to say this show did not have bubblegum appeal, and the band's LP didn't chart, despite a talented cast that included Mykelti Williamson (Bubba from *Forrest Gump*) and E. G. Daily, who later had a top-ten solo hit and voiced one of the *Powerpuff Girls* (Cartoon Network, 1998–present). *Dreams* (CBS, 1984) featured John Stamos, who had quit his fake band Blackie and the Riff Raffs on *General Hospital* (ABC, 1963–present) to star in this MTV-age show that used music video editing and graphics for the few numbers the band squeezed in during their one month on the air.

The saddest failure of all was *The New Monkees* (syndicated, 1987), which picked four puffy-haired rockers after auditioning more than ten times the wannabes that had tried out for the original Monkees. The high-concept show (they lived in a giant, magic mansion with rooms that opened up into weird fantasy scenarios) had little chemistry, and the music was awful. The show lasted a lucky thirteen episodes. Apparently Nesmith's conclusion is sound: the magic Screen Gems found with the Monkees couldn't be re-created. But . . .

The New Monkees. Courtesy Jake Austen

Twenty-one months after the Monkees left TV, Screen Gems debuted *The Partridge Family* (ABC, 1970–1974). Like *The Monkees* the show was heralded by a hit single that shot up the charts before the show debuted. Like *The Monkees* it was a popular sitcom about a made-for-TV band that consistently produced real-life hit records. Like *The Monkees* it promoted new singles with musical numbers built into the show. And like *The Monkees* it produced frenzy among young fans that sparked comparisons to Beatlemania, Sinatra bobby-soxer fever, and Rudy Vallee's swoon-inducing heyday.

Created by TV vet Bernard Slade and produced by Bob Claver and Paul Witt (who had helped turn Bobby Sherman into a teen idol on the nonmusical show *Here Come the Brides*), *The Partridge Family* was a fictionalized version of the Cowsills story. The Rhode Island–based Cowsills were a typical garage band made up of four brothers that became unique when their mother and seven-year-old sister, Susan, joined the act. Recording an armful of LPs between 1965 and 1971, having hit singles (including "The Rain, The Park, and Other Things" and a cover of "Hair"), making numerous TV appearances, and running the musical gamut from light bubblegum to conceptual rock, the family act was one of the more interesting groups of its day. But by the time Slade became interested in exploring the dynamic of a mom in a teen band, the Cowsills were too old (and other than little Susan, not quite cute enough) to star in the show themselves.

Another reason not to hire a real band was to avoid another Monkee mutiny. This show would unambiguously feature actors (not rockers) with the songs created strictly by studio musicians. When the casting was complete the Partridge family unit consisted of a beautiful, but too matronly to be sexy, mom (played by Broadway and movie vet Shirley Jones), two waiflike and enchantingly pretty teens (David Cassidy and Susan Dey), an adolescent comic prodigy (Danny Bonaduce), and two extremely quiet little kids (dual George Harrisons, without the brilliance, played by Suzanne Crough and Jeremy Gelbwaks, whom Brian Forster later replaced).

The family led a normal life by day (school, chores, pets) but was a popular band in the early evenings and on weekends. The show featured musical sequences highlighted by mimed drumstick motions, keyboard playing, and tambourine shakings, often completely out of synch with the music being played. In *The Partridge Family: Behind the Music* (VH1, 2000), Cassidy, the only serious rock fan among the kids, recalls screaming at Bonaduce for strumming instead of plucking his bass.

One of the most brilliant elements in the construction of *The Partridge Family* was making the mom a widow. By eliminating a patriarch they not only avoided the Ozzie Nelson castrated dad cliché, but also circumvented the sad reality that

The Partridge Family. Courtesy Jake Austen

the fathers of most musical family acts, including the Cowsills, the Beach Boys, the Jacksons, and even the Shaggs, were abusive dictators whose pursuit of family fame and fortune magnified existing dysfunction. It also suggested an unspoken subtext: the possibility that before settling down Shirley had been a loose and wild rock chick, as all her children clearly had different fathers.

Wes Farrell, who produced the music for the show, was similar to Don Kirshner in that he oversaw a brilliant stable of writers, including Neil Diamond and Barry Manilow. He composed a number of decent hits himself, but his fortune came from controlling the publishing of his gifted legion and from his ability to nurture a hit. In addition to using the finest tunesmiths Farrell also had the absolute best session musicians (including Tommy Tedesco, Mike Melvoin, and Hal Blaine) record the Partridge tracks; he also had a charismatic vocalist with a sexy voice in David Cassidy, who successfully lobbied to sing his own leads, despite being cast as a looker and lip-syncher. The resulting Partridge Family records were good enough to be hits. But they were *just* good enough, as Farrell didn't possess the intangibles that made Kirshner's best output so magical. The greatest Monkees songs transcend the disposable nature of their context, and that's why countless musicians credit that show with leading them down rock's glorious highway to hell. In contrast, when Joey Green, in his book *Partridge Family Album*, surveyed rock stars to see how the Partridges influenced them, he received the written equivalents of blank stares. "Phil is sorry he's unable to help you," Phil Collins's assistant responded in a typical reply, "as the Partridge Family didn't do anything to influence him."

Though they made some catchy songs—"I Think I Love You," "I Woke Up In Love This Morning," "Bandala," "I Can Feel Your Heartbeat," "Doesn't Somebody Want to Be Loved"—the Partridge Family did not rock. In fact, the Partridges were perhaps the greatest triumph in TV's long history of attempts to neuter the danger of rock 'n' roll. Although Ricky Nelson obviously came packaged with the parental seal of approval, at least his music stayed true to rockabilly, a genre with a raw, uncouth, rural heart. And while the Monkees may have been the definition of bubblegum, any interpretation of their antics must involve some threat to genteel society. (If you choose to ignore the obvious drug-laden counterculture themes and attribute their zaniness simply to Marx Brothers–style madness then you still have a scenario where America's kids are worshiping behavior fashioned by anarchist Jews.)

The Partridge Family, on the other hand, made pleasant pop presented in a wholesome and sober manner. More significantly, they removed all the unsafe accoutrements of rock. Their mom was in the band, so certainly there was no sex or drugs or even hanging out after the shows. And in contrast to that Woodstock thing everyone had heard so much about, Partridge Family concerts all seemed to take place in dinner theaters or lounges with fans seated at tables politely applauding. The band was *sort of* part of the counterculture, at least aesthetically (they have long hair and a psychedelic bus) and politically (they do concerts to help displaced Native Americans on one show and a ghetto social program on another—in that episode, featuring a guest appearance by Richard Pryor, Danny even joins the Black Panthers). But as positive as their music and motives were, the Partridges never ruffled any feathers.

This isn't an indictment of the program (which got better ratings and lasted longer than *The Monkees*). In general, *The Partridge Family* was a decent show. "We always figured," Slade explained in the book *The Partridge Family Album*, "that we were a classier show and that we had better scripts [than *The Brady Bunch*]." He's right. Many 1970s shows are still appreciated because of their camp and nostalgia value, but *The Partridge Family* has persevered because it was pretty good. Cassidy and Bonaduce possessed excellent comic timing; most of the writing, though hokey, was fairly sharp; and the overall look and feel of the program was solid (though mundane compared to *The Monkees*, the show was visually superior to the cheap-looking sitcoms that dominated the decade).

But the real legacy of the show isn't its content or even the hit records, but the fury it created surrounding David Cassidy. Like the Monkees before him, Cassidy was victimized by his own confusion about the legitimacy of his career. Like the Monkees he made the mistake of thinking his band wasn't real just because they were fictional. For someone who already had issues coming into the game, that crisis made it pretty hard for him to heed his own lyrical command to "get happy."

I won't be presumptuous enough to psychoanalyze Cassidy, but I will present the data and let you armchair Freuds have a go at it. The press had a field day with the charming fact that David Cassidy's TV mother was played by his real-life mom, Shirley Jones. He had a civil relationship with Jones, but she was actually his stepmother, the woman David's father left his mother for when David was five. His father rarely contacted David during his childhood ("a little boy shouldn't have been shunned like that," Cassidy told *Rolling Stone* in 1972). Jack Cassidy had been a stage and screen actor who stands as the all-time greatest villain on *Columbo* (NBC, 1971–1978; ABC, 1989–1990) because his cold, mesmerizing eyes conveyed a perfect balance between swarmy charm and brutal cruelty. He was a serial philanderer and a shitty father, rarely on good terms with his children. But when David decided to give showbiz a try (because, as he told *Las Vegas Weekly* in 1998, "I just wanted to act, like my father, and have him appreciate me for my talents") his dad made a gesture of reconciliation by setting him up with a super agent. Reportedly jealous of the success of others, Jack's relationship with David eroded again when *The Partridge Family* made his son a superstar.

Since he was the only Partridge who could sing (other than Jones, who was contractually guaranteed to do backup vocals on the records, earning her some royalties), David toured the country as a solo act on the weekends after filming the show, playing matinees to 56,723 screaming girls in the Astrodome one day, then to 20,000-plus in a sold-out Madison Square Garden another. His fans didn't miss the other Partridges; the singer and lead guitarist are the only ones anybody ever wants to see. But they did want to see a Partridge, as the songs he sang on that show, and the self-effacing character he played, were what made (to quote David from his *Rolling Stone* interview) "those girls leave behind thousands of sticky seats." David, however, was uncomfortable being white-bread Keith Partridge. He was a natural on stage, a decent rock guitarist and an aspiring songwriter who nurtured relationships with John Lennon and Brian Wilson. He wanted the credibility he felt he deserved, so he tried to get out of his TV contract and attempted to change his image (partially by doing the *Rolling Stone* piece, where he exposed his pubic hair, got high around the reporter, and let a girlfriend tell the magazine he "was a really good fuck"). After the show ended he laid low, eventually attempted to get back into acting, and spent decades sounding either hostile or ambivalent when discussing *The Partridge Family*.

Cassidy's bitterness is understandable. It's hard for bubblegum music idols, from Fabian to Vanilla Ice, to get any respect after their brief moment on top, and it's nearly impossible for the Gilligans and the Urkels of the sitcom world to move on after playing an iconic character. So David was double-screwed. That said, one of the keys to his redemption was realizing that Keith Partridge, despite being make-believe, was made real by the millions of little girls who believed in him. Today Cassidy is a doing well, both as a hot Vegas attraction and as a successful touring musician, and the key to these achievements has been embracing the idea that his loyal original audience was right to believe what they saw on TV, even if he thought it was bullshit.

Probably the most telling evidence of his troubled relationship with his Partridge past was a 2000 VH1 special about the show. Throughout the hour he seemed really upbeat and grounded, finally at peace with his legacy. But as the show progressed he began to seem a little *too* into the Partridges: he was producing a made-for-TV movie about the show, rerecording the songs with the original session men for that movie's soundtrack, and then re-rerecording the songs with New Age arrangements for a solo album. It seemed that he had reached a juncture in his career where it was prudent to be pro-Partridge, and perhaps his charming smile was pasted on to cover his still seething hostility. This theory proved to have merit when the show ended with Cassidy declaring that he has nothing bad to say about his Partridge days. He then paused, looked directly into the camera, and in a half-joking, half-scary tone declared, *"And don't let anyone tell you otherwise!"*

Because the Monkees' success with preteens was immediately followed by the Archies' success with pre-preteens, which was followed by the prepubescent popularity triumph of the Partridge Family, it became clear who made up the made-up band demographic. From then on the phenomenon mostly was relegated to kiddie shows, and for the next thirty years some of the more interesting TV rock appeared on Saturday morning instead of Saturday night.

The Banana Splits (NBC, 1968–1970) were four animals named Drooper, Snorky, Bingo, and Fleegle (live-action people in puppet suits) who played bubblegum flower pop while cavorting around playgrounds and their hip pad in Monkees-style music videos. Their real-life record sales were unimpressive, possibly due to the fact that all their best songs were given away free with breakfast cereal, but the songs were pretty good. Barry White worked on their sessions and wrote an R&B tune for them, and they even had a song where they name-checked America's greatest soul brothers: Ray Charles, James Brown, Otis Redding . . . and Yogi Bear! Joey Ramone years later would cite the Monkees and the Splits as two of his favorite bands.

Less influential were the *Bugaloos* (NBC, 1970–1972), though currently there are multiple *extensive* Bugaloos Web sites. Produced by Sid and Marty Krofft, the kings of psychedelic, drug trip–simulating kiddie shows, this was about a band of attractive, English magic bug-fairy people who live in Tranquility Forest and tussle with an evil Martha Raye. The music was okay, and the LP is pleasant, surely better than if Phil Collins had won the Bugaloo role he auditioned for—who wants to hear an insect buzzing, "Su-su-sudio"?

A less interesting act was *The Kids from C.A.P.E.R.* (NBC, 1976–1977), a Don Kirshner attempt to re-create the Monkees by designing a show about four super spies (from the Civilian Authority for the Protection of Everyone Regardless) with four distinct personalities and one indistinct music act.

My least favorite of the Saturday-morning rock bunch was the pseudo-glam Kaptain Kool and the Kongs. The unfortunately initialed KKK had one flop LP, a few comic books, and a gig emceeing the *Krofft Supershow* (NBC 1976–1978). Despite their name the Kongs were people, not apes.

My favorite of the kiddie TV rock bands is the Evolution Revolution, which appeared on *Lancelot Link, Secret Chimp* (ABC, 1970–1972). This live-action show starred an all-chimpanzee cast, and each episode featured a musical number by the band that would be introduced by Ed Simian (a monkey who did an Ed Sullivan impersonation then spun around like a whirling dervish). On a crazy psychedelic set, the band would "play" excellent bubble-psyche songs like "Yummy Love" and "Wild Dream, Jelly Bean." As far as filming the segments, they couldn't get the apes to strum or drum until they actually played the record for them . . . then the chimps grooved right along! Of course, actual symmetry between the music and the action is not nearly as important as showing chimpanzees in crazy hippie duds. Years later the Anipals on *TV Funhouse* (Comedy Central, 2000–2001) paid homage to the Evolution Revolution and the inanity of pretending animals can play instruments.

A new wave of live-action shows with kids and teens playing music emerged many Saturdays later. *Kids Incorporated* (Disney Channel, syndicated 1984–1993) was an odd program in which the rotating cast of dozens of children would sing, play, and dance their own versions of well-known pop tunes. The show is most notable for producing numerous somewhat successful performers, including Martika, Shanice, Fergie from Black Eyed Peas/Wild Orchid, actress Jennifer Love Hewitt (who has a healthy music career in Japan), and neo-soul artist Rahsaan Patterson. Patterson played "The Kid" on the show, a possible *Purple Rain* reference, though the most infamous episode involved him idolizing not Prince but rather guest star David Hasselhoff, who sang a painful Motown cover. Other live-action made-for-TV kid bands from that era include the New Kids on the Block rip-off *Guys Next Door* (NBC, 1990–1991) and the Party, who appeared on the *New Mickey Mouse Club* (Disney Channel, 1989–1994). The Party was made up of Mouseketeers, but Disney chose the wrong ones—they bypassed Britney Spears, Justin Timberlake, and Christina Aguilera, who were all on the show at the time.

Despite producing fewer stars than its peers, the live kids show that did the most with its Monkeeness was the long-running Saturday-morning sitcom *California Dreams* (NBC, 1992–1997). The show followed the comical adventures of a group of beautiful L.A. high school students who formed a garage band that somehow managed to make lush, sappy, adult contemporary music (this despite a theme song that promised "surf dudes with attitude"). With the guidance of a sleazy teenage manager, the band spent five years of high school trying to make it. This was the second of producer Peter Engel's live-action sitcoms that usurped Saturday morning from cartoons (the first was *Saved by the Bell* [NBC, in several incarnations between 1987–2000]). Engel's shows seem to operate on the theory that since they are for children the writing, acting, and direction can be vastly inferior to the already insipid prime-time sitcoms. It's no wonder the most infamous Engel graduate, Elizabeth Berkeley, didn't have the critical capacity to know not to star in *Showgirls*. California Dreams released a CD on MCA in 1992 to tepid sales, but they recorded dozens of songs over the next five years, and bootleg compilations sell for more than forty dollars on ebay. Though not really musicians per se, a couple of the cast members pursued music careers after the show wrapped. Brentley Gore has been in the trenches of the L.A. club scene and Jennie Kwan briefly joined the teen girl vocal group Nobody's Angel. For the most part, the members of California Dreams were attractive, moderately talented kids who held their own vocally. Bad boy Jake did the only significant lip-synching. His voice was provided by the composer and producer of the California Dreams' music, Barry Coffing, the man who was best positioned to be the Don Kirshner of 1990s TV fake rock.

Catwalk (syndicated, 1992; MTV, 1994) was a short-lived, forgettable Canadian-produced series about a struggling rock band that featured a few memorable light-rock songs (there was a CD on Atlantic), including some written by Coffing, who had spent time under the wing of legendary writer/producer Steve Tyrell. Coffing and Tyrell's next Monkees redux would prove to be more golden. *The Heights* (Fox, 1992) was a vehicle for singer Jamie Walters (who later broke hearts and bones as a girlfriend-beating sensitive rocker on *Beverly Hills 90210*). *The Heights* was the story of a blue-collar band, the Heights (you knew they were cool because of the black member's dreadlocks and the guy in the Hüsker Dü shirt), that made wussy music. The show couldn't find an audience, but the week it got canceled the Heights' "How Do You Talk to an Angel" (composed by Coffing/Tyrell) hit number one on the *Billboard* pop chart. So Coffing achieved CD sales success with a flop TV series, yet would spend the next half-decade making music for *California Dreams*, a successful kiddie show with no CD sales. Another generation failed to duplicate the Monkees magic.

Other than shows about a band's career, numerous "fake" bands have been written into fiction series for various reasons. Virtually every sitcom with teenagers had episodes or running subplots where the kids form a band. As the title character in *Gidget* (ABC, 1965–1966), Sally Field fronted a proto-goth combo called the Gories for one episode. Ron Howard (as Opie) had a preteen band on the *Andy Griffith Show* (CBS, 1960–1968), and as teenage Ritchie on *Happy Days* (ABC, 1974–1984) he had a regular gig at Arnold's Diner (Fonzie once sat in on bongos). Ritchie's younger sister Joanie was briefly in Leather and the Suedes (Leather Tuscadero was played by glam/garage queen Suzi Quatro). Later Joanie had her own brief spinoff sitcom, *Joanie Loves Chachi* (ABC, 1982–1983), where she and her boyfriend tried to make it as rockers in 1960s Chicago. The kids from *The Brady Bunch* (ABC, 1969–1974) formed several acts, including the Brady Six and Johnny Bravo. They released records and had two musical spinoff programs, a variety show, and a cartoon. On *Diff'rent Strokes* (NBC, 1979–1986) Willis had a funky band called the Afrodesiacs, featuring a pre-superstardom Janet Jackson. Even adults got into the act, as Homer won a Grammy with the Be Sharps on *The Simpsons* (FOX, 1989–present) and Drew played lounges with the Horndogs on the *Drew Carey Show* (ABC, 1995–2004).

Sillier still are the TV bands that are supposed to represent current trends. When the Beatles made it big, sitcoms were swarmed with comical bug bands. On a 1964 *Joey Bishop Show* (NBC, 1962–1964; CBS, 1964–1965) Bishop in a Beatle wig played in a band called the Grasshoppers. On a 1965 episode of *Gilligan's Island*

(CBS, 1964–1967) the island was visited by the mop-topped Mosquitos (featuring Bingo, Bango, Bongo, and Irving). On a 1965 episode of the *Bing Crosby Show* (ABC, 1964–1965) Bing is plagued by, but eventually sings with, the Love Bugs (played by L.A. garage kings the Standells). And most absurdly, in a 1967 episode of *F Troop* (ABC, 1965–1967), a comedy set in the 1870s, there was a battle of the bug bands with the Termites and the Bed Bugs doing covers of songs that wouldn't be written until ninety years later.

When the theatrical rock band KISS, with their face paint and shocking antics, made waves in the late 1970s, TV responded. In 1978 *Scooby Doo* (CBS, 1969–1976; ABC, 1976–1986, 1988–1991; WB, 2002–2003) and his gang foiled the Diabolical Disc Demon, a Gene Simmons look-alike (in 2003 the real KISS, in animated form, met the mystery-solving pooch). In a 1979 episode of *Love Boat* (ABC 1977–1986; UPN 1998–1999), Sonny Bono played Deacon Dark, an evil, violent, makeup-slathered shock rocker who falls in love with a deaf girl who turns him into a spineless acoustic singer-songwriter. Best of all was Moloch, the rocker played by Donny Most (Ralph Malph from *Happy Days*) on the 1982 Halloween episode of *CHiPs* (NBC, 1977–1983). Wearing a KISS costume and KISS makeup (supplemented by minstrel lips and a Barbra Streisand wig), Moloch's satanic rock apparently angered the Devil himself, as a series of macabre, seemingly occult accidents nearly killed him. In the end the would-be murderer was revealed to be his manager (played by Peter Marshall of *Hollywood Squares*), who figured a dead rock star would increase record sales (Tupac notwithstanding, I think he might have been mistaken).

During the *NSYNC/Backstreet Boys heyday fake TV bands were created in a more cynical, meaner spirit than were the parodies during previous fads. Comedy shows mocked the concept of boy bands outright, equating the fakeness of their own fake bands to the fakeness of the actual chart toppers. Some of the absurdities presented included 7 Degrees Celsius on *Saturday Night Live* (NBC, 1975–present) in 2000, Fingerbang on *South Park* (Comedy Central, 1997–present) in 2000, and Dudez A Plenti on *Late Night with Conan O'Brien* (NBC, 1993–present) in 2002. More telling were the two Monkees-like series cashing in on the craze. The British show *Boyz Unlimited* (BBC, 1999) featured a shyster assembling a band of awful teenagers who impregnate their tutor, stiff loan sharks, and feud with their more successful rivals, Boyz Limited. One might assume that *Boyz Unlimited* was never imported because it was too dark for a U.S. teen audience, but apparently that wasn't the case. When the U.S. equivalent premiered the next year it was sufficiently edgy, including a postscript that trumps even Andy Kaufman's most disturbing performance art.

2Ge+her (MTV, 2000–2001) was launched as MTV's first made-for-TV movie and became a series when the soundtrack album sold surprisingly well. Directed by Nigel Dick, who had previously made Radiohead and Guns 'n Roses videos, the story was a cynical comedy about a washed-up manager assembling a horrible prefab act. Much of the comedy derives from an articulation of the clichés of the trend. The band has to supplement the handsome lead singer with a bad boy (in this case a goofy white kid addicted to angry Ebonics), a quiet one (who is nearly retarded), a cute little one, and an older-brother type. Both *NSYNC and Backstreet Boys had one member substantially older (in his mid 20s) but in 2Ge+her this role was filled by Chris Farley's heavy-set, balding middle-aged brother.

Some of the show's humor was based on the insipidness of boy-band fashion, choreography, songwriting, and spelling; their faux hit, "U+Me=Us (Calculus)," for example. Despite being aimed at easy targets these jokes were somewhat daring considering MTV was telling the same audience that bought Backstreet Boys CDs that Backstreet Boys suck. But more interesting was the edgier material that dealt flippantly with teen pregnancy, homoeroticism (one episode is about jealousy over which member has the largest gay fan base), and, most notably, cancer. In the boldest incident of black humor ever on teen TV Michael Cuccione played QT, "the cute one," a doe-eyed character whose appeal played upon the sympathy felt for adorable terminally ill children. QT gets attention from the girls and a lot of comedic mileage out of the fact that his youthful, upbeat character could die any day. The sick jokes about a pubescent, mortally ill heartthrob were made sicker (and infinitely bolder) by the fact that Cuccione actually was a pubescent, mortally ill heartthrob. Before the second season finished airing the comically gifted sixteen-year-old died of respiratory complications related to Hodgkin's lymphoma.

Morbidity aside, the show was an interesting *Monkees* update simply because the prefab nature of actual boy bands complicates the idea of branding 2Ge+her as a fake band. They were assembled by a casting agent in a manner not dissimilar to the way 1990s Svengali Lou Pearlman cast his million-seller acts. Thanks to the complicity of MTV, 2Ge+her appeared on the popular video countdown show *TRL* (MTV, 1989–present) and had their own episode of *Making the Video* (MTV, 1999–present), just like *NSYNC. All members of 2Ge+her sang their own vocals, which is the extent of involvement of any boy band (writing one's own material was not an option for these acts). They toured with Britney Spears and had hundreds of thousands of rabid fans. There were even 2Ge+her dolls. Despite being actors using fictitious names and reading lines, in many ways this band was totally real (*too* real if you factor in the part about one of the members actually having cancer).

Even though it was a short-lived craze, the boy-band era yielded its own Monkees. But surprisingly the contemporary music movement that has most impacted the charts for the last two decades has failed to make fake band progress. Given how easy it would be to find good-looking kids who could sort of rap it is curious that there hasn't been a prefab TV hip-hop superstar (not counting Arsenio Hall's fat alter ego, Chunky A). But hip-hop's contradictory embrace of and disdain for artifice complicates the creation of a Rappin' Monkees. Though the mantra "keep it real" resonates throughout the culture, hip-hop is also a world of superhero pseudonyms, bizarre couture, and fantasies of extreme violence and extreme wealth. Sure, rap fans appreciate authenticity—consider the value of 50 Cent's bullet

2Ge+her dolls. Courtesy Jake Austen

wounds (though Mr. Cent claims that they furthered his musicianship, attributing his unique vocal timbre to being shot in the throat). But fans also understand that their heroes are engaging in make-believe. No one protests when a debut album by an unknown bulges with boasts of riches and platinum success.

Another reason there may not be a rush to put make-believe rappers on TV series is that TV series are chock-full of real-life rappers. In the 1990s the networks cashed in on rap's popularity by developing projects for rap stars, though they very deliberately cast them in non-rapper roles. Will Smith and Jazzy Jeff in *Fresh Prince of Bel Air* (NBC, 1990–1996), Queen Latifah in *Living Single* (FOX, 1993–1998), and LL Cool J in *In The House* (NBC 1995–1996, UPN 1996–1998) played nonmusical characters on conventional sitcoms. This was the best of both worlds for the networks and rappers—the networks gained the credibility of having hip rappers while not alienating viewers that disliked rap, and rappers got to be bigger stars without risking being branded as bogus Monkees types.

The only fake-band show vaguely about a rap group (a predominantly white one) was the awful *Shasta McNasty* (UPN, 1999–2000). Though it attempted to capture some of the frenetic anarchy of *The Monkees*, it tempered the zaniness with slacker laziness, so that the band rarely got around to making any music. Led by Gary Busey's rumpled son, Jake, Shasta McNasty was supposed to be a band trying to make it. But early on the producers realized that the sole attraction of the show was the participation of the tiny Verne Troyer (Mini-Me from *Austin Powers*). The program stopped being about a band and more about discovering what sort of wacky situations a midget can get into. When Shasta McNasty did make music it was absolutely awful. But that doesn't mean that they weren't a real band. It just means that they were a real band that was really bad.

The Monkees were a real band that was really good. They may not have been as talented or as smart or as funny as the Beatles, but that doesn't mean there is anything wrong with liking the pre-Fabs as much as, or more than, the Fabs. The audience is an integral part of the rock experience, and whatever you think about TV as a medium, one thing that cannot be denied is its power to capture, even entrance and immobilize, an audience. It is little wonder that several of the silly made-for-TV bands that pop culture addicts have seen while under TV's hypnotizing spell have made a more powerful impression on them than many of the critic's choices and Rock 'n' Roll Hall of Famers.

So if your favorite band is an all-chimp psychedelic act or a group where Susan Dey's keyboard isn't actually plugged in or a Make-A-Wish-Foundation boy band or even Shasta McNasty, keep your head up. Some might say you don't have the most sophisticated musical palette, and it's unlikely that you are ever going to get to see your heroes in concert. But if you sincerely dig that group and they genuinely do it for you, you are not being a chump by loving those "fakes."

You're just keeping it real.

4

The Hippest Trip in Town

Black-on-Black Music TV

t's 1954 and through the magic of TV, black Americans can get a glimpse of their cultural Mecca, and white Americans can go uptown without fear. As the speakers on their massive Dumont, RCA, or Coronado TV sets emit the wails of a slinky jazz trumpet, their proud picture tubes radiate with a montage of the landmarks of Harlem after dark. Flashy neon signs announce legendary locales like the Savoy, Smalls', Sugar Ray's, and Hotel Theresa, climaxing with the marquee of the legendary Apollo Theater promising the "Harlem Variety Review." America then welcomes into its collective living room the handsome, light-skinned bandleader, Willie Bryant (one of the many unofficial "mayors" of Harlem). Between comical interruptions by chitlin circuit comedians like Nipsey Russell and Mantan Moreland, Bryant brings to the Apollo stage the greatest stars in black entertainment: Duke Ellington, Lionel Hampton, Herb Jeffries, Amos Milburn, The Clovers, Dinah Washington, Nat King Cole, and more.

Or so it would seem. This short-lived production called *Show Time at the Apollo* (syndicated, 1954) featured some amazing live footage. However, it certainly wasn't shot at the Apollo. The introductions and some of the performances were shot in a studio, while the remaining performances (including Ellington's) were Snader Telescriptions. Snader produced thousands of short films of musicians playing jazz, country, and pop tunes. These ancestors of music videos were used for filling in gaps when TV scheduling was still an inexact science. To create the illusion of a live program *Show Time at the Apollo* occasionally cut to stock footage of an audience applauding. Shots of Bryant standing in the wings snapping his fingers were spliced into the Telescriptions. However, the illusion that this was a real Apollo concert was compromised when the curtains parted behind Bryant to reveal Telescriptions that opened with close-ups, or with musicians in a far different scale than the emcee, suggesting a surreal world where the giants of jazz were actual giants.

Show Time at the Apollo was a pretty good show: the comics were funny, and the musical performances were excellent. The lineup was diverse, with not only jazz and pop but also jump blues and R&B, the latter a rarity on TV in those days. (In 1949 Bryant hosted a similar program on CBS limited to jazz and pop, called,

alternately, *Uptown Jubilee* and *Sugar Hill Times* during its five-week run.) Though not exactly rock 'n' roll, some of the acts here certainly laid the groundwork, and one amazing number actually heralds not only the breakthrough rock 'n' roll of the 1950s but also that of the 1960s and 1970s. In a performance original to the show, Big Joe Turner unleashed a live version of "Shake, Rattle and Roll" (which became an early rock standard when Bill Haley and the Comets, and later Elvis Presley, recorded it) that sounds remarkable to contemporary ears because it is dominated by cymbal crashes that caught the TV soundmen unprepared. This resulted in the number being underscored by brutal, vibrant overmodulation that vividly invokes the Detroit power-punk that Iggy and the Stooges would create a decade and a half down the line. But despite being historic, and despite giving TV viewers some of their first views of the rock 'n' roll mayhem to come, *Show Time at the Apollo* failed to capture the magic of the real Apollo Theater and its audience, and consequently it failed to capture what could be so special about black musical programming.

Over the next half-century black musical programming would include the socially conscious political shows that emerged in the 1960s, the funky dance shows that boogied into the 1970s, the music video–heavy Black Entertainment Television cable network that was born in the 1980s, and the often criticized comedy shows that appeared on the upstart UPN and WB networks in the 1990s and 2000s. These shows were very different, but they all understood what was special about a black audience and knew how to speak directly to it. And to best appreciate that audience, the place to look is the Apollo Theater.

The modest palace on 125th Street, built in 1913 and reborn as the Apollo in 1934, was still establishing itself in 1935 when a Harlem riot got the media stirred up. Newspapers urged whites to avoid the dangerous streets of Uptown where reportedly savage blacks exhibited a bloodlust for white victims. Prior to that, Harlem had operated like a Third World tourist resort; whites frequented segregated nightclubs where they were served and entertained by the neighborhood's natives. Though it may seem like I am laying the jungle metaphors on a bit thick, the Cotton Club (its name an invitation to the lily white) and other legendary venues often presented stage shows with cartoonish "Darkest Africa" themes. Though the members of the community who were gainfully employed by the clubs were willing to suffer these indignities, obviously there were others who were not. The policies of the clubs were among the inequities that fueled one of New York's first race riots, a two-day event that injured dozens, killed three, and smashed the majority of windows in the 125th Street theater district.

Though owned by a white man, Sid Cohen, the Apollo was not modeled after the Cotton Club. Cohen had opened the previously segregated theater's doors to a black audience. The announcement in Harlem newspapers promised, "Courtesy and consideration will be the watchword of the management, truly a resort for the better people" (code for "black folk"). The Apollo was the first theater on 125th Street that courted a black audience, and over the years the white owner-ship (Cohen until 1936, the Schiffman family for most of the next four decades) was committed to a policy of hiring all black staff, stagehands, and personnel. Most importantly, Cohen empowered emcee Ralph Cooper, a bandleader and a race-film actor nicknamed "Dark Gable," to create Amateur Night at the Apollo shortly after the theater opened.

Banking that Harlem was brimming with untapped talent and that a black audience was anxious to cheer on (or jeer off) the girls and boys next door, Cooper developed a format that quickly caught on. Wednesday night in Harlem for the next four decades featured raucous crowds participating fully in the competition, determining the winners by applause and booing off delusional wannabes. Porto Rico, the "executioner"/rodeo clown (originally played by Norman Miller, later by Junkie Jones and C. P. Lacey), kept the mood light by using his broom to whisk off the ousted contestants. This formula was a smash and the legend of the demon-strative, vocal Apollo audience grew when Amateur Hour began broadcasting on the radio shortly after its inception. In the wake of the 1935 riot fewer whites ven-tured into the area. But on Wednesdays it became chic for white stars to attend. Jimmy Durante, Jack Benny, Jackie Gleason, Mae West, and others took great pride in being announced from the stage as they sat among the vocal locals. Leg-end has it that Joan Crawford practiced her screen screams by booing at Amateur Night. Though the Amateur Night stage introduced some of the greatest talents of the twentieth century to America (including Ella Fitzgerald, Billy Eckstine, Gladys Knight, Billie Holiday, Dionne Warwick, Luther Vandross, Stephanie Mills, and the Jackson 5ive), the true stars of the show were the people of Harlem who, from the front row to the Buzzard's Roost (second balcony), made their feel-ings known without restraint.

There has been criticism of loud black audiences ever since the early days of desegregated entertainment (a 1920s editorial cartoon in a New York newspaper shows a black couple in a theater with their lips padlocked shut) and it contin-ues today (a staple of contemporary hack stand-up comedy is mocking blacks who talk back to the movie screen). To dismiss this type of audience behavior as an indication of lack of class or as a sign of ignorance is wrongheaded. Active audience participation is one of the few opportunities for a minority to assert agency, as described in the writings of Ralph Ellison, James Baldwin, and Langston Hughes (who in his 1951 poem "Movies" celebrates a black filmgoer who knows it is appropriate to laugh at the bullshit on the screen). Contemporary studies by Henry Louis Gates, bell hooks, and Jacqueline Stewart have reexamined the relationships between the blacks in the audience and the action they are observing on the stage or screen.

For a simple tutorial in black spectatorship one need only observe the Apollo crowds. Gathered in that theater is a cross section of a marginalized people who can express themselves freely and demonstrate sound judgment. While it can be a great joy to use entertainment passively, as escapism, you can't really argue against using it as a way to be free and to be right.

Though it invoked the name of the Apollo, the 1954 TV show actually operated on a principle that predates that theater's reign. While it certainly wasn't guilty of dressing the performers in grass skirts or making the comedians "coon it up" (Charlie Chan movie fans were likely surprised to see Mantan Moreland's relative dignity on the show), like the pre-Apollo 125th Street theaters, this show was dressing up the black theater experience for a white audience. Certainly black TV viewers were delighted to see members of their race on TV, but by eliminating the energy and the interaction of the Harlem audience it was not providing them with what experience told them to expect at their theaters. When the Apollo stage returned to the TV screen three decades later this shortcoming was rectified.

Amateur Night remained an Apollo attraction until the mid-1970s when the poverty, drugs, and apathy that plagued Harlem forced the rundown theater to close its doors (its final concert, an appropriately futuristic attack on a night when past history was being laid to rest, was by P-Funk). Over the next five years the shell of the once-proud theater became more and more dilapidated. Then black businessman and Manhattan borough president Percy Sutton bought the building. In 1985 Amateur Night returned (amazingly still presided over, as it had been fifty-one years earlier, by Ralph Cooper, who would remain an Apollo presence until his death in 1992). Two years later it was TV time at the Apollo once again, and this time it was the real thing.

It's Showtime at the Apollo premiered in the fall of 1987. The syndicated show produced by Percy Sutton's Inner City Broadcasting Television was in many ways an old-time variety show in the *Ed Sullivan* mold. This "Harlem Variety Review" featured a charming emcee (actually several over the years, though few were as smooth as Willie Bryant had been), live performances by popular and up-and-coming R&B and rap acts, and a set by a black comedian (usually doing nasal impressions of how whites talk, making comic references to the black churchgoing experience, and working impersonations of black singers into the act). But the key to the show's success was a televised version of Amateur Night.

This segment became the signature of the show, a variation on the recent syndicated success *Star Search* (syndicated, 1983–1995; CBS, 2003–2004), a precursor to *American Idol* (Fox, 2002–present), and a revival of the principles of such early TV favorites as *Arthur Godfrey's Talent Scouts* (CBS, 1948–1958) and *Ted Mack's Original Amateur Hour*. What made the Apollo show stand out from these programs was that instead of being a formal, serious election of those with "star potential," the Apollo contest was a festive event that felt more like a family reunion. While a number of youthful, beautiful contestants clearly had aspirations of pop stardom, middle-aged and average-looking folks also showed off their talents on the fabled Harlem stage. And though the vocal jeers of the crowd would get one banished from the stage, this comic vote of disapproval wasn't nearly as cruel as *American Idol*'s adult panel of mean-spirited experts eviscerating vulnerable sixteen-year-olds.

What really differentiated *It's Showtime at the Apollo* from the other shows was that it was not really about the performers. Just like the radio version of more than a half-century earlier, *It's Showtime at the Apollo* was about the audience. The crowd reaction was far more important than the performance onstage, and the TV show reflected that, generously turning the cameras on the crowd. Before a collective roar of endorsement or disapproval was unleashed, the TV audience could witness the development of the crowd's opinion. This helped the TV viewer *be* part of that crowd. Like the teen dance shows that inspired viewers to dance in front of their TVs, *It's Showtime at the Apollo* invited viewers to cheer and boo along with the audience. Like no other show, this one was about black spectatorship, as the African American audience was not only a desired demographic but also the main subject matter.

The producers made the audience the star of the show partly by emphasizing its connections with the legendary Apollo crowds of yore through elements that invoked the classic Amateur Night (which still ran on Wednesdays, now an audition stage for the TV show). Porto Rico's clown suit and executioner duties were passed on to Sandman Sims, a legendary tap dancer who was no stranger to the Apollo stage, having performed upon it for decades doing his signature sand dance (he would spread sand on the floor to combine shuffling scratches with his percussive taps). Classic Apollo glamour was represented by Kiki Shepard (the black

Vanna White), a woman whose minor acting roles over the years in plays and cable movies more than qualified her to stand behind the amateur performers and hold her manicured hand over their heads to indicate for whom to applaud (audience applause determines the winner). Also present was a shellacked cross section of the stump of the Tree of Hope, a symbol of brotherhood for Harlem entertainers that had shaded the back alley of the Lafayette (the off-125th Street black theater that reigned before the Apollo opened). When Seventh Avenue was widened around the time of the Apollo's opening, necessitating the uprooting of the shade tree, Ralph Cooper got the idea to mount a scrap of it onto an Ionic column and allow Amateur Night contestants to touch it for good luck, just as rookie entertainers had hugged the tree during its lifetime. Though the entire show emphasized the Apollo's history, this element was the most overt manifestation of its ambition to be something bigger than Ed McMahon's search for the stars of tomorrow. It was not only exciting for the performers to touch something that they knew Billie Holiday had touched but it also was a profound symbol of taking part in something bigger than a talent show.

Another major difference between this and other amateur contests was that *It's Showtime at the Apollo* was a variety competition, with disparate modes of entertainment going head to head. This, of course, was neither sensible nor fair (what chance would a juggler have against a soul singer?), which fit perfectly with the Apollo vibe of being more fun than serious. With a number of disciplines to choose from, would-be Amateur Night contestants could look to the audience's reactions week after week to determine what kind of performance was likely to win the crowd over. Singing gospel was one of the safer routes, even for those with average voices, because the crowd was hesitant to boo Jesus. Nonetheless, truly bad gospel singing was treated as blasphemy. Stand-up comedy was the most dangerous area, as it usually required a crowd to be on the performer's side from the get-go, and the impatience that the Amateur Night format necessitated could have a comic drawing dead from "How you all doing tonight?" It's hard to be hilarious within five seconds; many would-be funnymen made quick dejected exits. Rapping fell into that category as well—it's challenging to instantly convey rap skills—and if LL Cool J wannabes lost the beat for even a second they were doomed. Acrobatic dancing, especially from young dance teams that combined athletic contemporary choreography with the classic tap or jazz dancing that were historic elements of Apollo lore, went over well. Doing a decent job playing a musical instrument, especially brass (usually playing the vocal line of a popular song), wouldn't get a contestant booed off, but he or she probably wouldn't win either. Little children doing *anything* usually received encouraging applause (eventually they were relegated to their own, less-competitive segment, "Apollo Kids"). The heart of the contest, and the most likely victors, were R&B vocalists. One running joke (Chris Rock loves making fun of this) was that certain songs always got the crowd jumping out of their seats with applause, especially "And I Am Telling You I'm Not Going," made popular by Jennifer Holliday in the musical *Dreamgirls* (though uptown Apollo fans probably knew the song from urban radio, not from downtown Broadway excursions), followed closely by Whitney Houston's "I Have Nothing." Though there was an absurdity to hearing these same songs ad nauseam (*American Idol* has a list of chestnuts *verboten* for auditioning hopefuls), it makes sense that familiar, melodramatic ballads that surge to tremendous climaxes and favor church-trained R&B voices with dynamic range were perfect for a contest like this. Subtlety was not a performer's friend at Amateur Night.

Nonetheless, that doesn't mean the crowd, with their raucous hollering and histrionic gestures, had a coarse palate that is easy to manipulate. The reason this format was so successful for so long is that the Apollo audience was usually right about who had the juice and who needed to limit his or her singing to the shower. Often demonstrating an impressive collective sophistication, the crowd en masse picked up on subtle elements that distinguished a seemingly proficient performer from someone who really had the right stuff. And the Apollo crowd did hope that the contestants would sing well. For while they loved to make Sandman sweep a delusional wannabe offstage, they also loved to be able to claim that they had discovered a new talent. Just as the legendary Amateur Night helped launch the careers of numerous stars, artists who appeared on the televised *It's Show Time at the Apollo* Amateur Night have gone on to professional glory, including Lauryn Hill, Fat Joe, Jaheim, and D'Angelo.

To guarantee that no week would go by without a comical "execution," there were always a certain number of absurd acts. White performers of dubious talent (or of talents incongruous with the Apollo's tastes, such as mimes) were set up as patsies. But unlike *American Idol*'s delusional William Hung, these were often performance artists or eccentrics who were excited about the opportunity to be booed by such an esteemed crowd. A white musician once told me that he knew he would lose but insisted on doing an original song so that he would get publishing royalties whenever the show aired. The racial angle certainly played a part, as the black audience seemed to relish having temporary power over whites and seeing them fail. But racial representation on the Apollo stage could also go the other way, as the black audience could enjoy the compliment of seeing another culture acknowledge their art form (as when a group of Japanese break dancers won the competition).

The Apollo audience was unpredictable. A white champion, Superbad Brad, dressed like a homeless person, seemed to be positioning himself to be the target of boos, but then launched into a soulful number (in a slightly above-average voice that in and of itself likely would not have cut it with the Apollo crowd), and his "soul" combined with his unusual appearance won the crowd over.

For the most part the Apollo TV crowd wanted to be supportive of its own people, with the Amateur Night hecklers being a playful exception. "The show is about hope and aspiration," executive producer Chuck Sutton (Percy's nephew) explained in 1997—but not in the same way *American Idol* is about the aspirations of an individual to become a superstar. When a young saxophonist mentioned that he was studying at a certain conservatory the crowd gave a roar of approval, not because they had heard of the school and knew of its prestige, but because they saw the idea of a black teen honing his craft in a music conservatory as an achievement worthy of acknowledgment. When host Steve Harvey preached to the crowd about black responsibility and the absurdity of black-on-black violence the audience was receptive and engaged, not impatient for the next act. Spoken-word performers with militant or positive messages were made to feel welcome and appreciated on the stage. The catchphrase that invited the audience to welcome a new act to the stage was, "Show them your love!" And despite being most famous as a show where a clown punished amateurs for failure, the Apollo was fundamentally a show about African Americans feeling love, pride, and connection with their people and their cultural history. In this way the show was profoundly different than the 1956 Apollo show, which evoked the Harlem landmark only as a code word for black entertainment, not as a venue to celebrate the collective black spectator experience.

Some may argue that *It's Showtime at the Apollo* was not merely directed at a black audience, but was designed to simulate a black audience experience for white viewers. While it is true that at the show's ratings peak, it had a broad audience (for a while it was the highest rated syndicated show among young women), a closer look at the demographics indicates that it clearly had a black audience in mind. According to the king of black syndication, Frank Mercado-Valdes, *It's Showtime at the Apollo* is the number-one syndicated show for black viewers, and "the crown jewel" in his empire. The Nielsen ratings consistently tallied the show as scoring five times higher in black households than in the general ratings. Comedians on the show regularly made cultural references few nonblacks would pick up on, with little or no attempt at contextualizing the jokes. The show booked musical acts that were popular on black radio but had little crossover appeal. And time was set aside for affirmations, pleas for black unity, and Afro-centric poets. But the most telling symbol that this show was aimed at a black audience was the presence of its two most popular hosts.

Steve Harvey (host 1994–2000) and Mo'Nique (host 2002–present) are two names synonymous with the gap between white and black TV audiences. Both stand-up comedians fronted their own sitcoms that ran concurrently with their *Apollo* reigns. Mo'Nique's *The Parkers* (UPN, 1999–2004) was notable because though it was by far the number-one show in black households, it ranked dead last in white homes. *The Steve Harvey Show* (WB, 1996–2002) is a bit more note-worthy for this book because it was music themed. Harvey played Steve High-tower, a 1970s funk musician who finds himself teaching music at an inner-city high school. His former band, the Hi-Tops, which included Ron Isley, often per-formed on the show to sing their hits "When the Funk Hits the Fan" and "Break Me Off a Piece of That Funk." Harvey's show was black America's *Seinfeld*, treas-ured by its viewers, towering in the black household ratings, and annually sweep-ing the NAACP Image Awards. Yet it was unknown in most white homes and was never nominated for an Emmy in any category.

Like the majority of black-cast TV shows in the last two decades, *The Steve Harvey Show* aired on one of the startup networks that began offering original prime-time programming in 1987 when Fox was launched, followed in the 1990s by the WB and UPN. Early offerings on each network, such as Fox's *In Living Color* (1990–1994), WB's *The Parent 'hood* (1995–1999), and UPN's *Homeboys in Outer Space* (1996–1997), catered to African American audiences that were eager to see black faces on TV. In a 1998 interview with the *Boston Phoenix* Jordan Levin, head of development for the WB, admitted that blacks are "a built-in audience that is open to trying new services," and that wooing them was part of the network's startup plan. Once established, both Fox and WB dropped their black shows and moved on to paler niches (Fox leaned toward edgy shows for radical dudes and WB went for teenage girls). So far UPN is the only network that has maintained a commitment to black programming.

While the abandonment of the black base may be disloyal, it is typical of busi-ness practices. Once the networks were established, to lure more lucrative (in terms of advertising dollars) white audiences they had to give up black audiences because blacks and whites simply refused to watch the same shows. In 1997 (the last year when UPN, Fox, and the WB all had significant black programming) the top ten shows in black households were startup networks' black-cast shows, none of which ranked higher than 115th in white homes. Among the top ten shows for white viewers four programs were in the black top twenty (three of which featured prominent black faces: *ER, Touched by an Angel,* and *Monday Night Football*). However, white ratings juggernauts *Seinfeld* and *Friends* were blips in black homes, ranking 59th and 118th respectively. Recently the reality TV boom closed the gap because despite the fact that African Americans don't love Raymond (ranking him 105th), apparently everybody loves Ruben, and *American Idol* rules across the board.

Black audiences had a good excuse for not watching *Friends* and *Seinfeld*: those shows were about urban characters who never encountered black people. Unfortunately, white people also had good reason to avoid the black sitcoms. Many black viewers found the content offensive (Chuck D called UPN the "United Plantation of Negroes" and Spike Lee declared in 1997, "I would rather see *Amos 'n' Andy*; at least they were straight-up about Uncle Tommin'"). Many of the shows also were poorly done. In 2004 African American TV historian Donald Bogle told the *Boston Globe* that these shows "appear thrown together. They're not well written. They're not well directed. You feel for the actors."

Harvey's show certainly suffered from some of the formal shortcomings Bogle lamented. The rhythm seemed off (occasionally the show would end at what felt like the wrong time), the writing was sloppy (token white kid Bullethead is supposed to live in a trailer park despite residing in trailer-free Chicago, and he speaks with a Brooklyn accent), and the plots seemed to recycle at a faster rate than even the most tired ABC sitcom. However, the reason Harvey's show was more beloved than its contemporaries was that it was sincere, warm, and positive. *The Steve Harvey Show* was produced and directed by Stan Lathan, a veteran of black TV. He worked on *Soul!* in the late 1960s and went on to direct episodes of *Sanford and Son* (NBC, 1972–1977), *Roc* (Fox, 1991–1994), *Moesha* (UPN, 1996–2001), as well as numerous white shows. *The Steve Harvey Show* was a proud program that was tremendously fond of its black audience, going out of its way to emphasize its characters' dignity (Harvey and his sidekick Cedric the Entertainer made a point of speaking properly, dressing well, and genuinely caring for the young men they mentored on the show). Though the craftsmanship was often suspect, the quality was there if you were willing to see it, and obviously many people were.

Harvey's show (which featured guest appearances by rappers Lil' Bow Wow, Busta Rhymes, and others) was also popular because of its use of black music, a common element in these programs. In addition to shows with musician protagonists, other popular shows cast musicians—such as Brandy on *Moesha*, Queen Latifah on *Living Single* (Fox, 1993–1998), and Eve on *Eve* (UPN, 2003–present)—

or used music locales such as a radio station on *Martin* (Fox, 1992–1997), a nightclub on *New York Undercover* (Fox, 1994–1998), or a record label office on *Half and Half* (UPN, 2002–present). This built on a tradition established a generation earlier when a wave of programming targeting black audiences also leaned heavily on the use of music. However, unlike the cookie-cutter nature of most startup-network sitcoms, the shows that emerged in the wake of the civil rights era were a dynamic showcase for black creativity.

As the 1960s became the 1970s many musicians, including acts with some counterculture inclinations, surrendered to TV's "fun for the whole family" aesthetic and refrained from rocking as they helmed hokey variety shows. Sonny and Cher, the Hudson Brothers, Glen Campbell, the Jacksons, the Bay City Rollers, and others performed baggy-pants vaudeville comedy in front of the cameras in efforts to appeal to the widest possible audiences. While the networks tried to please everyone, producers of local, syndicated, and, to some extent, public television realized that narrowcasting to a very specific demographic was an efficient way to connect sponsors with consumers. And though African Americans historically have lower median incomes than white Americans, by the 1970s studies were indicating that blacks were extremely avid TV watchers (according to Nielsen figures African American households watch, on average, around 13 percent more prime-time TV than any other demographic) and were active consumers of products aimed at their needs. From a commercial standpoint black programming in that era made sense. However, not all programming decisions were strictly commercial.

There were two types of black music TV productions that emerged in the late 1960s and early 1970s. One wave of conscious, positive programming was born out of the recognition of the need for such shows (and advertisers' and foundations' white guilt) in the wake of Dr. Martin Luther King's assassination. The other was low-budget local youth programming ("chocolate-flavored *American Bandstand*," as Marc Weingarten put it in his book *Station to Station*) that took advantage of the advertising dollars local businesses were willing to spend to reach a black market. The former produced remarkably ambitious and passionate programming. The latter helped propel one of black music's greatest eras.

In response to the racial unrest that erupted after King was killed, Lyndon Johnson's National Advisory Commission on Civil Disorders issued (with the FCC's blessing) the Kerner Commission Report, recommending that a black presence on urban TV would benefit race relations. In addition to adding black anchors and commentators to existing (white) newscasts, this also led to several all-black programs (frequently buried in early morning weekend time slots). New York became the base for the most prominent of these shows, and while many were news-oriented, including WABC's public affairs program *Like It Is* (which still airs), others were showcases for cultural and musical expression.

The greatest of these was WNDT New York's *Soul!* (PBS, 1968–1973), which eventually went national via a Ford grant. Created by Ellis Haizlip, a visionary producer (and an icon among black gays; on one episode he challenged Louis Farrakhan on the Nation of Islam's position on homosexuality), *Soul!* presented the most remarkable music of the era alongside poetry, dance, and radical black politics. Only the second national program ever to be a completely black production, in front of and behind the cameras (*Black Journal*, which is still in production as *Tony Brown's Journal*, preceded it by a few months), the show was a training ground for black media makers, including Lathan, who became one of the most prolific black directors in TV history. *Soul!* featured live music by dynamic acts like Stevie Wonder (a full hour-long set), Rahsaan Roland Kirk, and the Dells. "That show had some of the baddest performances," recalls Calvin Lincoln, who hosts the Los Angeles cable show *Soul School*. "Everybody from Kool and the Gang to Earth, Wind and Fire, they put these groups on when they were early in their careers and very hungry . . . they'd be playing pretty hard on that show."

Soul! showcased up-and-coming musicians, and it also gave them respect and a voice, interviewing them at length, allowing them to have their say on issues that mattered to young blacks. Most striking about the show, especially when compared to its low-budget talking-head contemporaries, was its look, which showcased camera tricks that married the languages of experimental film and psychedelia on a set that combined vibrant, shocking colors with sculptural modern-art props. Germany's rock show *Beat Club* was also messing around with the camera and superimposing strange backgrounds at the time, but on *Soul!* these bizarre angles and odd layered images had an almost opposite effect—instead of seeming absurd (as they do when applied to a Black Sabbath performance) they made the show's content seem more serious.

Another amazing show from this era was Brooklyn's *Inside Bedford-Stuyvesant* (WNEW, 1968–1970). Initially underwritten by the Robert F. Kennedy Bedford-Stuyvesant Restoration Project, the program was helmed by black journalist Charles Hobson (who later worked on the controversial 1986 PBS documentary *The Africans*) after it was passed on to him by a friend who, as Hobson explained in a 2004 interview, "(couldn't) get along with these white people at Kennedy." Hosted by Roxie Roker (later of *The Jeffersons*, and the mother of Lenny Kravitz), this show featured African American artists, activists, poets, and musicians such as the Persuasions, Ritchie Havens, and Eubie Blake. Harry Belafonte, in lieu of singing, gave a dire, brave treatise on racism that was remarkable coming from someone so embraced by white America. In an incredible segment, the Leroi Jones Young Spirit House Players, a group of children, performed an angry, militant musical poem under the direction of Jones (later Amiri Baraka), chanting, "What has America done for me . . . made me a zombie . . . a robot, a puppet, Franken-stein . . . you keep talking to us about Mary Had a Little Lamb—Mary was white— *the lamb was white!*"

Both *Soul!* and *Inside Bedford-Stuyvesant* were powerful because they were actually situated in the community. Like *It's Showtime at the Apollo*, these shows gave the responses and faces and presence of the black audience equal weight with the performers. The black audience at home had to appreciate that they were as much a part of the show as the Afro-bearing, fist-raising crowd on the screen. Anecdotal evidence suggests that home audiences did react. According to a New York producer at a 1969 public TV conference, thanks to shows like *Soul!* audiences in black neighborhoods were watching PBS for the first time (very soon *Sesame Street* would hire some of the black crew members who worked on *Soul!*). He also mentioned that a WNDT cameraman "who has occasionally run into some trouble filming in Harlem because he is white has told me that when things get really tight he says, 'Take it easy man. I'm just doing a little segment for *Soul!*'"

On *Inside Bedford-Stuyvesant* not only were the members of the community (on and off screen) integral characters but the neighborhood itself was a star. Nearly every segment was filmed outside, with the buildings, sidewalks, and pedes-trians in the background giving more flavor to the show than any set could (even the brilliant sets utilized by *Soul!*). In one of the best live performances I've ever seen on TV, jazz drummer Max Roach gave a brilliant outdoor demonstration of improvisational solo percussion. Roach was enveloped not only by the warm sum-mer air but also by a group of young Brooklynites who seemed to love him as much as he loved them. In many ways moments like these demonstrate the true prom-ise of a black production for black spectators: the performers are totally comfort-able (in a way they might not be around whites) and also sincerely invested in the audience.

Other contemporary local shows served black communities around the coun-try, mostly public-affairs interview programs. However, musical artists were occa-sionally featured on shows such as Detroit's *CPT* (WTVS, 1968–present, now called *American Black Journal*), D.C.'s *Harambee* (WTOP, 1968–1975), and espe-cially Boston's *Say Brother* (WGBH, 1968–present, now titled *Basic Black*). In

April 1968 Boston mayor Kevin White arranged for WGBH to broadcast a live James Brown concert the night after Martin Luther King's assassination. He gambled (and won) that blacks would stay home and watch the concert instead of rioting, so despite having equal or greater racial tensions than other cities with substantial African American populations, Boston's poor black neighborhoods remained intact while other ghettos around the country burned. It isn't surprising, then, that when the station funded a black-produced public-affairs program later that year, live music would be a valued (if only occasional) component. The show captured remarkable performances by the Impressions, Patti LaBelle and the Blue Bells, and Howling Wolf.

Some of these shows have remained on the air for decades, partly due to stealth (a combination of low budgets and obscure time slots makes them nearly invisible. Tim Meadows parodied this situation on *Saturday Night Live* as Lionel Osbourne, the host of *Perspectives*, a five-minute black-issues show that airs after the National Anthem). But the more ambitious shows disappeared when civil rights issues stopped being a trendy TV subject. By the time there were plans to expand *Inside Bedford-Stuyvesant* into a national show called *Black Is*, the pangs of conscience America had felt after the tragedy in Memphis were waning. "It just isn't chic anymore for advertisers to sponsor a black show," an anonymous WNEW spokesman explained to *Variety* in late 1969. In 1970 production on *Inside Bedford-Stuyvesant* ceased due to lack of sponsor money. Three years later *Soul!*, which was programming itself as a more traditional music show in its later days, disappeared for similar reasons. Both shows (as well as a number of episodes of *Say Brother*) are available for viewing in archives today, and Charles Hobson recently edited highlights of *Inside Bedford-Stuyvesant* into a documentary that has made the rounds of the festival circuit.

(In 1968, around the same time *Soul!* began airing, NBC developed a pilot for a black variety show called *Soul*, starring Lou Rawls, Redd Foxx, and Nipsey Russell. Though the show—which did not come to fruition—certainly would not have had the cultural integrity of the PBS *Soul!*, it was to feature black creative talent offscreen, as the scripting team came from the legendary Watts Writer's Workshop.)

These "conscious" shows, true originals that sought to uplift the race, shared the dial with black music programs that aimed for less lofty goals. Around the country black DJs, inspired by the massive successes of both Dick Clark and Motown, held televised versions of the record hops they normally emceed in gymnasiums and meeting halls on the weekends. While nearly all teen dance shows charm just by virtue of the form, these stood out. Unlike network fare such as *Julia* (NBC, 1968–1971), where Diahann Carroll looked like a supermodel, or *Amos* 'n' *Andy* (CBS, 1951–1953), which ran in syndication until 1966 and featured stereotypical caricatures, the dancers in these shows actually looked like the black kids watching them. Over the years, black youth routinely developed popular dances that gained the mainstream's attention once they were appropriated by white dancers. But now instead of seeing the *American Bandstand* kids show off the latest steps secondhand, audiences could access the primary source material.

What is most thrilling about these shows is the tunes, which document soul music at one of its artistic apexes. In the early 1970s black American music became the most happening thing on the radio. The Beatles' experimental late records had inspired rock bands to make ambitious, often progressive album-oriented music, and white pop producers responded by letting these geniuses have FM while they made infectious, disposable bubblegum for the AM dial. And all the while singer-songwriters strummed their way to a healthy share of the market. Black creative teams took a different route: they made their productions deeper, more nuanced, and more exciting while never abandoning the concept of hit radio singles. Though Motown became the Jackie Robinson of radio by calculating perfect, inoffensive crossover in the early and mid-1960s, those days were over and producers in Memphis, Philadelphia, Chicago, and Los Angeles were making some of the best records of all time for acts like the O'Jays, the Isley Brothers, Curtis Mayfield, and Al Green. James Brown's always impressive revue had become a powerful force, almost a cult of funk. Motown, which once had made its acts take elocution and etiquette lessons, was now giving artists like Marvin Gaye and Stevie Wonder the independence to make their own powerful music, and even their nonautonomous acts, such as the Jackson 5ive, were given seriously funky, textured tracks. Black music began selling better than ever in the early 1970s, migrating from the R&B charts to the pop charts, at times monopolizing the top ten.

Black TV shows helped promote the music to its black fan base far more efficiently than had high school record hops and small nightclub performances. Bigger black artists were certainly not locked out of the mainstream (white) music TV shows of the late 1960s and early 1970s. But for smaller acts, big acts interested in connecting with their core audience, acts trying to stay in good with DJs that controlled radio play, and even for righteous acts motivated to show unity and feel the comfort of being around their people, the local and syndicated black music TV shows made up a powerful new chitlin circuit.

Two of the earliest shows from this wave of programs, while they were not black-produced, ran on the belief that black content could be successful on the small screen. *Night Train* (WLAC, 1964–1965), from Nashville, featured an all

African American cast, with a black host, a black house band (Johnny Jones and the King Kasuals), and black musical guests. More like a low-budget soulful version of *Shindig* than a teen dance show, *Night Train* goes down in music history for one of its young participants—twenty-three-year-old Jimi Hendrix was a pickup musician in 1965 and can be seen backing up Buddy and Stacey on their version of "Shotgun."

Much more interesting is the 1966 nationally syndicated series that developed out of *Night Train, The !!! Beat*. Hosted by white (but jive-talking) Hoss Allen, the show featured a black house band (the Kasuals, renamed the Beat Boys, now fronted by Clarence "Gatemouth" Brown), black go-go dancers (shimmying atop exclamation marks), and the best soul and blues musicians working at the time. The first national black variety show since Nat King Cole's had gone off the air in 1957, and the first to feature R&B since *Show Time at the Apollo* in 1955, *The !!! Beat* lasted one short season before dismal ratings buried it. Despite telecasting in some of the most soul-filled major cities, often after midnight on the weekends, for some reason the show bombed. Only 7,600 people watched it during sweeps week in Chicago, and in Detroit it got a "negative 1" rating, 1,100 percent worse than a competing *Flipper* episode. I'm somewhat baffled that it did so badly; in my view, the show was riveting. Taped on a bizarre Technicolor set (shot in Texas, because Nashville didn't have a color TV studio), the show had amazing live (and occasionally even more amazing off-kilter lip-synch) performances by such marvels of soul as Johnnie Taylor, Carla Thomas, Joe Tex, Z. Z. Hill, Etta James, Mitty Collier, and even the great proto-rocker Louis Jordan. Hoss, a former record promoter for Chess, had plenty of connections, and the talent appeared for free, often asking to be on, excited that the medium of TV was finally available to them. The great guitarist Freddie King begged for a slot and was featured four times (his performances have been compiled on a home video). The short-lived show died young but left a good-looking corpse by ending its twenty-six-episode run with a blowout featuring Otis Redding, Percy Sledge, and Patti LaBelle. In hindsight, the problems this show faced may have stemmed from being a white production, as it didn't seem to know how to syndicate itself to a black audience or to line up the right sponsors. Maybe the producers expected the show would have universal appeal, but unlike Motown stars most southern soul singers found themselves supported mostly by a broad black fan base without the crossover appeal of Berry Gordy's golden children.

An excellent example of the low-budget local dance show is San Diego's *Soul Time USA*. In the late 1960s and early 1970s it showcased some of the deepest soul acts in the business, including Joe Simon and Dyke and the

Blazers. *Soul Time USA* supposedly had opportunities to go national, but its enigmatic producer, Chuck Johnson, fueled by black power philosophy and a tremendous ego, was not willing to make concessions or relinquish any control. A soul DJ who spun records on Tijuana and San Diego radio in the 1960s, Johnson established himself as a low-end black TV/music video pioneer in the 1970s and 1980s. In 1978 Johnson launched Soul Beat, an all black TV network, two years before BET. Operating on a nonexistent budget on local leased-access cable channels (leased-access is the semicommercial cousin of cable access), Johnson presented decades of black programming that included talk shows, religious shows, gospel music, and hours of music videos. He was not only a presenter of video clips but also a creator. In the early days when few black music videos existed Johnson would make arrangements with Los Angeles A&R guys to shoot low-budget clips of black radio acts and then he'd show them on his programs. Soul Beat was one of the reasons black artists and record labels started creating music videos. Johnson's unique, raw programming (the network's talk show hosts sometimes ate lunch on the air) at times invokes a ghetto *SCTV*, but for all the people he's alienated and enraged over the years (with everything from creative financial practices to giving airtime to controversial figures), nobody can accuse Johnson of not keeping it black. Unfortunately Soul Beat hit a bump recently. In November 2003, after a quarter of a century on the tube, Comcast took Soul Beat off its cable system, claiming Johnson (who had declared bankruptcy) owed several hundred thousand dollars in missed fee payments (he apparently owed a comparable amount to the IRS). Amazingly, Johnson's Web site recently announced the channel's return, so perhaps the Beat will go on!

Though not a black show, Detroit's mid-1960s integrated dance party *Teen Town* (hosted by white DJ Robin Seymour, who also hosted a better known rock 'n' roll dance show called *Swingin' Time*) is notable because virtually the entire Motown roster appeared on it, including the Temptations, the Supremes, Stevie Wonder, and even George Clinton's Parliaments. Clips from the show often pop up in Motown documentaries.

Soul Is (later *The Jay Payton Show*) was an early 1970s Bay Area show starring Jay Payton, best known as the pimp convention emcee that gives Goldie the "Mack of the Year" award in the blaxploitation classic *The Mack*. "I can speak from a personal perspective," recalls Calvin Lincoln. "People were just glad to see themselves on TV. It basically was a *Soul Train* rip-off. The quality of the production was definitely like a moms and pops store, you know, your corner liquor store type of deal—'I got a dollar, you got a dollar, lets make a TV show.' But it had a different philosophy from *Soul Train*—no scramble board, nothing to separate the crowd from the action. It was just a bunch of people up there dancing."

Chicago's *Red, Hot, and Blue* (WCIU, 1967–1973), a black-music youth-dance show that predated that station's 1970s hit *Soul Train*, was inspired by *Kiddie-a-Go-Go*, which featured preschoolers and preteens grooving. Popular DJ Big Bill Hill sought to develop a South Side version featuring African American kids ranging from five to fourteen. Not the most likely guy to be around kids, the towering, gravel-voiced Hill was a pioneering blues DJ on WPOA-FM, fondly remembered for broadcasting from black clubs (including his own) between live sets. DJ Darryl, a TV historian, was a big fan of the show growing up. "The dancers danced in groups and sometimes there'd be three or four kids dancing together to a particular song. Sometimes the kids would lip-sync to a record, instead of the artist doing the lip-synch. They also had actual guest performers, like Archie Bell and the Drells. . . . Alvin Cash was on there once." Sponsored by South Side and West Side businesses (like Dell's Upholstery), the show was a favorite in black neighborhoods, especially because the kids on *Kiddie-a-Go-Go* were all white in the show's early days (not a policy—black kids just didn't come to dance on the show for its first few years). "In the 1960s, music was becoming polarized," DJ Darryl remembers. "*Kiddie-a-Go-Go* would have a lot of top-forty music like the Box Tops and Tommy James and the Shondells, stuff that you would not hear on *Red, Hot, and Blue*, which would be exclusively R&B music and some blues and jazz. Also, for the most part, even as little kids the African Americans seemed like better dancers."

Because the other shows around the country were mostly local live broadcasts, few of them were ever committed to videotape or kinescope, and the few that were often were taped over or thrown away. The hosts of many of these shows were also their driving forces, men who saw TV as just another medium for selling ads and another pie to stick a thumb in. The shows were not archived because the producers weren't thinking of each individual episode as a work of art or a treasured memento to value. They were movers and shakers, but not visionaries, and that is why they were good fits in local markets. But one among their rank had a far grander vision, a vision in which local TV was not an end, but merely a stepping-stone. That DJ was Chicago's own Don Cornelius.

Born in Chicago on September 27, 1936, Cornelius attended DuSable High School, whose legendary music education program produced Nat King Cole, Von

Freeman, and Johnny Hartman. That rich environment encouraged Cornelius to study the arts, but a stint in the Marines and a wife and kids led him down a more pragmatic path to become a salesman. Inspired by customers who said his rich baritone sounded like DJ Sid McCoy (Cornelius's hero), Cornelius enrolled in broadcasting school in 1966 and soon found himself an auxiliary member of the WVON Good Guys. WVON (the Voice of the Negro), founded in 1963 by Chess Records' Phil and Leonard Chess, was one of the most influential black radio stations of its day and the all-star Good Guys were some of the most popular DJs in the country. Their ranks included Lucky Cordell, Ed "Nassau Daddy" Cook, Bill "Butterball" Crane, the still active Pervis Spann (today he hosts a local TV show called *Blues and More*), and the still popular Herb "Kool Gent" Kent (who in the late 1990s hosted *Steppin' at Club Seven*, one of the only dance shows aimed at older dancers). With such a stellar lineup of DJs, Cornelius had little chance of getting his own WVON radio slot. He became WVON's newscaster, and filled in shifts for sick colleagues while looking for opportunities elsewhere.

Cornelius began reading the sports on a black news show on WCIU-TV, a small UHF station (so small that it continued to broadcast in black and white well into the 1970s). Channel 26 featured a lineup of minority and ethnic programming at the time, including a show with Olympics great Jesse Owens as an anchor, and Cornelius fit in well there. Excited by the potential of the medium (and no doubt encouraged by the station's existing black dance show, *Red, Hot and Blue*, which Cornelius reportedly criticized for airing too late for its young dancers), Cornelius convinced management to let him use the station's cramped studio in the attic of the Board of Trade building. There he shot a pilot for a dance show inspired by one of his radio promotions in which a caravan of local R&B entertainers barnstormed several high schools a day, forming a "soul train."

The 1969 pilot impressed a local Sears-Roebuck executive enough to sponsor the show, so Cornelius invited soul star Jerry Butler, a gaggle of Chicago high school kids, and the home TV audience to ride the *Soul Train* for the first time on August 17, 1970. Immediately the show (telecast live Monday through Friday after school) became the talk of black Chicago. "Two days after it went on the air," Cornelius told Warner Saunders during a public interview at the Museum of Broadcast Communications (MBC) in 1995, "you couldn't go anywhere and brothers and sisters weren't talking about it. It was one of those ideas whose time had come."

The set was simple (just the words "Soul Train" on the wall) and the dancers were regular kids. The most unique feature of the show was the Soul Train line, where couples boogied toward the camera flanked by two parallel lines of dancers, showing off moves like "the bop" and "the cold duck." Everything was smooth and successful, but unlike local black dance-show producers around the country who were satisfied with regional fame and its trappings, Cornelius had grand designs. His vision, and his local success, convinced Johnson Products Company, a black-owned hair care and cosmetics manufacturer, to underwrite the show. The substantial backing (commitments of more than a million dollars a year by the end of the first season) was beneficial to all. Cornelius was able to relocate the show to Hollywood, where he could produce a high-quality nationally syndicated weekly series. Johnson's sales doubled soon after.

The Hollywood *Soul Train* was very different from the local version. By using his own production company, syndicating the show, and enjoying healthy financial backing, Cornelius answered to no network authority. He brought in his idol Sid McCoy as announcer (a role McCoy still fills today), and McCoy later directed the show. He invited local teenage dancers, and unlike the normal-looking Chicago kids, they had spectacular threads, the most happening hair, and sophisticated moves. The set design evolved throughout the 1970s but always maintained its original train motif. Over the years train tracks covered the floor and walls, stages looked like trains (smaller stages were train wheels), and wooden signs announced train stops (basically every city with a black population in Amer-

Courtesy Jake Austen

ica). Cornelius introduced songs in front of a relief of an oncoming train with funky colored headlights. Other signatures included the scramble board (where dancers unscrambled the name of a prominent African American), an animated train mascot, and the distinctive Johnson Products commercials ("Beautiful people use Afro Sheen"). And presiding over the funky proceedings, sporting a proud afro, audacious cravats around his neck, and *bad* vines, was Cornelius himself, with his sexy, too-cool voice delivering such signature introductions as, "Greet them with a thunder that giants like them are deserving of . . . the Four Tops!"

As soon as Gladys Knight and the Pips rode the *Soul Train* as the show's first nationally televised guests on October 2, 1971, the show was a hit. Originally shown in only seven target markets, it quickly expanded to 25, then 45, then 75, and eventually 105. (However, it was not initially broadcast in Chicago, where the original daily *Soul Train* continued broadcasting live on weekdays until 1976. Hosted by Clifford Ghent, a member of the band Sons of Slum, Chicago's *Soul Train* welcomed great local acts like the Mandells and Otis Leavill and middle-of-the-charts national acts like the Escorts (an all-convict vocal group, though only the ex-con members appeared on the show) and Dexter Redding, Otis Redding's eleven-year-old son. Eventually, to black Chicago's delight, the city had two *Soul Trains* running.)

Though dismissed by some as a black version of *American Bandstand*, the early *Soul Train* was far superior to early 1970s *American Bandstand* ("*Soul Train* is to *American Bandstand*," Clayton Wiley wrote in the *New York Times* in 1973, "as champagne is to seltzer"). Before (and during) *Soul Train*'s run, black kids watched *American Bandstand*, excited to see the black and white performers who did songs they liked. But when the shows were programmed against each other in many markets, Dick Clark's show lost significant black viewership. His response was to introduce *Soul Unlimited* (ABC, 1973), an all-black show hosted by L.A. DJ Buster Jones that alternated with *American Bandstand* in its time slot every few weeks. The attempt of a white production company to co-opt *Soul Train*'s success did not sit well with Cornelius, who told *Rolling Stone* that *American Bandstand* was "obsolete" because while all the biggest black artists did *Soul Train*, few of the biggest rock acts (most of whom were making album-oriented rock, not bubblegum dance music) wanted to be on Clark's show. Reverend Jesse Jackson wrote an angry letter to ABC about the situation and Clark responded by accusing the *Soul Train* camp of "ghetto paranoia." He also offered, "I don't dig black people not liking white people. I've been seeing too much of that for too long already," absurdly assigning the blame for America's racial problems to its victims. Worse still, a spokesman for his company called Jackson's letter "inhuman" and pointed a finger back at Cornelius, whining, "an all-black show—that's segregation!" Cornelius summed up his feelings about Clark in a recent interview: "Any comment I make would have to be honest and if I were honest it would be badmouthing him." No comments were necessary. *Soul Unlimited* was a failed experiment that quickly disappeared.

Cornelius had little to worry about. His show was the best of its kind in the early 1970s. "I think it's the most sophisticated dance format that's ever been done," Cornelius told *Billboard* in 1974, "and it takes a great deal of money to produce it." The money was right there on the screen. While many *Soul Train* guests lip-synched, especially those from labels known for textured studio-production like Philadelphia International, dynamic live performances were also welcome on Saturday mornings. "Performers would come to us and say, 'We don't want to do the lip-synch jazz, I want to play live,'" Cornelius told *Billboard* in 1990, "and we said 'OK, do it.'" Live performers included Barry White with a forty-piece orchestra, the awesome funk band Mandrill, and James Brown, who crammed his full revue on the tiny train-shaped stage (two wheels had to be added to the train for his horn sections). As his mighty performance peaked, Brown led the unamplified but fully audible *Soul Train* crowd in chanting "I'm black and I'm proud." Then popular dancer Damita Jo Freeman joined him on stage for a spectacular routine that featured her shooting black-pride fists in the air and then going into that *Soul Train* favorite, "the robot."

As dynamic as Brown always was, it was Freeman who stole the show, and as a rule, the dancers (known as the Soul Train Gang) were the stars and the reason *Soul Train* had no competition. The dancers auditioned at an open call in 1971, and since then the producers have maintained a strong lineup of dancers via a referral system. "We've found over the years that kids who dance really well and groom themselves really well and have a sense of style and behave well know other kids who can do the same thing," Cornelius explained on his 1996 twenty-fifth anniversary TV special. The dancers were paid only in fried chicken and pop, standard practice on dance shows ("The unions agreed to look the other way and treat dance shows as 'audience participation,'" explained Cornelius in his MBC interview). But many of them later found numerous professional opportunities: touring with musicians; doing choreography for movies, TV, and eventually music videos; and teaching dance classes. They also were treated like royalty in L.A. nightclubs. Dancers such as Little Joe Chism and Scooby Doo became national celebrities.

And they earned it, as their work on the show was profoundly important. Mark Anthony Neal in the *Journal of Popular Music and Society* called the show "a dynamic, visually mediated example of the power of black social dance." Clayton Riley in the *New York Times* called it "a grooving, swinging, moving thing of beauty, a video sampler of soul carried into a spirited, collective ritual where human feeling is extended, is contained within but also carried without the body." Cornelius has been less poetic, but no less grandiose over the years, likening the dancers to improvising jazz musicians and pointing out that his show powerfully influenced black dance in America, creating an America where every black party and nightclub features *Soul Train*–style moves, as opposed to being dominated by regional dance trends as in the pre–*Soul Train* days.

The greatest visual delight of early *Soul Train* may be the dancers surrounding the stage during the guests' performances, dancing in couples without facing the stage, completely invested in their groove and the music, ignoring the performers (which is astounding considering the stage featured sights like the Jackson 5ive doing their "Dancing Machine" routine). The camera respected the entire, dynamic space of the room, tempering artist close-ups (which highlighted awesome fashion like David Ruffin's outrageous brown polyester gaucho outfit) with wide shots that maroon the star in a kinetic ocean of crisp, staccato dance movements.

But it was also magic when the guests and dancers mingled. Classic segments include the great soul shouter Joe Tex lustily pulling dancer Freeman to the stage during "I Gotcha"; Marvin Gaye singing "Let's Get It On" while wading through the crowd of dancers, embracing them lovingly; and the early episodes where the dancers were allowed to help conduct the interviews, politely offering sincere softball questions and nonquestions ("Tito, we understand it was your birthday recently so we'd like to give you a birthday card"). In a transcendent scene that could only happen on *Soul Train*, Stevie Wonder improvised a song about the show from a piano on the dance floor. With confidence in the crowd's soul quotient, Stevie requested that they "soft clap" then sing a chorus that went, "All the brothers and sisters get together." Of course the mighty Soul Train Gang got together and the result sounded like a hit record.

Over the years the show has welcomed the greatest black performers in the pop world, plus white acts that had a black following (including Elton John, David Bowie, Gino Vanelli, Teena Marie, and Duran Duran), and even black acts that cultivated white audiences (including Fishbone, Lenny Kravitz, Darius "Hootie" Rucker, and, in a wild 1973 live performance, Chuck Berry backed by white stoners doing a boogie version of "Johnny B. Goode"). In the 1970s and 1980s, in addition to musical acts, *Soul Train* welcomed comedians (Paul Mooney, Tom Dreesen, Redd Foxx, and even Cheech and Chong, who boldly did the potentially offensive-to-blacks "Basketball Jones"), contest winners (national dance contests, Hal Jackson's Talented Teens), and dance troupes made up of L.A. dancers who frequented the show. Two of the greatest acts ever to grace *Soul Train* were the Lockers and Electric Boogaloo, each wearing outrageous oversized costumes that brought to mind zoot-suit versions of jockey uniforms. Both acts were masters of the ultra-cool L.A. "locking" dance moves that were made famous on *What's Happening!!* (ABC, 1976–1979) by Fred "Rerun" Berry (who appeared with the Lockers on *Soul Train*) and were the harbinger of break dancing, brought to the mainstream in the movie *Breakin'* (1984), starring Shabba Doo (who also appeared with the Lockers on *Soul Train*).

The early 1970s was an artistic peak for *Soul Train*, but its popularity didn't wane as the decade progressed. The disco years (1976–1979) were the show's most popular. And though MTV revolutionized the ways kids watched music on TV and made pop stars more famous than ever, the 1980s were not lean times for *Soul Train*. "When the major pop stars said, 'I don't want to do shows that pay scale,' that doesn't affect *Soul Train*," Cornelius explained in a 1995 interview, "because black artists don't get to do *Barbara Walters*, they don't get to do the *Tonight Show* and they hardly can get on MTV." In response to the slick new aesthetics music video introduced, *Soul Train*'s style shifted from the look of a house party that just happened to have the most stylish kids to more of a nightclub vibe. It was a showcase for highly stylized dancers who seemed like professionals, certainly as good as or better than the dancers in music videos (many of whom were *Soul Train* dancers). Though some of the homey charm of the original *Soul Train* was lost, the 1980s Soul Train Dancers (they stopped being called the Soul Train Gang when Cornelius introduced a music group by that name) were some of the most memorable, including Cheryl Song, an Asian dancer with knee-length hair; the beautiful Nieci' Payne (who as a young teen danced on Clifford Ghent's local *Soul Train* in Chicago); Odis Medley, who wore masks and costumes; the handsome Derek Fleming, whose signature was affixing foxtails to his wardrobe; and Rosie Perez, whose dynamic dancing (and lovemaking) sequences in Spike Lee's *Do The Right Thing* made her famous as a choreographer and actress. Other *Soul Train* alumni who went on to greater fame include Carmen Electra, actress Vivica A. Fox, Nickelodeon TV star Nick Cannon (who rejoined the Soul Train line when he returned as a musical guest), and even NFL Hall of Famer Walter Payton, who won a spot to compete on a dance-contest episode.

As the show has gone through changes Cornelius has served its legacy well through his endeavors to spread the soul beyond Saturday morning. In the mid-1970s Soul Train Records was home of the Soul Train Gang and Shalamar (which featured *Soul Train* dance partners Jody Watley and Jeffrey Daniel). The *Soul Train* name has also been licensed to package R&B hits compilations since 1973 (for the "As Seen on TV" label Adam VIII) and as recently as 2000 (Rhino's *Soul Train: The Dance Years* collection). And while tie-ins as obvious as T-shirts and as ambitious as a Bay Area nightclub have come and gone, one idea that has certainly strengthened the Soul Train brand name is the Soul Train Music Awards.

Launched in 1987, this awards show carved out a niche as a high-profile, glamorous black music event without peer. (The NAACP Image Awards were first given in the late 1960s, but didn't begin televising until Cornelius's awards show launched, and did not become a glitzy, prime-time affair until, with help from Cornelius Productions, it moved to Fox in the mid-1990s.) With rap, gospel, and R&B artists underserved by the Grammy Awards, Cornelius's annual event became an important affair for black music superstars. Over the years, as BET and hip-hop crossover success made *Soul Train* a less frequent stop for established artists, the carrot of an award (and the fact that a Soul Train Awards appearance had more effect on record sales than a weekly show appearance) was enough to keep the movers and shakers from putting call block on Cornelius's phone number. In the 1990s Cornelius added the Lady of Soul Awards and the Christmas Star Fest as annual syndicated TV events. Rival shows arose, but most were no competition. (The Source Awards became a sad joke when violent gunplay occurred during the taping. At the Soul Train Awards violence only occurred off-camera and after the fact, as when Biggie Smalls was slain after the 1997 edition.) But BET, now owned by media conglomerate Viacom, has recently challenged Cornelius's dominance and launched its own black music awards show. I have no fear, however, that Cornelius will persevere because, to quote a 1974 *Crawdaddy* magazine article, he is "the leading authority on the past, present, and future of blacks on television."

As far as longevity, *Bandstand*, in its various forms, ran thirty-six years, eleven months, and three weeks. If *Soul Train* can make it to August 18, 2007, it will have surpassed that mark. However, there's no guarantee the show will make it to that magic date, as numerous challenges have threatened to derail the *Train*. Though I'm not alone in declaring my loyalty to the show (in 1996 noted booty-hound and leader of the free world Bill Clinton admitted, "I've been a fan for a long time"), the rumble of critics has been increasing in volume over the last decade.

As the 1990s dawned, *Soul Train* became a target of criticism and ridicule even among those who had traditionally supported it (in 1990 Ice Cube rapped, "*Soul Train* done lost they soul. . . . It almost look like *Bandstand*"). This was due in part to changes that started in the 1980s. The dancers began to look older than high school age, in part because many of them were, but also due to the women's couture journeying into fashion model/street walker/superhero territories. The set evolved into a series of levels and platforms (the better to shoot a camera up a dancer's skirt) with train motifs giving way to less specific neon and scaffolding. Though a large group of amateur dancers still attended, most of them were visible only during the guest performances and the Soul Train line, with the sexy professional dancers serving as the sole camera fodder during most songs. The Soul Train line ceased to be a couples dance and became two lines segregated by sex. The cameras gave the female dancers (often doing strip club moves) long, sensuous ogles, punctuated by tiny bursts of male dancers doing intense acrobatics so that their five seconds would be memorable. In some ways the new sexier *Soul Train* was an excellent response to music videos: while T&A were regular components of MTV and BET, music video leering was limited by the quick-cut editing style that had become the medium's standard. *Soul Train* offered lingering lechery, which was sure to make loyal watchers of adolescent boys, dirty old men, and prison inmates (apparently *Soul Train* and its Latino equivalent *Caliente* are must-see TV in America's correctional facilities).

The most major change to *Soul Train* came in 1993 when Cornelius gave up hosting duties. Dick Clark had replaced himself with a bland game-show-host type, but Cornelius (who continued to produce and write the show) tried to do something different; he had the next three seasons hosted by a different emerging black celebrity each week. While seeing a series of young, pretty soap stars, models, sitcom actors, and comedians preside over the "hippest trip in town" may not have seemed cohesive, it was an interesting idea, mostly because (unlike Cornelius) the new hosts were required to dance, which gave fans a lot of insight into just how funky Tyra Banks, Jamie Foxx, Traci Bingham, and Kristoff St. John really were. Then from 1997–1999 *Def Comedy Jam* (HBO, 1992–1998) comedian/Gulf War vet Mystro Clark became the regular host, but his style, humor, and posturing did not mesh with the format (according to a *Soul Train* fan Web site the 1998–1999 season is the show's all-time low point). Despite having stellar guests to launch the 1999–2000 season, including Destiny's Child, DMX, and Christina Aguilera, Clark was replaced midseason.

The new host was soap hunk Shemar Moore, a fair-skinned, muscle-bound model. Over the next four seasons he helped the show regain its footing. Moore was an easy target for criticism because of his prettiness (a Brother Ali rap lyric proclaimed: "You ain't hardcore/you soft more/than Shemar Moore/in a tight shirt"), his awkward use of street lingo (both his jive talk and his dancing made one think Moore was taking hip-hop classes), and his problematic crudeness around the sexy women (as if to say "See, Brother Ali, I ain't gay, I'm putting my face next to this woman's big ass and pointing!"). However, he had a number of redemptive qualities. He did a lot of his own writing, and his preachy affirmations as well as his extended train-ride metaphors were endearing. His Ken doll looks meant hip-hop fashions looked good on him. And his artist interviews were oddly revealing, as he didn't hesitate to betray jealousy of rappers who scored feature film acting roles that he found elusive and he was eager to discuss his biracial background with mixed-race guests like Alicia Keys and Sean Paul. Late in the 2003 season, as Moore prepared to move on from the host role, Old Navy confirmed his cultural acceptance as *Soul Train* conductor, launching its high-profile "Cargo Train" ad campaign with Moore fronting a 1970s *Soul Train*–style set.

The show suffered more setbacks post-Moore. The 2003–2004 season started well, with excellent camerawork, and more shots of the group of dancers (in addition to the hoochie mamas). However, new host Dorian Gregory was a huge step backward. Though seemingly Moore-like (a light-skinned marginal actor who strained to engage in street lingo), Gregory was ill-suited for the job. His mature face looked absurd under a cocked hip-hop hat, his histrionic hand gestures were awkward, and his dialogue was spare, a far cry from Moore's elaborate pleas to reach for the stars. Perhaps Cornelius granted Gregory the position because he got to hire him away from Dick Clark (Gregory cohosted, with Danny Bonaduce and Clark himself, *The Other Half*, a male response to the estrogen chat fest *The View*). Gregory's *Soul Train* proved to be weaker even than Mystro's worst shows, partly because as the season progressed it became obvious that *Soul Train* was struggling for guests; relative unknowns were being supplemented with music videos and clips of old *Soul Train* performances. Far too many concessions were made to music video aesthetics, including dancers sharing split screens with videos, and a music-video choreographer bringing his dance troupe on the show to posture and strut. Like the Negro Leagues, ghetto public schools, and historically black colleges, Cornelius was finally suffering from integration, as the best and brightest black stars entered higher-profile institutions like MTV and BET (which had recently given up its black ownership). This was due in part to the massive mainstream acceptance of hip-hop, a genre with which Cornelius had an interesting history.

Soul Train had put rappers on the air as early as 1980 (Kurtis Blow doing "The Breaks," followed quickly by Sugarhill Gang, Planet Patrol, Run-DMC, the Fat Boys, Whodini, and nearly every major *black* rapper since—Vanilla Ice and Eminem were notable exceptions). In 1993 the *Soul Train* theme song became a rap by Naughty by Nature. That said, Cornelius has given mixed signals on rap.

He obviously doesn't want to disparage black art forms, especially when talking to white media. He has told *Billboard,* "I think rap goes deeper than just music, partly because of the social commentary." In the liner notes to the 1996 *Soul Train* twenty-fifth anniversary CD set he explained, "*Soul Train* hasn't shied away from rappers coming on, looking tough, acting mean, being angry. That's not a negative image." But contrasted with his 1970s position that "the *Superfly* thing . . . disgusts me," it's unclear what he really feels about gangsta rap. Perhaps more tempered is his 1995 MBC interview in which he offered, "I see the value (in rap music) and I understand it and I love it," but, "I don't think all rap records are great." He also offered a seeming indictment of hip-hop culture when explaining why he gave up his *Soul Train* conductor chores. "The era of a guy in a suit and a tie with good diction keeping a groove alive was not going to be the future," he explained, also offering that kids feel connected to rap because the rappers, unlike artists like Luther Vandross, are not more talented than the audience.

Perhaps the most revealing moment came back in 1986 when LL Cool J first performed on *Soul Train.* The dancers in the audience went absolutely ape-shit for the duration of his number, giving the young rapper the most enthusiastic response I had ever seen on the show (of course, in the 1970s the dancers danced during the performances in lieu of cheering). During his post-song interview LL was glowing, vibing off the audience's energy. Cornelius did not seem to be feeling it, and despite having been supportive of rap since its inception, his dismissive, condescending interview betrayed how unimpressed he was with the direction in which black music was heading.

Cornelius's frank and stubborn personality is a key to *Soul Train*'s success. Unlike Dick Clark, who puts on an "aw shucks" grin when he's on the air but practices ruthless business tactics and (if his *Rolling Stone* interviews are any indication) curses like a sailor when he's off camera, Cornelius's cool emcee act did not require a second face. Cornelius's cool is that of a tough guy, an old-school gangster, someone you shouldn't mess with. And even when he preaches "love, peace, and soul" (the mantra that ends every *Soul Train* episode) you never doubt that Cornelius practices tough love and keeps the peace by any means necessary. His defensive maneuvers against Clark's *Soul Unlimited* were only one example of this take-no-shit philosophy. In 1989 he bumped heads with the AFTRA union (he was upset because MTV, whom he considered his white competition, were not required to have similar union contracts), and AFTRA's executive director claimed Cornelius struck him. In 1996 Cornelius charged that *Billboard* magazine "literally leaped at the chance to spread negative publicity regarding an event controlled by African Americans" after the magazine reported on an altercation

Tupac had outside the Soul Train Awards. In August 2002, in perhaps the most publicized incident, fifteen-year-old Rommel Zamora posted an Internet petition challenging R&B singer Ashanti's worthiness to receive the Aretha Franklin Entertainer of the Year honor at the Soul Train Lady of Soul Awards (his protest was based, in part, on the absurdity of linking the thin-voiced Ashanti with the mighty Franklin, of whom Cornelius once said, "I consider myself very fortunate to live on earth during her career"). An unsigned Soultrain.com response labeled the petition an "insidious Internet hate campaign," and called the high school sophomore "a fucking loser," who didn't "know shit about the music industry" and needed "to get a motherfucking life!" Though he did not author the posting, Cornelius defended it, telling the *Los Angeles Times,* "After thirty years in the business, I should be told by a fifteen-year-old white kid who should get an award on my show?" He amended his position upon learning that Zamora was Filipino, telling *Time* magazine, "It's a patriarchal syndrome when any fifteen-year-old non-black kid can get on a soapbox and raise questions about a program like ours."

Cornelius's fearless address of racial prejudice has been a hallmark of his career, and his independence as a syndicated producer has allowed him to air his opinions uncensored for years, from refusing to "cooperate with that kind of bull-shit" when do-gooders insisted *Soul Train* should feature discussions of social issues, to rebuffing suggestions he make the show more racially mixed to challenging his competition's character. "MTV and some of those major formats are so racist," Cornelius declared in his MBC interview, going on at length and naming names before coming to a satisfying conclusion by offering with sly joy, "The music video was designed to put *Soul Train* out of business, but instead it put *Bandstand* out of business."

Like Don Cornelius, Robert L. Johnson is a driven, individualistic black entre-preneur. But unlike Cornelius and many of the other black visionaries who have attempted to create TV dynasties with a foundation in black music (ranging from Oakland's low-rent Chuck Johnson to ultra-successes Quincy Jones and Russell Simmons), Johnson was driven not by the pulsating beat of the music but by the hard thud of the bottom line. In January 1980, with a $15,000 loan that he finessed into a $500,000 investment, Johnson, an ambitious cable TV lobbyist and American dream poster child (the Mississippi-born son of a factory worker, the only one of ten siblings to attend college, is now a self-made *billionaire*) launched BET. He conceptualized BET as a sound business plan, not as a social movement. "I'm not a programmer," Johnson told Fortune.com in 2002. "That was never my thing, because I didn't see the connection between huge expenses in programming and advertisers stepping up their ad rates. They were only going to pay so much." Thus Johnson filled his programming hours with the least expensive black content available.

Black viewers were excited to have a home of their own, and if that home was decorated with reruns of *The Jeffersons* (CBS, 1975–1985) and *Sanford* (NBC, 1980–1981) and with low-budget music videos by Midnight Star and Mtume, so be it. Perhaps BET wasn't the best that black programming could be, but it was important to black viewers that it existed. Columnist Clarence Page wrote, "BET to Black America is sort of like a beloved cousin. It embarrasses us sometimes but we still love it and don't want it to go away." And it didn't, quickly expanding from several hours a day to round-the-clock programming, with a handful of talk, news, and gospel programs supplemented by hours of back-to-back music videos in "shows" called *Video Soul* (originally without a host, later with the smooth Donnie Simpson seducing the camera), *Video Vibrations*, and *Midnight Love*. Before BET existed, and while MTV practiced video apartheid, there was little reason for black artists to make promotional clips, so in BET's early days white artists like Foreigner and Scandal got unexpected promotion in the hood as the network struggled to fill the video time slots. But as BET became a familiar guest in African American homes, virtually all black artists made videos. Soon the world of black videos was employing *Soul Train* dancers, providing new outlets for urban visual artists and choreographers, and helping to develop a new generation of black directors (F. Gary Gray, the Hughes Brothers, and Hype Williams all made feature films after launching their careers making music videos for black artists). With the explosion of hip-hop, BET became the main home for rap videos, with other outlets looking to it as a farm team, waiting to snatch up the next Fresh Prince or Puff Daddy. Shows like *Rap City* were second homes for rap stars (especially after BET moved to New York from Washington, D.C., in 2000), and unlike *Soul Train*, which had trouble booking some black artists who had crossed over to mainstream, no rap star was too big to stop by BET's studio. And most importantly, since the original MTV era in the 1980s, when every kid in the free world became obsessed with music videos, it has been awesome for black kids to have their own to obsess over. That said, the fact that it was young kids watching these videos fueled BET's harshest critics.

Though other BET programming has done its share to offend sensitive viewers (the stand-up comedy show *Comic View* features broad, coarse comedy, and BET's animated *Cita's World* featured a melon-breasted diva who specialized in nasty ghetto attitude), the videos have consistently been the main target of criticism. Half-naked black women shake their asses as they appear as decorations in rap videos. White women played similar roles in 1980s metal videos, but "heavy metal sluts" (not my term, it's the name of a Web site devoted to these women) soon became less ubiquitous than "rap video hoes" (another Web site), not because rock fans became more enlightened but because Nirvana made the trappings of the 1980s glam era uncool. But as rap became more lucrative—and materialistic themes became dominant—the women (who represented success) in rap videos became more abundant both in volume and in anatomy. This sexist imagery, the sometimes violent content of the videos, and the reruns of 1970s and 1980s black sitcoms chock-full of stereotypes all seem to validate charges that BET is a hub of negative black imagery.

One of the problems with running a specialized network for a marginalized population is that when drawing from the pool of existing programming, you are bound to choose from material that perpetuates stereotypes. These audiences have rarely had genuine options so they have come to embrace the scraps TV has given them, and have found ways to enjoy this questionable material. So the southern core audience of The Nashville Network cheered along with the whoops and hollers of *The Dukes of Hazzard* (CBS, 1979–1985) reruns and BET's viewers laughed as the overweight mammy sassed her son on old episodes of *That's My Mama* (ABC, 1974–1975). And therein lies the excuse for some of the most critiqued programming on BET. The sexist, violent music videos, the offensive stand-up comedians, and the sitcom reruns of questionable quality may be embarrassing for many older or bourgeois or religious or socially conscious African Americans, but not only are they all that is currently available but they also seem to be what many of the people want.

Johnson complicated the issues in 2000 when he made a deal that allowed Viacom (owner of CBS, MTV, VH1, Comedy Central, and UPN) to buy BET for $3 billion (mostly in stock). Suddenly the critics who had been all over BET about its content were aghast that the most prominent black-owned media outlet in the world was no longer owned by blacks. But the idea that Johnson wronged his people by selling BET to a white-owned corporation (a majority of respondents to a BlackPlanet.com poll called Johnson a sellout) is inconsistent with the other criticism. TV is a dominant cultural force in America, especially among impressionable kids. So for people who were offended by BET's foundation, under Johnson, of violent and sexist music videos, black ownership didn't solve that problem. If one believes that a TV network owned by an African American is a powerful symbol, then the results of that sale—a black-owned sports franchise (Johnson purchased an NBA expansion team, the Charlotte Bobcats), the prospect of a black-owned airline (Johnson almost launched DC Air in 2000 and may try again), and a prominent black billionaire—also seem like pretty powerful symbols.

Of course, there was also the question of whether the sale was bad for BET. A reasonable argument is that since Johnson was more a bottom-line guy than a programmer, Viacom's acquisition meant that BET now had the capital to create more and better shows to serve the community, rather than just being a low-rent black MTV. That's not exactly what happened. In 2002 the station drastically cut back on its already meager public-affairs programming, canceling its highest-profile news show, *BET Tonight*; its weekend black panel discussion *Lead Story*; and its longstanding youth-issues program *Teen Summit*. The news programming was not replaced and "responsible" teen content was reduced to a music video show called *The Center* where R&B singer Amerie gave questionable advice between clips (she once encouraged kids to download term papers off the Internet). The high-profile new programming strived to turn the network into a black MTV. BET duplicated MTV's behind-the-scenes series *Making the Video* with *Access Granted*. BET mimicked MTV's lifestyles-of-the-rich-and-famous program *Cribs* (which already featured black content) with *How I'm Living*. MTV's live video countdown show *TRL* begat BET's *106 and Park* (though the seething hatred between *106 and Park* hosts Free and A.J. is no match for the utter charmlessness of *TRL's* Carson Daly). While black versions of popular white media didn't represent a new phenomenon and were often entertaining (*Blacula,* anyone?), one of the key results was to reveal the usual racial inequities: the production values were far lower on BET than on MTV, despite their common rich daddy. Apparently Viacom was no Mr. Drummond, and when BET played Arnold to MTV's Kimberly, it found itself eating in the kitchen with the help.

Not to say there weren't ratings and artistic improvements. BET launched a spectacular awards show (again modeled on MTV's awards), which became the network's highest-rated program of all time. Then it launched *College Hill*, an all-black reality show based on MTV's *Real World*, which became its new highest-rated show. *College Hill* countered *Real World's* narrow stereotypes of negative black behavior with a broad array of negative black behavior. Viacom also made some commitments to existing programs, including taking over the production duties of the BET's longest-running program, *Bobby Jones Gospel*, previously produced by Jones for as low as $5,000 an episode (and it showed). "I've waited twenty-two years for this," Jones told the *New York Times*, expressing relief that BET was finally giving his show the respect he felt its ratings had earned.

Johnson was still involved in BET as its chief executive officer, and as the twenty-first century got underway he ignored or attacked his critics. In his *Emerge* magazine, he published a two-page response to what he called "people who try to shoot arrows at [my] back." He refused to accept or even consider any of the criticism that came his way. Gadfly comic strip creator Aaron McGruder (*The Boondocks*) was too young, simple, and irresponsible to express opinions on how BET serves the black community. Civil rights icon Julian Bond was too old to appreciate booty-shaking music videos. But most importantly, the ends overshadow the means. A blustery Johnson's reaction was to address the economics, not the content, in response to *Washington Post* reporter Paul Farhi's question, "When will BET finally grow up?"

"BET has grown up," Johnson offered, "grown to [a company] that today commands a market value of more than $2 billion." (Given the eventual sale price of the network, he was being modest.) And though he is not fully considerate of the perspectives of his detractors, his money-driven response makes it possible to appreciate his perspective. Decades earlier, in the years many consider the apex of American black pride and consciousness, "black power" was a mantra. No one can deny that Johnson, a billionaire, has achieved what many Americans value as true power. Why should he have to justify airing music videos that are in demand?

While writing this I decided to click on BET. The youth-oriented video show *The Center* was on, and the clip featured Murphy Lee and Nelly throwing a party in their lavish mansion. A harem of black women in hot pants parades before Lee, holding up different items from his wardrobe so he can pick his party outfit (each, upon Lee's request, also presents her ample bottom for inspection). Lee expresses his appreciation by rapping, "I loves my hoes, pimping ain't easy but it's under control." The poolside party features booty, bikinis, and a potpourri of comic stereotypes ranging from watermelon eating to an obese female shake dancer. Julian Bond would have hated it, so I could see where BET's critics were coming from. But the video was pretty lively and fun, so I could see where the teenage BET fans were coming from. And after seeing thousands of videos like this over the years I have never refused to pay my cable bill, sending money to this network and its peers without protest, so I guess my actions agree with where Johnson is coming from as well.

The challenges *Soul Train* and BET have faced pale by comparison to those of the show whose very title invokes the greatest glories of black entertainment. *It's Showtime at the Apollo* has spent the last few seasons as a serious drama off screen, and an absurdist farce on the tube.

Though low-budget by Hollywood standards ("if you knew TV, you'd fall on your face [upon hearing *Apollo's* budget]," an insider told *Variety* in 1997. "It's the most inexpensive variety show"), *It's Showtime at the Apollo* was not profitable in its early years, and the expenses of owning and running the Apollo Theater became burdensome to Percy Sutton. In 1989 his Inner City Broadcasting Television partnered with Western International Syndication to produce the show, and in 1991 Sutton created the Apollo Foundation and transferred ownership of the theater. He then gave himself, as they say in the hood, "the hookup." A sweetheart deal had him paying a pittance for the right to use the Apollo's stage and name for his TV show, a show Inner City and Western (and not the Apollo) fully owned.

He deserved his hookup—Sutton is the historic Apollo's savior, its first black owner, and if he doesn't deserve a deal, who does? And for a while it worked; after thirteen years in the red the show turned a profit in its fourteenth and fifteenth seasons. But by that time capitalism had reared its ugly American head, and fellow black media mogul Frank Mercado-Valdes had exposed the questionable contracts between the Apollo and Sutton and forced the TV franchise to open for competitive bidding.

With Johnson no longer in ownership of BET, Mercado-Valdes had positioned himself as the most powerful man in black TV programming by developing Heritage Networks, a TV syndicate for 1970s blaxploitation movies, 1980s black sitcoms (such as *The Cosby Show*), and, most lucratively, the beloved *Steve Harvey Show* reruns. His plans for expansion included original programming, and his method of raising the profile of his hip-hop lifestyle programs, *Livin' Large* and *Weekend Vibe*, was to supplement them with the mighty Apollo program.

Heritage virtually guaranteed winning the Apollo contract not only by throwing money at the foundation but by enlisting an excellent minority-owned production house, de Passe Entertainment, which was sure to put Western's chintzy production to shame. Suzanne de Passe, a 1970s Motown production assistant who worked her way up to president by ably handling the Jackson 5ive, has enjoyed tremendous success producing black shows with crossover appeal. These include the *Motown 25* special, which has been credited with launching the Michael Jackson phenomenon; the sitcom *Sister, Sister* (ABC, 1994; WB, 1995–1999); the excellent made-for-TV biographical miniseries *The Temptations* (NBC, 1998); and even the *Motown Returns to the Apollo* special, which she did with Sutton in 1985 to celebrate the theater's relaunch.

If the story had ended with Sutton punked, Mercado-Valdes grinning, and *It's Showtime at the Apollo* still on the air it wouldn't exactly be a happy ending for everyone, but at least it would be fairly neat. However, Western International had amazingly slipped a clause into its existing syndication contracts stating that it was not obliged to deliver *It's Showtime at the Apollo*, but rather any similar "urban variety show." Western International still owned the sets, the talent, and the syndication contracts, so when Heritage's new Apollo show hit the air in 2002 it found itself head to head with shows that seemed eerily familiar. Peppering the airwaves were the titles *Showtime In Harlem* (shot at the Brooklyn Academy of Music), *Showtime*, and *Showtime Live*, all featured a stage set up to look like the Apollo's and starred familiar Apollo faces Kiki Shepard and Rudy Rush (who hosted the show after Harvey).

Both sides filed numerous lawsuits against each other. Each show appeared on more than a hundred stations around the country, in many markets (including Chicago, New York, and L.A.) in direct competition with each other. Collectively the same number of viewers watched both *Showtime*s as had watched the original program, so the existence of fighting clones guaranteed lower ratings for each show. *Showtime in Harlem* briefly won the Neilsen war, but soon *Showtime at the Apollo*, with a more lavish production, and the most important affiliates (network stations that weren't intimidated by bizarre contract clauses or fooled by Western's alleged spreading of rumors that the Apollo's renovations meant Heritage's show wouldn't get made), was on top.

For the 2003–2004 season, under the weight of lawsuits from their adversary, Sutton and Western parted ways, though Western continued to produce the show, albeit without the word *Showtime* in the title. The new program boiled the formula down to its essence, putting Kiki front and center, minimizing celebrity performances, and expanding the amateur competitions and child-performer segments. They left Harlem altogether, renaming the show *Live in Hollywood* (though it was never telecast live), and, in a swipe at its evictors, declaring the new incarnation "the *only* talent show with R&B soul and hip-hop flavor." *Live in Hollywood* is a bit of a hollow shell, with the L.A. audience and Ms. Shepard (who rarely spoke in her Apollo role) not quite up to simulating Apollo magic. However, to keep things interesting Western also began aggressively distributing old episodes of *It's Showtime at the Apollo* (which they own) as *The Best of It's Showtime at the Apollo*, whenever possible programming them opposite the current *Showtime at the Apollo*, making baffled viewers choose between new hostess Mo'Nique and old favorite Steve Harvey.

Heritage Networks' *Showtime at the Apollo* (the "It's" seems to have been officially dropped) is certainly slicker than its counterpart, but it has a strange vibe that is probably due to pressure to differentiate itself. While the show, now distributed in partnership with Warner Brothers, looks far better (there's a fancy new set and the innovative lighting design is rich and warm, which makes each performance look beautiful), several new elements have been added to a format in no need of repair. Chris Reid, "Kid" of the rap duo Kid 'N Play, interviews participants backstage. There are also interviews with the audience during acts, their talking heads and critiques superseding the performance. This seems extraneous, since the audience already owns the show's predominant voice. Each segment also has an awkwardly announced corporate underwriter ("Fannie Mae presents Apollo Legends . . . ," "McDonald's Apollo Kids"), which, while hearkening back to the early days of TV, makes it feel more like a telethon than a variety show by today's TV standards.

This "Showdown at the Apollo" controversy, along with Robert Johnson's sale of BET and the challenges *Soul Train* faces maintaining its position as a player in today's music industry, are all harsh indicators of changing times. When monolithic media conglomerates make independent operation nearly impossible and hip-hop's billion-dollar bottom line means mainstream outlets are readily available to African American artists, it becomes far more difficult for black TV producers to connect with a black audience. But despite the problems, there are still moments when everything is as magical as it was in 1977 for *Soul Train*, 1987 for *It's Showtime at the Apollo*, or 1997 for BET. When a dreamy-eyed African American teenybopper hangs on every word of Dorian Gregory's Omarion interview, when a black family screams along with Mo'Nique to get some crank off the Apollo stage, or when Harlem high school kids dance along at home to an Usher video on *106 and Park*, then it doesn't matter how hard it is to keep things going and how ugly things get behind the scenes. During those magic moments viewers know they are watching something that is for their people—something that they, and *only* they, can connect with in a special way. Despite the hate, discord, and soullessness that has infected far too much black programming in the twenty-first century, in those moments the audience feels nothing but "love, peace, and soul!"

5

Never Mind the Bollocks: Here's the Chipmunks!

Rock 'n' Roll Cartoons

Of course Bugs Bunny is Johnny Rotten and Woody Woodpecker is Little Richard. From a twenty-first-century perspective, it makes perfect sense that the subversive, rebellious tricksters that populated animation cells of the 1930s, '40s, and '50s laid the groundwork for the rock 'n' roll takeover of American popular culture. But certainly parents of yore giving their precious kids a nickel for the show had no idea that race mixing, fornication, and cultural revolution were being gestated on the silver screen ("Isn't that cute, son, Daffy Duck is a violent anarchist!"). Though tricksters and violence had always been a part of children's stories (from fables to the funny pages), movies with sound added a volatile element with the potential to stir the savage beasts within viewers of all ages. However, when children's cartoons and rock 'n' roll meet, concessions and compromises cause the anarchy and danger that mark both art forms' finest moments to disappear.

While musical scores for children's animation have a complex, amazing history, the history of cartoons' diegetic songs (music that the characters sing or play, as opposed to background music) is a little less complicated. Not long after the rock 'n' roll era took hold of American culture, the record-buying tastes of the kids—from the British Invasion to MTV to hip-hop—influenced the musical content of cartoons for kids. During the early days of rock 'n' roll, TV began its assault on movies and radio as America's prime entertainment source. To some, the transient nature of Top Forty rock 'n' roll styles may have seemed inappropriate to the elaborate, expensive full-animation cartoons that screened theatrically in the days before TV. More logical was the marriage between cheaper, limited-animation cartoons made specifically for TV and that "low" musical form that the kids dug.

In pre-TV cartoons, diegetic music tried to teach culture to the kiddies (Bugs, Daffy, or Tom the cat picking up the conductor's baton to lead an orchestra, or Disney's *Fantasia*, for example), or was limited to innocuous nursery-rhyme melodies or floral Hollywood harmonies. With a few exceptions (notably Disney's *Fantasia* sequel, *Make Mine Music*), when popular music of the day appeared in cartoons it would either be a nod to the adults in the theater (Sinatra and Bing references in Warner Brothers cartoons) or, as in the case of Cab Calloway's *Betty Boop* appearance or the minstrel crows in *Dumbo*, a signifier of decadence. Basing a cartoon's entire premise on the exploits of pop musicians is another matter. Certainly the misadventures of traveling minstrels is a theme older than *The Canterbury Tales*, but the idea of presenting it as appropriate material for the wee ones was something that would involve baby boomer influence, TV's hypnotizing capabilities, and the (somewhat) unstoppable power of rock 'n' roll.

TV began to saturate living rooms during boomer adolescence, and in the early 1950s, despite the fact that its programming was heavy on violence (professional wrestling and westerns), TV was considered relatively safe fare for children. Parents believed that TV, like the cartoon-heavy Saturday movie matinees that preceded it, was a harmless, vanilla babysitter— it didn't have anything to do with such issues as sex, race mixing, and delinquency.

The same couldn't be said about the other emerging passion of the kids: rock 'n' roll. The massive power of the new generation became evident when Elvis Presley mania trumped the Rudy Vallee/Bing Crosby/Frank Sinatra swoonings of previous teen scenes. This generation would prove to be so massive in size and influence that its allowance money would force record, TV, and movie execs to ignore protesting church groups and give the public the Pelvis they demanded. It was during this same period that the classic theatrical cartoons of the 1940s began making their way onto the small screen, with Woody Woodpecker and Bugs Bunny getting their own shows in 1957 and 1960, respectively. The reintroduction of these hooligans nicely complemented the emergence of the savage Elvis.

Though economics allowed America's teenagers to have their Elvis frenzy, the country wasn't yet ready to hand over its preteens. Earlier in the 1950s, comic books had been successfully neutered by Dr. Frederick Wertham's congressional hearings. But comics were produced by obscure, creepy, small publishers that needed to be kept in check. For many parents, TV's contents were controlled by accountable cultural authorities, so they felt little need to worry that the rock 'n' roll ills Elvis might unleash would get at their well-guarded offspring. The fact that the public didn't consider the bizarre *Andy's Gang* (NBC, 1955–1960)— which featured a clearly drunk Andy Devine and the near-satanic Froggy the Gremlin—and the sly *Soupy Sales Show* (ABC, 1955, 1959–1962; syndicated, 1965–1967, 1979) subversive is a testament to the faith parents had in children's programming. Not surprisingly, the first cartoon to reach the airwaves that dealt with the career of a young band in the rock 'n' roll era clearly had no intention of featuring any rock 'n' roll at all. However, it did manage to sneak in some genuine subversion.

Ross Bagdasarian, an Armenian American novelty-song writer and bit-part actor, turned tape speed manipulation into gold when he had his first big hit with the record "Witch Doctor" in 1958. He recorded as the "witch doctor" at a slow speed while articulating clearly, then played the tape back at regular speed, producing the pygmy medicine man's comic, high-pitched voice. He followed "Witch Doctor" with a Christmas single ("The Chipmunk Song"), introducing the Chipmunks, three performing rodent siblings with an ambiguous relationship to their Svengali father figure, David Seville (Bagdasarian's nonethnic alter ego). How this human came to adopt (or father) three chipmunks was unclear, but what was clear as soon as the record was released, and sold faster than any single to date, was that Simon, Theodore, and especially the mischievous Alvin, were here to stay. For the next decade, the Chipmunks enjoyed success on novelty records, on

© Ross Bagdasarian. Courtesy Jake Austen

live TV (as puppets on *The Ed Sullivan Show*), in comic books, as dolls, and as an animated TV show.

The success of the Chipmunks is due in large part to the care their cartoon received. Originally pictured on record sleeves as inhuman little rodents, when the cartoon was conceived the production house, Format Films, exerted great efforts to come up with a more suitable design for the bucktoothed siblings.

There were high hopes for *The Alvin Show* (CBS 1961–1965). Like *The Flintstones* before them and *The Simpsons* after them, The Chipmunks were believed to appeal to adults and kids alike, and thus their cartoon debuted as a prime-time show. It was hilarious, featuring excellent Bagdasarian songs (he also did the voices) and funny, expressive designs that capitalized on low-budget animation techniques by making the herky-jerky movements part of the humor. Bagdasarian's exquisitely constructed recordings proved perfect for animation, and since the characters were a musical group, it made sense for them to be performing songs (and viewers performed along as they followed the bouncing ball across the song lyrics, a segment of the show revived from the Fleischer brothers' late 1920s and early 1930s *Song Car-Tune* shorts). One of the strengths of the show was the fact that Bagdasarian represented the generation gap without fully submitting to it.

Unlike Sammy Davis, Jr., wearing hot pants to fit in with the kids, Bagdasarian knew he didn't grasp rock 'n' roll (a pop music devotee, he cowrote the Rosemary Clooney hit "Come On-A My House"), and he didn't fake it. When the Chipmunks usurp Seville's recording sessions with "rock 'n' roll," it's a charming fantasy version featuring clean-sounding, professional, swinging horns and the rodents chanting "cha cha cha." But despite avoiding rock 'n' roll rebel music, Alvin proved to be as antiauthoritarian as his cartoon predecessors and punk-rock followers. There were never any consequences to his nastiness, a fact that almost certainly led many impressionable children down a delightfully wicked path.

The show was not particularly appealing to adults, and was rerouted to Saturday morning in its second season, where it appeared in reruns until 1965. By that time, actual rock 'n' roll had enjoyed its breakthrough into the wholesome mainstream.

The Beatles' film *A Hard Day's Night* (1964), with its absurd chase scenes and comical bantering, is often cited as the first instance of the cartoon-style anarchy that made them natural heirs (hares?) to Bugs Bunny's trickster throne. However, the moment America was truly invaded was months earlier, during the Beatles' press conference at Idlewild Airport after the Fab Four landed on U.S. soil. The American press was surprised and delighted by the quick-witted, goofy, comedic shtick that Ringo and company delivered in lieu of regular answers.

Actually, this was nothing new. Elvis Presley's interviews and stage banter were filled with borscht belt one-liners and bad puns. But at the height of Elvismania, this aspect of his personality was ignored; the unleashed sexuality, the foreboding danger, and the juvenile delinquency he symbolized were all that the terrified fogeys and awestruck teens allowed themselves to acknowledge. Fans and foes alike refused to see the Shecky Greene side of the King. Though some kiddie ephemera was produced (bubblegum cards, toy guitars), something like an Elvis Presley cartoon was unthinkable. Parents may have begrudgingly acknowledged that their thirteen-year-olds were lost, but the idea of willingly giving up the six-year-olds to jungle music was unthinkable. Adults still believed they were in charge, that they were the ones who decided what was appropriate for their kids. They believed they were the gatekeepers of popular culture, and as the 1960s dawned, America still thought that the Rat Pack in tuxedos was running the show. Even the Dick Clark–promoted twist craze, where adults went to posh nightclubs and took lessons to learn the top teen dance, was essentially dismissing the cultural revolution as cute and exotic. By treating rock 'n' roll culture as some romantic novelty, like the tango or a tiki bar, they tried to tame and compartmentalize it.

But by 1965, the inevitable was underway, and the old guard was primed for a fall. The road to Rolling Stones credit cards, Ramones songs being played over the public-address system at baseball games, and casual Fridays was being paved. The Beatles got their own cartoon.

In addition to the Beatles' British charm and wit, a far more American reason ultimately hastened the decision that rock 'n' roll was appropriate for tiny tykes. There was a lot of money to be made by marketing the Beatles to tots as well as teens, and toymaker A. C. Gilmer understood that. Financing the show, with the understanding that the merchandising of the cartoon images of the Beatles would make him a fortune, Gilmer worked with King Features and a British animation design house to make *The Beatles* (ABC, 1965–1969) the first real rock 'n' roll cartoon, creating the mold for all rock 'n' roll cartoons to come. Although they borrowed the "follow the bouncing ball" sing-along aspect from Alvin, they innovated a frantic style of incorporating the songs into the story that would later become known as "MTV style." Of course, this was riffing off similar nonanimated segments from *A Hard Day's Night*, which would be perfected in 1967 by *The Monkees* TV show. The other aspect *The Beatles* introduced that would become a constant in rock 'n' roll cartoons was shoddy animation. The Beatles cartoon alter egos were charmingly designed, and the cartoon was funny, but unlike *The Alvin Show*, it did not make the most of the limited animation. Also, although the cartoon boasted that it featured the voices of the Beatles, it did so only in the songs. The spoken voices were performed by actors (including the great Paul Frees, one of Presley's cronies who was known for doing the voice of Boris Badenov on *The Bullwinkle Show*). One area in which the show didn't skimp was the music. The show included virtually the entire Beatles musical catalog up to 1965, including the German-language "Komm, Gib Mir Deine Hand."

Gilmer's calculations proved accurate. The show was a huge success, and the stellar early ratings were unprecedented in daytime TV. Apparently, the limitations of cheap animation and halfhearted Beatles impersonators were not a problem for the little kids. Despite sporting long hair, the Beatles (who were perpetually in their 1964 mode on the cartoon) were portrayed as clean-cut kids. Girls chasing them never led to sex, and Ringo's goofiness was never a result of drugs. When the smoke (never from cigarettes) cleared, marketing black-influenced music to toddlers had put a lot of loot in businessmen's pockets, and it seemed to have left American civilization intact.

In the immediate wake of *The Beatles*, a number of cartoon rock 'n' roll bands emerged, but, like the Chipmunks before them, their producers had little grasp of rock 'n' roll and were simply making fun of it or exploiting it halfheartedly (as bubblegum music later demonstrated, in rock 'n' roll, only wholehearted, unambiguous exploitation is smiled upon). The shows rarely featured songs, and there was little evidence of the baggage of the rock 'n' roll lifestyle (gear, rehearsals, gigging, vans). Cartoon bands included the Impossibles, a goofy superhero trio whose alter egos were a rock band (they appeared on Hanna-Barbera's *Frankenstein, Jr. and the Impossibles*, CBS, 1966). Depatie-Freleng's *The Super 6* (NBC, 1966–1969) featured Super Bwoing, a rock superhero with a flying guitar. Total Television's *The Beagles* (CBS, 1966–1967; ABC, 1967–1968) were a duo of dogs that played music (their relationship to the Beatles ended at the pun name). The Beagles did release an LP, but it consisted of mostly upbeat kiddie folk music.

Despite the moderate success of these post-*Beatles* cartoon bands, the cartoon rock revolution wouldn't begin until the end of the decade. This came about by way of the convergence of two factors: the raising of bubblegum music to an art form and Hanna-Barbera's lowering of TV cartoon standards.

Although the Beatles liberated rock 'n' roll for the preteens by making it safe for Saturday mornings in the early 1960s, the phenomenal success of their *Sgt. Pepper's Lonely Heart's Club Band* LP in 1967 essentially liberated (or enslaved) the adults by changing *rock 'n' roll* to *rock*, a serious art form deserving of its own *New York Times* critics and academic conferences. When the mature incarnation of the Beatles returned to animated form it was in a work of art, not a tool of toy-store commerce. In 1968, the more sophisticated, psychedelic *Yellow Submarine* feature film was a far cry from the chintzy, goofy TV cartoon (though, surprisingly, both were animated by the same production houses). The introduction of the idea that rock musicians were serious artists who couldn't possibly make music that the milk-and-cookies set could understand, however, opened up a gaping hole of opportunity for some joyously crass impresarios.

In 1966, the Monkees revealed the limitless possibilities of prefab gold by going head to head with the Beatles on the charts, despite the fact that they were a fabricated band who had most of their songs written, produced, and performed (except for the singing) by slick studio hotshots. If they could be successful, why not market records by studio musicians as groups who didn't even exist? If the songs became popular, *then* worry about who's in the band! Who needs a real-life band at all?

Bubblegum music does not avoid the kiddies of cartoons-and-Cocoa Puffs age; it ignores everyone else. It combines the finest pop craftsmen (on a mission to make a hit, not a piece of art), the slickest studio musicians, and singers whose voices somehow combine total innocence with almost creepy seductiveness. It gives these people a mandate to make a song so catchy as to be almost a jingle, and to make the subject matter about things little kids dig: candy! games! roller skates! But the writer also must, somehow, make candy, games, and roller skates overt, yet ambiguous, metaphors for sex. (Bubblegum scholars debate whether this methodology purposefully tapped into preteen sexuality—with a premeditated goal to make the songs seem naughtier and more authentic to the kids—or whether it was instead simply a form of in-joking among sleazy songwriters.) Most important, the process can't be about glory or immortality or individual achievement; it has to be about brutally honest commerce (give the kids *exactly* what they want, and they'll pay), so no performer's egos are allowed. The architects of bubblegum, Buddah records owner Neil Bogart and the Super-K production team of Kasenetz-Katz, knew when they started in 1967 that bands like the 1910 Fruitgum Company and the Ohio Express didn't really have to exist to have hits. If someone in the studio could come up with a winner, it didn't matter what band name was slapped on the label. But despite their prowess, the ultimate bubblegum achievement wasn't made by Bogart or Super-K. It was made by a little Jewish man who set the wheels of cartoon rock 'n' roll in fast motion.

The Archies had the only bubblegum superhit, "Sugar Sugar" (it hit number one on *Billboard*'s chart in 1969), an amazing eleven-year tenure on TV, and one of the most interesting stories in rock 'n' roll history. The *Archie* comic, featuring the adventures of the wacky teenagers of Riverdale, was launched in 1942 by John Goldwater, but the Archies, the band, owe their creation to a different patriarch. In 1968, after Don Kirschner was ousted by those ungrateful louts, the Monkees, he vowed to show them all. He found himself producing for the perfect band, one that would do his bidding, play the songs the way they were supposed to be played, and never rebel. How could they be difficult? *They were only cartoons!*

Working with songwriter Jeff Barry, hit-making songwriter/artist Andy Kim, pop singer extraordinaire Ron Dante, and sexy vocalist Toni Wine (as both Betty and Veronica), Kirschner crafted a bevy of surefire pop winners to be performed by the "band" on Filmation's *Archie Show* (CBS, 1968–1976; NBC, 1977–1978, 1987–1989). Every episode would end with the animated Archies playing a song, and if you dug the tune, you could go out and buy it on vinyl at your local record

©Archie Comics Publications, Inc. Courtesy Jake Austen

shop. Their first single, "Bang-Shang-a-Lang," just missed the top twenty. But when "Sugar Sugar" hit the top of the charts the following year, it made the Archies the *ultimate* cartoon rock 'n' roll band. Their huge hit allowed them to record five LPs of absurd, joyous, undeniable pop, including such naughty album cuts as "Hot Dog," which is either about penis worship or bestiality, and "Jingle Jangle," which equates an erection with Pinocchio's nose. Their contagious music was a perfect bubblegum balance of nice and naughty, and the program proved to be the perfect marriage of music and cartoons. Despite Filmation's limited animation style, the songs looked good being sung by the band, and fit into the show's structure well. The tunes kept the cartoon popular, and the cartoon (in the days before MTV) kept the songs on the tube and in the kids' heads. As cartoon rock 'n' roll reached the pinnacle of its success, it became clear that, though TV cartoon characters were making no attempt to capture the dangerous, contrarian spirit of their cinematic ancestors, the absurd, fun music was closer in spirit to the simple, sexy tunes of early rock 'n' roll than the mature post–*Sgt. Pepper* music on FM radio.

Filmation's attempts to replicate its Archies success proved fruitless. *The Hardy Boys* (ABC, 1969–1971) featured a rock 'n' roll version of the famous mystery-solving brothers, who now moonlighted in a rock band. This production was meant to take the Archies model one step further. To coincide with the cartoon's debut, they cast a band that looked like the cartoon characters (a fat one, a black one, etc.) to record and tour. They released two LPs of moderate quality, with no commercial success. *Groovie Goolies* (CBS, 1971–1972; ABC, 1975–1976) was ostensibly an Archies spin-off, as these monster musicians were cousins of Archie's classmate, Sabrina the Teenage Witch. They released a decent bubblegum LP, but it also failed to catch on with the public. *The Brady Kids* (ABC, 1972–1974) was an animated, parentless version of *The Brady Bunch* sitcom, with an emphasis on the kids' musical career. However, any success their recordings enjoyed could be attributed to the songs also being performed on the real *Brady Bunch* show. *Mission: Magic!* (ABC, 1972) featured then-teenage Rick Springfield as an enchanted rock star, but the cartoon, and his LP that coincided with it, tanked, leaving Springfield in obscurity until the 1980s.

Also entering the cartoon rock fray was the Rankin/Bass production house, which attempted to re-create the success of the 1965 Beatles cartoon. Using that same model, Rankin/Bass licensed the likenesses and music of two bubblegum-era acts whose genuine talent made them rise above the transient nature of the genre: the Jackson 5ive and the Osmonds. Running back-to-back for much of their time on the air, *The Jackson 5ive* (ABC, 1971–1973) and *The Osmonds* (ABC, 1972–1974) mimicked the Beatles cartoon by having adventures built around cartoon videos of their currently popular hits. These programs were better than *The Beatles* (and the cookie-cutter Filmation and Hanna-Barbera shows), however, because of Rankin/Bass's whimsical, confident signature style (courtesy of *Mad* magazine's Paul Coker) that would also be featured in their popular holiday cartoons and stop-action animations (such as *Frosty the Snowman* and *Rudolph the Red-Nosed Reindeer*). Also, since rock 'n' roll was now a more established part of the cultural landscape, these cartoons could include references to the lifestyle that *The Beatles* left out. Motown executive Berry Gordy appeared in the Jacksons' cartoon, and some of the mechanics of the record industry were demonstrated, while the Osmonds (the show featured the boys touring the world to promote goodwill) took the "screaming fans" aspect to a new level by featuring a recurring character (Hortense Byrd) who was Donny's obsessed stalker.

While Rankin/Bass was getting into the groove and Filmation was striking gold with the Archies, Hanna and Barbera, the cartoon kings, were ready to dive in deeper than Tito's and Jughead's bosses could imagine. Hanna-Barbera Studios opened in 1957, after Bill Hanna and Joe Barbera had spent nearly two decades directing high-end theatrical cartoons for MGM, winning an armful of Oscars for their work on the *Tom & Jerry* series. Hanna-Barbera Studios had a mandate to exploit TV's potential as a home for original animation, as opposed to a place where old theatrical cartoons were repackaged. By 1960, the Studio had established a foothold on Saturday morning TV and had introduced *The Flintstones*, a show that trumped Alvin and his Chipmunk crew by becoming the first successful prime-time cartoon. They also perfected cost-cutting techniques that they accurately calculated wouldn't adversely affect the show's appeal.

Hanna-Barbera's "planned animation" consisted of a series of techniques to cut down on labor. If a character ran or walked one time, why animate it again? Just use the same footage every time! If the only thing moving in a scene is an arm or mouth, why not paint the rest of the body as background and just animate the moving part? So what if the colors of the moving sleeve and the still shirt don't quite match? On the audio side, the frugality involved "needle drops" (the incidental soundtrack equivalent of stock footage). The studio developed an innovative but limited library of sound effects to be used in every cartoon. While the theme songs for many of the programs were excellent, catchy compositions, the real sound of Hanna-Barbera consists of the eerily familiar musical cues that go along with a character shaking its head in disbelief or falling on its ass.

But by the late 1960s, new sounds were appearing on competitors' cartoons, specifically the *Archie Show*, and Hanna-Barbera wanted a piece of the rock 'n' roll pie. Unfortunately, by this time the Hanna-Barbera machine was so well oiled that the sparks of innovation that made *The Flintstones*, *The Jetsons*, and *Top Cat* special had long since burned out. The phenomenal success of the studio's 1969 *Scooby-Doo* cartoon established what was essentially their last great model, and for the next decade the idea of kids and a companion creature solving mysteries and getting into adventures was the cornerstone of the studio's assembly-line production. What the *Archie Show*'s success added to the mix was that now these kids would also be a band! Though Hanna-Barbera had dabbled in cartoon rock before (most successfully with rock 'n' roll episodes of *The Flintstones* and *The Jetsons* that featured musical characters like the Way-Outs, the Beau Brummelstones and Jet Screamer), they suddenly threw themselves into it. They made efforts to work with bubblegum impresarios, and even had their own label, Hanna-Barbera

Records. But on the animation front, the studio did not want to take risks. The shows that resulted took the notion of planned animation to an extreme. Since each program would now feature a musical number or two, Hanna-Barbera would simply animate the band playing one time and then run a nearly identical sequence weekly, with only the song changing. They played the second musical number during a chase scene (a la *The Monkees*), meaning they relied on a series of visual sequences and actions that became very familiar very quickly.

The shows that came off this assembly line included *Pebbles and Bam Bam* (CBS, 1971–1976), featuring the rock 'n' roll adventures of the teenage progeny of Fred, Wilma, Barney, and Betty; *The Amazing Chan and the Chan Clan* (CBS, 1972–1974), in which Charlie Chan's huge brood of children played pop music and solved crime; *Partridge Family: 2200 A.D.* (CBS, 1974–1975), featuring the family rock band in the future; *Butch Cassidy and the Sundance Kids* (NBC, 1973–1974), featuring the voices of Monkee Micky Dolenz and future Charlie's Angel Cheryl Ladd as rock 'n' roll secret agents; and *Jabberjaw* (ABC, 1976–1978), about a giant shark who drums for the aquatic rock band the Neptunes. Rock bands also hosted two Hanna-Barbera cartoon anthology shows, the pop art–influenced *Cattanooga Cats* (ABC, 1969–1971) and *The Banana Splits* (ABC, 1968–1970), who were live-action puppets (they were reborn in the twenty-first century as animated Web-based cartoons). Also notable is the series *The New Scooby Doo Movies* (CBS, 1972), which featured animated versions of guest stars from real life, including such musicians as Davy Jones, Mama Cass Elliot, Sonny and Cher, and Jerry Reed.

Though Hanna-Barbera was interested in Archies-style pop chart crossover success, they only produced three solid bubblegum bands from the entire brood, and none of them hit it big. It seems they all suffered from the unlikely malady of Too Much Soul. The Banana Splits' LP featured some catchy bubble-soul (including some session work by Barry White), but only managed to slip one single into the top 100. *Josie and the Pussycats* (CBS, 1970–1974; NBC, 1975–1976) became one of their most popular cartoons, and was a coup for Hanna-Barbera, as it was a license from the Archie Comics Group, who owned the rights to Filmation's competing cartoon rock 'n' roll juggernaut, the *Archie Show*. Attempting to replicate the soul music variation of bubblegum that the Jackson 5ive scored with, the producers hired a black singer (note that Val of the Pussycats, voiced by Patrice Hollaway, was one of the first black Hanna-Barbera characters) and stocked the studio with top soul session men. It was initially fruitless, as the songs never charted, but the theme song eventually proved memorable enough to keep the Pussycats in the collective consumer consciousness, meriting a live-action movie revival in 2001. Not yet aware that the formula combining bubblegum/soul and Hanna-Barbera was a bust, Josie's contemporaries, *The Harlem Globetrotters* (CBS, 1970–1972; NBC, 1978), went all out. Produced by Monkees and Archies guru Don Kirschner, the album that accompanied the bizarre cartoon—in which the Globetrotters traveled the world playing ball, solving mysteries, and playing music (they were *very* talented)—should have reached the heights of the *Billboard* charts, or at least the *Jet* top twenty. Unfortunately, it never found an audience. In addition to Meadowlark Lemon, the leader of the Harlem Globetrotters at the time, the LP features an all-star voice cast of R&B/doo-wop legends, including members of the Coasters, the Drifters, the Platters, and the Cadillacs. Although the record is now beloved by collectors and connoisseurs, at the time it was too much for the target audience.

With the few noted exceptions, the music featured in Hanna-Barbera cartoons was weak, and one reason for this is that they failed to fully exploit the naughty double-entendre nature of classic bubblegum, instead featuring didactic songs designed to teach the kiddies life lessons. This tactic failed to generate memorable music; even toddlers could recognize the insincerity and two-dimensionality of the planned-animation/needle-drop company's concern for their welfare. In 1969, *Sesame Street* (PBS, 1969–present) had debuted, and with its sister show, *The Electric Company* (PBS, 1971–1976), it presented educational pop music of a quality and genuineness that few questioned. Hanna-Barbera shared no mandates with the Children's Television Workshop, and consequently, its efforts to educate

©The Cartoon Network

through song seem about as genuine as the food coloring in the sugary breakfast cereal advertised during their programs.

The only bubblegum-era cartoon rock 'n' roll band that convincingly made "message music" (in this arena that means "don't smoke" and "avoid peer pressure" rather than "stop the war in Viet Nam") was Filmation's *Fat Albert and the Cosby Kids* (CBS, 1972–1984). On the long-running program, comedian Bill Cosby brought the characters of his youth (who had been central to his stand-up comedy since the mid-1960s) to cartoon life, and the motley group of urban African American youth would meet up in the afternoons at the junkyard and bang out tunes on musical instruments made out of garbage (an accordion made from a hot water bottle and a radiator, a harp made out of a bedspring). Their songs, which ended every show in the early seasons (a TV in the clubhouse playing the *Brown Hornet* serial usurped band practice in the 1980s), would reiterate the lessons learned in each week's narrative. While the music wouldn't make the Jackson 5ive nervous, Fat Albert's smooth baritone was memorable, and the songs were catchy. Most important, the intention seemed sincere, possibly stemming from the idea that Cosby (a successful actor and comic) didn't need to do a cartoon, but was genuinely interested in making a quality product for young people, particularly black kids with little representation on Saturday morning. Though Cosby opted against a pop crossover Cosby Kids LP (Fat Albert's two LPs were made for the kiddie market, not the pop charts), more recently the black clothing manufacturer FUBU (and a host of bootleggers) made Fat Albert and his friends a ubiquitous part of contemporary black fashion. This revival led to a 2004 live-action movie. Though Mr. Cosby had made bold (or curmudgeonly) public statements criticizing the hip-hop generation (he told *Jet* magazine that he dismissed many of the young African American producers who approached him about working on the movie because they would have made "*Soul Plane* meets *Fat Albert*"), the movie did feature numerous young pop stars (including bubblegum rapper Aaron Carter, and members of B2K, IMX, and Good Charlotte), and Fat Albert himself does some rapping in the movie.

One would expect the hip-hop generation to produce some genuine cartoon superstars. The combination of comical rap names (Flavor Flav, Yo Yo, Ice Cube), the exaggerated personalities (Busta Rhymes, Biz Markie, Redman), the Dr. Seuss–like rhyme schemes (especially in early rap), and the nursery-rhyme melodies that frequent the hooks of hip-hop hits would suggest that a successful kiddie show with a rapping protagonist was a natural. When you factor in budget-minded Hanna-Barbera logic (rap music can be produced less expensively than rock), you'd almost think a slew of touring, crime-solving rap acts was inevitable.

©Filmation. Courtesy Jake Austen

Perhaps the failure of the Globetrotters record made the big boys hesitant to explore black music. Also, rap's interest in authenticity is possibly recognized by even the youngest fans, who can rap along obliviously to adult-themed radio hits while still digging Elmo and Barney (both, incidentally, played by black men) on their TV screens.

Despite no success stories emerging, there were some attempts at hip-hop animation, including two short-lived series. Kid 'N Play were a marginal teenybopper rap act when the Hudlin Brothers noticed an interview that mentioned they were interested in expanding into movies. Casting them as the leads in their successful *House Party* films launched the duo into a series of multimedia projects, despite the fact that their recording career remained lackluster. The cartoon *Kid 'N Play* (produced by Motown/Saban/Marvel, NBC, 1990–1991) only lasted thirteen episodes. On the show, Kid 'N Play was a teenage performing act looking for their big break. But the ultra-cheap Japanese animation and dull rap sequences didn't really capitalize on anything unique about hip-hop. It is notable that the voice cast featured black actors and actresses from prime-time TV and feature films including Tommy Davidson, Dorian Harewood, Cree Summer, Dawnn Lewis, and Martin Lawrence (who also appeared in the *House Party* films).

Artistically more successful, but just as doomed by the "Where Are They Now" nature of pop music, was *Hammerman* (produced by Bustin' Productions/DIC, ABC, 1991–1992). MC Hammer's show used Fat Albert as a model of an urban kiddie cartoon, and the humorously didactic stories dealt with juvenile delinquency and peer pressure. Whenever trouble brewed in Oaktown (Hammer is from Oakland), Stanley (Hammer's real name), a normal Joe who worked at an Oakland recreational center, would don magical dancing shoes (that talked) and become Hammerman, a superheroic extension of Hammer's stage persona. The show was entertaining and convincingly urban. Like *Fat Albert* every episode had a musical number. But the quality of the program wasn't really an issue, because by 1992 MC Hammer was a punch line. Renewal for a second season wasn't a remote possibility.

Outside of hip-hop, the music-video era has produced a few interesting blips for cartoon bands. Less interesting are animated music videos by real acts (Madonna, A-Ha, Master P). More fascinating is the attempt to create Archies-like animated bands to compete with real acts. The new medium of music video made it possible to have such an act without the commitment of a TV network's time slot. This has been much more successful in England, where pop music traditions make the landscape for cartoon stars more inviting. *Top of the Pops*, the English equivalent of *American Bandstand*, is bizarrely populist; if a record sells, the artists will appear on the show, be they pop, punk, gay disco, or even completely fictional. When the Smurfs had a kiddie record on the charts, *Top of the Pops* managed to get the Smurfs to perform on the show. In the wake of success stories like that of the Wombles (a British furry puppet band that began producing hit records in 1974 and charted as recently as 1998), it was little surprise that the MTV era would produce new cartoon superstars in England.

The first big success story was Jive Bunny, who in 1989 proved that the shoddiest animation imaginable and a goofy mix of oldies songs was enough to impress the Brits. Over the years the JB has sold over three million records, proving once again that the critics and the public come from different planets. Everyone agrees, however, on Gorillaz, a collaboration between cartoonist Jamie Hewlett (of *Tank Girl* comics fame), Blur frontman Damon Albarn, rapper Del Tha Funky Homosapien, and various hipster all-stars. The odd-looking cartoon band plays a punked-up hip-hop pastiche with a bored, jaded patina that matches the deadpan looks of the characters. The fact that the human participants make their presence known instead of totally pretending the cartoon characters are real, however, seems like too radical (and unendearingly ironic) a departure from the Archies model. The band actually went on a world tour, mixing the live musicians with their animated counterparts on video screens, both playing up and playing down the cartoon rock authenticity of this act.

In America, the best we've come up with is MC Skat Kat, who rapped a duet with Paula Abdul ("Opposites Attract," which hit number one on the *Billboard* chart in 1990) and fruitlessly attempted to follow it up with an album by his band the Stray Mob. On a more traditional, though not more successful, note, Dick Clark's DIC production company tried to integrate music videos and Saturday morning cartoons. *Kidd Video* (NBC, 1984–1987; CBS, 1987) told the tale of a live-action teenage rock band who gets sucked into a cartoon dimension, where they become animated, and must fight the corporate rock villain Master Blaster, who plans to steal their rock 'n' roll magic. Clips of top-forty music videos were woven into the plot. A slight variation on this theme was *Wolf Rock TV* (ABC, 1984), in which a cartoon version of legendary DJ Wolfman Jack hosted the video hits while trying to help teenagers save a doomed TV station.

Other MTV-era cartoon rock series include *California Raisins* (produced by Murakami-Wolf-Swenson, ABC, 1989–1990), a cheapo animated version of the minstrel Claymation creatures that sang Motown music on raisin commercials; Hanna-Barbera's *Bill and Ted's Excellent Adventures* (CBS, 1990–1991; Fox, 1991–1992); and Sunbow's *Jem and the Holograms* (syndicated, 1986–1987), a series based on an MTV-era Barbie-doll rip-off. Although Mattel had created its own musical line of Barbie dolls (called Barbie and the Rockers), the hipper Jem dolls proved popular enough to warrant a series featuring an all-female group of new wave, orphan-saving rock stars who battle an evil rival band, the Misfits (a punky all-girl band, not Glenn Danzig's New Jersey–based horror-rock band of the same name). The show featured video-style music numbers, and Jem cassettes were available not at the record shop but at the toy store alongside the dolls.

Fittingly, the most successful, enduring cartoon to emerge during this era was a revival of the first cartoon rock band, the Chipmunks. The original series ran in Saturday morning reruns until 1965, around the time the Chipmunks' record sales were petering out as well. Though Bagdasarian would make low-profile Chipmunk LPs until 1969, he had obviously lost interest after the success of the Beatles. Rock 'n' roll held less musical interest for him than novelty-tinged pop, and when it became necessary to make records where the Chips sang real rock songs (starting with a Beatles cover LP in 1964), he was just going through the motions. Bagdasarian retired to his vineyard and died a relatively young man in 1972. However, the Chipmunks story was far from over.

In the late 1970s Bagdasarian's son, Ross, Jr., became interested in reviving the act. NBC began running reruns of *The Alvin Show* in 1979, inspiring morning DJs around the country to do comedy segments where they would speed up recordings and pretend the Chipmunks were making a comeback and recording Cheap Trick and punk rock songs. This led to Ross, Jr., doing the voices on an album called *Chipmunk Punk* in 1980, which became a minor hit. That resulted in a full-blown revival that, while never reaching the frenzy of the first Chipmunks singles, would burn longer and more steadily for the better part of the next two decades. After a sentimental animated Christmas special in 1981, Bagdasarian Productions (partnering with Ruby-Spears) plunged into a weekly cartoon, *Alvin and the Chipmunks* (NBC, 1983–1991). The animation was less stylized and more "rad" for the 1980s, the gang was cuter, more "Smurf-ified," and they now had female equivalents, a rival rock band called The Chipettes (Brittany, Jeanette, and Eleanor). Although the new show was more squarely aimed at kids (the humor was less sophisticated, and there were more lessons to be learned), it proved to be more durable and marketable than the original. Musically, it was not comparable to the classic show, since the new Chipmunks made simple, cute cover versions or mild parodies of contemporary songs. But by aiming the music toward kids only, and not the *Billboard* charts, they were able to release more recordings over a longer period of time than the original Chipmunks. Although the show has been off the air for more than a decade, videotapes, some with new material, are still being released and are exceedingly popular with kids. In 2004 the Chipmunks underwent a direct-to-video 3-D computer animation makeover. Ultimately, the first cartoon rock 'n' roll band is the last one standing.

In the 1990s and the new century, cable TV, the Internet, cheap computer animation, and kids-only music outlets such as Radio Disney have carpet-bombed pop culture with rock 'n' roll/cartoon hybrids. Postmodern references to Hanna-Barbera's bubblegum heyday not only pepper parodies (*Saturday Night Live's* cartoon *X-Presidents* always ends with a dead-on Hanna-Barbera song sequence takeoff) but also genuine kiddie fare (*The Powerpuff Girls* and their Cartoon Network colleagues are virtually pastiches of past cartoon references). Just as Duran Duran and *NSYNC ultimately failed to live up to their labeling as the next Beatles, however, it's likely we'll never again see cartoons with the charm of the Chipmunks, the bubblegum synergy of the Archies, or the shamelessly unchecked mediocrity of Hanna-Barbera's 1970s cartoon rock renaissance. But with luck, we will someday see something far different and greater. While *The Simpsons* (on which three-fourths of the Beatles made animated returns) and *South Park* certainly have taken up the antiauthoritarian mantle of Bugs, Alvin, and company, we've yet to see the seemingly inevitable marriage of truly rebellious rock 'n' roll and an amazing children's cartoon. But let us dream—for perhaps some young mind, contaminated by hours of animated adventures of music makers (no matter how crappily done), will one day create the ultimate cartoon rock 'n' roll band.

6

Rock Concert

1970s TV Rock

If rock 'n' roll was born in the mid-1950s, then by the early 1970s it was a teenager with an identity crisis. In the late 1960s it seemed clear where the kid was headed: rock 'n' roll (its music and fashion and philosophy) became recognized as both a social force and a genuine art form. But by the early 1970s, that was changing. President Nixon's hard-line stance against student demonstrators, culminating in the death of four kids shot by guardsmen at Kent State in 1970, proved to be relatively effective. It exposed much of the peace-and-love generation as bandwagon jumpers whose dissidence was merely a fad that they were not willing to die for. This was signified by a folk music movement that had quickly morphed from political activism into an army of sensitive singer-songwriters reflecting upon their individual feelings and relationships.

More confusing was the schism between AM radio pop and FM radio album-oriented rock (AOR), as fun, poppy top-forty singles had little to do with the heavy, hard rock and the progressive album-side epics that stoners were listening to through their headphones. Throw in an "outlaw" country movement and soul music that was reaching new levels of sophistication (and, ignoring the white trend, becoming more focused on social issues) and you have the most interesting, complex decade in rock 'n' roll history, a decade whose music would resonate for generations to come.

To document these real, tangible developments TV rock decided to become more real, as efforts were made to close the gap between the live music experience and the televised music experience. The results were certainly mixed, as some of the most daring, exciting musicians got a chance to use the airwaves to spread their message, but at the same time, many of the most important TV rock lessons of the 1950s and 1960s were ignored. And by decade's end it was all moot—rock TV was turned off, the channel changed to a station that had a disco beat vibrating the shag carpeting of America's living rooms.

At the dawn of the 1970s the departure of two shows from the airwaves marked the death of two different TV rock landmarks. One died of old age, and one was stillborn. In June 1971 CBS canceled *The Ed Sullivan Show*. The program was still relatively popular but head of programming Fred Silverman had decided to remake the network as urbane and youthful by purging the schedule of all shows that were rural (*Beverly Hillbillies, Green Acres, Hee Haw*) or old-timey (*Lassie, The Ed Sullivan Show*). As a result, Sullivan's Sunday night showcase, where rock and soul acts had long enjoyed intergenerational prime-time audiences, was gone. The other program that died early in the 1970s was far less famous than Sullivan's, but its demise was no less significant for TV rock fans.

While still in the talking stages *The Music Scene* (ABC, 1969–1970) was touted as the most important rock show of all time, a return of youth music to prime time in the post–*Sgt. Pepper's*/Woodstock world, in which rock had become respectable and important. The festive silliness of *Shindig* and *Hullabaloo* could be left behind as this show, which had commitments from the Rolling Stones, Sly and the Family Stone, Crosby, Stills, Nash & Young, and even the Beatles, was to usher in a new age of TV rock.

The *Music Scene* was from the same production team that had created the *Smothers Brothers Comedy Hour* (CBS, 1967–1969, 1988–1989; ABC, 1970; NBC, 1975), which in its original incarnation used the clean-cut looks and goofy comedy of Tom and Dick Smothers' act to covertly program the most radical content on TV. They made jokes about the clergy, sex, miscegenation, and politics, and they had musical guests that were both literally explosive (The Who, during an amazing 1967 appearance, blew up their drum kit, contributing to Pete Town-shend's tinnitus) and socially explosive (many anti–Viet Nam folk singers played the show, including Pete Seeger, making a triumphant return to the public eye after being blacklisted for Communist Party ties in the 1950s). CBS canceled the show due to the controversies, but there was a feeling (as expressed in *Rolling Stone* magazine) that *The Music Scene* would act as a continuation of the edgy, socially conscious programming of the Smothers Brothers' series. To assure that vibe the show's producers wanted the show to be hosted by the Committee, a longhaired San Francisco theater group that practiced the then-radical improvisational comedy techniques developed by Chicago's famed Second City troupe.

Weeks before the show aired several things began to indicate that *The Music Scene* was in for some trouble. Disputes between the producers of the show and the director of the Committee led to the group's dismissal, with only two members remaining among the final sextet of young hosts. The most prominent comic handling the emcee duties was former *Smothers Brothers Show* writer David Steinberg, a member of the original Second City whose delivery and youthful Semitic looks slightly brought to mind the danger of Lenny Bruce. However, his Jewish comedy style also brought to mind the Catskills comics that had been a fixture on *The Ed Sullivan Show* and the *Tonight Show*, making his TV presence far less jarring to older viewers than a frenetic, hairy youth ensemble might have.

Another problem was *The Music Scene*'s length. Due to a contractual dispute between the network (which wanted the show to run thirty minutes) and the producers (who insisted on an hour) *The Music Scene* ran at an unusual forty-five minutes. To accommodate the return of base-fifteen TV length (which hadn't been in use since the medium's early days) the show was coupled with another program of the same length and packaged as ninety minutes of progressive youth programming for the new generation. Following *The Music Scene* was Rod Serling's *The New People* (ABC, 1969–1970), *Gilligan's Island* reimagined as a multicultural, flower power drama (a plane carrying a group of young people from all races who are participating in a cultural exchange program crash-lands on a deserted island, and the survivors must start a new society).

The biggest problem with *The Music Scene*, however, was that when it finally reached the airwaves on September 22, 1969, it satisfied no one. Once conservative middle-American viewers heard Sly Stone sing "Don't call me nigger, whitey," they would turn the channel. On the other side, radical youths were put off by the tame comedy and by bookings that mixed the likes of Steve and Eydie and bubblegum singer Bobby Sherman with acts they considered legitimate rock, soul, and folk voices like Janis Joplin, Isaac Hayes, and Buffy Ste. Marie. After several weeks on the air Ben Fong-Torres declared in *Rolling Stone* (a magazine that had been salivating for this series since its announcement) that the show, "so full of potential and promises in its talking stage, has turned out to be another floating object in the toilet bowl we call television."

While the show featured live singing instead of lip-synching, it too often created hokey staged productions instead of letting the artists do their own thing. And for every effective production number—James Brown singing "World" while walking through a group of indifferent multiethnic, multigenerational people—there would be a corny number—Lou Rawls singing a love song to the back of a blond girl's head only to find out that he is actually singing to a long-haired dog. Thus, a segment that opened by hinting at the interracial love seen on *Smothers Brothers* ended in a neutering Elvis-and-the-basset-hound scenario straight out of 1956. The show did feature several outstanding performances, including Stone's, Joplin's, and a chilling "Down by the River" done by Crosby, Stills, Nash & Young. But overall it was a bore to rock fans.

Top acts cooled to appearing after the first disappointing episodes hit the airwaves. The ratings were abysmal. Perhaps the producers should have reconsidered the Committee; *The Music Scene* was thrashed in the ratings by *Laugh-In* (NBC, 1968–1973, 1977–1979), a comedy show featuring faux radical pseudo-improvisers. When *The Music Scene* was canceled after less than five months, airing its last episode on January 17, 1970, audiences could wave good-bye to the idea of a prime-time broadcast network series dedicated to rock performances. If fans of 1970s guitar slingers and rad singers wanted to see TV devoted to their music they would need to score some No-Doz. Rock TV was heading into the wee hours.

More than two years after the *The Music Scene* bombed, one of its key producers, Stan Harris, returned to TV with a new show conceived by Burt Sugarman, a music-awards-show producer who wanted to do a rock series. Because of the poor track record of prime-time rock Sugarman had to think outside the boxes that made up the network scheduling grid. He proposed to do a ninety-minute rock music special/pilot episode that would air at 1:00 a.m. EST. No network had ever programmed that time slot before, as the existing practice was to turn over the airwaves to local affiliates after *The Tonight Show* and its contemporaries signed off (ninety minutes was a standard talk-show length at the time, so *The Tonight Show* ran from 11:30 p.m. to 1:00 a.m. until it was shortened to sixty minutes in

1980). NBC was wary, but after Sugarman offered to front the cost in exchange for ownership of the show (an unusual arrangement in an era when the networks owned many of the programs they aired) the Peacock relented. Sugarman enlisted Harris, and they prepared a program that was billed as a youth-voter-registration drive, presaging MTV's Rock the Vote by more than a decade. Popular musicians such as John Denver, Mama Cass Elliot, Helen Reddy, War, and the Isley Brothers would (between live performances of their hits) urge newly suffraged eighteen- to twenty-year-olds to exercise their constitutional right to be heard.

Midnight Special (named after a blues song by Leadbelly that had become a standard during the 1960s folk revival) was a tremendous ratings success. Though it did little to affect the election—Nixon eviscerated the youth-friendly McGovern—it did persuade the network to offer Sugarman a series. *Midnight Special* (NBC, 1973–1981) premiered six months later, airing every Friday evening after Johnny Carson's *The Tonight Show*. The format featured a musician host singing a few numbers and introducing four to eight eclectic guests from all genres of pop music, ranging from what would eventually be known as adult contemporary (Reddy, Don McLean) to super-funky soul (Curtis Mayfield, Ohio Players). There were brash rock acts like T-Rex and Aerosmith, classic rock 'n' rollers like Little Richard and Bo Diddley, and country acts like Willie Nelson and Charlie Daniels. Even blues and R&B singers who rarely made it onto TV, such as Big Mama Thornton, Bobby "Blue" Bland, and John Lee Hooker, graced the *Midnight Special* stage.

Though TV sound (both in the TV studios and in the home TV sets) wasn't designed to capture a live rock mix that was up to the standards of 1970s audiophiles, the main conceit of *Midnight Special* was that it captured the rock concert experience more authentically than the contrived shows that came before it had done. Bands always played live, never lip-synching; a real audience was there to react; and hosts and guests consistently employed youthful language (much of it by the ageless, gravel-voiced on-air announcer Wolfman Jack, a rock 'n' roll DJ who made a name for himself in the 1960s spinning records on border stations in Southern Texas and Tijuana). But despite its efforts to keep it real, what made *Midnight Special* lively and exciting was its classic TV fakery. Instead of looking like a 1970s rock concert, the show's stage looked like a 1970s Vegas revue, or the set of the establishment-friendly variety show *Hollywood Palace* (ABC, 1964–1970), with flashing lights, mirrors, and glittery excess. (The *New York Times* offered a more generous description, declaring the set authentically "rock," but hopelessly outdated, as it was "reminiscent of the psychedelic ballrooms that went out with the sixties"). Most performances on the show used bright TV lighting rather than employing spotlights and pools of color as concerts did. Most importantly, the show's early seasons featured a mishmash of genres, with icons from all walks of music and different generations mingling in a thrilling, organic manner. While this was perhaps the very best way to capture the essence of the early 1970s rock scene, it also inevitably conjured up the bizarre, heterogeneous booking practices Ed Sullivan had once used. Despite the groundbreaking nature of the show, the elements that called upon a quarter-decade of mainstream-pleasing TV—the gaudy set, the bright lights, the vaudeville vibe—were what made *Midnight Special* special.

It is difficult to generalize too much about the show, because over the years the producers were often willing to alter their format. Some performers were shot in a very straightforward manner (super-pro live acts like Patti LaBelle, Sha Na Na, and Ray Charles needed little dressing up). But if an act required visual mood setting, as Genesis, who performed partially in black-light with Peter Gabriel wearing a glow-in-the-dark bat outfit, did, or Jermaine Jackson, who needed to be shot in a trippy, wild manner when he played his extensive, instrumental psyche-funk "Bass Odyssey," *Midnight Special* could adjust. More dramatically, the entire format could be changed, as when Flo and Eddie did a talk-show segment with Lou Reed, or Andy Kaufman took over an entire episode with bizarre comedy. Even when the show became more cautious in the mid-1970s ("There aren't enough rock fans . . . the music's changed," Sugarman told *Rolling Stone* in 1975), installing Helen Reddy as semipermanent host and booking less challenging acts, the show still held some surprises, like the all hard-rock 1978 episode with AC/DC, Thin Lizzy, and Ted Nugent.

Some of the most ambitious episodes of the show were concerts shot on location. A bizarre London revue assembled by David Bowie (see Appendix 2) and a full-length Marvin Gaye concert shot in Atlanta did not have the feel of classic episodes, but they were important endeavors for the producers. This was not merely because these shows were entertaining and historical. *Midnight Special* needed to push its limitations in shooting live concerts because, despite being trailblazers for late-night rock, by the time they hit the airwaves as a series, their followers were already in place.

When ABC saw the impressive ratings of 1972's *Midnight Special* voter-drive episode it was convinced that a live rock show would be a perfect fit for its new half-ambitious/half-defeatist late-night scheduling concept. Finally ready to wave a white flag and concede the 11:30 p.m.–1:00 a.m. time slot to Johnny Carson, the network created a "program" called *Wide World of Entertainment* (ABC, 1973–1976), later renamed *ABC Late Night* (ABC, 1976–1982), which would be a catchall weeknight programming block featuring sporadically scheduled talk shows, specials, documentaries, movies, and reruns of prime-time shows. *In Concert* (ABC, 1973–1975), ABC's answer to *Midnight Special*, would broadcast performance footage of rock stars twice a month as part of *Wide World of Entertainment*.

Overseeing *In Concert* was an old friend to TV rock, Don Kirshner. While one cannot overstate Kirshner's importance to the success of *The Monkees* and *The Archies* (the hit singles he helped execute made those multimedia projects the phenomena they were), legend, and Kirshner, have overstated Kirshner's role in creating those TV programs—he did little beyond coordinating the music. But for *In Concert*, which was to be nothing but music, Kirshner's booking of guests and conceptualization of the project would define the show. Kirshner promised rock fans that he would deliver "a Fillmore of the air." Unlike *Midnight Special*, *In Concert* would not have the feel of a studio production but would take TV viewers to real rock concerts in real concert halls with concert lighting and (thanks to radio simulcasts on ABC stations) stereo sound. Instead of two songs for each guest, *In Concert* would spend thirty minutes or more on featured bands. Theoretically, *In Concert* would capture the excitement of being there.

TV, however, proved to be a poor substitute for the actual concert experience. "At a live rock concert," Loraine Alterman wrote in her *New York Times* review of *In Concert*'s premiere, "you're plunked right into a throbbing unit of energy—the audience . . . the magic of any live performance happens when the performer and crowd become one. That just can't happen sitting home where you're an observer, not a participant."

By shooting the show like a concert movie (though on a lower budget and with less interesting camerawork and editing than a good concert film) instead of like TV, Kirshner failed to utilize the medium's power to control the viewer's attention and make things feel intimate. Certainly most *Hullabaloo* performances seemed less gritty and real than most *In Concert* performances, but they were also more entertaining. Because of this, *In Concert* was in the unenviable position of only being good if the guests were really great.

Luckily for *In Concert*, Kirshner was up to the task of booking great bands. The first show featured Alice Cooper, a genuine showman whose haunted-house antics from his extremely narrative stage show were riveting on TV. As he went through costume changes (from leather-clad monster dude to formalwear showman) he presented everything from a gang rumble to his own execution. Other guests whose dynamism compensated for the imperfect format included the Allman Brothers, Curtis Mayfield, and the original TV rocker, Bo Diddley. After com-

pleting the first four shows Kirshner became ill and was booking future episodes
from his hospital bed when he learned that ABC (who fully owned the show—
Kirshner had no Burt Sugarman–type deal in place) had decided to proceed without him. They had the show's youthful production team and ABC's king of rock,
Dick Clark, trade production duties episode to episode. Clark's *In Concert* productions were technically more adept than Kirshner's, but this change in command, combined with the show's strange schedule and varied locations, made it
the least cohesive of the rock shows on the air. When the going got rough for rock
TV, *In Concert* was too mixed up to survive. It was canceled after two short seasons. More than a decade later it was revived in updated formats as *ABC In Concert* (ABC, 1991–1998) and *ABC In Concert Country* (ABC, 1994).

Though he was bedridden, Kirshner did not take his dismissal lying down.
Immediately he assembled an identical product that he delivered to more than a
hundred stations (including some ABC affiliates) as a syndicated weekly show
called *Don Kirshner's Rock Concert* (syndicated, 1973–1982). Using his stature in
the industry to assemble powerhouse bills, his first four shows featured the Rolling
Stones, the Allman Brothers, Sly Stone, and Van Morrison. While the actual production values varied (the Stones produced their own concert film for the show,
and later Led Zeppelin's appearance was a clip from their film *The Song Remains
the Same*), the show was much more cohesive than *In Concert*. Kirshner introduced each episode, looking like the ultimate 1970s industry sleaze. With his
heavy New York accent, open-shirted polyester suits, and thinning hair he was
an aging Studio 54 habitué presenting youthful longhairs. But what he lacked in
follicles he made up for in vision. Just as his Alice Cooper *In Concert* demonstrated an understanding of theatricality, he seemed to know which bands would
make great TV, and it was on *Don Kirshner's Rock Concert* that KISS, the New
York Dolls, and the Ramones got their best TV exposure, playing extended sets
for confused home viewers. Though bookings became less impressive over the
years ("a lot of the 'A' groups won't do TV anymore," Kirshner told *Rolling Stone*
in 1975, citing as cause that bands were trying to protect their mystique and box-
office draw), Kirshner continued to showcase entertaining acts. These included
Black Oak Arkansas (a band whose shtick involved lead singer Jim Dandy wearing tight pants that made the outline of his penis the star of the show) and classic acts like Chuck Berry.

A low-key counterpoint to the bombastic late-night rock shows was public television's live music slate. In 1974 PBS stations began airing *Soundstage* (PBS,

Alice Cooper. Courtesy John Battles

1974–1982, 2003–present), a show that presented dignified, full-length concerts showcasing significant artists like Bob Dylan, Tina Turner, Jose Feliciano, Bonnie Raitt, the Temptations, and Harry Chapin. From the first episode—Muddy Waters in concert, joined by Michael Bloomfield, Koko Taylor, Dr. John, and Johnny Winter—*Soundstage* made it clear that it was presenting what it considered important music without commercial considerations. With no emcee, no fancy lighting tricks, no dramatic camerawork, and no commercial interruptions, viewers were rarely reminded that they were watching a TV show.

Of course, watching TV is never the same thing as being at a live concert. Without manipulative directing or bombast, *Soundstage* producers expected viewers to soberly drink in the performances—and artists to capture the audience's attention with their talents. One of the advantages of being noncommercial was that bookings could be even bolder and stranger than *Midnight Special*. Comedian Martin Mull, who released a series of musical comedy concept albums in the 1970s, shared a bill with ex-Turtles/Zappa coconspirators Flo and Eddie. The Blasters played a set with Carl Perkins and Willie Dixon sitting in. And in one of the series' late episodes, doo wop pioneers the Jive Five, the Harptones, Randy and the Rainbows, and the Mystics performed.

That episode proved prophetic. Decades later PBS would have some of its highest-rated shows with a series of "oldies but goodies" concert specials featuring original doo-wop artists from the 1950s (which led to similar R&B, folk, vanilla pop, and disco specials). These bland, nostalgic productions aired during extremely successful pledge drives in which local PBS personalities begged for contributions during the equivalent of commercial breaks. These and other music specials have proven to be some of PBS's most popular programming, as evidenced by their proliferation during pledge season. All this has led to a revival of *Soundstage*. The twenty-first-century version boasts high-end digital video and sound production and continues the tradition of bold booking, including a Wilco/Sonic Youth tandem, a concert of Ron Isley collaborating with Burt Bacharach, and even a set by Elvis Presley's daughter, Lisa Marie.

PBS's other straightforward live music show is *Austin City Limits* (PBS, 1976–present), which quietly has become one of the longest-running music series on TV. In the early 1970s Willie Nelson helped establish the Texas state capitol as the home base for "outlaw" country that eschewed the gloss of Nashville. Marrying the relatively new tradition of hippie freedom with the old time country & western tradition of hard-living, enigmatic, songwriting troubadours (downplayed by Nashville during the Lee Greenwood/Barbara Mandrell/Olivia Newton-John era) Nelson led a group of long-haired rebels that helped turn Austin into the hipster town it has become.

Austin City Limits aimed to capture that maverick spirit, but wanted to do it, like *Soundstage*, in an unpretentious manner with a minimum of edits and camera trickery. Musicians do a thirty- or sixty-minute set in front of a small enthusiastic audience. The program has showcased music artists from the mainstream and fringes of country, folk, blues, and rock over the years, including George Strait, Ray Charles, Leonard Cohen, George Jones, Townes Van Zandt, Johnny Cash, Jerry Jeff Walker, Lyle Lovett, Guy Clark, Marty Robbins, Jerry Lee Lewis, Garth Brooks, Freddy Fender, and, of course, the red-headed stranger himself (Willie Nelson did the pilot episode, which became a pledge-drive powerhouse, and has appeared several times since). Recently bookings have expanded to include alternative hipsters (Beck, Spoon) and jam bands (Phish, String Cheese Incident). It is hard to call the PBS music shows great TV, as they fail to utilize the medium's awesome, manipulative powers to maximize their subjects' effectiveness, but the shows are definitely fine documents of good music. Over the years, PBS viewers who have been willing to relax and pay attention without being told what to pay attention to find themselves soundly rewarded.

Though rock concerts had made an exit from prime-time network schedules, rock, pop, and soul performers had not. Between 1969 and 1980 it seemed that every unthreatening musical performer, from smiling R&B singers to pop-oriented country acts, was given a TV variety series (hard rockers need not apply). Based on old-time vaudeville shows as filtered through Las Vegas glitz, these would usually feature a mix of lounge-style songs and extremely corny comedy. The comic relief generally involved stiff stand-up routines by the host(s) to open the show and several skits from the stars and the supporting cast (composed of such comics as Jeff Altman, Paul Lynde, Tim Reid, and Jim "Ernest" Varney). The star would sing a few songs, including duets with guests, and musical guests would participate in skits and then do their latest hits, either lip-synched or, if live, accompanied by the house orchestra (even acts that played their own instruments might have orchestral accompaniment).

The dozens of different pop star–fronted variety series during this period included *Bobbie Gentry's Happiness Hour* (CBS, 1974), *The Bobby Darin Amusement Co.* (NBC, 1972–1973), *Bobby Goldsboro* (syndicated, 1972), *Bobby Vinton* (syndicated, 1975–1978), *The Captain and Tennille* (ABC, 1976–1977), *Dolly* (syndicated, 1976–1978; ABC, 1987), *Don Ho* (ABC, 1976–1977), *Easy Does It . . . Starring Frankie Avalon* (CBS, 1976), *Gladys Knight and the Pips* (NBC, 1975), *The Glen Campbell Goodtime Hour* (CBS, 1969–1972), *Helen Reddy* (NBC, 1973), *The Jacksons* (CBS, 1976–1977), *Johnny Cash* (ABC, 1969–1970; CBS, 1976), *Mac Davis* (NBC, 1974–1976), *The Manhattan Transfer* (CBS, 1975), *Marilyn McCoo and Billy Davis* (CBS, 1977), *Pink Lady . . . and Jeff* (NBC, 1980), *Rollin' on the River with Kenny Rogers and the First Edition* (syndicated, 1971–1972), *Sha Na Na* (syndicated, 1977–1981), *Starland Vocal Band* (CBS, 1977), *This Is Tom Jones* (ABC, 1969–1970), *Tony Orlando and Dawn* (CBS, 1974–1976), and *Wolfman Jack* (syndicated, 1977–1978). Many of these were summer replacement series. During that era, instead of running reruns during the summer (or short-run reality series, as is done today), networks would launch series that would only run for four to eight episodes. By basing them around pleasant celebrities who already had a fan base it assured they would be at least moderately popular. If any of these shows became really popular a regular series could be developed.

One replacement series that showed just such promise, developing into a long-running hit, was the quintessential 1970s musical variety show, *The Sonny and Cher Comedy Hour* (CBS, 1971–1974). Salvatore "Sonny" Bono was an ambitious songwriter (he penned "Koko Joe" for Don & Dewey) and a fledgling record producer working under Phil Spector when he met charismatic teenage session singer Cherilyn Sarkosian LaPierre. Despite an age difference of almost a decade, the two were soon married and recording as Caesar and Cleo. That act quickly remade itself as Sonny and Cher, a faux-hippie duo who gained popularity by using Spectoresque pop production to create pseudo-social commentary singles like "The Beat Goes On." When the hits faded Bono, confident in Cher's star power, financially ruined the couple by producing a flop movie *Chastity* (a would-be radical drama with Cher as a drifter-lover-whore).

Career salvation came when the duo reinvented themselves as a comical Vegas act, which led to the TV show. Their lounge experiences wiped the rock right off of the former mod poseurs. Bono's fur vests and shag haircut were replaced with a tux and a cop's moustache. Cher's casual hippie gear was replaced with dazzling Bob Mackie gowns that showed off as much of her impossibly thin body as the censors would allow. Musically the show also veered away from the counterculture themes that defined their first period of fame. While TV Cher often sang rocking songs like "We Can Work It Out," "Stagger Lee," "Rip It Up," "Bad Moon Rising," and "Rockin' Pneumonia and the Boogie Woogie Flu," she was just as comfortable doing an Al Jolson medley of "Mammy" and "Rock-a-Bye Your Baby with a Dixie Melody." And while an interesting rock or soul act occasionally graced the stage (the lesbian rock group Fanny did their hit "Charity Ball," the Honey Cone performed "One Monkey Don't Stop No Show," the Temptations sang "Smiling Faces Sometimes," and Australian Rick Springfield made his American TV debut), more often the guests were sitcom stars such as Ken Berry or Jean Stapleton.

The show's signature segment featured the tall, exotic beauty insulting her squat Italian husband. The act was not new to TV. One of Ed Sullivan's greatest guests was the proto-rocker Louis Prima who, at the height of his career, grounded his frenetic jump-blues lounge act with humor, as his beautiful wife, Keely Smith, directed funny insults at her Italian goofball husband. Responding to her ethnic slurs Prima countered by making fun of Smith's Native American background. Though Cher was not really part American Indian (though she played one in song on 1973's "Half Breed") the couple's update of the Prima-Smith banter was perfect for the politically incorrect Archie Bunker era. In fact, the show's skits often featured ethnic humor with Sonny running a pizza parlor or with Cher's vague, dark looks allowing her to fill whatever role was needed (on a single episode she once played a Native American, a gypsy, and Tokyo Rose). Despite their bickering and seeming incompatibility, Sonny and Cher made America feel comfortable because beneath the put-downs everyone knew they had domestic bliss, as symbolized by the ending of each show when the couple would hold their infant daughter Chastity (named after their whore movie) and sing the love anthem "I Got You Babe."

However, it turned out that Sonny and Cher's *Bickersons* impersonation was more truthful than the show's loving closing number. The couple's appearance of marital bliss was maintained for TV only, as they lived in separate rooms and slept with different partners during the show's run. When they officially broke up, the show was still popular enough to give the former mates two separate prime-time hours instead of one. Alas, *The Sonny Comedy Revue* (ABC, 1974) and *Cher* (CBS, 1975–1976) were coolly received (though Cher's show did feature some spectacular style, as the sets were often designed to match her skimpy couture). They reunited professionally in *The Sonny and Cher Show* (CBS, 1976–1977), but that just made viewers uncomfortable. With TV variety no longer an option, Cher took advantage of the notoriety her silly show afforded her and became one of the most durable pop icons in history, scoring chart hits decade after decade and acting in numerous acclaimed films. Bono became a second-tier celebrity, guest-starring on *Fantasy Island* and *Love Boat*, before once again reinventing himself, this time as a clueless but well-advised Republican congressman. His notoriety helped him become one of his party's most successful fundraisers and led to the passage of the Sonny Bono Copyright Extension Act, an awful procorporate piece of legislation. Bono died in a skiing accident in 1998.

Another iconic 1970s variety show was *Donny and Marie* (ABC, 1976–1979). The Osmonds are a musical family act whose Mormon values have led to their amazing longevity, the group sticking together in various incarnations for almost five decades. Formed in the mid-1950s as a kiddie barbershop quartet, the brothers regularly appeared on *The Andy Williams Show* (NBC, 1957, 1962–1967, 1969–1971; ABC, 1958; CBS, 1959; syndicated, 1976) and *The Jerry Lewis Show* (ABC, 1963; NBC, 1967–1969) with four-year-old Donny stealing the show when he joined the act in 1962. In the early 1970s they were remolded in the Jackson 5ive's image and became a fringed-jumpsuit-wearing bubblegum act singing pop candy like "One Bad Apple." The group played their own instruments and wrote much of their own material. They decided to take a stab at rock credibility by releasing the heavy, funky *Crazy Horses* in 1972 (absurdly listed as the sixty-sixth best heavy-metal album in the universe by Chuck Eddy in his book *Stairway to*

Donny and Marie. Courtesy Jake Austen

Hell). They followed it up with *The Plan*, an ambitious rock concept album about Mormonism. After Donny left the group in the mid-1970s the act took a country turn, and starting in the early 1990s they became fixtures in Branson, Missouri, the vice-free Vegas.

While all of the brothers were talented and kind of cute, all of them were also a little funny looking, save for the radiant Donny who somehow managed to supplement his beauty with stage presence comparable to his primary rival, Michael Jackson. Not surprisingly it was seventeen-year old Donny and his equally pretty fifteen-year-old sister Marie who nabbed their own variety show. Dressed in glittery formalwear (Donny in his signature purple socks, Marie in Bob Mackie outfits more modest than Cher's showgirl gowns), the squeaky clean teens gave little indication that they were from the rock generation as they traded jokes seemingly lifted from *Bazooka Joe* comics with guests like Bob Hope, Farrah Fawcett, Vincent Price, Art Linkletter, the Harlem Globetrotters, Rip Taylor, Kate Smith, and Charro.

But each show also featured a duet between the siblings in which Marie declared she was a little bit country to which Donny countered that he was a little bit rock 'n' roll (with a little bit of Motown in his soul). This would lead into production number medleys of famous country and rock 'n' roll standards, linking the kids to earlier, romanticized eras (the 1970s featured the first wave of 1950s nostalgia, evidenced by *American Graffiti*, *Happy Days*, and successful rock revival concerts). This look backward was reflected in the bookings for the show, as metal and glam rockers never graced the Osmonds' stage, but old-timers like Chubby Checker, Bo Diddley, Little Richard, Chuck Berry, and, for Marie's little bit, Roy Rogers and Dale Evans, were more than welcome.

But even when a great performer like Diddley or Berry appeared on these shows they rarely were given the respect or performance space that teen dance shows or *The Ed Sullivan Show* had given them. Sullivan allowed every trained monkey act and puppeteer to do something close to what they normally did, with the TV professionals directing them to make it better fit the TV screen, and then using manipulative camerawork to get it just right. Rock acts got the same treatment as those monkeys and puppets. But on the 1970s variety shows the formats were so rigid, the writing so bad, and the tone so condescending toward the audience that acts were rarely able to convey what made them special. I am as big a fan of lip-synching as you'll ever find, but on these shows canned applause, laugh tracks, terrible arrangements, and offensive lighting supplemented the miming in ways that even I couldn't dig. Most 1970s variety shows were hard to appreciate beyond their kitsch value (which was plentiful). Together they represent one of the few moments in rock TV history when the power, possibilities, and appeal of TV's glorious artifice were mangled beyond repair by misguided micromanaging production teams with no appreciation for the music or the medium's strengths.

This was not the case with all variety shows—just virtually every one hosted by a 1970s pop musician. Some of the best televised musical performances of the 1970s were on shows that differed from that cumbersome model. *The Flip Wilson Show* (NBC, 1970–1974) featured comedian Clerow "Flip" Wilson in a series of sketches (many in drag as the sassy Geraldine) that were occasionally grounded in the African American experience (Geraldine's antics involved plenty of jive talking, and Wilson often played a lecherous clergyman, a staple of black film since Paul Robeson's powerhouse performance in Oscar Micheaux's 1925 masterpiece *Body and Soul*). But most of the humor on the show was pretty universal, which allowed all of America to enjoy the program, making it a top-five show for two years, and earning a *Time* magazine cover that declared Flip "TV's First Black Superstar." While the comedy on the show may not have been particularly ethnic, the music sure was, as *The Flip Wilson Show*, which preceded *Soul Train* by a year, was the best place to see sizzling performances by James Brown, the Temptations, B. B. King, Aretha Franklin, Stevie Wonder, the Jackson 5ive, and the Chi-Lites. White acts also appeared (like Johnny Cash, Bobby Darin, and Kris Kristofferson), but it was soul music that made the show groove. Unlike its hokey contemporaries, which made guests fit into their awkward worlds, Wilson's program relied on the excellent techniques of the 1960s music shows to shoot the musical acts in ways that maximized their impact, making it one of the most exciting 1970s variety programs.

Better still was *The Muppet Show* (syndicated, 1976–1981), which featured a wide array of guest musicians from every genre, including Lou Rawls, Roy Clark, Liberace, Alice Cooper, Leo Sayer, Harry Belafonte, Arlo Guthrie, Dizzy Gillespie, Joan Baez, and Gladys Knight. Puppeteer Jim Henson introduced Kermit the Frog and his felt colleagues to local TV audiences in Washington, D.C., on *Sam and Friends* (WRC-TV, 1955–1961). The menagerie then appeared on *The Today Show* (NBC, 1952–present), *The Jimmy Dean Show* (CBS, 1957–1959; ABC, 1963–1966; syndicated, 1974) and *The Ed Sullivan Show* before finding their perfect home on the educational series *Sesame Street* (PBS, 1969–present), where Henson collaborated with great songwriters like Joe Raposo and Jeff Moss on memorable musical numbers that often mimicked or spoofed contemporary pop and rock music. Seeking an adult audience for his creations Henson spent 1975 creating unappreciated Muppets for his short stint as a *Saturday Night Live* contributor and also crafting a huge world of Muppet vaudevillians to populate his British production that would become a syndicated American hit.

A brilliant and extremely music-oriented program, *The Muppet Show* featured its guest stars doing elaborate production numbers of their hits, acted out by puppets, and informed by humor infinitely more sophisticated than the knock-knock-level jokes on *Donny and Marie*. Though only a few rock performers, including Elton John and Debbie Harry, appeared on the show, every episode featured the rocking house band Electric Mayhem, with their Keith Moon–esque drummer Animal. Of all the variety shows of the 1970s, this was the one that came closest to capturing the vitality and energy of contemporary music. In fact, even when presenting opera arias *The Muppet Show* rocked more than *Sonny and Cher*. Despite taking artifice to the extreme (what could be more artificial than puppets?) and embracing the corniest of showbiz traditions (the show was based backstage and onstage at a vaudeville theater), *The Muppet Show* was honest and authentic. The guests and the audience not only believed the characters were real, everyone also accepted that they sincerely wanted their revue to be great. This show proved that the hokey, synthetic qualities of the other 1970s variety programs weren't the problem—it was their lack of ingenuity, honesty, and soul.

In addition to dozens of variety series that featured pop stars in the 1970s, one-shot variety specials (sometimes featuring live concert material) brought the number of music programs in that decade into the hundreds. One of the golden eras of network specials, hour-long TV romps by Three Dog Night, Petula Clark, Ringo Starr, Roberta Flack, Paul Anka, Paul Simon, Neil Diamond, Natalie Cole, Nancy Sinatra, the Beach Boys, the Carpenters, Wings, and numerous others (including most of the Motown stars) filled TV airwaves in the 1970s. While usu-ally as vanilla as their variety-show cousins, a good special could restart a career (as did Elvis Presley's famed 1968 special) and a bad one could throw dirt on a career's coffin (as did the Monkees' awful *33 1/3 Revolutions per Monkee* in 1969).

More interesting than the prime-time 1970s variety shows were their daytime rel-atives. Compared to the blander and more sycophantic talk-show hosts of the 1990s (Rosie O' Donnell and Wayne Brady come to mind), the hosts of the 1970s were a different breed. As showbiz veterans (ready to start singing at any moment) they had seen decades of fads go by, and they understood that new music and new fashion and new politics were interesting. Also, with their ninety-minute formats they had plenty of time to actually *talk*. Consequently, the interviews consisted

Mike Douglas welcomes some dancers to his show. Courtesy Jake Austen

of lengthy discussions instead of quick little formalities. Programs like *The Mike Douglas Show* (syndicated, 1963–1982), *The Merv Griffin Show* (NBC, 1962–1963; syndicated, 1965–1969, 1972–1986; CBS, 1969–1972), and Dinah Shore's *Dinah's Place* (NBC, 1970–1974) and *Dinah!* (syndicated, 1974–1980) featured rock and youthful pop acts all the time, and these hosts' comfort level with the kids was impressive. One reason for this was Mike's, Merv's, and Dinah's understanding of the entertainment omnibus—they saw how everything fit together, even if it wasn't obviously related (which is why Bowie hung with Henry Winkler on *Dinah!* and borscht belt comics met heavy-metal stars on *Mike Douglas*). They also were braver and more intelligent than they were usually given credit for; Griffin boldly bringing controversial guests like Abbie Hoffman and Richard Pryor to TV and Douglas, who prided himself on being a good listener no matter what position his guest took, welcoming incendiary figures like Malcolm X and Jimmy Hoffa.

Rockers who appeared on *The Merv Griffin Show* over the years included Blue Öyster Cult, Spanky and Our Gang, the Righteous Brothers, and Sonny and Cher. Griffin also spotlighted dynamic artists in other genres, such as Village People, Ian Whitcomb, Dwight Tilley, James Brown, and, in an early championing of hip-hop, the NYC Breakers in 1983. Over the years Dinah Shore welcomed ABBA, the Treniers, the Bay City Rollers, Diana Ross, and Iggy Pop. But among these giants it is Mike Douglas who stands tallest, for he presided over some of the greatest daytime TV rock moments of the 1970s.

The Douglas format had him sharing hosting duties with a celebrity guest who would visit for a week and was sometimes invited to book his or her own guests. In his most legendary episodes Douglas invited John Lennon and Yoko Ono to cohost from Valentine's Day until February 18, 1972. Lennon and Ono were given complete autonomy to choose guests, so progressive political and cultural figures had their say to America's housewives that week: Jerry Rubin, Ralph Nader, Bobby Seale, and comedian George Carlin visited the show and had ample time to express themselves. The programs also featured Ono doing a number of performance art projects as well as performing two of her experimental music pieces each day. Lennon also did musical numbers every day, including "Imagine" and "It's So Hard." The musical highlight of the week had Lennon inviting his personal hero Chuck Berry on the show so that the duo could play "Memphis" and "Johnny B. Goode" together. Their set was far from a technical triumph, as the show's sound was notoriously bad and Berry, who had built a reputation as a sloppy performer, was a mess. But the real revelation of the program was Lennon's performance—he was so excited to play with Chuck that he was also stumbling. Here were two of the pillars of rock 'n' roll teaming up and they sounded like kids in a garage. This made the moment more magical because in addition to creating raw, shitty sounds like a high school kid with his first guitar, Lennon was grinning in ecstasy like a high school kid with his first guitar. To see a Beatle be so unjaded and so un-self-conscious that he could lose himself in the presence of his hero made for one of the great TV rock moments.

Another landmark came two years later when Douglas welcomed KISS, making their national TV debut. Gene Simmons, the spokesman for the band, in his demon face paint and cheap stage costume, sat down next to Mike and a duo of Jewish comics. The hip Robert Klein seemed confused by Simmons's Halloween vibe and remained quiet, but the dumpy Catskills legend Totie Fields was amused by the absurdity. Fields, born Sophie Feldman, was one of the most popular female comics in America in the 1960s, but by the mid-1970s her health was failing and she was far less active. But Simmons's ridiculous getup was enough to light a spark, and she pondered, in a veteran comic's deadpan, "Wouldn't it be funny if, under this, he's just a nice Jewish boy?" Rock's proudest, boldest, most stereotypically shrewd Semite slyly answered, "You should only know . . ."

Totie, on the beat, responds, "I do . . . *you can't hide the hook!*"

After some silliness about a KISS kissing contest, Gene got up to perform "Firehouse" with his band. With smoke machines spewing and a red police light spinning, the New York rockers kicked out their heavy tune as the director and cameramen adjusted to this unusual act. Amazingly, about halfway through the song the crew seemingly had a revelation and started making dynamic, improvisational edits on the drum beats. By the time the song built to a climax (which had Simmons breathe a ball of fire like a circus performer), the technical direc-

KISS. Courtesy Jake Austen

tor had become a far better rock documentarian than most of the crews that worked *Midnight Special*. Surely KISS's theatrical presentation was inspirational, but nonetheless, the cameramen and switchers on this crew deserve credit for helping the band, and America, rock 'n' roll all afternoon.

A few months later Douglas shared hosting duties with professional disaster Sly Stone. Stone was resplendent in his giant afro, huge Star of David medallion, and rhinestone-adorned, open-chested Captain Marvel superhero costume covered in glittering moons and stars (he told Douglas he spent $100,000 a year on clothes). But he was also slightly (deliberately?) out of control, at one point doing a two-minute, nonlinear FM radio DJ rap and then smacking Douglas's shoe, knocking the host's crossed leg off his knee. As Douglas announced Sly's personal guest, Muhammad Ali, Stone couldn't stop inanely blathering about how a karate guy would *definitely* beat a boxer. When Ali sat down he was grim faced, explaining that he refused to go on TV and be a laughing, grinning Negro with all the racism and suffering that existed in America. Sly (who had been clowning) took this as a personal insult, which led to a tense exchange between the two.

After Ali agreed that a karate man would whoop a boxer's ass, a Caucasian congressman came out to discuss campaign finance reform. When Douglas asked Ali if he would ever run for office Ali gave a lengthy, dead-serious diatribe against the government, citing his belief in Allah and his refusal to represent or help the white Americans responsible for the slave trade and killing Native Americans. He was building up a rhythm and just as he began to demand reparations for slavery Stone started saying stupid things, which pissed off Ali, who was taking the forum seriously. This led to another argument between the two. Though *he* was the one who had been acting like a fool, Stone then decided to mediate between the boxer and the congressman who were sitting on either side of him. The politician, a colleague of Barbara Jordan, began to bristle as he perceived that Ali was calling him a racist and denigrating black representatives. Ali started barking about lynching and rapes and throwing the word *nigger* around when Stone, histrionically overreacting, made moves to physically restrain both men. When the discussion finally ended so that Sly and the Family Stone could play a few numbers it was obvious to all who were watching that this was some crazy, serious shit going down, and that daytime TV wasn't a joke.

The show ended with the band doing "Stand" as a whispering meditation. Shot abysmally (the lessons learned during KISS's visit had obviously been forgotten), the goofiest video effects imaginable took viewer's minds off the bad sound. The number got interesting when Stone left his keyboard and started doing pop-locking kung fu moves as he approached the audience while the music began to build in intensity. Stone strolled out to the crowd and then the home audience saw the real highlight of the show. A small portion of the crowd, made up of young black women, was getting down! The rest of the audience was white non-hipsters, and all of them seemed to want to get up and clap, but, bizarrely, none of them were able to even remotely clap to the beat. You could not cast actors to do what these white people were doing, and that TV moment became a perfect metaphor for the combustible discourse between Ali and the congressman. The white people wanted to understand, but they didn't have the tools. But before we could really contemplate this central problem in post–civil rights era race relations, Stone had the band kick into "I Want to Take You Higher." Seizing the moment, Douglas grabbed a tambourine and shook his way into TV rock history.

Though the occasional daytime show, and the whole late-night TV rock scene, initially indicated that the 1970s was the era when big, nasty hard-rocking, guitar music would finally make it to the airwaves, one trend emerged late in the decade that took the rock out of the rock concerts. Black music in the early 1970s, which featured brilliant productions from the Curtom label from Chicago, the Gamble-Huff production team from Philadelphia, and the P-Funk family from outer space, became a more powerful commercial and artistic force than it had ever been before. Factor in a more progressive Motown that featured Marvin Gaye and Stevie Wonder breaking new ground, and you had a soul/funk renaissance.

Dance clubs with DJs who spun funky records in lieu of presenting live bands began to signify urban hipness in a way that extended beyond the core black, Latino, and gay audiences that had long frequented such venues. After John Travolta starred in the 1977 movie *Saturday Night Fever*, which yielded a massive hit soundtrack album highlighted by the Bee Gees' dance tunes and the Trammps hit "Disco Inferno," disco stopped being an emerging trend and became a colossal fad. The record industry remade itself, dedicating huge resources to the music, much of it heavily orchestrated with strings and some of it (especially the productions of the ubiquitous Giorgio Morodor) relying on electronic instrumentation. Even rock bands like the Rolling Stones and KISS began to make disco tracks. More people, of all generations, were learning the dance steps of the day than at any time since the twist craze.

Of course, TV recognized this trend (though rather late, as most of the TV disco shows were from 1979, the year disco reached the tipping point and the reactive "Disco Sucks" movement gained prominence). Dick Clark produced *Le Disco;*

Solid Gold (syndicated, 1980–1988) used athletic trained disco dancers to help count down the top hits of the week; local TV dance shows caught disco fever; and several national shows attempted to hop the disco train.

The most ambitious disco show was *Makin' It* (ABC, 1979), which was supposed to be *Saturday Night Fever* as filtered through the hit sitcom *Happy Days* (ABC, 1974–1984). To guarantee that no viewers failed to associate the show with the movie, John Travolta's older sister Ellen was cast as the mom, Bee Gees music was used during the dance sequences, and the discotheque the characters frequented was named "The Inferno," referencing the hit song from the movie's soundtrack. The soundtrack proved to be the only hit associated with this TV show, as the star of this short-lived flop, David Naughton (better known for *American Werewolf in London* and the "I'm A Pepper" TV commercials), had a number-five *Billboard* single with the show's theme song.

The most successful disco-themed show was *Dance Fever* (syndicated, 1979–1987), a disco dance contest hosted by Deney Terrio, Travolta's *Saturday Night Fever* dance coach. Couples performed dance routines in front of a panel of celebrity judges who then voted for a winner. Though initially it was disco only, as the fad died down contestants were allowed to choose other styles of dance.

But the real effects of disco could be seen on preexisting series. Sitcoms made disco jokes (George became addicted to the boogie on *The Jeffersons*), cops solved disco crimes (the *CHiPs* officers thwarted roller disco robbers in a two-part episode guest starring Leif Garrett), and *American Bandstand* became a sea of satin, polyester, and mustaches. *Soul Train* played black dance music before and after the disco boom; consequently, it was less visibly and outrageously affected.

And in a symbolic death knell for 1970s TV rock-concert shows, head banging was replaced by booty shaking. *Don Kirshner's Rock Concert*, once the TV home of Led Zeppelin and the Ramones, began spotlighting artists like ABBA and Shaun Cassidy and even added an in-house dance troupe called Don's Disco Dancers. *Midnight Special* continued with somewhat eclectic bookings, but it too began careening toward Funky Town: Village People hosted an all-disco episode; there was an audience dance segment; and even an episode hosted by the original late night TV rocker Alice Cooper was populated by acts like Chic, Olivia Newton-John, and Instant Funk. Debbie Harry of Blondie, a band that frequently played the show, put it best on a January 1979 episode: "Our band plays an ancient form of music that is still seen and heard in some places today. It's called rock 'n' roll. But now *everybody* is dancing to a heavy bass line beat . . ." The singer— whose ragged punk band became superstars when they allowed production magic to add a disco element to their songs—then went on to introduce Sarah Dash and Peaches and Herb.

Though disco decimated the straightforward late-night rock shows, one nocturnal youth-oriented offering kept rocking far beyond the 1970s finish line. In 1975 NBC executive Dick Ebersole told *Rolling Stone* magazine that the new program he and Canadian-born producer Lorne Michaels were preparing would be a comedy/variety show that would consist of 20 percent music. *Saturday Night Live* (NBC, 1975–present) was scheduled to run live from 11:30 p.m. to 1:00 a.m. every Saturday and would be a showcase for sketch comedy featuring young, shaggy performers schooled in improvisational comedy techniques at Chicago's Second City theater and its Toronto offshoot. NBC did not make the same mistake ABC had when it neutered the edgy comedy of the Committee on *The Music Scene* five years earlier. This new show would push drugged-out, sick, rock 'n' roll comedy to the far edges of the network censor's parameters.

Saturday Night Live quickly became a hit as the young comedians featured on the show (particularly Chevy Chase, John Belushi, and Gilda Radner) and the characters they portrayed became national obsessions. Each show spotlighted a celebrity guest host and at least one musical guest who typically did two numbers. Two or three songs in ninety minutes doesn't quite equal Ebersole's 20 percent estimate, but over its thirty-year history the show has had quite a bit of musical content beyond the guest artists. Some of the original cast members had musical backgrounds (Chevy Chase had been in the 1960s psychedelic band Chamaeleon Church, and Dan Aykroyd was an avid blues fan who fancied himself a fair harmonica player), so it wasn't surprising that music showed up in numerous skits. Impressions of famed musicians over the years included Belushi's Joe Cocker impersonation (which he once performed as a "dueling Cockers" duet with the actual British blues rocker), Eddie Murphy as the Godfather of Soul on "James Brown Celebrity Hot Tub" (a skit that consisted of Murphy doing a series of Brown's signature grunts and moves, all in response to sticking his toe into scalding water), and Chris Farley as a wasted Hank Williams, Jr., recording *Monday Night Football* promos.

There were also music skits featuring original characters and songs by cast members. Many were memorable (though not always good). These include Gilda Radner's Patti Smith parody Candy Slice; Jim Belushi's "White Guy Rap"; the TV debut of The Folksmen (Michael McKean, Harry Shearer, and Christopher

Belushi as Cocker. Courtesy Jake Austen

Guest as the band that later starred in the mock documentary *A Mighty Wind*);
Michael Myers's guitar shredding on "Wayne's World" ; Will Farrell's numerous
musical characters (who exploit the alleged humor of hearing a stiff Caucasian
reference 1970s funk and 1990s R&B lyrics); and juvenile acoustic guitar songs
by Adam Sandler (somewhat unimpressive at the time, but eventually revealed
as brilliant in comparison with the on-air songs of his successor, Jimmy Fallon).

The most famous music bit the cast ever devised was the Blues Brothers. Originally presented as an absurdist concept gag in the premiere season (John Belushi,
Dan Aykroyd, and the *Saturday Night Live* band dressed in bee costumes while performing Slim Harpo's blues classic "King Bee"), the act reemerged in 1978 dressed
in black suits and sunglasses, performing blues standards, with Belushi's barely adequate vocals made acceptable by the stellar musicians backing him up (including
Steve Cropper of Booker T. and the MGs). Through a combination of Belushi's
massive popularity and the strength of the material (the superior original records
were unknown to the young, white kids hearing the songs for the first time), the

Blues Brothers became a popular touring and recording act, ultimately starring in their own 1980 movie.

Saturday Night Live was grounded in music in several ways. Toscanini had used the studio where *Saturday Night Live* was originally shot to conduct the NBC orchestra (though it needed to be substantially remodeled to accommodate rock). Howard Shore, the show's music director, had assembled (as the musical heart of the show) an ace house band equally adept in R&B, jazz, and rock 'n' roll. (The band was fronted by Paul Shaffer, who later became a fixture on *Late Night/Late Show with David Letterman* [NBC, 1982–1993; CBS, 1993–present].) Most importantly, the early *Saturday Night Live* booking policy fostered an atmosphere of sonic eclecticism reminiscent of the free-form stations of the early days of FM rock culture.

On paper *Saturday Night Live* seems like the best music show of all time. It has spent years boldly booking unusual, important acts. In the first six seasons a partial list of musical guests includes Randy Newman, Gil-Scott Heron, The Stylistics, Bill Withers, Jimmy Cliff, Desi Arnaz, The Band, Brian Wilson, The Kinks, Taj Mahal, Ray Charles, Willie Nelson, Sun Ra, Frank Zappa, Kate Bush, Peter Tosh, The Doobie Brothers, Paul Butterfield, Eubie Blake, the Chieftains, Bette Midler, Bob Dylan, Chicago, David Bowie, Marianne Faithfull, Sam and Dave, The Specials, Captain Beefheart, and James Brown. The bookings became more hit-oriented in the 1980s (by 1979 artists were seeing an increase of up to 300,000 copies of their albums sold after a *Saturday Night Live* performance, so record labels began aggressively trying to book their star acts) and by the twenty-first century the show rarely featured a musician who wasn't promoting one of the music industry's high-priority releases.

But from Janis Ian in 1975 to Green Day in 2005, *Saturday Night Live* has had one unifying thread: it has consistently featured some of the most boring, ineffective presentations of rock music in TV history.

From the beginning Lorne Michaels was dedicated to presenting a show that broke TV conventions. There would be no spit takes or mugging, there would be no guest hosts who were TV regulars, and music acts would not be presented the same way they had been in the past. Unlike the 1960s shows, there would be no lip-synching (except for ABBA in the first season, recent dance-based stadium acts like Janet Jackson, and an embarrassed Ashlee Simpson, whose prerecorded vocal tracks were revealed by a technical malfunction). And unlike the other live concert shows of the 1970s, there would be no TV rock clichés (Michaels reportedly did not want any close-ups of fingers on instruments, stating, "We're not giving music lessons").

Michaels was right in his sense that lip-synching would have been inappropriate on a show so grounded in being live, though many times bands on the show sounded disappointing compared to their recordings (most famously the Rolling Stones did a lackluster set with weak Jagger vocals in 1978, and more recently, numerous rap acts have been unable to re-create their recording studio sheen in the NBC studio).

But unfortunately, the way the show eschewed decades of TV rock development, particularly the Jack Good camerawork that became cliché as it was continuously copied, resulted in incredibly dull music segments. *Saturday Night Live* was genuinely young and really hip—it wasn't some middle-aged Don Kirshner with a gold chain and open collar (Paul Shaffer's scathing *SNL* impersonation of *Rock Concert*'s host made that position clear). Because the show's producers considered themselves to be of the same generation as the show's performers, perhaps they didn't feel it would be appropriate to tell these artists where to stand so that the shots would look best or when and where they should move. As the unambitious cameras shot whatever was going on, the spread-out musicians, under boring lighting schemes, blend into a distracting set (which changed annually, but usually reflected urban decay or urban clutter); audience reaction is never tangible and rarely documented.

Not to imply that bands are free to do whatever they want to or that no shots are blocked in advance. The week's band performs several times on the stage prior to the live performance, including a Thursday afternoon rehearsal and a taped dress rehearsal that precedes the actual show. (The taped rehearsal came in handy in 1992 when the innocuous rehearsal version of Sinead O'Connor's cover of Bob Marley's "War" aired on the West Coast and in reruns after the live telecast performance ended with her ripping up a photo of the Pope to protest sexual abuse by the clergy.) Also, all song lyrics have to be cleared with the network censors in advance, so there is little room for lyrical ad-libbing or improvisation. This came up in 1977 when Elvis Costello, protesting not NBC's rigid censorship policy, but rather his dissatisfaction that his record label demanded he play his next single, began playing an approved song on-air, and then went into the unapproved, but inoffensive, "Radio Radio."

But despite the rehearsals and restrictions, *Saturday Night Live* has always kept its instructions to the bands to a minimum, allowing them to treat a TV stage the way they would a club or concert stage. This often resulted in several minutes of TV that, during the show's better years, were a dull distraction from exciting comedy skits and films. A band like the Grateful Dead (who were on the show twice in its early years) obviously is quite adept at playing live, but an outdoor concert performance for thousands of fans is quite different from a multicamera shoot for TV. The band played for their Deadheads (they choreographed nothing for the cameras), and the director didn't do anything to compensate. Perhaps that was how the band wanted to present itself—to let their music speak for itself. But *Saturday Night Live*'s worst crimes occurred when an act demanded to be shot well and the show couldn't accommodate it.

When Prince came on to perform "Party Up" in 1981 it was his only TV appearance promoting his amazing, raw *Dirty Mind* LP, and he clearly wanted to make it classic. His band had worked on dynamic stage moves; they were wearing absurd, eclectic outfits (which were neutered by the distracting set, which looked like buildings with several patterns and colors of bricks). Also working against the performance was sparse lighting, with the band casting shadows across each other and often moving into darkness. For the most part the director used a full cover shot of the group and three-quarter shots from either side of Prince, every once in a while going to close-ups of singing and a two-shot of Prince and his bassist. There was virtually no camera movement (one zoom opened the performance, and that was it) and the edits, while adequate (in that they are on the beat), are perfunctory. Everything they shoot is good—Prince made sure that he was riveting the whole time—but what they don't shoot is a shame. Keyboardist Matt Fink is dressed in full surgical scrubs and appears to have been doing a hilarious robot dance the entire time, but because only a sliver of him is visible over the guitarist's shoulder I can't really say. And most disappointing is that it is not until the song is almost over that viewers find out that Prince is not wearing pants, but rather stockings and panties. If a director's guest is wearing black panties, I would think that director would want to show that pretty early; it's a visual that clearly says that this is something special. The obvious approach would be to start a camera at Prince's feet early in the song and pan up slowly, revealing his outfit, then stop the pan on his face, timing it to get there at an important vocal moment. Perhaps that is hackneyed, but it, or a more original approach to get the same effect, would have made the segment better. In the end this was a decent TV performance, but the fact is that with proactive TV direction it could have rivaled the best *Shindig* performance or the finest moments from the best concert films.

There have certainly been a few performances over the years that worked well within *Saturday Night Live*'s format. During the first several seasons, progressive jazz acts were given rare national media exposure, and some of these performers transcended the show's limitations. Though it's not shown often (because it occurred during an episode hosted by Milton Berle, whose comedy was so incongruous with the *Saturday Night Live* players that Michaels rarely reran the show), a 1979 Ornette Coleman number, in which he reconfigured the studio space by having his funky fusion/bop band play in a circle, was one of the most powerful *Saturday Night Live* performances ever. Another visually compelling number featured Brick (whose hit "Dazz" attempted to fuse disco and jazz by combining improvised flute with dance music). For some reason their performance was shot using the kind of close-ups and trickery (the funky drummer is shot through his transparent drum heads) that the show usually shied away from. But outstanding musical segments like these were rare, and as the show became more pop oriented and less daring with its bookings the blandness increased as less talented musicians graced the stage. For three decades *Saturday Night Live* has achieved the remarkable feat of putting some of the most interesting acts on TV and making people reach for their remotes when those acts start performing.

Despite the pounding disco beat, TV rock of the 1970s ended with a whimper instead of a wail. The 1980s would bring with them Reagan and the reinvention of idealistic hippies as materialistic yuppies. The greasy-haired masses, wanking guitar solos, and wafting aroma of cannabis that were hallmarks of real 1970s concerts (and were inadequately captured in 1970s concert TV shows) would become passé. They were replaced with puffy-haired masses, wobbling keyboard solos, and cocaine hazes. Most importantly, the commercial failures and intergenerational concessions of TV rock were about to become moot points with the explosion of MTV. But despite its shortcomings and nuttiness, TV rock served nobly during the Nixon and Carter administrations. Through the late-night concerts, talk shows, variety programs and specials, TV had presented contemporary music in an unfocused, goofy, absurd light. Sometimes it was unsatisfying, sometimes it was thrilling, but it was almost always giddily, joyously confusing. And considering the wildly eclectic music of that bizarre, legendary era—an era when rock 'n' roll reached its fullest potential for artistry, idiocy, intensity, and diversity—that's the only way it could have been.

> "Created by the TV screen/Cut your
> hair and act real mean/Don't believe
> in the music or what it means/Just
> want to be cool and be part of the
> scene"
>
> —Negative Element ("Media Punks")

7

BEEF BEEF BEEF BEEF BALONEY!

Punk Rock on TV

Punk rock as envisioned by Malcolm McLaren was a flamboyant, made-for-TV concept. Media-savvy early L.A. punkers, embracing British punk's spectacle, were gainfully employed as colorful TV extras. The Ramones expected what they called "punk" to land them on *American Bandstand*. And other New York 1970s scenesters, who viewed punk as a wide-open meeting place for the avant-garde, were preparing for an MTV that was never to be—an audio-visual landscape as daring as the animated bumpers the channel ran between videos in its early days.

The only punk rock that couldn't envision itself on a TV screen was hardcore. In some ways the hardcore movement of the early 1980s was punk's most American moment, with its regional communities embracing the mantra of D.I.Y. ("do it yourself"), a democratic ideal that is a fervent declaration of independence. But to many it seemed a profoundly un-American subculture that didn't fully embrace capitalism (valuing underground status over mainstream success) and borrowed liberally from such unpatriotic ideas as socialism, anarchy and, in some cases, Nazism. Consequently, hardcore was briefly held up before national TV cameras as a threat, both on news programs and fictional dramas.

But on its own terms hardcore celebrated only one remarkable moment of small-screen prominence, a triumph of authenticity that was a gob of spit in the face of the artifice that usually marked the best rock 'n' roll TV. After years of being mocked, demonized, and trivialized by Mr. TV, on Halloween, 1981, the punks egged his house and TPed his tree.

Because it has always been a stranger to mainstream media, hardcore is not widely understood. Defining it requires laying out a history of punk rock and its important benchmarks, an exercise that can come off as silly as a George F. Will treatise on baseball's cosmic significance. That said, here is my best attempt to summarize the history of a movement that often, by default, had amateur zine writers and teenage lyricists acting as its principal historians.

American garage bands of the mid-1960s made the first music that would be referred to as punk. Raw, rocking acts like Question Mark and the Mysterians and the Seeds were recognized as historically significant less than a decade after their reign by pundits like Lenny Kaye (who released the compilation album *Nuggets* in 1972) and Dave Marsh (who is credited with being the first to use the term *punk-rock* in print in a May 1971 *Creem* article). As the 1960s became the 1970s, *Sgt. Pepper's*–inspired artistes, overproduced stadium rock bands, and mild singer-songwriters ruled the charts, but strange musical brews were starting to bubble in unglamorous places like Detroit, Cleveland, and the lower east side of Manhattan. Bands like the Velvet Underground, the Stooges, New York Dolls, Dead Boys, and Television were making primal, ugly music that inspired a vibrant New York underground scene. From this fertile soil came the Ramones, a band that perfectly combined the direct rawness of this new breed with the primitive pop sensibilities of 1960s garage bands. In 1976 punk officially became "punk" with the release of the Ramones self-titled LP, the launch of *Punk* magazine (which helped solidify the name), and summer Ramones concerts in London.

Manager/impresario Malcolm McLaren had assembled the Sex Pistols several months before the Ramones' London tour. A visit to New York had inspired McLaren to propagate punk in England. Using his avant-garde clothing boutique,

The Ramones. Courtesy Jake Austen

Sex, as a base, he helped to promote punk as an outrageous, fashion-driven trend. And the Sex Pistols offended and amused their way to the top of the British charts with a combination of good music (solid, snotty anthems about anarchy, apathy, and abortion) and wild press manipulation, including Britain's most notorious punk TV incident. The Pistols and their posse appeared on *Today* (Thames, 1968–1977), Bill Grundy's newsmagazine show, on December 1, 1976. After Grundy propositioned Siouxsie Sioux, Sex Pistols guitarist Steve Jones responded, "You dirty sod. You dirty old man!" Delighted to have gotten a rise out of the punks, Grundy challenged, "Well, keep going, chief, keep going. Go on, you've got another five seconds. Say something outrageous," to which Jones replied, "You dirty bastard . . . you dirty fucker!" Not punk's most clever, articulate moment, but it grabbed headlines and served McLaren's desire to portray the subculture as both dangerously unsuitable for proper society and entertaining to all.

This cynical marketing of punk led to the media boom of 1977 and 1978. Mainstream newspapers and TV had a ball covering the wild-looking punk musicians and fans mugging for the cameras in the wake of the Sex Pistols' popularity. A 1978 Sex Pistols tour of America designed by McLaren to be a media-friendly disaster (the tour concentrated on conservative Texas, Louisiana, and Oklahoma, where it would be sure to draw detractors) resulted in countless nightly news novelty stories and the band's breakup. But later that year when bassist Sid Vicious allegedly stabbed his girlfriend, Nancy Spungen, to death and then died of a heroin overdose in 1979, the press (after treating the deaths as tabloid events) stopped seeing punk as a novelty. As far as the mainstream was concerned, punk was no longer amusing, and it soon ceased to be of interest.

The record companies' ready response to this development was to promote the concept of "new wave" music as an alternative to punk. While a movement of keyboard-driven acts who legitimately could fly the new wave flag had emerged parallel to punk, the music industry used that label to distance promising punk bands from scary things like Vicious's overdose. For some acts, like Talking Heads and Elvis Costello, this just meant recording their sounds cleanly and crisply, while for Blondie and the Go-Go's it meant major label overhauls in which raw, punk-club sounds were replaced with danceable pop grooves.

But some American fans of the nasty spirit of early punk had the opposite reaction. Rejecting sanitized new wave, they began developing harder, louder, faster strains of the punk virus. As the curtain on the 1970s was closing, two bands began making punk music more brutal and proudly noncommercial than any of their predecessors. In Los Angeles Black Flag emerged from a scene that had instantly taken to the Sex Pistols brand of punk in 1977. But unlike the Sex Pistols, Black Flag was a no-frills, no-costumes band. They focused on making direct, raging music that ignited their audiences. In the Washington, D.C., region Bad Brains, a group of African American youth with interests in progressive jazz and hard rock, unleashed some of the most furious punk ever.

This was the birth of hardcore, the regional, localized punk that was more about supporting a scene than worshiping iconic rock stars or creating hit records. Black Flag toured relentlessly, acting as punk Johnny Appleseeds, helping to foster local hardcore scenes in every town they played. Bad Brains helped launch Washington, D.C.'s hardcore scene, a (relatively) cohesive, self-sufficient punk community that would become a model for scenes around the country. Mini-societies formed in cities across America—societies populated by local bands; promoters who found alternative venues (bars barred underage hardcore fans, so VFWs, churches, and basements became their all-ages clubs); zine writers who photocopied their own periodicals; artists who made their own flyers, patches, and shirts; amateur video documentarians; and "record labels" that consisted of kids making small runs of cassettes or singles. Signifiers of hardcore included mosh pits (dance floors bursting with a stylized progression of punk's slam dancing); skateboards; and, occasionally, violent, racist skinheads, a small but vocal segment of the hardcore community that sometimes came to shows to fight.

Though hardcore still exists in several forms today—from 1980s bands still chugging along to contemporary strains that incorporate emo, grindcore, and even rap—the first wave of hardcore began to dissipate in the mid-eighties when its speedy, guitar-driven foundation made an unfortunate but natural progression toward heavy metal. "Crossover," as the hardcore-metal fusion was called, diluted the scene, and wanky guitar solos, the antithesis of straightforward, driving, selfless hardcore, was the death cry of the movement's early glory days.

In the decade between 1976 and 1986 punk pretty much exhausted its cultural relevance, but you would have been hard-pressed to get a good picture of its progressions and regressions by watching TV. After the first wave of Sex Pistols–fueled news stories, the pickings were slim. Music shows shied away from punk bands, and sitcoms used punks as occasional punch lines. When hardcore began scaring parents, punks became villains on TV dramas or topics of concern on talk shows. Though punk bands could make for good TV—they were outrageous, extremely visual, and prone to dynamic performances—they rarely got to show their talents.

Despite a reputation for bold bookings, *Saturday Night Live* did a poor job of promoting the innovative music of its fellow Manhattanites from 1976 to 1979, a classic era for both New York punk and the landmark comedy show. The show had an eclectic array of musical guests in those days, including free-jazz legends, reggae artists, and unclassifiable acts like Frank Zappa, but it ignored the critic's choices in its own backyard: Television, Richard Hell, Suicide, and the Heartbreakers. The only local act to make it on the show in pure punk form was Patti Smith in April 1976 (two years later Smith would be goofed on the show by Gilda Radner as "Candy Slice," a rocker with hairy armpits and a cocaine addiction—not exactly an insightful parody). Smith's appearance took place a week prior to the official kickoff of the punk game: the release of the Ramones' debut LP. The Ramones, perhaps the most telegenic band of the era, never were on *Saturday Night Live* and only had one real moment of American TV glory, appearing on *Don Kirshner's Rock Concert* in January 1977. Other than that appearance the godfathers of punk were limited to novelty shows like the *Sha Na Na* syndicated comedy/variety show and *Uncle Floyd* (various stations, 1974–present), a New Jersey *Pee Wee's Playhouse*/Howard Stern hybrid.

Saturday Night Live also fell short when booking British punk. The Sex Pistols were scheduled and announced as upcoming guests in 1977 (hearing Don Pardo say "Sex Pistols" in his game-show announcer voice was priceless) but reportedly couldn't get into the country. Elvis Costello, a performer I classify as new wave, replaced them.

Other acts that were in polished-pop form by the time they graced the *Saturday Night Live* stage were Talking Heads in 1978 and Blondie in 1979. The show's only amazing new-wave performance came from Devo, the most successful band of that genre to truly challenge pop conventions. In addition to their angular, electronic popular material like "Whip It," they also made jarring avant-garde music, and presented themselves visually with a series of costumes that invoked the best experimental films and theater of the early twentieth century. Their 1978 appearance (performing "Jocko Homo," a cover of "Satisfaction," and a sketch where their character Booji Boy disseminates information on "de-evolution") was a remarkably unique TV event, maybe the show's most exciting of that era.

Perhaps *Saturday Night Live*'s biggest oversight was not booking the Clash in the 1970s. The most talented, dynamic band of that era to maintain their punk credibility, the Clash were on a downward artistic slope in 1982, when they played material from their blatantly commercial (though excellent) *Combat Rock* LP on *Saturday Night Live*. The supposedly hip producers of the show had not only failed to book the five-year-old band previously, but they had also been trumped by their only rival.

Fridays (ABC, 1980–1982) was a cocaine-fueled, low-budget show that featured Larry David and Michael Richards (later of *Seinfeld*, a show that revived several *Fridays* jokes and characters). The show booked wonderfully diverse music acts. Guests on *Fridays* included the Beach Boys, KISS, Garland Jeffreys, Sir Douglas Quintet, Rockpile, the Four Tops, Jimmy Buffet, Journey, Ian Hunter, and Devo (who appeared on all three seasons). Punkish acts that played included the Pretenders, the Jam, author/rocker Jim Carroll (doing his nonhit "People Who Died"), and the Plasmatics. Led by the brutally sexy Wendy O. Williams, the Plasmatics were the ultimate TV rock act, more performance art than punk—they blew up/chainsawed/shotgun-blasted the stage while "playing." But despite Williams's pyrotechnics, the most remarkable *Fridays* performance was on the third episode, April 25, 1980. The Clash took the stage looking like three hooligans and a pimp (Mick Jones was wearing a purple suit reminiscent of something Batman's nemesis the Joker would wear). They attacked four songs (on *Saturday Night Live* bands usually only played two): "London Calling," "Train in Vain," "Guns of Brixton," and "Clampdown." They featured three different vocalists on these anthems, jumped and danced around like speed freaks, and showcased bad teeth, imperfect voices, and very British punk posturing. Though relatively low-budget, *Fridays* usually shot its performances better than *Saturday Night Live*, possibly because ABC had more experience with live rock acts. (*Fridays* was in the same slot vacated several seasons earlier by *In Concert*.) Joe Strummer was all over the stage, and as he bounced around the director framed amazing shots from unique angles as cameras deftly zoomed in and out. *Fridays* also was known for having terrible sound, which wasn't necessarily a problem in this case. Malcolm Danbury, who runs a punk record store in Connecticut, recalls the Clash's *Fridays'* audio being "like a flamethrower, so overmodulated and harsh, it was filthy, and that sound made it so much more punk. It was raw and immediate, like being smacked in the face. [That performance] felt like a real mass media revolution."

Punk found another dysfunctional TV home in the wee hours. In the era of ninety-minute talk shows and chain-smoking hosts and guests, late-late night TV was a fascinating mess, and nothing was messier than Tom Snyder's post–Johnny Carson gabfest *Tomorrow* (NBC, 1973–1982). While Carson would never have punk rockers as guests, Snyder did on several occasions, sometimes giving them the respect "normal" guests deserved (the Clash played live in 1981) and other times positioning them as silly sideshow freaks. For example, in 1980 Johnny Lydon, the former Sex Pistols member who was then fronting Public Image, Ltd., gave a combative, bizarrely philosophical interview on the show in which he stated: "We ain't no band, we're a company . . . nothing to do with rock 'n' roll. Doo dah!" The best of Snyder's benign looks at punk was a 1977 roundtable discussion featuring an articulate English punk (a teenage Paul Weller of the Jam), a mumbling American punk (Joan Jett, serving time with the Runaways), a jaded rock promoter baffled by punk (Bill Graham), a nerdy rock critic impressed by punk (Robert Hilburn from the *L.A. Times*), a scheming scene-maker cashing in on punk (Kim Fowley, who explains to the masses, "Punk rockers hate Springsteen . . . he uses horns . . . they find that offensive"), and a polyester wearing, hopelessly out-of-touch talk-show host (Snyder, who declares the show to be about "new wave," *not* that "Sex Pistols . . . urination, beating people up, bloody noses" stuff). When Fowley lamented the travesty of the Adverts' "Looking Through Gary Gilmore's Eyes" not making the top forty, poor Snyder got that confused deer-in-the-headlights look that was his signature.

Other 1970s and early 1980s shows that featured music rarely had punk guests, as the audiences for daytime talk shows and *The Tonight Show* had blue hair for a different reason than punk fans. *In Concert* was canceled just as punk was coming up and *Midnight Special* only occasionally featured new-wave acts, like Blondie, Devo, and the Police (they showed a Ramones video in 1980). But for the most part, any time you saw a punk band on TV in the 1970s it was accompanied by a laugh track.

Where punk got real TV time was on comedies like *Sugar Time!*, *Good Times*, *WKRP in Cincinnati*, *C.P.O. Sharkey*, *Square Pegs*, and *SCTV*. Some of these just made passing references to punk in its heyday. *Sugar Time!* (ABC 1977–1978), a sitcom starring the queen of Playboy bunnies, Barbi Benton, as one third of a musical act named Sugar, featured the band's brief foray into punk rock. To ABC's hack writers this meant wearing garbage bags for dresses and singing, "Garbage, garbage—we want trash!" (The music on this show was composed by the tiny but brilliant Paul Williams, so credit him with that poetry.) A 1978 episode of the black sitcom *Good Times* (CBS, 1974–1979) illustrated the extent to which Malcolm McLaren's message had spread when nosy neighbor Willona likens babysitting the Evans kids to looking after the Sex Pistols. On cue J.J. (Jimmie Walker) enters the room, prompting Willona to add, "Here's Johnny Rotten himself!"

Taking the punk themes a little further was *C.P.O. Sharkey* (NBC, 1976–1978), insult comic Don Rickles's 1970s update of military sitcom *The Phil Silvers Show* (CBS, 1955–1959). In a 1978 episode Sharkey's naval troop sneaks off to a punk club and sits in amused disbelief as a relatively authentic looking group of punks thrash about to a band. The authenticity of the crowd can be attributed to Janet Cunningham's C.A.S.H. talent agency. C.A.S.H. provided colorful extras for TV and film productions, and Cunningham realized that rather than have studios waste money on Mohawk wigs and fake tattoos they might as well tap directly into the large, cash-strapped L.A. punk population. Thanks to C.A.S.H., if you squint hard while watching punk rock scenes in late 1970s and early 1980s movies and TV you can see members of the Germs, the Screamers, the Bags, and the Circle Jerks. Of course, punks being punks, they weren't always model employees. Former extra Pleasant Gehman, in the online magazine *Request*

Line, recalled, "Basically, getting a job as an extra meant that you and your friends got paid to party. Everyone was sneaking off to smoke pot or pop pills, stealing food from the craft-service tables. A favorite game was to wreck the continuity of the shot: punk extras would gleefully change clothes or positions so there'd be glaring errors in the same scene."

Continuity wasn't much of an issue in *Sharkey*, as the incongruity of the sitcom actors in suits and the slamming kids was weird enough. But one touch of realism made this episode notable . . . the band on stage wasn't just a bunch of actors wearing punk Halloween costumes. In the late 1970s the goofy L.A. punk band the Dickies surprised themselves and others by finding a number of mainstream doors opened wide enough for them to stumble through (especially surprising when you consider that their logo was a flaccid penis and bulbous testicles spelling out their name). Not only were they the first post–Sex Pistols punk band signed to an American major label but they also got to play themselves on TV and in the movies. A humorous band that sang about giant robots and gorillas rather than angst and doom, the Dickies actually fit quite well into the sitcom world. In fact, what makes this episode stand out from most of the punk TV programs that followed was the humor of the production. The amused sailors learn that the punks are not a menace to be feared but a comical subculture to be enjoyed. Although obviously condescending, the show does end with some cross-pollination: Don Rickles learns how to pogo, and the most outrageous punk girl joins the navy.

In "Hoodlum Rock," a 1978 episode of *WKRP in Cincinnati* (CBS, 1978–1983; syndicated, 1991–1993), the radio station, with trepidation, sponsors a punk rock concert by a notorious English group, Scum of the Earth, fronted by the well-dressed, exquisitely mannered "Dog" (played by Michael Des Barres). Des Barres, a Led Zeppelin hanger-on and would-be rock star who fronted the 1970s rock band Detective, is best known for his marriage to Pamela Des Barres, who penned the book *I'm with the Band*, a rock lit classic about her life as a groupie. Though he had appeared as a teen in *To Sir, With Love* in 1967, the most successful part of his career was as an actor on American TV. He worked on dozens of sitcoms, action shows, and cartoons, including a role as a recurring villain on *MacGyver* (ABC, 1985–1992) and as a regular on the 1990s revival of *WKRP* (playing a different character). The punch line of the Scum of the Earth episode was that in contrast to the charming English manners that convince station management to go through with the concert, onstage the band is pathologically violent, hateful, and destructive, soiling WKRP's reputation. Although hardly an authentic portrayal of punk, musically or visually, according to a *Wall Street Journal* article, the show's original script had the band dressing and acting like the Sex Pistols; during rehearsals, however, the show discovered that it was impossible to parody something as intentionally absurd as 1977 punk.

Square Pegs (CBS, 1982–1983) has the distinction of being the only series of that period to have a punk rocker as a regular character. The sitcom, set in a Southern California high school, has nerdy outcasts Lauren and Patty (Amy Linker and Sarah Jessica Parker, later of *Sex in the City*) relegated to hanging out with the lowly Marshall Bleckman, an aspiring borscht belt comedian, and Johnny Slash, introduced by Bleckman as "the only authentic punk" in school. More an awkward, lumbering surfer burnout than a violent Sid Vicious type, Slash (Merritt Butrick) denies actually being a punk rocker: "I'm new wave, totally different head." Although he makes some pretty raw punk references ("Remember when the Dead Boys broke up? I ate eight bags of pork rinds"), his own band, Open 24 Hours (which inexplicably includes Doors drummer John Densmore), confirms his new-wave pedigree, as it sounds very much like Johnny's "ninth favorite band," Devo (in a later episode Open 24 Hours played with Devo at a "new-wave bat mitzvah").

In a bit of silly trivia, another episode has Johnny reluctantly joining the baseball team and being recruited by the Dodgers. Coincidently, at the time this episode was shot, there was a high school punk rocker baseball phenomenon from that region, Scott "Rad" Radinsky, who looked like Johnny Slash and years later played for the Dodgers (as well as recording albums with his bands Scared Straight, Ten Foot Pole, and Pulley). The real Johnny's future wasn't as bright, as Butrick, who also played Captain Kirk's son in the *Star Trek* movies, died of AIDS in 1989 just shy of his thirtieth birthday. Also worth mentioning is that the *Square Pegs'* memorable theme song was performed by The Waitresses, a new-wave band best known for the song, "I Know What Boys Like." Though Chris Butler, the creative force in the band, later headed underground, creating odd music using archival recording methods like wax cylinders, Tracy Wormworth, the Waitresses' bassist, became an extremely mainstream daytime TV fixture in the late 1990s, playing in the band on the *Rosie O'Donnell Show*.

Though it was five years removed from the Sex Pistols era, perhaps the funniest TV punk comedy bit was on a 1983 episode of *SCTV*. *Mel's Rockpile* (a parody of *Don Kirshner's Rock Concert*) was having a "punk rock tribute" episode with English band the Queenhaters as special guests. Led by a sneering Martin Short (and featuring a punked-out John Candy on drums) the band snarled through "I Hate the Bloody Queen," a hilarious punk protest song (" . . . I hate the bloody Queen/She made me go to school/I hate the bloody Queen/And all her bloody rules/I'd like to drown the Queen/Off the coast of Argentine/Throw her off a battleship/With her Falkland war machine . . . I feel sorry for you Lady Di/Havin' a mother-in-law like that!"). The segment ends with a slam-dance contest that flattens host Mel Slirrup (Eugene Levy) like a pancake.

Although the strutting roosters of 1970s English punk were still funny even a half-decade removed from their heyday, what was going on with suburban America's kids in the early 1980s was less humorous. Many parents were concerned about the emergence of hardcore, with its shaved heads, dour expressions, and abrasive soundtrack, so Hollywood responded the best way it knew how. It sent its make-believe cops to set those punks straight. A number of commercial movies may have warned of the dangers of punk, and a few hardcore kids with video and super-8 cameras did a decent job documenting the scenes, but amongst 1980s punks there were two holy grails of media representation. This dynamic duo of 1982 TV shows convinced them that the clueless mainstream they were rebelling against deserved their scorn.

The more absurd of the two was "Battle of the Bands," a January 1982 episode of *CHiPs* (NBC, 1977–1983), a show about handsome L.A. motorcycle cops. The drama opens as new waver Snow Pink has her band's van robbed by evil punk rockers. After speeding away (they are a psychopathic, homoerotic biker gang as well as a band) the punkers engage in rock 'n' roll crimes with Pink's gear, including defacing a graveyard by swinging around microphones and throwing her bass through a moving car's windshield, causing one of *CHiPs'* signature multicar collisions. When enlisting the cops' help, Snow Pink, played by Susan Richardson (Susan on *Eight Is Enough*), distances herself from the louts by explaining, "C'mon there is a whole different attitude to the music, man. Punkers are into an angry thing, new wavers, we're just having fun." The episode then satellites around a bizarre, multigenre battle of the bands that features not only Snow Pink and Pain (the evil hardcore band) but also the head CHiP himself, Ponch (Erik Estrada), performing with his disco band.

Pain—featuring members Trasher, Potatohead, and Fido—plans to lose the contest and then trash the club, expressing the nihilistic and sadistic violence that evil punk kids wallow in. Their theme song, the ridiculous anthem, "I Dig Pain," proclaims, "Take a hunk of concrete, stick it in my face, I like to play with razor blades, I hate the human race . . . I dig pain . . . the feeling my brain!" Amazingly, these oh-so-hip writers didn't call the song, "I Dig Pain, Daddio." But archaic slang aside, the funniest thing about this stupid song was that it wasn't so bad. Just as 1977 British punk couldn't be parodied because of its absurdity, 1982 hardcore was hard to get completely wrong. The song is a brutal, plodding slice of idiocy, but if the lyrics were different and it was sped up, this could have easily passed for a mediocre, but genuine, teenage hardcore single.

Amid all the *CHiPs* buffoonery there is one thoughtful exchange about the nature of suburban hardcore kids. It, however, is delivered by Officer "Grossie" Grossman (Paul Linke), the rotund provider of the show's comic relief. After some slapstick where Grossie demonstrates his slam-dancing technique in the police locker room, he is confronted by Officer Jon Baker (Larry Wilcox):

> JON: Punks, I mean, I don't get it, it's not as if they're underprivileged from the ghetto.
> GROSSIE: The suburbs can be a ghetto, too, Jon. An overprivileged kid can get just as lost. Try finding an identity in a place where every house is the same.
> JON: Well, uh, why don't you explain about the violence?
> GROSSIE: You can't, and that's why it's the perfect antisocial protest against the nine-to-five world.

Not surprisingly, this is followed by more portrayals of punks as two-dimensional comic-book villains. Pain arrives at the contest and improvises an evil plan, admittedly the most punk rock scheme I've ever heard of. They tie up the club owner, padlock the crowd inside and then force everyone to listen to "I Dig Pain," as they beat slam dancers with their guitar stocks. Ponch and Jon's heroics soon save the day, as they break into the club, arrest Pain and quell a riot with an anti-punk pep talk. The battle of the bands, amazingly, goes on after this chaos, and as a swivel-hipped Ponch croons Kool and the Gang's "Celebration" in his disco glitter shirt, all is right in the world. Punk has been vanquished by righteousness.

A more sincere piece of anti-punk propaganda was the December 1982 "Next Stop, Nowhere" episode of *Quincy, M.E.* (NBC, 1976–1983). Police medical examiner Quincy (Jack Klugman) gets involved in the local punk scene when the body of a punk rock runaway stabbed in a mosh pit (or "slam pit," as the TV punks call it) turns up on his slab. The actual crime involves a crazed punk girl who murdered the guy and is poisoning/gaslighting/framing her friend, but that's not the important part of the show. What is more significant is that Emily, Quincy's social worker girlfriend, convinces him that punk rock itself is responsible for the murder and that it must be stopped. "I thought [punk] was another silly fad," says Quincy.

"Silly fad, huh?" Emily challenges. "Kids come off that dance floor with crushed ribs and bloody faces like soldiers fighting some kind of insane war."

Quincy is instantly convinced, and officially blames punk in his report. He explains to the world, "Listening to that violence-oriented punk rock music does nothing but reinforce bad feelings." It can even lead to . . . *murder!*

One reason these shows are so memorable to punk fans is that, like 1950s shows that dealt with beatniks, 1960s shows that dealt with hippies, and 1990s shows that dealt with rave culture, "the man" got *everything* wrong. The punk rockers dress either like zombie extras in Michael Jackson's *Thriller* video or like cast members of *Cats*. Punkers throw cowboy-movie punches in the pit. They have beaded doors in their pad and eat tofu (apparently the writers were fifteen years off on counterculture clichés). And when the good girl shows up at the club, the bad girl takes her into the bathroom because she "needs some punking up" (which involves makeup, not drugs). The best bogus aspect of the *Quincy* show is the band at the punk club, Mayhem (not to be confused with the murder/suicide-plagued Norwegian black metal band of the same name). Mayhem's lead singer, Fly, is dressed like a space ninja, with a top-knot hairdo and circus-clown stage moves. The band's silly song, "I Wanna See You Choke," is the least threatening faux-hardcore song ever.

Like *CHiPs*, this show features one seemingly sympathetic scene, in which Quincy, on a talk show, pleads with punks to repent. The relatively articulate kids

"Mayhem" on *Quincy*.

respond, "We're not psychos, we're not bikers . . . we're artists!" Two other scenes that also seem designed to show the kids' perspective actually just reflect the producer's cluelessness. When the good girl's mom pleads with her to abandon her punk ways, the mother, with her perm, gaudy lipstick and thick eye makeup, looks far more grotesque and unnatural than her daughter. More tellingly, the cops catch the bad punk by being unapologetically corrupt, threatening to close down the punk club if the club owner doesn't cooperate with the illegal police tactics—fingerprinting every kid who comes to the show. Even as these scenes fit into the sensibilities of the producers, they also corroborated the dissenting position of the outsider kids—the acceptable world was pretty horrifying!

In the end the good girl is cured of punk and Quincy finds himself in a more sedate nightclub, one where he feels comfortable enough to ponder the week's events. "Why would you want to listen to music that makes you hate," a tipsy Quincy conjectures on the dance floor while holding his antipunk crusader woman tight, "when you could listen to music that makes you love?"

These shows both annoyed and amused the genuine hardcore kids around the country. Larry Hardy, owner of the In The Red record label, recalls, "It bothered me at the time to have the music and scene that were so important to me misrepresented. Living in suburban Orange County you caught a lot of flack from schoolmates and people in general for being a 'punk rocker,' so it didn't help when shows like Quincy made out as if punk rockers were violent miscreants. But it was also very funny in a Reefer Madness kind of way, too."

Though some were genuinely upset by the portrayals (Alex Totino, of the New York hardcore band the Misguided, told a TV news show, "They made a punching bag out of our scene, the Quincy thing made everybody look like drug-taking maniacs"), most recognized the shows' inherent absurdity. Several bands covered "I Dig Pain," including the Ohio hardcore group Starvation Army and California's the Sickos, and other bands, including New Jersey's the Wretched Ones, covered "I Wanna See You Choke." The shows inspired band names (Minnesota's Quincy Punx and Illinois' Chips Patroll) and even a few songs, including Sacred Order's "Erik Estrada."

"I responded to the CHiPs and Quincy shows," Negative Element songwriter Barry Steppe recalls, "by writing a song called 'Media Punks,'" which was kind of a watered-down version of 'Nazi Punks Fuck Off' by the Dead Kennedys. The song isn't an indictment of Hollywood TV producers (who were as relevant as Martians to a Midwestern hardcore kid), but rather of the influx of kids into the scene after the shows aired."

Sacramento's Scott Soriano laments, "The thing that annoyed us about *CHiPs* and *Quincy* wasn't the portrayal of punks as bad people or the shows themselves, but that jocks would come to punk shows after seeing those TV shows and figure they were free to brawl."

There was a positive side to this as well. "At least after the airing of those programs people were a little less willing to pick fights with me," Steppe recollects. "Better than being called 'Rock Lobster' every time I walked down the hallway during high school."

Less amusing to hardcore kids were the TV antics of Serena Dank. In 1982 the usually harmless Tom Snyder welcomed Dank, leader of Parents of Punkers, to *Tomorrow*. Dank was making the media rounds, on both daytime shows like *The Phil Donahue Show* (syndicated, 1970–1996) and nighttime gabfests, explaining how her organization was positioned to deprogram and rehabilitate kids enslaved by this evil music. Part of her shtick was to read the lyrics of the Dead Kennedys' absurdist song, "I Kill Children," in a serious voice as if the song was a how-to manual. Though it evoked Steve Allen's old comedy bit where he would denigrate rock 'n' roll by reciting nonsense lyrics like "Be Bop A Lula" as if they were poetry, this is one of the rare cases where punks didn't share a *Quincy* laugh.

"At first I found [it] humorous," wrote Janine Frenken in the Canadian hardcore zine *No Cause for Concern* in 1983. "But not once you consider that people really do believe them. Not once you realize there are no doubt parents out there who have watched these shows and are now shitting their pants because their offspring dresses differently."

"What pissed me and my friends off the most was the endless appearances of Serena Dank on talk shows," recalls Soriano. "I remember the two *Donahue* shows very well. Serena also came to Sacramento to do our local TV talk show, *Flaherty and Co.*, and we packed the studio. She lost that battle because there were intelligent punks and punk defenders represented. My mom even called the show and said that she would rather have her kids slam dancing than playing high school football, because the pit was much safer than a football field. The reason Serena pissed us off was because she actually was a threat. We knew kids who were packed up and sent to Utah to be deprogrammed or sent to children's homes or even juvenile hall because parents listened to that bitch. In reaction to Serena's Parents of Punkers, my mom and a few other moms formed a group called Moms of Punks.

They would meet with their punk kids and talk about things that disturbed them, like the lyrics of 'I Kill Children.' This was done over pizza and cokes and in a very nonconfrontational/nonjudgmental manner. They did this outside the media, did not include dads (because they thought dads were too macho), and there was absolutely no religious angle to it. It lasted for a couple years. So there is a positive spin-off of a pretty fucked-up TV publicity hound."

Dank's appearance on *Tomorrow* wasn't the only negative spin on hardcore the show aired. In 1981 gossip queen Rona Barrett (Snyder's co-host from 1980 to 1981) did a lengthy segment about hardcore, built around the conflicts between L.A. hardcore fans and the LAPD at local Black Flag shows. Preceding the interview with Black Flag's Chuck Dukowski (wearing a short Mohawk certainly more inspired by Travis Bickle than British punk) was a nearly eight-minute introductory piece explaining punk to the viewers. It showed the Plasmatics blowing up a car, a flyer for a Phranc show, a nonmusical clip from the faux-punk movie *Times Square*, footage of the Cramps, X, Surf Punks, and Dead Kennedys (Rona pronounced the latter's name with disgust), and several bizarre bits of information that ranged from the obvious to the curious. "Punk also has its own history," Rona related. "It has been around since 1978, maybe earlier" (maybe so, considering that *Tomorrow* covered punk in 1977). She inexplicably declared that the heroes of punk were Elvis Presley, Jim Morrison, Charles Manson, and Adolf Hitler. And she brought it home with, "Many of these rebels are our own children; the majority of these punks seem to be young WASPS who masquerade at night in leather and chains," not only making (fairly accurate) assumptions about hardcore kids, but also assuming that none of her audience is nonwhite, non-Protestant, or too young to have kids. She segued into the interview by showing amazing live footage of Black Flag (describing them as a band "with a particularly violent following") and the subsequent unrest after the police shut down the concert. The footage showed, in response to what they interpreted as the cops' storm-trooper tactics, the kids taunting the police with Nazi gestures. This was the launching point for Barrett's interview with Dukowski.

With a pained look on her face, Barrett asked why the kids wanted to be associated with Nazis. Chuck calmly explained that they were indicating that the police were behaving like Nazis. This information confounded Barrett; her confusion was likely compounded by the fact that Dukowski's version of articulate restraint involves scrunching up his face and talking slowly and deliberately in a manner that invokes equal parts Pee Wee Herman and Dustin Hoffman in *Rain Man*. But in spite of his idiosyncrasies, even Serena Dank would have to agree that Chuck seemed like a genius compared to Barrett, who conducted the entire interview in a kind of stupor, as if Black Flag's existence were more than her circuits could handle.

A similar TV reaction to the band occurred on *Entertainment Tonight* (syndicated, 1981–present) in a 1981 report on MCA Records backing out on a distribution deal for Black Flag's upcoming record on the grounds that it was, among other things, "antiparental." Sitting in what seemed like a rec room were a baby-faced Henry Rollins, a mellow Dez Cadena (the band's guitarist), and Dukowski, whose shaved dome and striped shirt make him look like a hardcore Charlie Brown. "This is the music MCA finds offensive," Rollins barks, and then the trio starts pounding their fists and shouting an a cappella version of "Rise Above" ("Jealous cowards try to control—RISE ABOVE, WE'RE GONNA RISE ABOVE—they distort what we say—RISE ABOVE, WE'RE GONNA RISE ABOVE!"). At that point, cameras cut back to the studio where poodle-haired Ron Hendren and his cohost Marjorie Wallace sat saucer-eyed and slack-jawed in response to the raw intensity of this performance; the footage was profoundly incongruous with the slick Hollywood subjects usually covered by the show. Shaking his head and scratching his temple, Hendren stammers, "There's . . . really . . . there's not a lot you can say after that. . . ."

"You're right," a stunned Wallace adds. "I'm speechless."

That short segment demonstrated both the power of the genre and how ill a fit hardcore was with mainstream TV. But it also demonstrated that, unlike some of the 1977 punks who mugged and tried to shock the cameras, these serious, sober hardcore kids usually articulated their position well. So regardless of the programmers' intent, on the rare occasions when they got to express themselves on the tube, the kids held their own. On local shows around the country there were snippets of positive coverage, including the Sacramento show where Dank was outmatched, an appearance by the band Verboten on the Chicago children's show *Kidding Around,* and an excellent segment on a 1982 New York news program that offered, "We [talked] to these kids called punks and we were surprised to find out that what they had to say was very interesting." That show not only featured live footage of Bad Brains (although the band went unidentified), but also a nice defense of hardcore by the mother of Queens punker Alex Totino (Misguided, Das Damen), praising her son's courage for standing up against the establishment.

But these were small TV moments—blips that had little possibility of impacting the viewers. Only once was hardcore given the national stage on its own terms, on October 31, 1981. Curiously obscure, the incident was one of the most real rock moments in TV history and one of the few times that the danger supposedly inherent in rebellious youth music had TV people genuinely scared.

The fabled original cast of *Saturday Night Live* disbanded after the 1979–1980 season. After the disastrous launch of the new cast/new producer 1980–1981 season, Dick Ebersole (one of the show's creators) came in to right the ship. The show also rehired Michael O'Donoghue as head writer. And to really bring back the flavor they made arrangements for John Belushi, the greatest of the show's alumni, to make a cameo on the October 31 show. His participation was conditional: he would come only if the punk band Fear were booked as musical guests. O'Donoghue, who had taken a particularly proactive role in crafting that week's show (Halloween appealed to his macabre sense of humor), was delighted to add this chaotic element to the mix. To increase the energy the show arranged for three dozen or so actual hardcore kids to create a mosh pit on stage.

The show that night was particularly dark and gruesome, including a short film where pumpkins oozed blood when carved and a real juggler who juggled three apples while taking bites out of one—the other two containing razor blades! In a skit that was cut before airtime Ronald and Nancy Reagan ate Jane Fonda. And in a musical number cut *during* airtime, TV and hardcore met intimately for the first time.

Numerous odd elements converged to make this particular episode happen. Belushi had been hanging around hardcore shows and had become a big fan of Fear. Ebersole had just begun wooing his future wife, actress Susan St. James, leaving O'Donoghue in charge of arrangements for that week's show. Belushi took it upon himself to ask filmmaker Penelope Spheeris for advice. Spheeris had recently screened her punk/hardcore documentary *Decline of Western Civilization* to a lively crowd in Washington, D.C., so she recommended that *Saturday Night Live* import authentic punks from the nation's capitol to liven things up. Early one morning Ian MacKaye (of Minor Threat, the most influential Washington, D.C., band after Bad Brains) got a call about coming on *Saturday Night Live*. He was skeptical, but believed it when (as MacKaye told *Verbicide* magazine in 2002), "Belushi gets on the phone, and says, 'Hey, this is John Belushi, here's the deal—I got Fear on the show, and I really wanna get some cool punks to come up here to dance, and Penelope gave me your number.'" Twenty or so punks came up a day early on Friday, October 30 to see Midwestern hardcore band the Necros open for the Misfits. So it was the crew from Washington along with the Necros posse and a few New York hangers-on that arrived at *Saturday Night Live*'s midtown Manhattan studio the next night. That all-star lineup included MacKaye, Sab Gray from Iron Cross,

Photo from the book *Banned in DC*, ©2005 Cynthia Connolly. Used with permission.

Tesco Vee from the Meatmen, Barry Henssler from Necros, Eric from Double-O, Sean from Void, and Corey Rusk of Touch and Go fame. O'Donoghue reportedly was delighted that Ian was bringing his "neo-Nazi friends" to enjoy the festivities.

O'Donoghue, a former *National Lampoon* scribe who sometimes appeared on camera as Mr. Mike, was the *SNL* writer responsible for the darkest, ugliest material on the show. Since his death in 1994 he has become as well known for skits that were rejected as for things that made it on air. Legendary censored skits include "Original Shaft" (a thirties movie in which Shaft, played by Chevy Chase (!), is a stereotypical shuffling "coon" character) and two Nazi-schemed sketches set to air in the 1981 season. The "Silverman's Bunker" sketch equated fired NBC chief Fred Silverman with Hitler, and "The Good Excuse" had a concentration camp officer whispering the reasoning behind the Holocaust to several people, who concur that his explanation makes sense. With Nazis on his mind it isn't surprising he was delighted to reel in what he mistakenly thought were actual Nazis (Sab Gray's Iron Cross was perhaps the first American skinhead band, but Gray has always disavowed Nazism, despite the band name, which he claimed was a coincidence).

Though he was wary of Fear and the kids, Ebersole was excited about Belushi's return and approved the appearance. Still, after some minor chaos with the hardcore kids at the rehearsal, there was discussion of cutting the pit from the show. "I remember Eddie Murphy telling us to fuck off as we made our way back up to the green room overlooking the studio," MacKaye recalls. "We were told that we had misbehaved and therefore wouldn't be able to be on the actual show, but it was Belushi to the rescue. As I understood it, he told them that if they didn't let us on, he wasn't going to do his cameo, so they relented."

Ebersole proceeded cautiously. Fear's first number, performed early in the show and without the pit, was "I Don't Care About You." The performance felt raw and spare on the *Saturday Night Live* stage. With a spray-painted, stenciled "FEAR" banner behind them, and a coarse, hollow tone to their music, the band was abrasive and pummeling as they sped through their song in under two minutes, dropped their instruments and walked off stage, acting out the indifference of the song title.

The second set was far more eventful. Guest host Donald Pleasance announced, "Look out for surprises," clearly expecting Belushi (who had only appeared wordlessly in a bathroom in the opening sketch) to join the pit. But John was an old man compared to these sixteen- to nineteen-year-olds and thought better of it. Good move. As soon as Fear launched into "Beef Balogna" the mass went ape-shit, giving TV viewers their first real view of slam dancing. Instantly they were on the stage with the band, skanking around and jumping off. Their rubber-limbed, kinetic energy was aggressive, joyful, and ridiculous. After they finished their first song, Fear slowly made some adjustments, then they went into a second number as the kids again exploded. According to *Saturday Night: A Backstage History of Saturday Night Live*, "Michael O'Donoghue watching backstage had a look of pure ecstasy on his face, convinced this was one of TV's greatest moments ever."

Led by Lee Ving, Fear was an obnoxious, powerful California punk band that was older, more professional, and more musical than most teen hardcore bands. Their 1978 debut single, "I Love Livin' in the City," was a catchy tune that could have been a mainstream hit if it didn't contain lyrics like "chock full of shit and puke" and "crabs are crawlin' on my balls." Ving's hulking, crude, hate-spewing stage persona fit TV's idea of punk rock. In fact, it seems likely that the lead singers of Pain and Mayhem (the *CHiPs* and *Quincy* bands) were modeled on the muscular, threatening Ving. He was playing a character on stage, and after his *Saturday Night Live* appearance he would return to the small screen as an actor, appearing in many shows, including a role as a singing Keystone Kop in a 1984 episode of *Fame* (NBC, 1982–1983; syndicated, 1983–1987) and as Jake the Snake, a tough guy on a 1987 *Who's the Boss* (ABC, 1984–1992). But his finest role was as the snarling front man of Fear. As his appearance in Spheeris's *Decline of Western Civilization* documented, Ving's chief talent was in insulting the crowd (perhaps Fear should have starred opposite Don Rickles in *C.P.O. Sharkey* instead of the Dickies).

Lee Ving. Courtesy Jake Austen

On *Saturday Night Live,* Ving lived up to his reputation for abusing the audience, disdainfully barking, "Great to be here in New Jersey," and generally treating the crowd with contempt. Lyrically Ving bit the hand that was feeding him by choosing songs from Fear's catalog (with no hits they were not obligated to play anything specific) that viciously attacked the Big Apple, its inhuman living conditions, and its cold population. In "I Don't Care About You" he shouts, "I've seen an old man have a heart attack in Manhattan/Well he died while we just stood there lookin' at him. . . . Ain't he cute?" In "New York's Alright If You Like Saxophones" he posits, "New York's alright if you wanna be pushed in front of the subway. . . . New York's alright if you're a homosexual. . . . New York's alright if you like drunks in your doorway. . . . New York's alright if you wanna freeze to death. . . . New York's alright if you wanna get mugged or murdered!" The band even threatened the tri-state area in "Let's Have a War" (Fear performed three songs in their second set—highly unusual for the show), as Ving suggested that the violence "can start in New Jersey." The only nonpolitical tune Fear performed that night was "Beef Balogna," a song about Ving's penis.

But to the hardcore kids in attendance, Fear was pure baloney of a different kind. "To us Fear were careerist punk rockers," explained Henssler. "Only in LA would they think that you could take something as fucked up as punk rock and make money off of it; certainly if you were a kid in high school you weren't thinking like that." The idea that there was something Hollywood about Fear permeated the idealistic Washington, D.C., scene that provided the troops for NBC's pit that night. Although the kids were not humorless, they were very serious about their ideals, even to the point of being quixotic. The scene adhered to a set of unofficial commandments that included bands breaking up when members left, the "straight-edge" lifestyle (abstinence from drinking, drugs, etc., as referenced in Minor Threat's "Out of Step": "Don't smoke, don't drink, don't fuck—*at least I can fucking think*"), and a dedication to accessible, all-ages shows that continues today with MacKaye's current band Fugazi's low-priced concerts. Not surprisingly an aging Ving (he was over thirty and backstage at *Saturday Night Live* he introduced the punk kids to his niece who was nearly their age) and his band were not this crowd's style.

"Ian and Lee Ving in the same room is just weird," remarks college DJ Brian Collins. "It's like a movie where Superman meets Godzilla . . . separate worlds that are not supposed to coexist." In the book *American Hardcore*, Ian MacKaye recalls, "We weren't big fans of Fear—they were kind of a joke band."

But somehow this posing, silly band, with Ving glaring out from under sculpted Norma Desmond eyebrows, managed to preside over an amazingly accurate re-creation of a local all-ages show. Perhaps they knew this would be more historical if they played to the expectations of the pit and not the cameras, or maybe they had been conditioned by so many hardcore-type shows that this was the only way they knew how to act on stage. Regardless of the reason, what was broadcast that night felt exactly like a real hardcore show. And it wasn't the music or the explosive pit that gave that impression (though the pit was awesome). What made it so gloriously real was the downtime. Between the first and second songs Fear took a full thirty-six seconds. They fumbled around, talked to the kids a little, and threw out a few insults. But basically it was thirty-six seconds of network TV with nothing happening. That's unheard of on TV, where time is money. But it's standard procedure at a hardcore show, where amateur bands rarely have it together enough to play one song after another and would be almost ashamed to have a slick, stage show with planned transitions between numbers. Also contributing to the genuine hardcore vibe was the lack of distance between the band and the crowd—they *all* were the show. Though the moshers literally were part of the entertainment as far as *Saturday Night Live* was concerned, the director didn't show the broader audience (who reportedly hated both the band and the moshers), so the camera treated the punk kids as the audience, making home viewers feel as if they too were in the pit and were of equal stature to the band. And when the kids knocked over microphone stands and bumped into musicians, the missed notes, unsung lyrics, and lost rhythm didn't matter. This was a real live, vital, imperfect, shoddy, fun show. The most Hollywood of the 1980s punk acts allowed themselves to be unprofessional, and that was the key to this triumph. "No one had seen anything like that on TV," Henssler recalls. "That was the real deal!"

Since the band was doing what they would normally do at a real hardcore show, the kids decided to do what they would normally do. John Brannon promoted his Detroit hardcore band during the dead time between songs by yelling, "Negative Approach is gonna fuck you up!" Positioned at a poor angle to the microphone (anticipating that the kids might voice such inappropriate sentiments, Ebersole had arranged for only Ving's microphone to be on), Brannon's testament to his band's prowess was muffled as it went out over the nation's airwaves. Ian MacKaye, however, was at a perfect angle to verbalize his opinion, and his thoughtful declaration that "New York sucks!" was clearly audible.

That was enough for Ebersole, who at one point had crawled around the floor off camera telling certain rowdy punks to take it down a notch. He had prepared a rerun of a filmed skit, "Prose and Cons" (in which Eddie Murphy plays a poet prisoner reciting his piece, "Kill My Landlord") to roll just in case things got out of hand. Right before the engineers hit play, there came the sound of a mosher's barely audible voice yelling, "Get the pumpkin." As the scene fades to black, Fear having just declared, "Let's start a war," D.C. punk-scene denizen Billy McKenzie is seen lurking on the other side of the stage gleefully holding the biggest pumpkin anyone in the studio had ever seen.

As Eddie Murphy's satire on Norman Mailer's championing of prison authors went out over the airwaves the pumpkin went flying through the air. The details of what happened after the cameras stopped rolling are unclear for a number of reasons, including inaccurate press reports; hazy memories; boastful, hyperbolizing punks; and, reportedly, Ebersole's desire not to appear out of control. Some say the pumpkin splattered all over Ebersole's silk jacket. Others claim that the floor, covered in mush, became slippery, causing a kid to fall into a camera and damage it. What definitely did happen was the band finished its song and the kids were brusquely herded into a room and locked in, away from the respectable humans, before being kicked out of the building. Soon the *New York Post* and the *Daily News* were reporting that there had been a violent riot with the skinheads destroying the studio, resulting in "smashed furniture, equipment, and props," totaling $200,000 in damages. Although there certainly was no riot, the damages are a point of contention. It has been reported that all that was damaged was a plastic camera case lock worth about $40. Ebersole at the time told *New York* magazine that a dancer knocked over "a support box for a handheld camera resulting in a rewiring job that cost $42 in engineer overtime." In a 2002 interview for the book *Live From New York* he revised that to $2,500 in general damages. Regardless of the physical damage, Ebersole was suffering from a bruised ego and raised dander. ("I'm mad at those kids who were slamming," Ebersole told *New York* magazine.)

And Michael O'Donoghue? He was on his way out, having finally succeeded in pushing things too far.

Great TV rock moments usually reflect the ways artifice can enhance real rock 'n' roll energy, but this event ended up being solely about realness. And that, ultimately, is why it was a failure, rarely cited by media critics as a significant event in TV history and severely underappreciated by punk fans. Despite its triumph of authenticity, the show had surprisingly little impact, neither raising the profile of hardcore among the general population nor working as a recruiting tool. After polling more than a hundred musicians, zine editors, and fans active in hardcore, none of them cited Fear's *Saturday Night Live* appearance as their point of entry into the scene (the most frequently cited TV moment that led pollsters to punk/hardcore was actually Devo on *Saturday Night Live* in 1978) and few cited it as their favorite punk TV moment. One reason for this may be that very few people were watching *Saturday Night Live* at that point. Fear appeared on one of the first shows of the 1981–1982 season, following a 1980 season that was the series' all-time low in quality and popularity. Later in 1981 viewers would recognize Eddie Murphy's talents, but by Halloween many couch potatoes, especially those with the kind of critical, cynical rejection of the mainstream that fits the punk profile, had given up on the show. Also, the fact that the Fear segment had the genuine feel of an all-ages hardcore show was something that could only be appreciated by those who had already been to such shows. The evidence of its realness—the downtime between songs, the lack of distance between audience and artists, and the imperfect performance—may have been unappealing to those not familiar with the hardcore experience.

Hardcore would eventually have profound impact on mainstream pop culture. In the early 1990s a number of former teen hardcore performers became the young adults that led the "alternative rock" fad that dominated MTV and radio (including Dave Grohl of Nirvana/Foo Fighters who had been in Washington, D.C., hardcore band Scream; Jay Yuenger of White Zombie, formerly of Chicago hardcore band Rights of the Accused; and former Black Flag singer Henry Rollins, who fronted the Rollins Band). Even dance music (Moby, former member of the Vatican Commandos) and rap (Beastie Boys, originally a hardcore band) felt the impact of hardcore. Most significantly, due to ESPN's lucrative promotion of extreme sports, the acrobatic "vert" skateboarding that was an integral part of the hardcore scene became a billion-dollar industry.

But all this would unfold more than a decade after the night pumpkin flesh went flying in NBC's Studio 8-H. Doing what it does worst, TV that night showed real youth culture as it actually was, and to paraphrase Jack Nicholson in *A Few Good Men*, though they may have wanted the truth, they couldn't handle the truth. By the time the pumpkin seeds settled, the kids were escorted out to the midtown street, Donald Pleasance waved good-bye, and it was all over . . . and it hadn't meant much at all. A Halloween punk-rock moment that should have been a triumphant treat ended up being nothing more than an obscure trick.

8

Video Vanguard

MTV, Music Videos, and the History of Rock 'n' Roll on TV

" didn't have cable in the mid-1980s," filmmaker Russ Forster recalls, "but I always knew when Madonna had a new video out. Every few months the Mexican teenage girls in my neighborhood would suddenly all get a new look, and that meant Madonna was back on MTV."

Urban (as well as suburban and rural) fashion wasn't the only sector of culture affected by the cable network MTV (an abbreviation for the never-used network name Music Television). Upon its launch at midnight on August 1, 1981 (with stock footage of a rocket launch followed by the Buggles' clip "Video Killed the Radio Star"), the twenty-four-hour music video channel began flexing its cultural muscles. Kids camped out in front of it much as they had for *American Bandstand*, but now they could remain camped infinitely instead of for a mere hour each day. Elements of youth culture that once had to be spread from teen to teen, or in short bursts on weekly music shows, now were available continuously on MTV, where cues on couture, speech, attitude, dancing, and all things hip showed up in loops of hypnotic repetition.

Hollywood began to employ music videos within the body of their movies, with films like *Footloose* (1984) and *Rocky IV* (1985) using a series of rock videos to narrate the stories. A more sophisticated response was the use of what instantly became known as the MTV style—quick edits, bright colors, music-driven action—most famously utilized by Michael Mann in his TV series *Miami Vice* (NBC, 1984–1989). Sporting events began showing music video–style montages on their Jumbotrons; video installations became a fixture in modern art; and even print media was affected, as America's national newspaper *USA Today*, founded in late 1982, used flashy graphics that mimicked MTV's visual style and short capsule reporting that paralleled the channel's quick edits.

The most obvious effects of MTV took place in the practices of the music industry. Though hesitant at first to invest in the production of music videos for its artists, American record labels changed their tune after the new British Invasion—bands like Duran Duran, Culture Club, and the Police all hailed from a country where videos were a part of the pop scene before the United States caught on. Soon labels were signing acts based on their prospects as music video stars, and new artists like Cyndi Lauper topped the charts because of their distinct looks as much as their music. Established artists that adapted well to the new medium, such as Tina Turner and ZZ Top, increased their record sales exponentially.

MTV was a quick success; it delivered a very desirable demographic to advertisers, and sold $7 million worth of ads in its first eighteen months. By 1984 MTV was reaching $1 million a week in ad revenues. And it achieved this corporate triumph while presenting the channel as an edgy voice of the underground. Some critics were excited by the eclectic playlist and experimental film techniques of early MTV, and by music video's possibilities as a new art form. But there were many who found MTV's exclusion of black artists and the sexist imagery (which quickly became a music video cliché) problematic. Others were disturbed by the corporate co-opting of avant-garde styles, and the disservice the medium does to the music itself, both by making it secondary to the visuals (rewarding image over talent) and by providing imagery once created in listeners' own imaginations, resulting in a more passive role for the audience.

Cheered or jeered, MTV's impact was immediate and powerful. Playing God with rock 'n' roll, MTV remade the pop charts in its own image, and as far as it, its advertisers, the music industry, and *many* fans were concerned, it was very good.

Despite its tendency to present itself as the center of the universe, MTV did not invent music videos. Music video is a freestanding form, the ultimate synthesis of TV and pop music, one that allows our rock stars to showcase themselves at their most powerful, doubling our sensory indulgence by presenting visuals as finely honed as the sounds that come from our stereos. But what MTV did create, by harnessing the power of music videos, is a world, a *cool* world, where the music is forever married to the picture. It is a world whose fan base can feast upon manipulative, image-conscious, highly choreographed artifice without shame.

MTV's 1981 birth certainly launched the first era when music videos influenced the aesthetic of America's culture at large, but by the time MTV planted its flag, music videos already had a forty-year history behind them. On February 12, 1940, the Mills Novelty Company, America's most successful jukebox manufacturer, joined forces with James Roosevelt, FDR's businessman son, to begin manufacturing the Panoram, a movie jukebox that played special three-minute musical films called Soundies, featuring popular and obscure songs performed by popular and obscure artists.

Eventually more than four thousand Panorams were installed in bars, ballrooms, hotels, and restaurants around the country. Though the machines were somewhat well received by the public, they did not challenge standard jukeboxes in popularity, never achieving even 1 percent of the market saturation their record-playing relatives enjoyed. And with good reason: unlike a jukebox, with numerous records, each featuring two songs, a Panoram held only eight songs, and you could not choose a tune, but rather had to watch all of them in a row. Thus, with a very limited number of songs playing in monotonous rotation, the Soundies truly set the precedent for early MTV.

Aesthetically the films were very different from contemporary music videos. While MTV's ancestors shared some of modern music videos' artifice (artists lip-synched—and in a preview of MTV favorite Milli Vanilli, they sometimes lip-synched to other people's vocals, as when comedian Dudley Dickerson performed a Big Joe Turner song) and themes (sexist cheesecake abounds), Soundies were essentially unlike their 1980s counterparts. Because Soundies producers had to turn out many films very quickly (the eight song reels changed once or twice a week) the performances were often very straightforward without gimmicks or elaborate production. The camera captured brilliant performers like Nat King Cole, Louis Armstrong, Fats Waller, and Gene Krupa from a static distance, similar to the vantage point of a club audience, instead of choreographing the artist for the camera with abundant edits and mobile framing. Pretty gals like Dorothy Dandridge, Gale Storm, and Yvonne DeCarlo (later the matriarch on *The Munsters*) did little more than look pretty and pretend to sing in their Soundies without the bells and whistles that would later accompany videos for Whitney Houston or Beyoncé. The closest Soundies came to matching the innovative absurdity that marked early MTV videos was when novelty acts like Borrah Minnevitch and his Harmonica Rascals, Spike Jones, or even proto-rocker Louis Jordan created manic music that made surreal or bizarre visuals almost mandatory.

Between August 1940 and December 1946 more than fifteen hundred Soundies were produced, featuring hundreds of artists as prominent as Count Basie and as obscure as Freddie Fisher and his Schnickelfritz Band. Several companies tried to compete with Soundies in the movie jukebox biz, each producing their own films, but none could match the Soundies' modest success. Vis-O-Graph was a short-lived rival that most prominently featured films of the company's president, Rudy Vallee. Featurettes was a company on artistic par with Soundies that only managed to produce thirty shorts. Lesser companies to try their hand at music movie jukeboxes included Phonovision, Nickel Talkies, and Phonofilms.

As TV took off in the 1940s Soundies lost their appeal and eventually disappeared, but their production model inspired an even more direct predecessor of today's music videos. Between 1950 and 1954 Snader Telescriptions produced more than a thousand short musical segments for TV. In TV's adolescence local stations often had dead time during their schedule, ranging from a few minutes after a sporting event or news broadcast to fifteen-minute blocks between programs. These gaps could be plugged by the works of director/writer Duke Goldstone (who had a background in Soundies, as well as on the groundbreaking George Pal Puppetoons) and producer Louis D. Snader, a pioneer of early musical shows like *Korla Pandit* (KTTV-Los Angeles, 1949–1952) and *Liberace* (NBC, 1952; syndicated, 1953–1955; ABC, 1958–1959; CBS, 1969). Creating up to a dozen shorts daily, Goldstone documented exciting performances with his multicamera shoots, capturing greats like Duke Ellington, Cab Calloway, Peggy Lee, Herb Jeffries, Bob Wills, the Weavers, Merle Travis, the Jordanaires, Frank Yankovic, the Ink Spots, Tex Williams, and Yogi Yorgenson. Most exciting for fans of some of these pop, country, polka, and jazz artists, the performances were all live, captured expertly with excellent microphones. In addition to pinch-hitting for dead airtime, these clips also found their way into the bodies of programs, including the original *Show Time at the Apollo* and Philadelphia's *Bandstand* program, which later became Dick Clark's juggernaut. As TV program lengths became standardized, Snader Telescriptions eventually disappeared.

The first musical shorts that were true antecedents of MTV's visual style came in 1960 when a new video jukebox was introduced in France. There the concept had never died out (during the 1950s, long after the death of Soundies in the United States, Telescriptions were sent to Europe to play in their machines). During World War II many French warplanes came fitted with 16-millimeter film cameras, and the late 1950s saw this glut of equipment repurposed by turning the cameras into projectors, fitting them into cabinets, and selling them as movie jukeboxes. And thus were born the mighty Scopitones.

The films that played in these machines were far more exciting than Soundies and Telescriptions for many reasons, not the least of which was their Franco heritage, which guaranteed far naughtier content than their American predecessors. Also, not only were these the first music clips shot in color but they were shot in rich, bizarre, lurid color. "The colors are absolutely gorgeous," avant-garde filmmaker and Scopitone collector Joel Haertling gushed in a 2002 *Denver Westworld* interview. "They're extremely vibrant. And because the films were made using magnetic sound, they give you fantastic fidelity compared to optical soundtracks. And that's not to mention the planning and the set design and the beautiful locations and the subject matter. Scopitones weren't for kids; you usually found them in bars. So they're suggestive, but they have a playful sexiness."

The machines hit America in 1963, but by that time the coin-operated amusement industry was so deeply connected to organized crime that within a few years prominent investigations by the feds (*Wall Street Journal* headline: "Movie Jukebox Probe: Grand Jury Looks into Everybody Linked with Scopitone") doomed the innovation, and by the Summer of Love it was a faint celluloid memory. But in its few active years the American arm of the company managed to create exciting clips for Nancy Sinatra's "These Boots Were Made for Walking," Timi Yuro's "If," Herb Alpert's "Tijuana Taxi," and Neil Sedaka's "Calendar Girl."

The French flicks by icons like Juliette Greco, Vince Taylor, and Johnny Hallyday boasted plenty of sex and sexiness, and the American clips were determined to compete in the naughty department. Perhaps the greatest Scopitone of all time is "Web of Love" by Joi Lansing, the buxom bombshell who played Lester Flatt's wife on *The Beverly Hillbillies*. Bellowing (she wasn't hired for her voice) her seductive song in a jungle-print bikini, the glamorous Ms. Lansing does a cage dance behind a giant steel spider web and later finds herself naked in a cannibal's stewpot.

By the time Scopitones disappeared rock bands like the Beatles were already making promotional films for their songs, even without a prefab outlet to air them. Occasionally these would be sent to *The Ed Sullivan Show* or *American Bandstand* in lieu of an actual guest appearance (though often the band would still be listed as guests). Simple, economical, and often innovative clips like these were popular throughout the 1970s and early 1980s, occasionally playing on shows like *Solid Gold* and disc jockey Casey Kasem's *America's Top 10* (syndicated, 1980–1990), just waiting for MTV to happen.

But the music channel's most directly influential predecessor was the Monkees' own Michael Nesmith, who became a music video producer by combining his frustrations about lack of creative control, his desire to promote his own music, and the fortune he inherited when his mother (who invented Liquid Paper) died. *The Monkees* program itself, with its freestanding visually dynamic song segments, is an obvious ancestor of MTV, but it was Nesmith's understanding of these segments that led to the MTV revolution. He had become convinced of the power of video when an elaborate clip he produced to promote his 1976 song "Rio" was well received in England and Australia. In the late 1970s and early 1980s avant-garde artists using videotape (excited about a medium that was far cheaper than film) were starting to work with artsy new-wave musicians to make music videos to accompany their songs. Impressed by this movement, in 1980 Nesmith produced America's first music video program, *Pop Clips* for Warner Communications' Nickelodeon network. The program was aesthetically groundbreaking, featuring Nesmith's signature quirky, humorous, frenetic visual style that would become the look and feel of early MTV. This short-lived program was in fact a pilot of sorts, as it helped convince Warner-Amex (American Express was partnered with the communications company during explorations of cable TV possibilities) to launch an all-music video network the next year. Though Nesmith continued to get some acclaim for his style (his 1981 project *Elephant Parts*, which combined videos and comedy, won the first video Grammy), his formal contributions to MTV are rarely acknowledged. However, on the FAQ section of Nesmith's Video Ranch Web site, the question, "Did Nez invent MTV?" is answered with "In a word, yes."

Despite the long history of music videos, MTV was more than the sum of its content. The network was packaged by Robert Pittman, a visionary AM radio "wonder boy" (he boldly saved several stations around the country) turned TV programmer, as a cutting-edge youth movement. MTV's signature was its "bumpers," short station identification films that ran between videos. The most famous one alters footage of Buzz Aldrin's lunar walk so that he is planting an MTV flag on the moon. The MTV logo on the flag is crudely animated by hand coloring the film stock with markers, a technique popular—and identifiable— with teenage art students. MTV was always a sophisticated exercise in corporate marketing, but the bumpers' raw, amateurish, do-it-yourself aesthetic sent a different message. Bumpers methodically drew from art school and the underground, using surreal animation, striking text-based pieces that referenced the work of artist Jenny Holzer, and irreverent comedy clips that positioned MTV as a genuine upstart. This, they declared, was a dangerous new entity that was profoundly different from other stodgy, old networks.

This claim was somewhat accurate. MTV was truly new, despite on the surface being nothing more than a radio station that showed videos instead of playing records. VJs (video jockeys) replaced DJs (in fact, two of the first VJs, Mark Goodman and the late J. J. Jackson, came from radio) and they would introduce video after video in the hip, conversational style associated with radio jocks. But MTV's content was different, and more diverse, than rigidly structured commercial radio. Because record labels were slow to realize the promotional value of producing videos for their artists, early MTV featured a small number of videos representing a wide variety of (white) music styles. A block of videos could go from heavy metal (Iron Maiden) to rootsy rock (Rockpile) to arty new wave (Talking Heads) to power pop (Shoes) to singer-songwriter (Carly Simon) to classic rock (the Who). Suddenly Kate Bush, Styx, Elvis Costello, Lee Ritenour, and April Wine belonged together. And though the station was broader in scope than radio, it was more specialized than broadcast TV networks. Like many cable channels, instead of broadcasting MTV was narrowcasting, targeting a specific audience. This was fundamentally different than *The Ed Sullivan Show*'s philosophy of giving something to everyone in the family, and because this was the first network to market exclusively to the (highly desirable to advertisers) youth demographic, it really was revolutionary.

Formally the early videos were simple and raw, heavy on corny special effects and often shot with the ham-fisted grace of porno movies. And the kids loved them. MTV was one of the highest-rated and fastest-growing cable channels (originally carried on three hundred cable systems, it expanded by almost 600 percent in its first two years). Watching videos became an obsession for America's kids, and the influence of popular videos on teen fashion was instant. More importantly for the industry, a link between videos and record sales was quickly revealed,

MTV bumper

prompting major labels to invest heavily in slicker, more expensive clips and a new breed of rock superstars for the video age.

The bread and butter of 1980s MTV, the music videos themselves, are perhaps the greatest triumph in the history of TV rock 'n' roll, trumping even the seemingly more historical moments on *Ed Sullivan*. Suddenly TV wasn't merely an outlet to advertise music (though videos were ads, and MTV was pretty much a twenty-four-hour commercial) but rather a medium that completely dictated the direction of the music industry. While Dick Clark's teen idols had demonstrated this to a degree, they were a blip, a footnote compared to the massive impact of MTV. And while the Monkees' success was significant, it was an exception, an example of TV alchemy that could not be re-created. MTV told the music world that artists had to be televisual and as instantly identifiable as the Pillsbury Doughboy or Ronald McDonald. Musicians wrote songs with the video in mind. Fashion, modern dance, and filmmaking became as important to a record's success as songwriting, instrumentation, and production. Music videos created their own distinct language and the artists who could speak this language thrived.

This did not sit well with all observers. In a 1987 issue of *Artforum* Greil Marcus declared music videos an "art form born dead" and MTV "the pornography of semiotics . . . where nothing outside of its own frame of reference is allowed to intrude . . . so ugly, so directly productive of aesthetic and moral shame, as to be fundamentally obscene." Less eloquently, others lamented that music videos rewarded the most superficial aspects of rock (looks, marketing) at the expense of skilled songwriting and actual talent. While criticism of the visually homogenous formal aspects of videos or the unjust (but socially omnipresent) system of rewarding looks over ability may be fair and even accurate, it overlooks one important factor that accounts for the hypnotic spell these promotional clips cast over teenagers: music videos are *awesome!*

Many early videos were actually profoundly clever, visually exciting short films, and the new form (which offered opportunities to make fully funded visionary statements) attracted numerous innovative filmmakers. But even discounting the videos that are good by film-scholar standards, videos are still compelling and seductive, and even the crappiest ones can offer fans a slice of pop perfection. Seeing a favorite artist present a fundamentally false, heavily manipulated performance/visualization of a song is a dream come true for many fans. Unlike a live performance (in which the song doesn't sound as perfect as the pristine studio version) and unlike a guest spot on a lip-synch TV show (where the act is at the mercy of the camera crew and the interpretation of the song is bound by the limitations of the studio) a music video allows fans to enjoy visuals that are just as polished as even the slickest music. While this may read to some purists as a celebration of the fakest elements of pop, music video devotees often read the clips as a profound statement of artistic vision as weighty as any other element of the pop craft. And often they're right.

The genuine energy of a live music experience cannot be truly captured on film (or video), but in many ways videos that simulate live concerts can improve on the aspects that the artist finds important. Prince is (according to a 2004 *Spin* feature) the greatest live performer in rock history, but his early music videos made a point of not presenting Prince playing live but rather presenting make-believe concerts, stiffly (though playfully) posed and choreographed. Though Prince became an icon in the wake of his 1984 film *Purple Rain*, which featured more organic live concert sequences, he solidified his original fan base with his earlier cartoonish faux-concert videos for "Controversy," "1999," and "Little Red Corvette." These clips unambiguously articulated the fantasy reality Prince wanted to create and helped his fans see him as he wanted to be seen. While this is perhaps less honest than a truly live performance, it is the kind of manipulation many pop fans want—to be swept up into the world their heroes create.

More illuminating than the case of Prince's video work are the incidences of successful videos by less talented artists. Without music videos Tiffany, Vanilla Ice, Adam Ant, MC Hammer, and Britney Spears would have had extremely lim-

Prince "1999" video. Courtesy Jake Austen

ited success. One could argue that these performers deserved to do poorly because they weren't particularly good. But if one weighs the video as heavily as the song (or heavier, in some cases) then these artists become viable. MC Hammer may not be as good at writing raps as Rakim or Nas, but his spectacular dancing compensates. Britney Spears may not have the voice of Patti LaBelle, or even Debby Boone, but her curvy body manipulations and Lolita-like teases create videos compelling enough to make up for her limitations. Powerful music videos could survive and thrive without being connected to the life-support system of a great record, as artists such as Twisted Sister and Wham proved. Acts that would have been marginal in the pre-MTV era could become stars. And artists who mastered the new form could become superstars.

Michael Jackson was the god of 1980s MTV. His *Thriller* album was written with music videos in mind and his "Billie Jean," "Beat It," and "Thriller" videos (the latter covertly financed by MTV) not only broke the color line at the network but also shot MTV into the stratosphere. But Jackson was a remarkably talented singer and dancer, an experienced songwriter, and a seasoned performer when he conquered MTV. Without the video channel he would have done fine. A more interesting example of a video-age rock deity is MTV's other megastar. Madonna had the training and experience to sing and dance adequately at best. However, the young diva had charisma and a sense of style that commanded people to mimic her. Radio could not adequately convey these strengths. Because of MTV she was able to become one of the most influential pop figures of the last twenty years and a lightning rod for fascinating cultural criticism. Her videos allowed her to disseminate a message of sex-positive feminism to a wider audience than Camille Paglia could ever hope for and afforded her a platform for chameleon-like "reinventions" on par with Cindy Sherman's. She has boldly practiced multicultural minstrelsy, appearing in her videos as a Latina, an East Indian, and a Japanese woman, and she has also consumed subcultures and underground movements, packaging them for the masses without being branded a traitor. These are achievements, be they heroic or dubious, which could not be realized through the pre-MTV means of radio, touring, and Dick Clark. When an act like Madonna becomes Beatles-big it makes us rethink what constitutes talent and redefine what makes an artist legitimate. The powerful voodoo of combining TV's mighty sway with pop music's perfect three-minute confine made Madonna possible. It also created videos that were—and are—legitimate, exciting art.

Despite the inherent awesomeness of music videos, before the 1980s ended MTV began weaning itself from the video teat. Though originally bold and boastful about being a twenty-four-hour music video channel, MTV's format presented problems as a business model. The network eventually learned that Neilsen ratings, which determine advertising rates, were not as high when showing videos as when a much-hyped new show came on, and over the years MTV has found that not only does traditional programming rate higher than blocks of music videos, but often nonmusic shows rate higher still. While MTV made its reputation with heavy rotation of videos, as the years went on it devoted less programming to videos and more to game shows, sitcoms, reality shows, documentaries, bikini contests, and cartoons. Ironically, just as Mike Nesmith's video work and *The Monkees* show were inspirations for an all-video network, they also helped doom the concept. When MTV ran a *Monkees* marathon in 1986 the ratings and press it generated helped the network decide that airing series was the way to go.

Originally some of the shows were merely extensions of the radio model, with personality VJs showing videos in a particular genre, while appropriate celebrity guests stopped by to chat. These programs included MTV's longest running show,

120 Minutes (MTV, 1986–2000, MTV2, 2001–2003), which was the network's weekly late-night refuge for alternative rock, *Headbanger's Ball* (MTV, 1987–1995, MTV2, 2003–present), which features heavy metal and hard rock, and *Yo! MTV Raps* (MTV, 1988–1995), the hip-hop program that became a surprise hit after MTV's early resistance to black artists.

One of the network's earliest nonmusic video series was the game show *Remote Control* (MTV, 1987–1990), an irreverent and self-referential trivia test that rewarded a lifetime of TV addiction. Future game shows, most notably *Singled Out* (MTV, 1995–1997), which launched the TV careers of Jenny McCarthy and Carmen Electra, were bawdier and cruder. Collectively, they painted a grim picture of America's future, as the nation's colleges appeared to be churning out oversexed dimwits. Though it was cutting back on music videos, MTV seemed determined to keep the most prurient elements of its more controversial videos highly visible.

MTV has also produced a number of soft-core pornography shows. The most blatant of these was *Undressed* (MTV, 1999–2002), an anthology series that featured serialized vignettes about young, attractive people getting into sexual situations (hetero- and homo-). Produced by the English director Roland Joffé (acclaimed for 1984's *The Killing Fields* but derided for 1995's sexy version of *The Scarlet Letter* starring Demi Moore), the stylized show, with its wooden acting and ample shots of teens in underwear, clearly invoked dirty movies, despite its didactic, moral overtones. MTV's perennial spring-break specials are its most notorious programming. In addition to concerts and music-themed contests, the shows feature screaming, drunk college students "gone wild" as they compete in sexually suggestive games, often getting naked or simulating oral sex with strangers. In terms of being irresponsible to the preteens who make up the bulk of MTV's viewer base, this material is probably the least defensible, as it is neither innovative nor particularly funny. MTV has another peep-show program that may also be morally questionable, but at least it can justify its voyeurism as innovative— especially as it is one of the most influential shows MTV ever produced.

The Real World (MTV, 1992–present) is the program most responsible for the reality TV boom. Originally it was designed as a weighted sociological experiment in which a volatile group of young people moved in together and was constantly monitored by cameras for weeks. By building a cast that included such explosive combinations as a gay with a homophobe, an angry black with a prejudiced Southerner, and a weakling with a predatory jerk, the show guaranteed fireworks. Early seasons included relatively normal looking youngsters who flirted and hinted at sex. Eventually the casting was altered so all participants were extroverts that looked like models who were provided with a hot tub and kept drunk for the run

Beavis and Butt-head. Courtesy Jake Austen

of the show so that they would be perennially naked and have sex constantly. The "pornography of semiotics" was replaced by the semiotics of pornography.

Though extremely popular, *The Real World* was never MTV's flagship show, and for the last decade the cornerstones of the network have been two programs that were built around music videos, yet managed to keep the actual playing of videos to a minimum, *Beavis and Butt-head* and *Total Request Live*. The animated *Beavis and Butt-head* (MTV, 1993–1997) was a scathing critique of MTV's audience that became the network's highest-rated show. The cartoon featured a duo of adolescents whose steady diet of music videos (and, presumably, parental neglect) had turned them into imbecilic, vulgar, semicoherent cretins. Unlike the suburban dumb-ass, metal-head duos that preceded them, Bill and Ted (from the 1989 movie *Bill & Ted's Excellent Adventure*) and Wayne and Garth (from "Wayne's World," a 1988 *Saturday Night Live* skit, that begat two feature films), there isn't even an implication that Beavis and Butt-head were stoners, as their time-consuming and brain cell–destroying habit of watching videos has left them so socially inept that they would be unable to buy drugs. Between crudely rendered cartoon vignettes (with hilarious voice work by the show's creator Mike Judge, who would go on to create the more sophisticated *King of the Hill* for Fox in 1997) viewers watched the characters watching popular and obscure MTV videos and giving their own critiques, which usually boiled down to headbanging and screaming "YESSS!" at cool metal videos with explosions, and chuckling at anything that sounded vaguely dirty ("heh heh . . . he said *hole*"). Though the show was a celebration of stupidity, it wasn't actually a stupid show, as the adults Beavis and Butt-head encountered were either so awful or so hopelessly inept that the boys' aversion to becoming functional human beings seemed like a reasonable response.

The show that replaced *Beavis and Butt-head* as MTV's cornerstone is *Total Request Live* (MTV, 1998–present), more popularly known as *TRL*. The video countdown show (in the tradition of *Your Hit Parade* or *America's Top Ten*) shoots live every weekday afternoon in MTV's Manhattan studio with a small teenage audience in front of it and a large window facing Rudolph Giuliani's wholesome, corporate Times Square behind it. Every afternoon during *TRL's* broadcast, hundreds (sometimes thousands) of screaming teens holding signs and cheering for the show's hosts and guests flood into that once seedy midtown district. The show's format features an emcee and celebrity guests presenting the viewer's choices (voted online) for the most popular videos of the day.

There are several good things about *TRL*, but there are also problems that make it difficult for even a staunch proponent of music videos to defend it. The most positive result of *TRL* is a return to an MTV where kids are psyched about music videos. However, the show usually plays only a short sliver of each video, and that portion is obscured by inset shots of the Times Square teens shouting dedications and declarations of love for their favorite pop stars, as well as scrolling e-mail messages from home viewers. Another positive is that the show is genuinely democratic; the viewers vote for the content. Unfortunately it is a democracy that mirrors America's flawed two-party system, as MTV offers a small, controlled pool of videos to choose from. The imperfect voting process also favors obsessive fans with Internet access, skewing toward a very specific demographic and creating a fairly homogenous playlist. For the first 109 episodes either Backstreet Boys or *NSYNC held the number-one spot. Because of the viewers' loyalty to their idols, *TRL* had to invoke a retirement clause, wherein a video could only appear on the show for a total of 65 days, and within the first two years dozens of videos met that generous criterion.

Another good thing about *TRL* is that the show's energy is provided by the young music fans in the TV rock 'n' roll tradition that made *American Bandstand*, the Beatles on *The Ed Sullivan Show,* and *Soul Train* so successful. In fact, *TRL,* like early *American Bandstand,* became a weekday afternoon ritual for pop-obsessed kids across the nation. But *TRL* is *American Bandstand* without the dancing. The message seems to be that the most appropriate reaction to a band performing in a video (an act less interactive than performing in person) is to stand there and watch (an act less interactive than dancing).

The biggest caveat is that the host, Carson Daly, is a creepy (he mentions his fondness for strippers on the MTV Web site) L.A. DJ in his late twenties who seems like a problematic romantic fantasy for the army of twelve-year-old girls screaming "We love you, Carson!" With his expressionless face and cold, blank eyes, the charmless Daly's detached, monotone interviews mark him as both a sycophant and a dullard. MTV's book about *Total Request Live* devotes two pages to gushing over Daly's brilliant comeback to Madonna teasing him about his

Carson Daly and *TRL.*

rumored affair with Christina Aguilera. Daly, that master of wit, mumbled that she "had a big mouth." Touché!

But the real problem with *TRL* is that it is a fundamentally vanilla, middle-of-the-road show that complicates MTV's unspoken agenda. As a network, MTV serves three masters. It is theoretically bound to the concept that it is a network whose foundation is music videos (master #1—videos). MTV is willing to look the other way on this requirement if it produces programming that captures the rock 'n' roll spirit by being edgy (the "attitude" originally marked by its experimental bumpers in 1981). Thus, even as it works with major-label acts and constantly helps define the mainstream, it is also beholden to being somewhat cutting-edge (master #2—edge). As *TRL* demonstrates, this is complicated by the fact that MTV also has to serve its core audience: adolescents (master #3—the twelve-year-old), who may appreciate the outsider attitude but may not be interested in particularly challenging content. This results in an audience that either doesn't connect with more interesting programming or digs it for the wrong reasons.

While it was a well-oiled business machine from its outset, the corporate overlords at MTV did allow the youthful foot soldiers to create unusual, loose programming, and there are several stories of young interns working their way up to becoming important content creators. In the book *MTV Uncensored*, director Ted Demme recalls, "MTV is the only place you could think of an idea on Monday . . . it would air Saturday, and if it sucked, who cared?" Bold programming on MTV included its animation package *Liquid Television* (MTV, 1991–1993), which featured, among other things, cartoons based on the work of artists appearing in Art Spiegelman's underground comix anthology *Raw*. Two programs were spun off of that anthology series, the stylized *Æon Flux* (MTV, 1992–1995), which featured sensuous violence and designs based on Egon Schiele's paintings, and *Beavis and Butt-head*, a show that pushed some adolescents too far over the edge. The comical cartoon that parodied mindless TV viewing proved to be prescient—some MTV watchers were as dense as Beavis and Butt-head. They watched and then imitated the pyromania and animal abuse that the characters occasionally engaged in (meant to signify their damaged mental health), which led to at least one lawsuit. MTV excised every reference to fire from the reruns.

Other forward-looking programming included *Austin Stories* (MTV, 1997), a genre-challenging sitcom based on Richard Linklater's 1991 movie, *Slacker*. MTV mined the underground by bringing cult local cable shows like *Squirt TV* (MTV, 1996) and *The Tom Green Show* (MTV, 1999–2000, 2003) to the network and allowing them to stay true to their original visions. Even MTV's prank shows *Buzzkill* (MTV, 1996–1997) and *Punk'd* (MTV, 2003–present) were somewhat intelligent, the latter a deconstruction of the very cosmology MTV had helped to create. On it Ashton Kutcher, an ostensibly dumb stoner from the Midwest, continuously plays upon the gullibility and arrogance of Hollywood celebrities thereby revealing that the rock stars who have been built up as the emperors of cool are wearing no clothes (the show's signature prank involved faux federal agents seizing Justin Timberlake's possessions, transforming the *NSYNC member's brash, cocky Ebonics into meek, suppliant King's English).

For the most part MTV's most popular programs were the ones that could be appreciated on a juvenile (often puerile) level, and truly challenging shows had brief half-lives. Only during a short period in the early 1990s (bookended by late-1980s hair metal and mid-1990s boy bands), when Nirvana's straightforward rock and the Lilith Fair's singer-songwriter movement heralded a "credible" mainstream, did MTV's façade of outsider integrity really resonate with the audience. During this era the network was inspired to cultivate its most musical show, *Unplugged* (MTV, 1989–1997, 1999; MTV2, 2000–2002). In a move unusual for the network, this live program was more a nod to the noncommercial PBS shows *Soundstage* and *Austin City Limits* than to the more commercial and flamboyant 1970s late-night rock-concert shows. *Unplugged* featured popular contemporary and classic rock artists playing their greatest hits and new songs in an intimate setting using acoustic instruments. Originally the show featured a number of artists already associated with this pseudo-coffeehouse setup (Indigo Girls, Syd Straw) or hair metal bands flexing their melodramatic power-ballad muscles (Ratt, Great White). But by its second season, in the wake of the Milli Vanilli scandal, the show became important to both fans and the industry, as it symbolized authenticity. By playing with live musicians rap acts such as LL Cool J, De La Soul, and Arrested Development were able to further legitimize their music with white audiences at a time when hip-hop was on the verge of a commercial breakthrough. Older acts were able to expose themselves to a younger audience as valid and important artists, the most notable episode featuring a reunion of the original members of KISS, which led to the band getting back together for a series of lucrative tours. And MTV was finally heralded by rock critics as not only culturally notable but artistically valid, as the Nirvana episode was celebrated in print not as some absurd milestone, like a writhing Madonna, but as a cultural achievement on a par with Dylan's work. CD soundtrack albums of many of these episodes became top sellers, meaning that MTV was not only helping album sales but also *creating* albums to sell.

The artistic merits of *Unplugged* aside, the groundbreaking aspects of MTV (the way it reshaped the industry, the way it affected visual pop culture) never really turned kids into the revolutionary rebels its edgier programming suggested. Perhaps the tepid *TRL* is MTV's most honest program.

While the content of MTV may be milder than it pretends to be, the boardroom is vicious, and over the years the cable station and its parent have threatened to become a monolithic corporate monopoly that controlled all channels showing music videos. In 1985 (the same year media giant Viacom purchased the network from Warner) MTV introduced a sister station, VH1, originally an easy listening MTV for the baby-boomer generation, with Fleetwood Mac ruling its airwaves. When weak ratings disproved the maxim of boomers being a constant, loyal economic force, VH1 determined that it would be more prudent to serve each new generation of thirtysomethings rather than count on its original demographic, and shifted from 1970s nostalgia programming to 1980s nostalgia programming to 1990s nostalgia programming. VH1, like its big brother, eventually deemphasized music videos in lieu of original programming, though it maintained musical themes more overtly than MTV with such shows as *Pop Up Videos* (VH1, 1996–2000), *Behind the Music* (VH1, 1997–present), and *Rock 'n' Roll Jeopardy* (VH1, 1998).

To make up for the dearth of videos, MTV introduced MTV2 (originally called M2) as an alternative channel that would play videos exclusively, and would be broader in musical scope than MTV—a minor league where less established artists would get a shot at the bigs. Initially MTV2 didn't play in many markets, but in 2000 Viacom expanded its scope considerably by buying out an established basic cable channel, The Box Music Network, and replacing it with MTV2. Though MTV2 boldly declared itself to be the all-music video channel it quickly became a home for recycled MTV specials and series.

The station MTV2 usurped, The Box (not to be confused with the popular British music-video channel of the same name), was a televised video jukebox that showed nothing but music videos. Viewers called a toll number and paid a few dollars to choose the clips they wanted to see. Rap and metal were heavily represented, and occasionally independent or local artists (each city had its own Box) would get significant airplay. The promos the network ran explained that record labels were allowed to call in to request their own videos, so for some labels and artists it was cheap promotion (apparently Ja Rule came to the attention of Def Jam this way), but even with that variation on payola, populism ruled and the programming was decidedly different from MTV's. When MTV2 took over The

Box it transitioned by keeping some interactive programming, eventually limiting it to one show, *Control Freak* (MTV2, 2001–present), which involves free online voting and a choice of only two or three videos at a time, making it a far different animal (MTV later added a similar show called *Video Clash*). Later in 2000 MTV's parent company bought out Black Entertainment Television (BET), the cable home of rap and R&B music videos. Viacom also owns CMT, the country-music video channel. So with control of MTV, VH1, MTV2, BET, and CMT, Viacom effectively created a music-video monopoly. While this opened the door for the tiny upstart music network Fuse (Motto: "More Music, Less Crappy TV"), and Fuse's Box-like interactive sister network Fuse On Demand, these channels are a slingshot-free David up against the mighty Viacom Goliath.

Since its dramatic moonwalk-metaphor inception, MTV has invested in its reputation as a historic entity. One way it did this was by staging events that not only celebrated MTV and the rock culture it was shaping, but that also would gain prominence as pop culture landmarks. In 1984 it premiered its annual Video Music Awards, or VMAs, a hip riff on the Grammys (hipper even than Dick Clark's American Music Awards) that deemphasizes the awards and focuses on elaborate performances by the year's hot artists. These performances have ranged from the truly remarkable (Madonna's shockingly absurd 1984 performance of "Like a Virgin," featuring her writhing on the floor in a wedding dress, called one of the greatest moments in rock 'n' roll history by *Rolling Stone*) to the contrived (2003's Madonna performance featuring faux-lesbian kisses with Britney Spears and Christina Aguilera). But more blatant examples of MTV declaring its historical relevance came in the late 1990s when PBS, of all networks, set the stage for MTV to tell its story.

TV specials that set out to document the history of rock 'n' roll have appeared every few years since the 1970s first decided to get nostalgic for the 1950s. *Dick Clark Presents the Rock and Roll Years* (ABC, 1973–1974) coupled new performances by classic 1950s and 1960s acts with footage from the *American Bandstand* archives. *Rolling Stone* had two TV specials, each intent on telling the history of rock since the magazine's inception. *Rolling Stone: The Tenth Anniversary* (CBS, 1977) was an awful mess, with CBS imposing variety show tropes—disco dance numbers and guest stars galore—thus diluting the journalism. But *Rolling Stone Magazine's First 20 Years* (ABC, 1987) was a much more effective, serious look at the 1960s and 1970s. Ambitious histories followed, including *The Roots of Rock* 'n' Roll (syndicated, 1981), *Rock & Roll: The First 25 Years* (syndicated, 1982), and *Rock and Roll: The Early Years* (syndicated, 1984). These all gave a pretty standard take on rock history—hailing Elvis Presley, the Beatles, the Rolling Stones, and Woodstock—with a lot of archival footage that was great to see in the days when home video was scarce.

But the 1990s became the golden age of TV documentaries thanks to Ken Burns, who brought respectability and popularity to made-for-TV talking-head histories. Burns's *The Civil War* (PBS, 1990) was a high-profile TV documentary miniseries that received much fanfare. But it was his follow-up, *Baseball* (PBS, 1994), that really raised the bar. Unlike its predecessor, which featured historians jabbering away, *Baseball* mixed gushing scholars with actual regular-guy ball players, thus dignifying a "low" American pastime and its undereducated participants. The most memorable figure in *Baseball* was the elderly Negro League veteran Buck O'Neil, who was equally effective as a genuinely charming witness to history and as a cloying cliché who bordered on camp. The way *Baseball* presented corny material about the game with Biblical gravity made the slew of made-for-TV "rockumentaries" to follow inevitable. If you thought Buck O' Neil's thoughtful analysis was something, wait until you hear Vince Neil's!

In 1995 two different ten-hour rock history series aired. *The Time-Life History of Rock' n' Roll* (syndicated, 1995) was a very good overview of rock history, especially when compared to its less impressive predecessors. But PBS's *Rock & Roll* was excellent. It featured a sophisticated analysis of the racial politics of pop music and ample rarely seen archival performances by rockabilly, glam rock, funk, and hip-hop artists. Though imperfect (it predicted techno was the future of rock, and claimed that New England's Modern Lovers were the godfathers of American punk) it was TV's most intelligent, entertaining rock history TV yet (PBS later aired two other music documentary series, Burns's Satchmo-deifying *Jazz* in 2001 and 2003's *Blues*, which featured disparate episodes directed by such prominent filmmakers as Charles Burnett, Martin Scorsese, and Wim Wenders).

Despite the PBS documentary's excellence, it was the lesser productions that followed that proved to be the most fascinating. MTV and VH1 began producing a lot of documentary programming in the 1990s. Other cable networks had established documentary making as a cost-effective approach to original programming (most notably the History Channel and A&E, whose *Biography* series premiered in 1987), but MTV upped the ante by producing a slew of documentaries about itself. One of its high-profile specials featured the original five MTV VJs reminiscing about their heady days making groundbreaking TV. 1999's *MTV Uncensored* had talking head after talking head tell behind-the-scenes stories of

MTV with Ken Burns–like gravity. Every VMA had a documentary postmortem, with producers giving back stories (like the time they helped Snoop Dogg escape from the police), and even less ambitious MTV programs earned elaborate documentary treatment, so that history could note that Jean-Claude Van Damme was ungentlemanly during MTV *Spring Break* and Tom Cruise, according to an MTV intern, was a joy when he visited *TRL*.

What each of these specials had in common is that they treated the production of MTV as truly historical, with each mundane anecdote marked as a cultural benchmark. In a review of 2000's *Video Killed the Radio Star*, a VH1 documentary about the history of music videos, *Spin* magazine chided the special for reaching "a feverish pitch of importance . . . from its initial equation of the launch of MTV with the JFK assassination to its later evaluation of music TV's heroic role in the downfall of communism." Unlike the throwaway nature of the pop music MTV promotes, apparently the programming that features this pop music is far from disposable—it must be documented, revisited, and genuflected upon. One bizarre example of this was *VH1 Goes Inside The Real World* (VH1, 2003), a behind-the-scenes special about *The Real World* series that featured candid footage and the cast members as talking heads reflecting on the show, even though the original show consisted of nothing but candid footage and the cast members as talking heads reflecting on the show. Pornography of semiotics indeed!

What is this obsessive self-historicizing about? In some ways it is certainly a charmless exercise in branding engineered by the corporate drones at Viacom. However, in other ways it is a practice that certainly resonates with many MTV devotees, who not only bask in the warm glow of nostalgia ("I remember when that guy was on that show!") but also can feel like an insider ("So that's what he *really* said to that other guy!") and can bask in the satisfaction of being a part of something so historical ("And to think I was watching that show when that happened!").

To be fair, MTV also makes documentaries for young viewers that are not self-referential, including a series of specials that deglamorize drug use and many well-made films done in the series *True Life* (MTV, 1998–present). But even these can't avoid the MTV circle jerk. In one memorable special an attractive young dwarf decides to become an entertainer but is disillusioned by the degrading circumstances she finds herself in. However, the awful job that convinced her to reevaluate her dreams was as an elf at a heavy-metal Christmas concert—a concert that turns up (degraded dwarfs and all) on an episode of MTV's *The Osbournes*. For the most part the extremely active documentary division of MTV (according to the *New York Times* it produced seventy-five films for cable in 2000) has done fine work when it turned its cameras away from itself. And when it finally tackled the history of rock as it existed outside of the MTV/VH1 box, MTV actually created one of its best series.

Behind the Music was born after a successful VH1 special on heroin abuse sparked interest in a recurring documentary series. Jeff Gaspin, VH1 vice president, and producer Gay Rosenthal had the idea to do a sympathetic profile of shamed lip-synchers Milli Vanilli. The resulting show was magnetic: a fascinating, respectful human story that made you care about the protagonists even if you (inevitably) hated their music. Like its fellow iconic 1990s shows *Seinfeld* (NBC, 1989–1998) and *The Simpsons* (Fox, 1989–present), *Behind the Music* is fundamentally a triumph of writing. Certainly it is hackneyed writing at times, but the key to the show's success is its tight, formulaic construction that mixes absurd clichés with clever, florid narration, scripted to have power and force when delivered in the dire tones of announcer Jim Forbes. The formula is as set as ancient kabuki theater or, more appropriately, a Christian morality play. *Behind the Music* imposes a moralistic structure of vices receiving punishment and redemption coming from repentance, with a story arc as rigid as that other 1990s favorite *Law and Order* (NBC, 1990–present). A humble beginning is followed by a meteoric rise, a devastating fall, and ultimately a redemptive mini-rise ("Leif is back in the studio . . . ").

Classic episodes told the stories of either marginal musical figures like Tony Orlando or MC Hammer or trashy screw-ups like David Crosby or Rick James. The show basked in the lurid scandals and shame, tempered by staged footage of the now-redeemed heroes taking reflective walks along the beach or playing with their kids. At its best *Behind the Music* was the ultimate TV rock 'n' roll show. It paradoxically glorified and demystified the myths and legends of the rock 'n' roll lifestyle, making that fabled path more real and accessible to the fans than it had ever been before.

Unfortunately, success crept in. As *Behind the Music* became the network's top-rated show, the corporate culture of Viacom took over. The music biz began to realize that the show was impacting record sales. After an episode featuring an inspired splicing of two pieces of stock footage that imagined a cow in a field looking up just in time to see drummer Rick Allen lose his arm in a car crash, Def Leppard's weekly record sales doubled. For artists with miniscule sales like Vanilla Ice, sales increased exponentially. These figures led to episodes that featured current acts like Green Day, Alanis Morissette, and Creed, the shows coinciding with CD release dates. The show featured these artists, who had little history or tragedy behind them, at the expense of more obscure acts with much more interesting stories (in 1999 producer George Moll boasted, "We're moving away from heritage artists").

Because the structure did not serve trendy, new artists well, the ratings suffered and *Behind the Music* slowed down production (it currently airs only a few new episodes each year). VH1 developed shows that worked better for this current crop of performers, such as *Driven* (VH1, 2002–present), which shows family and friends describing the subject's early days leading up to stardom (the show purposely does not interview the overexposed subject). The channel then moved away from in-depth documentaries and toward a new style of show in which comedians and celebrities flippantly deliver scripted, empty quips about pop culture. Instead of spending an hour discussing one subject, these shows, including *I Love the 80s* (VH1, 2002), *One Hit Wonders* (VH1, 2002), and *Best Week Ever* (VH1, 2004–present), covered, with little insight or analysis, dozens of subjects each episode, broken up into short, separate segments.

By 2004 this style of show dominated VH1 and popped up on MTV and in reruns on MTV2. With quick edits, flashy design, and freestanding, delineated segments, these were basically the music videos of documentary programming, clearly influenced by early MTV. Despite the boardroom decisions to limit music video airings (which, combined with an ailing music industry, resulted in record labels cutting back on music-video budgets), the network couldn't deny the Frankenstein it created. Even in this bastardized form, MTV still looked like MTV because after over a quarter-century the manic, manipulative, superficial aesthetic it started with is still grooving. MTV as a channel may be an arrogant, problematic, socially irresponsible corporate bully, but the commodity upon which it built its empire, the music video, still stands as TV rock 'n' roll's most powerful example of entertaining artifice. The video may not be the social force it once was, but it is far from dead. A good video can still break a band (the White Stripes' innovative debut clip elevated them out of the underground) and video auteurs like Spike Jonze, Little X, and Michel Gondry are celebrated for their artistry. Ultimately, music video is a legitimate, expressive art form worthy of the university courses devoted to it, high culture's embrace of its aesthetics, and the amens of four generations of teenagers who have worshiped before its altar.

And music videos are totally *awesome!*

9

Idol Bands Are the Devil's Workshop

Rock 'n' Roll Reality TV

As we settle into a new millennium TV rock 'n' roll has reached either a stellar apex or a yawning nadir, depending on where you stand. A half-century of transparent, often joyous artifice has congealed into a shameless smorgasbord of blatantly inauthentic, contrived, inorganic programming. Incredibly, this tsunami of lies is branded "reality."

Rock 'n' roll reality TV is a kaleidoscope of absurdity: a coast-to-coast battle of the shitty bands on *Bands on the Run* (VH1, 2001); rapper-turned-evangelist MC Hammer counseling his new roommate, Motley Crüe's Vince Neil, on *The Surreal Life* (WB, 2003–2004; VH1, 2004–present); Sugar Ray's roadies competing for an entry-level job at a record label in *On the Road* (Spike, 2004); retired B-list rockers burying the hatchet on *Bands Reunited* (VH1, 2004–present); attrac-

217

tive youngsters being stalked like great white buffalo by Ted Nugent on *Surviving Nugent* (VH1, 2003–2004).

Reality TV, which takes the prefab nature of the Monkees to its logical end, has also given us the world's most popular talent show and MTV's most gloriously fucked-up programming slate ever. A return to the early days of TV history, it is also a posthistorical exercise in *über*-TV. Rock 'n' roll reality TV is an inside joke between audience and programmers, both of whom feel joyously empowered, in an interactive environment of absurdity and awfulness. It is as profound and thought-provoking as a philosophical debate and as shallow and festive as a drunken sing-along. Rock 'n' roll reality TV is the karaoke bar of network programming.

Reality TV isn't exactly a genre, as much as it is a catchall for the numerous seemingly untraditional shows that fill network TV schedules here in the early years of the twenty-first century. Some shows, like *The Osbournes* (MTV, 2002–2005), represent themselves as *cinéma vérité*, with omnipresent cameras acting as flies on the wall, ostensibly documenting their subjects' regular lives as they would occur even if the cameramen weren't there. A variation on this is the manipulated surveillance show, where the camera's constant gaze observes situations crafted by the producers, with participants documented in awkward scenarios (as in MTV's *The Real World*). Some shows are merely televised talent contests. Others are hidden-camera shows in which unsuspecting victims fall prey to pranks. Some of the programs are game shows, albeit grander than their daytime counterparts. And many of the shows combine these formulas. Manipulated surveillance + game show = *Survivor* (CBS, 2000–present); talent contest + game show = *Last Comic Standing* (NBC, 2003–present); hidden-camera prank show + manipulated surveillance = *My Big Fat Obnoxious Fiancé* (Fox, 2004).

What all these disparate programs have in common is that they are cheaper to produce than traditional TV dramas or sitcoms. They also share a long history. With the exception of the *cinéma vérité* shows, reality programming returned TV to the 1940s. The long-running *Candid Camera* (ABC, 1948; NBC, 1949, 1953; CBS, 1949–1950, 1960–1967, 1990, 1997–2000; syndicated, 1974–1978, 1991–1992; Pax, 2001–2004) was an early hidden-camera prank show that had predated TV as radio's *Candid Microphone*. Numerous amateur talent contests appeared on early TV (also with radio precedents). And game shows were some of TV's earliest hits. While a reality show–filled prime time may seem like a drastic, contemporary departure, in many ways it is a cozy return to TV's infancy.

Not that programmers decided en masse to look to the postwar era for inspiration. The flood of reality shows actually developed as a slow trickle before reaching today's tipping point. The first distinctly recognizable forebear of today's shows was *American Family* (PBS, 1972–1973), an experiment in ethnography in which a film crew, in an ostensibly unobtrusive manner, shot hundreds of hours of footage of the Louds, a seemingly typical family unit. While the show didn't invent a new kind of filmmaking (Jean Rouch defined *cinéma vérité*—"film truth"—in 1960's *Chronique d'un été* and Frederick Wiseman became known for exhaustive documentation in films like 1968's *High School*), *American Family* was a revelation because of its shocking results. Decades before Jerry Springer's heyday, *American Family* stumbled upon a cornucopia of painful dysfunction, documenting the Loud parents' divorce as it happened and their son, Lance Loud, as he made his way out of the closet. Though *American Family* didn't have an immediate effect on network programming, its trashy yield certainly was an inspiration for MTV's *The Real World*.

A more direct ancestor of contemporary reality TV is *Cops* (Fox, 1989–present), where cameramen accompany real police officers on patrols, documenting domestic disputes, drunken confrontations, and interrogations of strung-out, toothless victims of poverty. While not a formal model for the programs to come, *Cops* demonstrated that a prime-time audience would watch an extremely inexpensive show, its sparseness contributing to how "real" it felt (the unscripted nature and uncertain outcome titillating the audience, who watched it like a sporting event). 1992's *The Real World* was the next reality landmark, priming the adolescents who would become the key demographic a decade later. The show that sealed the deal for the reality boom was *Who Wants to Be a Millionaire* (ABC, 1999–2002), an American version of a British game show, which proved that programming unfamiliar to contemporary prime time could be massively successful. Due to network incompetence, the show nearly destroyed ABC, which greedily ran it nearly every night for months, forcing the public to tire of the show, and sacrificing all existing programming in the process. But despite ABC's failure in execution, *Who Wants to Be a Millionaire* clearly demonstrated reality's massive potential.

All this has very little to do with rock 'n' roll. After *American Family* aired, Lance Loud became an obscure pop punk singer in the 1970s band the Mumps; indie rocker Calvin Johnson of Beat Happening was rumored to have been arrested on the *Cops* clone *Real Stories of the Highway Patrol* (syndicated, 1992–1996); and musicians occasionally appeared on special episodes of *Who Wants to Be a Millionaire* and its British-import cousin *Weakest Link* (NBC, 2001–2002; syndicated, 2002–2003), on which rappers and rockers proved incapable of simple arithmetic. But it wasn't until after Dick Clark dropped the millennium ball on Times Square that music-themed reality shows would have an impact, entering the field with a whimper, but eventually ruling the airwaves. Their voices soon became so mighty that they managed to turn TV sets into time machines, setting TV rock 'n' roll back fifty years.

The show that launched reality TV rock 'n' roll was *Making the Band* (ABC, 2000–2001; MTV, 2002), a production by the MTV team responsible for *The Real World*. The show capitalized on how the popularity of 1990s boy bands Backstreet Boys and *NSYNC made the controversies surrounding the Monkees moot: their audience was fully aware of how these bands' Svengali manager constructed and controlled them. *Making the Band* declared that little girls should not be concerned that their heroes were not "real" bands with shared artistic vision, but rather puppets with a smarmy, middle-aged gargoyle pulling their strings. In fact, the show seemed to say that the fans should celebrate this fact and lionize the man behind the boys, Lou Pearlman.

Pearlman's showbiz career was an outgrowth of his earlier vocation: chartering private airplanes for musical superstars. Upon seeing the frenzy of attention afforded one of his clients, late-1980s boy band New Kids on the Block, Lou decided to go into the production business. With Johnny Wright (who helped manage the New Kids) he started Trans Continental Management. Drawing from the pool of local talent in his Orlando, Florida, base, Pearlman was able to assemble groups of talented local boys, many of whom were drawn to the area because of Disney-affiliated performing opportunities. Using slick production teams from Sweden to produce the music, and seasoning the acts by touring them throughout bubblegum-friendly Europe, Pearlman's dual boy band juggernauts, Backstreet Boys and *NSYNC, debuted in America fully polished and became two of the biggest-selling acts of the late 1990s.

In pop music's always sleazy behind-the-scenes world, Pearlman comes off as a particularly grotesque figure, not because of his obesity, but rather because of his unbridled creepiness. This manifests itself in Pearlman's lusty appreciation of his young boys (and older boys as well: Pearlman is an owner of the Chippendales exotic male dancer franchise) and young girls (a VH1 special showed Lou lecherously adjusting a teen female singer's clothing, under the auspices of "no detail is too small"). Apparently his lust is surpassed only by his greed. All of Pearlman's successful acts have sued to get out of what they deemed exploitative contracts, eventually settling for terms very favorable to Pearlman.

Despite this somewhat soiled reputation, MTV productions and ABC (the Disney-owned network that bought the series) still viewed Pearlman as an icon who would make a fine focal point for a reality show. *Making the Band* documented Pearlman constructing a new potential hit act, to be called O-Town (the name, style, and personality of the band were determined before he chose the band members). Omnipresent cameras documented the auditions, training, and early career of the act. The series began with a large open-audition process out of which

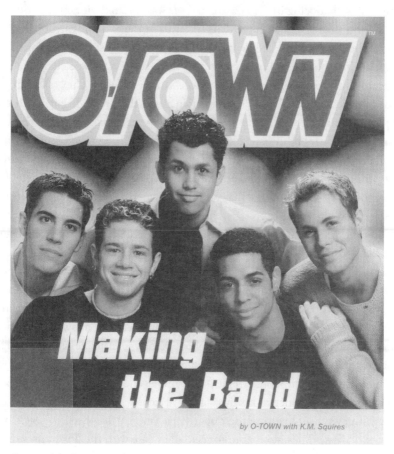

by O-TOWN with K.M. Squires

Courtesy Jake Austen

twenty-five potential band members were assembled. This group performed before judges who whittled down the ensemble to the eight young men who had the right balance of looks and singing ability to be the new New Kids. Then the eight moved in together while going through a training/hazing period to determine which five would make the final cut.

Several tropes of this type of musical reality series quickly established themselves. The audition process was the most interesting part of the series, where home viewers could sit in judgment along with the judges. When that process ended, far too early in this series, and the ins and outs of being a media-friendly twenty-first century pop act became the focus (going on *TRL*, doing press, being an opening act), things became pretty mundane. Another aspect of the show that would repeat in subsequent band-making reality series was the phenomenon of members quitting, usually out of discomfort with the stalking cameras, or the nagging feeling that being in the constructed act was not in their best interests.

One of the reasons for these exits seems to be the extreme career consciousness of the participants. Unlike hungry musicians who just want to play or sing or rock out, all of the young men on this show seemed to be calculating what developments would help further their success in the industry. They talked in platitudes straight out of a Tony Robbins seminar and their relationships with their bandmates seemed to be based on who would help them make it to the top rather than on loyalty, friendship, or respect for talent. While a group of musical middle managers living in mandatory cohabitation in a corporate compound may be more of a reality than the Monkees pretending to be best-friend roommates who go on adventures together and play rock 'n' roll when they feel like it, it certainly isn't as much fun. Not surprisingly, the show was not a big hit.

Making the Band was initially somewhat successful. Early ratings were decent and, like the Monkees, TV served record sales well. O-Town's CD, *Liquid Dreams*, made the *Billboard* top ten and eventually went double-platinum, yielding a number-one song, "All or Nothing." But the ratings soon dwindled (ABC eventually canceled the show, which finished its run on MTV), and the band began to unravel before viewers' eyes. Like their simian predecessors, midway through the series O-Town became uncomfortable about being the ultimate prefab act. They broke their ties with Pearlman (all documented on the small screen) and hooked up with a more worthy icon, Atlantic Records' legendary executive Clive Davis, who had recently launched his own label, J Records. They began playing their own instruments and writing their own songs (mostly dismissed by Davis, who insisted on hits). They also began to seem ill at ease with the TV show, expressing their misgivings in the press and on the show. They were rocking a leaky canoe, and they soon sunk. The show died, CD sales diminished, and O-Town disappeared from the public eye.

When *Making the Band*'s early ratings were still encouraging, the WB (a network that courted the teens that buy bubblegum pop) launched a copycat show, *Popstars* (WB, 2001–2002). Unlike its boy-band predecessor, this show created a girl group, called Eden's Crush. Like *Who Wants to Be a Millionaire*, *Popstars* was a franchise, launched in England, with different versions in simultaneous production in numerous countries (there was actually a different *Popstars* group, Sugar Jones, in Canada). While musically, and as a TV production, the American *Popstars* was far from groundbreaking, it did feature one fascinating experiment as its unspoken centerpiece. After an audition process that aired on TV in a longer, more interesting manner than on *Making the Band* (instead of quickly choosing a small pool and then training them all, this featured a more traditional series of auditions and eliminations), Eden's Crush was cast with five beautiful young women. While that was no surprise, Eden's Crush featured five "Exotic-Americans," a term coined by media scholar L. S. Kim.

Exotic-Americans, be they from Latin, Asian, Polynesian, or mixed-race backgrounds, share dark-haired, dark-eyed, relatively fair-skinned looks that suggest ethnicity while still adhering to European standards of beauty (check out twenty years of Prince's girlfriends and wives to see a catalog of them). Kim posited, in a study of the show done with Gilberto Moisés Blasini, that in response to multiculturalism and to recent protests about poor minority representation on TV, the *Popstars* producers deliberately cast only women who were neither black nor white, exotic yet not *too* ethnic, boldly banking on a new American beauty standard and on a cross-cultural demographic. The theory was that American teens of all races would connect with a group that wasn't any race at all.

As notable as that formula may have been to academics, it became strictly academic when it proved fruitless. Teen pop and innovation go together like oil and water, and America apparently wasn't ready for the new face of America. Ratings for the show were modest, which did not help CD sales. After an initially successful first single, "Get Over Yourself" (which went gold), Eden's Crush's full-length CD flopped. The group, which debuted in January 2001, played their last show in December and announced their dissolution the next year.

A second season of *Popstars*, crafted while the first season still held promise, was even more disappointing. Scrapping the experiment in Exotic-Americanism, the producers decided to simply re-create the British pop-group model in America. The English version of *Popstars* was a ratings smash, but British TV regulations prohibit promoting products in the body of a TV series, so the band couldn't release its CD while the series was still on the air, limiting the cross-marketing opportunities. In America capitalism is allowed to run amok, so the *Popstars* franchise decided to present the United States with an act that resembled the popular British *Popstars* act, Hear'say. But to do that meant breaking some American teen pop commandments about gender and race.

Because this particular type of boy band/girl act bubblegum is marketed to teen and preteen girls primarily (and gay men secondarily) it is very important to offer them either boys they can lust over or girls they can model themselves after. A mixed-gender group is unnecessarily confusing, and in America no such act has ever really made it huge (ABBA was not marketed as a teen act—the full beards are the giveaway; the nontouring Partridge Family was marketed as Keith only). Similar prohibitors exist for mixed-race acts; different demographics want their own kiddie groups to worship, and the Jackson 5ive, New Edition, and Menudo were crafted to make marketing simple (Frankie Lymon and the Teenagers, arguably the very first boy band, had both African American and Latino members, but they thrived in the days before *16 Magazine* set the rules).

But in Britain there had been a number of successful acts with mixed gender teens, featuring token ethnic members, including Hear'say. One possible reason that different teen pop formulas work in England may be that the public accepts the disposability of pop acts more easily than Americans do. The American Dream posits that Horatio Algers make it to the top and live happily ever after. Even if we may revel in *Behind the Music* fall-from-grace postscripts, we don't initially expect our stars to crash down to earth. Perhaps the more caste-comfortable United Kingdom doesn't mind enjoying singers they know will be back on the dole in a year. Thus, band configurations that are obviously artificial and calculated (three white boys, a black boy, and two girls as "best friends") are more palatable.

Alas, such palatability eluded Scene 23, the American *Popstars 2* band, which featured boys and girls, whites and blacks, and a repertoire of songs that had previously been hits for English pop acts. The show was a ratings failure (and a formal failure—once again the show was a bore after the initial auditions) and the band had only one flop release, which was padded with previously released songs by R. Kelly and Mariah Carey. The band broke up soon after the CD's release.

Even the golden touch of Simon Fuller, a British pop impresario who had guided the Spice Girls to huge success, couldn't convince America that this type of band was viable. After the Spice Girls defected from his management company he crafted a mixed gender/mixed race act that he originally wanted to call Spice Club 7, but was convinced to name the less-litigious S Club 7. They became a smash in Britain, and an international sensation, but when imported to America they had no chart success and barely made ripples when their TV show *S Club 7* (Fox Family, 2000–2001; ABC Family, 2001–2002), a kiddie sitcom, not a reality show, aired on American cable. However, Mr. Fuller was far from defeated. He soon would become the mighty emperor of the reality-show kingdom.

When Fuller began pitching to American TV networks a franchise version of his new British hit show *Pop Idol* (ITV1, 2001–present), they were skeptical. After the soft ratings of *Making the Band* and *Popstars*, a televised search for a new musical star seemed like an idea that America had considered and rejected. However, it intrigued Mike Darnell, the visionary Fox programming executive who had helmed some of TV's most crass—and most successful—reality specials, including *Alien Autopsy: Fact or Fiction?* (Fox, 1995), *When Animals Attack* (Fox, 1996–1998), and *Breaking the Magician's Code* (Fox, 1997). "All I liked about [*Making the Band* and *Pop Idols*] was the audition process," Darnell told *People* magazine. "So when Simon Fuller came in here with what was really just one big audition, that intrigued me—making it like *Survivor* meets singing." Darnell's instincts proved correct. *American Idol* (Fox, 2002–present) soon became Fox's cash cow.

Each season of *American Idol* begins with a massive open audition, where tens of thousands of young, unknown singers try to make an impression on judges by singing one a capella selection. This portion of the show, which lasts several episodes, is an irresistible lure to TV viewers, as there are always several excellent vocalists along with numerous incredibly bad or bizarre singers, some of whom are truly funny (and some of whom seem to be media-jamming performance artists). While seducing viewers with these fascinating car-wreck performances, the show also establishes narratives for the better singers, showing their families and briefly interviewing them, creating viewer loyalty for the hopefuls. One hundred promising singers then advance to Hollywood where they go through several formal auditions to whittle down the assembly to thirty-two singers. They then get divided into smaller groups and get a chance to perform solo songs on TV for home viewers who can vote by telephone for their favorites, eventually narrowing the group to ten (in season one) or twelve (in subsequent seasons) finalists.

These singers then perform every week with home viewers voting for their favorites. The singer with the least votes is eliminated each week until one is crowned the American Idol, a title that comes with a record contract and a powerful hype machine (Clive Davis, apparently unburned by O-Town, is involved in the postshow phase of the winner's career).

The show's hook is that the contestants must face a tribunal of judges. One of the adjudicators is late-1980s pop star/choreographer/Laker Girl Paula Abdul, who draws upon her cheerleading experience to cheerily offer positive platitudes after even the most pitiful performances. Another judge is record producer/songwriter/session musician/former Journey bassist Randy Jackson (not to be confused with Michael's youngest brother or with 1980s metal band Zebra's frontman) who provides affirmations and criticisms in a surfer dude/faux hip-hop patois that makes Beavis and Butt-head seem articulate. So the actual critiques are left to the third referee, Simon Cowell, an English music executive who oversaw hit British boy bands Westlife and Five, as well as a sea of pop acts that included an all-puppet novelty group. The metrosexual Cowell, a Tony Blair/Oscar Wilde hybrid, unleashes snap queen insults on the contestants ("If you lived two thousand years ago and sang like that they would have stoned you") ably filling his role of painful truth teller and becoming the mean-spirited star of the show. One interesting aspect about the judges is that after they stock the initial talent pool (a significant task—the first season they chose only pretty people, which made for blander shows than when they chose fatter, geekier, odder folks in later years) their judgments are nonbinding. They comment after each performance, but the phone-in votes from viewers are the sole basis of advancements; Cowell and company have no actual say other than what they actually say.

American Idol became Fox TV's biggest hit, and one of the most popular shows in international television history. The final episode of *American Idol's* second season, the face-off between the finalists Ruben Studdard and Clay Aiken, drew nearly forty million viewers. A staggering sixty-five million votes were cast in the 2004 *American Idol* finale. Fox averages $100 million profit per season on the show, and RCA/J Records (white winners' CDs are released on RCA, black winners on RCA subsidiary J) also fared well, with season one and two winners Kelly Clarkson and Ruben Studdard, and season two runner-up Clay Aiken, averaging sales of two million copies for their debut CDs. (At this writing season three winner Fantasia Barrino's CD has just gone platinum, and her single debuted at number one.) With its American franchise as its anchor (albums by U.S. winners and runners-up have outsold those of England's original *Pop Idol* winners), the show has yielded more than twenty international spin-offs (yes, there is a *Kazakhstan Idol*) and has earned billions of dollars worldwide.

Courtesy Jake Austen

Not bad for a televised amateur talent contest. Though *Idol's* success may make it seem like a groundbreaking show, in fact it is a continuation of one of the oldest genres on TV. In the 1940s *Original Amateur Hour* and *Arthur Godfrey's Talent Scouts* (both of which had lengthy radio tenures preceding their TV incarnations) were popular programs. Other early shows that featured amateur pop singers included *Doorway to Fame* (Dumont, 1947–1949), *Paul Whiteman's TV Teen Club* (ABC, 1949–1952), *Talent Jackpot* (1949, Dumont), *The Horace Heidt Show* (CBS, 1950–1951), *Lights, Camera, Action* (1950, NBC), and *Chance of a Lifetime* (ABC, 1952–1953, 1956; Dumont 1953–1955). Each of these was similar to *American Idol*; most used the panel of evaluating experts, and some (notably the very popular *Original Amateur Hour*) featured home viewers voting for the winners. Over the ensuing decades this model continued with shows like *Dick Clark's World of Talent* (ABC, 1959), *It's Happening* (ABC, 1968), *Star Search* (syndicated,

1983–1995; CBS, 2003–2004), *Big Break* (syndicated, 1990), *The Cut* (MTV, 1998–1999), and *Fame* (NBC, 2003).

TV amateur talent searches haven't been limited to pop music. Country music stars have been sought on several shows, including *Talent Varieties* (ABC, 1955), *You Can Be a Star* (Nashville Network, 1983–1989, 1991–1992), *Charlie Daniels Talent Roundup* (Nashville Network, 1994–1996), and *Nashville Star* (USA, 2003–present). There have been a few gospel talent searches on Christian networks, most recently *Gifted* (TBN, 2004). *The Road to Stardom with Missy Elliot* (UPN, 2005) sought out an unknown hip-hop talent. Even high-culture musicians received the *American Idol* treatment back in TV's formative days with *Metropolitan Opera Auditions of the Air* (ABC, 1952).

There have also been numerous variations on this simple theme over the years. On *Talent Patrol* (ABC, 1953–1955) gifted military personnel competed for a five-day pass and a date with a pretty girl. On *Showcase '68* (NBC, 1968) young musicians, still unknown but already with record contracts, had a panel of experts vote on their potential for success (the winners, Sly and the Family Stone, already had a single on the charts by the time the series ended). *You Write the Songs* (syndicated, 1986–1987) showcased amateur songwriters instead of singers, and *Puttin' on the Hits* (syndicated, 1985–1988) and *Lip Service* (MTV, 1992–1994) actually rewarded talented lip-synchers.

But despite dozens of offerings in the last half-century, some very successful, none has matched *American Idol*. Many factors contribute to the show's popularity, including Simon's bitchiness, the program's hypnotizing shiny glitz, the clever manipulative design of the early episodes, the appeal of the individual contestants (ratings were highest when the show featured Studdard and Aiken, two performers who quickly developed loyal fan bases), and the instant satisfaction of an empowering democratic process (keep in mind that this show emerged in the wake of 2000's drawn-out, flawed, contested presidential election). But there are two main reasons for *American Idol*'s phenomenal impact.

Every reality show intentionally exposes production methods, and the home viewers are often more aware of the show's direction than the on-screen participants. This allows the audience to feel in the loop and intimately involved. *American Idol* takes this feeling to a whole new level, not merely because of the interactive voting process, but more importantly, because we sit in the same chairs as the stars of the show, Simon, Paula and Randy. As they see the performances unfold so do we, and as Paula and Randy make so overtly clear with their inarticulate assessments, we are just as qualified as they are to pass judgment. Despite being an amateur contest, *American Idol* doesn't really invite the home viewers to feel like we are the ones onstage; most of us know we don't sing that well. Instead, it directs us to have opinions about the performers and then, via the show's structural presentation of punditry, validates our position as appraisers, making us feel like a crucial element of the program whether we vote or not.

The other secret ingredient to *American Idol*'s success is its offering of gentle, edgeless, family-friendly fare in an age of harsh, offensive, narrowcast fare (a media atmosphere heavily influenced by Fox's pre–*American Idol* offerings). At a time when the TV powers that be assume teens respond to obscene rap music, raging hard rock, and oversexed teen icons, *American Idol* presents clean-cut kids performing pop standards with lush orchestration. It is a rejection of decades of rockin' teenage pop culture and influence, and a return to the vanilla pop era that preceded rock 'n' roll. "Rock and hip-hop," Clive Davis offered, "have been ignoring the traditions of great entertainment and the values of songs well sung." And apparently, the rock and hip-hop generations, having never experienced this "tradition of great entertainment," saw it as a revelation—and their parents and grandparents, excited to see young people singing Sedaka, Carpenters, John Lennon, Gershwin, and (in the wake of Gulf War II) a lot of Francis Scott Key, hopped aboard as well.

The secret of *American Idol* is not that it conceptually references 1940s TV favorites *Talent Scouts* and *Original Amateur Hour*, but more importantly that it aesthetically nods to 1940s TV favorites *The Perry Como Show* and *Your Hit Parade*, which hypnotized their audiences with bland, pleasant performances. One fascinating aspect of the show is that, assuming that rock 'n' roll is a rawer, more aggressive form of popular music than the vanilla pop it usurped, *American Idol* becomes progressively less rock 'n' roll during the course of each season. The first round of auditions has the would-be idols singing without musical backing, and this is the most riveting part of the process, with the bad singers seeming wild and the strong singers presented in a naked manner that evokes street corner doo-wop, or even singing in the mirror at home while fantasizing about rock stardom. These performances, terrible or triumphant, bubble with energetic youthful ambition and (sometimes delusional) cockiness that has a relationship to the rock 'n' roll energy of young Elvis Presley letting loose (even if they are singing Celine Dion songs).

In the first two seasons, after open auditions yielded a crop of hopefuls, the next round had the singers accompanied by a versatile pianist. While this, to a degree, could transform a rock aesthetic into a lounge act sensibility, there was still a stripped-down power to the performances. If the singer requested it the accompanist even unleashed barrelhouse pounding (though after one such performance the tribunal chided the singer for attempting upbeat material with only a piano). In the third season a small, tight live band accompanied the second-round singers, also adding a jolt of energy to the performances. However, after the next round of dismissals, all subsequent singer-survivors are backed by a fully orchestrated prerecorded karaoke track complete with ridiculous backup singers. While I'm sure the top arrangers and session musicians in Hollywood were laying down these tracks, it would be an understatement to call the musical backing uninspired. Thus, if any of the *American Idol* contestants want to represent the youthful, electric, sexual energy of rock 'n' roll, as opposed to the safe maturity of the adult contemporary genre, they are required to transcend the "band" they are fronting. And few seem to want to do this.

The hokey nature of the arrangements and performances often puts the acerbic Cowell at odds with the show. One of his biggest insults is to tell a singer that his or her performance is like the entertainment on a cruise ship or at an amusement park. However, the ensemble of finalists regularly performs silly group songs on the show; they sing in unison, not harmony, and strut into the audience to shake hands with the fans. Those productions are so akin to an amusement park stage show that you can almost smell cotton candy while you watch them. Of course, Simon, despite his jabs, fully appreciates that the nature of the show is to find the most talented, marketable performer who fits perfectly into the toothless world of mature, cross-generational pop. Though he occasionally can't hide his disdain for the performers who conform with the least resistance to the show's culture of image manipulation and clichés (he once mocked a Marine for getting his hair frosted, despite the fact that the hair-care company that sponsored the show clearly required all contestants to get makeovers), he knows as well as anyone that the controlled corniness of *American Idol* is its magic formula.

Perhaps the most interesting story to come out of *American Idol* is the one that evolved beyond, and eventually outside of, the producers' designs. William Hung, a Chinese American Berkeley student, appeared on an early audition episode of season three. He sang an a cappella version of Ricky Martin's ridiculous sex song "She Bangs" in a comically flat, off-key voice, accompanied by bizarrely stiff dance moves. His ostensibly terrible performance was enhanced by his geekish appearance, with his clothes and haircut recalling the characters from the *Revenge of the Nerds* movies. While the befuddled and bemused judges initially began insulting him (Simon: "You can't sing, you can't dance, so what do you want me to say?"),

William Hung. Courtesy Jake Austen

Hung won them over with his affirmation, "I already gave my best, and I have no regrets at all" and his absurdist declaration "I have no professional training of singing."

While *American Idol* had exploited the "bad" singers on the show before, William Hung was different. They created a special episode called *American Idol: Uncut, Uncensored, Untalented* to bring back Hung and some other notable misfits. Because his famous performance was a cappella, amateur DJs and sound engineers began to make mash-ups that appeared online, marrying Hung's singing with famous recordings (a mash-up is a hybrid of two well-known recordings, the most famous being *The Grey Album* which laid Jay-Z's raps over Beatles music). Hung got a record deal and a TV special by MTV's rival Fuse network (working with Koch records). *American Idol*, notorious for holding its participants to iron-clad management contracts, wanted nothing to do with this endeavor, going so far as to muscle Koch into changing the title of the CD from *Real Idol*. Perhaps the

American Idol franchise should have been more open minded: The CD (retitled *Inspiration*) debuted in the Top Forty, sold nearly 400,000 copies (more than doubling the sales of *American Idol* first-season runner-up Justin Guarini), and featured several popular legal downloads.

Hung spent the rest of the year touring and making promotional appearances at race tracks, day camps, and baseball games. When he sang "Take Me Out to the Ball Game" at a Toronto Blue Jays game, there were more media representatives on hand than there had been on opening day. The Los Angeles Dodgers attempted to use Hung as their mascot, but Hung refused to allow his singing image to appear on the scoreboard when he learned he would not be paid (it wasn't exactly an honor: the Dodgers' neighbors, the Anaheim Angels, used a monkey in a similar capacity). Hung made a hero's return to his childhood home of Hong Kong, where he played a charity concert and filmed a comedy movie. His success even inspired a new show, *Superstar USA* (WB, 2004), a parody/prank version of *American Idol* designed to discover the next William Hung (amazingly, even a talent-show parody was an idea revived from early TV, as NBC had aired *Henry Morgan's Great Talent Hunt* in 1951). Bizarrely, unlike the *Popstars* and *Making the Band* alumni, William Hung was a star.

Hung's act is nothing new. There have been numerous performers who have made notable recordings despite possessing less than perfect singing ability. But unlike infamous "outsider" musicians such as the Shaggs, Wild Man Fischer, and Wesley Willis, whose cracking vocals match the discordant sensibilities of their songwriting (invoking the musical equivalent of the mutterings of a mentally ill street person), Hung sings covers of well-known songs. Thus, his music may be challenging to the ear, but the content doesn't challenge the listener to think about anything beyond how funny it is to hear bad singing. While pundits expressed outrage at Hung getting a record contract (Chuck D said it was a musical insult, but was still amused enough to highlight Hung's music on his Air America radio show), his recording career has very specific precedents.

Florence Foster Jenkins was a socialite who self-financed a career as a chamber music "diva" in the 1940s, singing operatic arias in a weak voice handicapped by a tin ear. Jenkins held numerous recitals, drawing an enthusiastic crowd of novelty opera music fans (a previously untapped demographic), culminating in a sold-out Carnegie Hall concert. Her recordings for RCA were popular at the time and are still in print. Several decades later, fifty-nine-year-old Elva Connes Miller made the *Billboard* charts and sold more than a quarter of a million LPs. As Mrs. Miller she sang pop hits of the day in a squeaky, off-key voice, shifting tempos mid-song in a way that suggested a record player powered by a tiring rodent on a hamster wheel. The novelty of a frumpy, older woman singing Beatles and Petula Clark tunes in a bizarre voice was a winner and for several months in 1966 Miller appeared on every major TV show, charming Johnny Carson, Ed Sullivan, and others with her unique gifts.

These are the foremothers of William Hung, and it is significant that both of them were frumpy women. To laugh at them involves taking a position of superiority (which would be more difficult if they were more attractive than you), and Hung is presented to the TV audience as inferior in every way. Certainly his singing and dancing are vastly worse than the *American Idol* finalists, but a masculine, handsome, white man who sounded and moved identically to Hung would not gain an audience. For the joke to be funny Hung has to be emasculated before he sings his first sour note about sexual conquest.

Hung's groundbreaking performance played on both the contemporary stereotype of nerdy Asians who may overachieve academically (he is repeatedly identified as an engineering student), but are awkward socially. However, it also brought to mind older, more vicious stereotypes. With his puffy, slanted eyes and buck teeth Hung looks like a 1940s cartoonist's caricature of an Asian, and this look was part of his appeal. This kind of racial caricature implies that nonwhites are inferior, even that they are not quite human. This is the basis of Hung's wacky absurdity: how can an obvious "inferior" consider himself a candidate to become an iconic American superstar?

In a broad sense, that question applies to the hundreds of sour-singing wannabes who populate the funny audition episodes of reality music shows. While most people have a hard time being objective about the quality of their own work and few have the ability to see themselves as others see them, the delusions of these contestants run deeper. Phil Milstein oversees the American Song-Poem Music Archives, which documents an industry that, like *American Idol* audition episodes, exploits such delusions. Song-Poems are a scam in which people pay money to have their poems set to music with promises of fame and fortune. Usually the people who fall for this grift are innocents who compose awkward, graceless, bizarrely bad verse that they believe is high-quality poetry. "It's a psychological condition," Milstein explains, "that is like an anorexic looking in the mirror and seeing a fat person. The mirror lies, and with these people blinded by the promise of fame it's a real funhouse mirror effect, distorting their sense of rational perspective. Often it is caused by what others are telling them filtered through an extreme amount of wishful thinking." Like the scam artists that egg on potential Song-Poem victims, the *American Idol* staff carefully chooses bad singers along with good ones, setting them up for ridicule by encouraging them to boldly face Simon and company (despite the way it is portrayed on TV, the *American Idol* hopefuls sing for screeners before they face the famous tribunal, which sits through less than 2 percent of all auditioners). Keith Beukelear, whose fey, squawky "Like a Virgin" was the centerpiece of the second season's auditions, recalled in *People* that the preliminary judges "said they liked my singing. No one told me I was bad until Simon." But despite the disingenuous maneuvering of these outcasts toward the TV screen, it is the singers' own delusions that get them to the initial audition, and this aspiration-beyond-reason attitude provides the nonrace card William Hung fans can play.

"I'm not famous for my sheer talent," William Hung told journalists upon the release of his album. "I'm famous because I inspire other people." The marketing of Hung's CD, while obviously about novelty, and less obviously about race, on the surface seems to be about Hung's ability to inspire others and the mighty power of his positive thinking. By repeating this mantra over and over, Hung's label, management and fans sidestep issues of exploitation, condescension, and racial prejudice. The central question with most outsider performers is: are they in on the joke? Though it is difficult to decode Hung's level of agency, perhaps a more relevant question is: who exactly is the joke on? While the goofy vocalist and the record-buying public are the most likely answers, *American Idol* itself is also a possibility. While Hung's success clearly demonstrates the massive power of *American Idol* exposure, it also throws into doubt the show's reputation as a perfectly calibrated money-making machine. Though Hung is a tribute to the show's influence, he is also a symbol that some things are beyond its control.

Another challenge to *American Idol*'s seamless image came in the form of accusations of racism that, unlike the inspiration-themed Hung phenomenon, did not have a built-in defense mechanism. On *American Idol*'s first season a talented African American singer, Tamyra Gray, placed fourth, behind the white Nikki McKibbin, an obviously weaker singer who exploited her biography of teen motherhood to get sympathy votes. It should be noted here that whatever rank a contestant finishes on the show, appearing on *American Idol* is a massive career boost for all participants, with tens of millions of people seeing the performers each week. Though only the winner is guaranteed the full force of the entertainment industry behind them, any *American Idol* contestant could have a career in music by exploiting the show's name, especially those with the humility to become working lounge singers, small-time musical theater performers, or, in the case of

McKibbin, a karaoke company owner. Famously the second-place winner of season two (Aiken) has become a more successful recording artist than the first-place winner (Studdard). And it is notable that the first-, second-, fourth-, and fifth-place contestants on season one, the first- through fourth-place contestants on season two, and, so far, both top finalists of season three, all received prominent recording contracts. So finishing fourth was no disaster for Gray. That being said, Gray's dismissal caused many black fans (including a brilliant professor I know) to label _American Idol_ (or at least its fans) as racist. Though _Idol_ is viewed in a far higher percentage of black homes than white homes, because the population of white Americans is substantially greater than that of black Americans, white voters are the majority of viewers. After one episode during the third season, when three black women (including eventual winner Fantasia Barrino), who certainly seemed to be the best singers in the competition, had received the fewest votes that week, Sir Elton John himself declared, "I find it incredibly racist."

This accusation demonstrates a total misunderstanding of the nature of teen idolhood. Despite _American Idol_ having a broad, cross-demographic audience, the actual voting skews toward teenagers. The success of the finalists is really based on the same formulas for success applied to rock 'n' roll since the music's birth. One of the misconceptions about early rock history is that white stars who either performed in styles informed by R&B and black gospel (like Elvis Presley) or who made sanitized versions of black hits (like Pat Boone) were villains who were ripping off black artists. Publishers who stole songs ripped off black artists, record labels that didn't pay ripped off black artists, but white artists who sang in a black style or did covers of black songs did not. Perhaps Little Richard would have sold a few more copies based on song quality alone if Presley and Boone hadn't recorded his tunes, but nothing was going to make Richard or Chuck Berry or Big Joe Turner, or even Jerry Lee Lewis, as big as Presley. They may have been more talented, but pop music isn't a meritocracy, it is pop—as in popular—and popularity in rock 'n' roll history has very often been based solely on whether or not little girls think a singer is cute. Deeming someone cute isn't a hiring preference or a school segregation situation, it is a primal feeling. And this decision can be based on race without being racist.

Even when these preferences are based on ugly reality, that doesn't necessarily reflect on the artist or the genuineness of the attraction. If a little white girl likes Pat Boone more than she likes Little Richard because she is fundamentally more attracted to someone who reminds her of her dad, that's OK. If she is fundamentally attracted to someone who reminds her of her dad because she was molested at home, that's awful, but it doesn't reflect poorly on Boone. If a white girl doesn't dig Chuck Berry because she is racist that is a bad thing, but even the most love-thy-brother, righteous, open-minded youngster in the world can still find Elvis sexier than Chuck Berry . . . Elvis *was* sexier than Chuck Berry! Thus, when little white girls find certain white *American Idol* boys dreamy, or see certain white *American Idol* girls as pretty role models/fantasy best friends, that's not racist—it's just silly, instinctual, and a devaluation of talent. If there's any election where you should be allowed to make a silly decision without censure, I think the *American Idol* determination qualifies. And clearly white kids often do find black artists attractive and appealing, as evidenced by the fact that two out of the first three American Idols have been African American.

So, while racism is certainly a value that much of mainstream America shared during the 1940s and 1950s, it isn't one of the values for which *American Idol* revived nostalgia. On the contrary, *American Idol* re-imagines TV's bygone days of wholesome, bland, family viewing as a multicultural celebration where blacks, whites, Latinos and Polynesians can work together to create a more soulful, yet just as safe, army of Perry Comos.

While *American Idol* was returning viewers to the Eisenhower era, MTV decided to use the reality boom to push the limits of TV beyond its own usual pseudo cutting edge. Its music-themed reality programs would collectively harmonize violence, scatology, obscene excess, minstrelsy, and elective mutilation into a bizarre, hypnotic song that kept the channel a must-see destination for young viewers. Despite its best efforts, though, MTV often found itself producing retro shows—tributes to 1950s family values dressed up in nose rings and tattoos. But, ultimately they were able to produce some programming that was jarring even by reality TV standards.

MTV had launched the modern reality boom with its nonmusical series *The Real World*. However, when network TV followed *The Real World*'s lead, MTV responded with a slew of reality shows that would be more "branded" to its music-network image by sticking with music themes. Its biggest hit was *The Osbournes* (MTV, 2002–2005), a reality show edited as a sitcom (with reels and reels of tape, MTV's creative editors can craft footage to fit familiar models—*The Real World*, for example, is billed as a soap opera). In theory, *The Osbournes* is supposed to read as the obituary of domestic sitcoms. Just as aging musician Ozzie Nelson launched the genre in the 1950s, with his straitlaced, white-bread nuclear family, aging musician Ozzy Osbourne (the heavy-metal vocalist of Black Sabbath, infamous

The Osbournes. Courtesy Jake Austen

for orally decapitating small, flying creatures) came to bury the genre with his foul-mouthed, tattooed, substance-abusing brood.

But *The Osbournes* quickly became MTV's biggest hit precisely because it wasn't diametrically opposed to *The Adventures of Ozzie and Harriet*. Ozzy, like Ozzie, was a bit of a doddering chump (though years of drugs, booze, and over-medication caused the Ozz-man's genuine slow-wittedness, as opposed to the shrewd-in-real-life Nelson's calculated sucker act). Like Nelson, Osbourne came off as a bit of a fogey to his wisecracking kids (Ozzy would rather watch The History Channel than MTV). And like the TV Nelsons, the Osbourne matriarch was the real brains behind the family. Most importantly, what drew viewers in was the genuine love, affection, and loyalty the family demonstrated, theoretically a continuation of a hokey sitcom tradition, but functionally more organic and convincing than its predecessors.

Another way in which the Osbournes differed from the Nelsons was in their TV rock 'n' roll influence on the actual rock 'n' roll charts. When Ricky Nelson hit the recording studio he was a focused, determined musician whose subsequent hit records kept the show popular. When Ozzy's daughter Kelly Osbourne launched a recording career based on the program's popularity, fans of the show and the rock audience in general wanted nothing to do with it, and her surprisingly boring album (surprising because Kelly on the show seemed to have a good ear for what sucked) tanked.

The first season of *The Osbournes* was genuinely excellent, with Ozzy's mumbled expletives delivered with comic timing reminiscent of Richard Pryor's Mudbone character, and wife Sharon's shrill, English silliness providing genuine laughs. Their imperfect, doughy, immature teenage kids, Jack and Kelly, were original voices on TV, their smartass comebacks sounding more like Johnny Rotten than Eddie Haskell. And if all that weren't enough, the show featured dogshit jokes galore. Unfortunately, the following seasons were somewhat doomed. The first shows were shot before the family knew what it was like to be on reality TV. Subsequent tapings had the brood, now international celebrities, more self-conscious and less charming. The show also became self-reflective, as much of the content involved the kids' lives being affected by the show. Even as real-life problems weaved their way into the text of the episodes (Jack had to go into drug rehab, Sharon got cancer, Ozzy was in an ATV accident), the heart of the show felt less and less real and more and more like that of a regular network offering.

However, MTV was ready with replacements on the bench. *Newlyweds* (MTV, 2003–present) had a camera crew document hunky boy-band vocalist Nick Lachey of 98° and buxom pop singer Jessica Simpson as they entered married life. The comedy on the show gravitated around Midwestern regular guy Nick being flustered by his new bride's domestic incompetence (she had been living in hotels and tour buses since childhood). Simpson is supposed to come off as a hilarious airhead—as witnessed by Lachey's elaborate eye rolls—but those "Jessica moments" often have less to do with her intelligence than with the fact that she is a decade younger than Lachey. She's not a bimbo because she never heard of *Scarface* or *Raiders of the Lost Ark*, she just happened to be an infant when they came out. The moderate success of *Newlyweds* resulted in two other reality series, *The Ashlee Simpson Show* (MTV, 2004–present) about Jessica's little sister's entry into the music industry, and *'Til Death Do Us Part: Carmen and Dave* (MTV, 2004), a show following *Baywatch* babe Carmen Electra and her rock star fiancé Dave Navarro (Jane's Addiction, Red Hot Chili Peppers) as they prepare for their dream wedding.

None of these shows matched the quality of early episodes of *The Osbournes* (though the Simpson girls' shows influenced CD sales more than the Osbournes' show), but they all verified that there was a new vision for MTV programming. Since the network had launched its nonmusic video programming in 1986, the bulk of its series had been about the lifestyles (fantasy as well as reality) of young people meant to mirror the MTV audience. Shows like *Remote Control, Singled Out, Real World, Dead at 21* (MTV, 1994), MTV *Spring Break, Club* MTV, *Daria* (MTV, 1997–2001), *Road Rules* (MTV, 1996–present), *Love Line* (MTV, 1996–2000), *The Grind, Undressed, True Life, My So-Called Life* (ABC, 1994–1995; MTV, 1995), and even *Beavis and Butt-head* featured theoretically regular kids in their teens and early twenties, dating, dancing, playing, loving, hating, etc., always with a tangible sense of cool (or in the case of *Beavis and Butt-head*, uncool) that represented the rock 'n' roll lifestyle that MTV was all about. But the twenty-first century slate of MTV reality programming skewed in a different direction. Instead of documenting or manipulating the lives of regular teens, MTV's new focus was a presentation of the lifestyles of its music video stars.

The most straightforward of these shows is *Diary* (MTV, 1999–present), which MTV describes as "the first ever invitation into the life of an artist, narrated first-hand, directly into the camera . . . untraditional and uncut." Though not as groundbreaking as that description, the show, shot primarily by MTV producer/documentary filmmaker Jesse Ignjatovic with a single hand-held camera, is direct and raw enough to be riveting if the subject is interesting. "A lot of the inspiration for *Diary* is from the Bob Dylan movie *Don't Look Back*," Ignjatovic explained in the book *MTV Uncensored*. "I wanted to be like D. A. Pennebaker, just hang with this person for days and days and days. You get those moments when their guard is down . . . if anyone wants to know about Dylan at the time, you watch *Don't Look Back*. That's where you really get the idea of who this person is." One of the ideas you get from *Diary* is that Bow Wow, Mandy Moore, and Lindsay Lohan are no Bob Dylan.

The most blatant example of MTV's celebrity-worship reality programming is *Cribs* (MTV, 2000–present). Templates for this show include the legendary celebration of 1980s excess *Lifestyles of the Rich and Famous* (syndicated, 1984–1996; ABC, 1986) and the numerous home shows cropping up on Home and Garden and other cable networks. But by sticking exclusively with young musicians (and occasionally professional athletes), *Cribs* distanced itself from the other shows by focusing primarily on the nouveau riche, many of whom came from poverty. To understand what this show is really about, one need only visit Graceland.

Elvis Presley's Memphis mansion has been one of the top tourist sites in the world since it opened to the public in 1982. While a number of elements are memorable (gauche but stately paintings of Mr. Presley, three TVs installed side by side so the King could watch several football games simultaneously), one feature stands out from all others. The Jungle Room is a den filled with a massive, absurd set of heavily shellacked wooden furniture crudely carved in a pseudo-Polynesian motif.

It also features grass-like shag carpeting (on the ceiling as well as the floor), a waterfall, and ceramic jungle cats. Graceland tour guides always note that Presley bought all the furniture himself at a local store in less than thirty minutes. He was a huge star when he did this and huge stars are supposed to hire designers and decorators and end up with tasteful decor featuring custom-made imported furniture. That he did not do this spoke directly to his fans in a very specific, very American way. The American Dream encourages regular folk to fantasize things like, "If *I* had a million dollars I'd give Cadillacs to all my friends, buy a private plane with a king-size sex bed in the middle, or turn my living room into a tropical jungle." When Presley made it he followed through on all his tacky dreams.

When hip-hop became a billion-dollar business in the 1990s all of a sudden a multitude of rich young stars with ample money and a "keep it real" attitude complicated the idea of consultants. Ghetto-fabulous jungle rooms were now popping up all over the place and MTV was there to document them. Fans can watch the show with jealous eyes or sit in snappy judgment (easy to do when tackiness, such as Missy Elliot's aquarium couch, or tastelessness, like Outkast's stripper pole in the rec room, abounds). There is often a melancholy subtext to certain segments, as modestly successful musicians with uncertain futures gloat over homes and luxuries that seem certain to slip from their possession sooner rather than later. Rappers, with their huge jewelry collections and customized vehicles, are notorious for spending beyond their means, the most famous example being MC Hammer, who blew a massive fortune partly by overdoing his crib. The rap community, however, does not view Hammer's fall from grace as shameful. Living for the moment is a respected attitude, as indicated in Nelly's hit "Country Grammar," which lists as a career goal, "blow thirty million like I'm Hammer."

It was interesting (and inevitable) how *Cribs* became almost instantly formalized, and the idea of the reality show capturing something real became inconsequential. After several early subjects had magnums of Cristal champagne in their refrigerator and a DVD of *Scarface* prominently displayed, all subsequent subjects either made sure they followed suit or prepared some funny variation, or ironic comment, on the bubbly beverage and the bloody Pacino movie. Instead of giving us a snapshot of our icons' home lives we instead see a snapshot of how their home lives would be if they ever got to be on *Cribs*. Similarly, in MTV's reality series *FANatic* (MTV, 1998–2000), in which the number-one fan of an artist got to meet and hang out with the object of his or her obsession, it wasn't long before artists became less interested in the fans and more conscious of the show's format. This peaked when the Mary J. Blige episode featured Blige shopping for "a gift for my FANatic." The ultimate example of this unreality came in the second season of *The*

Osbournes. When it became obvious that Sharon's cancer scare would color the mood of the season, an appropriate new sibling was "cast." In addition to their crude biological kids, that season Ozzy and Sharon took in an adorable teenage hunk with cancer (the ploy failed; cancer boy didn't become a *Tiger Beat* cover story and despite plummeting ratings Kelly and Jack maintained their unlikely celebrity).

Of course one has no expectations of noninvasive, impartial ethnography on an MTV show about rock stars. And dishonest documentary not only has precedent, it also is in many ways the model for success. The most popular ethnographic film of the early twentieth century was the romanticized portrait of Inuit life *Nanook of the North* (1922). It was filmed on location in Quebec, but outside of that it was completely fake. Nanook's igloo was a Hollywood-style set, the producers cast Inuit women to play Nanook's wives, and "Nanook" was an actor named Allakariallak. In fact, the original print of *Nanook of the North* burned and the director Robert Flaherty had to return to Canada to restage his already staged scenes. The African giraffe hunt that was the centerpiece of John Marshall's *cinéma vérité* masterpiece *The Hunters* (1957) was engineered for the film. Michael Moore's *Roger & Me* (1989), which was at the time the most financially successful documentary ever (since superseded by Moore's later films), was based on a completely dishonest premise: that a busy CEO was an asshole because he wouldn't respond fondly to a scary looking film crew's ambush. What makes MTV's forays into deceptive reality interesting is that they embrace the falsehoods. A "Best Of" episode of *Cribs* featured a montage of disingenuous fridge innards; and the Osbournes have performed scripted versions of their disheveled Ozzie and Harriet shtick for various MTV functions (including a Christmas special and several awards shows) without regard for what such staged antics might do to the public's perception of their show's veracity.

Perhaps this has to do with the idea of audience hipness that MTV trades in. In an age when everyone is an insider and a pundit (Neilsen ratings are printed in newspapers, voters choose candidates based on electability, and everyone has opinions about the box office performances of blockbuster movies), MTV makes the viewers feel more in the game by revealing the man behind the curtain. Network shows like *Survivor*, *Big Brother* (CBS, 2000–present), and *Fear Factor* (NBC, 2001–present) do more to cover up anything that would make the viewers question the purity of the situation (since these shows involve substantial cash prizes they likely do this to avoid any shades of the 1950s game show scandals). But to be cool enough to want your MTV is to be above the suckers who confuse reality TV with reality (in fact, in 2003 MTV2 renamed the Lord's Day "Sucker Free Sunday").

But even if they are primed to question the veracity of reality shows, MTV viewers are willing to be suckers when it comes to star worship. MTV's celebration of celebrity lifestyle did not pull the plug on programming featuring regular young folks, but rather inspired series in which noncelebrities got a taste of the glamorous life. On *Pimp My Ride* (MTV, 2004–present) rapper Xzibit helps out teenagers burdened with shitty cars by taking their automobiles to West Coast Customs, the legendary auto shop that customizes the vehicles of rap stars, and then getting MTV to pay tens of thousands of dollars for hydraulics, chrome, custom rims, and an obligatory entertainment system with multiple TV screens, DVD players, and video game modules installed throughout the automobile. Though the entire body of the auto receives an overhaul, no mechanical work is ever done to the engine, so despite the owner's auto insurance increasing exponentially, his or her $30,000 vehicle will still drive like a hooptie. At each episode's conclusion we see the newly "pimped" ride being presented to the (usually white) teenager who then breaks into joyful Ebonics.

Becoming (MTV, 2001–2002) was a show in which fans could mimic rock stars by allowing MTV to give them makeovers and a modicum of professional training so that they could reenact their favorite music video as celebrity lookalikes. This silliness gave little indication of the lunacy to follow. Inspired by *Extreme Makeover* (ABC, 2002–present), MTV brought forth *I Want a Famous Face* (MTV, 2004–present), a program on which young people got plastic surgery so that they could look like their favorite star. The show, which documents both the gory surgery and the more disturbing psychological problems of the participants, has featured transformations from the moderate—a blond woman getting a boob job to enhance her resemblance to Britney Spears or an Elvis impersonator getting a chin implant to improve his career—to the insanely extreme. On the ultimate episode Jessica (née Michael), a pre-op transsexual, got breast and cheek implants, eyebrow bone shaving, and a lowered hairline to look like Jennifer Lopez. Though MTV made numerous statements that they were not paying for the operations and were merely documenting surgeries that were already planned, that didn't stop the American Society of Aesthetic Plastic Surgeons from denouncing the show as a dangerous misrepresentation of their profession, certain to inspire unwise surgeries. The fact that MTV sent out a casting call for a second season implies that they were aware the first season would influence further face wanters.

Of course, it was MTV productions that originally brought to screen the show that blurred the line between regular kid and rock star by making unknowns into icons before our eyes: *Making the Band*, the series that initiated TV rock 'n' roll reality programming. Fittingly, MTV also served up the program that seemed most likely to kill the genre, with its obnoxious cast, terrible music, and the most problematic ethnic representation in a field cluttered with racial-themed car wrecks.

While *Survivor*, *The Real World* and other staged reality shows (as opposed to the programs that are presumptively more legitimate documentaries, such as *Cops*) regularly feature black participants, they frequently seem uncomfortable and unhappy. On competition shows like *Survivor* and *Temptation Island* (Fox, 2001–2003), blacks are often the first eliminated. On the first season of *The Real World*, Kevin Powell, who would go on to become an eloquent cultural critic, was so enraged by what he perceived as active and passive racism from his housemates that his polemics became semicoherent, misogynist attacks. Comedian Dave Chapelle on his sketch-comedy program *Chapelle's Show* (Comedy Central, 2003–present) once posited that the reason black participants on these shows fare poorly is because they are put in a situation with a group of the craziest white people imaginable. Chapelle then presented a skit, *The Mad Real World*, which featured a reality show that has a Caucasian living with a group of the craziest black people imaginable. While the skit was funny, it was a little late, as MTV had already begun airing just such a program, but without any on-camera whites in principal roles.

Making the Band II (MTV, 2002–2004) was a glorious mess. Like the original show it featured a massive open audition to join a new act, with 40,000 wannabes trying out. Unlike the original, which resulted in a pop boy band, this would create a hip-hop act for Sean "P. Diddy" Combs's Bad Boy Records label, with Combs overseeing the act's career. Also differing from the original show, which whittled down the prospects to a handful of very motivated pretty boys, *Making the Band II* culminated in the formation of the laziest, homeliest, most dysfunctional band ever to show up on TV, or as Renee Graham in the *Boston Globe* dubbed them, "The Gang That Couldn't Rap Straight."

The harshest of all reality shows (*Black Beat* magazine said it made "*Survivor* look like *Sesame Street*"), *Making the Band II* assembled six acne-ridden, immature, disheveled black youths and set out to turn them into a hit rap group called Da Band. This proved difficult as the members had a penchant for disappearing, leaving to hang out with friends, and missing planes, resulting in a show that rarely had the whole cast together at any given time. Strangely uninterested in cashing in on their golden opportunity, the wannabe stars seemed bent on reviving the

1930s black screen stereotype of the shiftless Stepin Fetchit/Willie Best "Sleep 'n' Eat" character (one band member actually falls asleep sucking his thumb during Combs's lecture on laziness).

This uncomfortable racial representation is made more troublesome because, unlike the black-cast UPN comedies or *Soul Train*, more whites than blacks watched *Making the Band II*. As a mainstay on MTV and MTV2, the show obviously sought to appeal to the network's core demographic, and even if it drew the largest black audience of any MTV show it would still have overwhelmingly white viewership. This is significant because to say this show presents problematic images of black life would be a ridiculous understatement. In contrast to shows like *The Real World* where a light slap to the face is the basis for an immediate eviction, on this show the participants constantly had genuinely violent fistfights. One fight came about because a cast member teased his bandmate about being functionally illiterate. One bandmate could participate in the show only after Combs pleaded with his parole board. The band members mumbled profanities as their main mode of communication (one parental-watch Web site counted seventy-two obscenities, most of them bleeped, on one half-hour show). Band members talked on cell phones constantly, even during events that they knew would be used in the show. During auditions one teenage female rapper left when she found out she was pregnant. Another auditioning rapper left because her sister's body was discovered dismembered (to make her horror worse, when she returned to the show after the funeral she was cut from the band). Shani Saxon, music editor of *Vibe* magazine, told the *New York Times* that she feared *Making The Band II* suggested "all young black people live lives filled with murder, family problems, and legal issues." As the third season ended with Combs disbanding (or un-making) Da Band, he expressed disappointment in the way the show constantly demonstrated the worst stereotypes about the hip-hop generation.

If embarrassing stereotypes were the show's only crime that would be bad, but *Making the Band II*'s main offense was that other than the guilty pleasure one might derive from watching poor behavior, the show was boring. Bad Boy as a label is known for valuing unusual rap voices, with the distinct marble-mouthed flow of Biggie Smalls being the label's artistic high point and the mumbling monotone of Mase being one of Bad Boy's biggest commercial successes. So for Da Band P. Diddy chose rappers based on their vocal quality instead of looks or personality. *Real World*, *Survivor*, and other such shows know that casting shameless extroverts is the way to guarantee riveting TV. But half the cast of *Making the Band II* was sleepy-eyed and quiet. These kids displayed the remarkable aptitude for break-

Da Band. Courtesy Jake Austen

ing into spontaneous fistfights while simultaneously showing no emotions. The "villain" of the show, Dylan (pronounced "Die-Lon," for no particular reason), never acts sad, happy, angry, or reflective as he faces prison time, acts treacherously toward his bandmates, even when he gets kicked off the show.

And to complicate the bad casting, the editing doesn't even manipulate Dylan to be the sole villain. The most successful reality shows cast one member as a rogue, giving the audience a character to latch on to, booing with glee at the obnoxious Puck on the third season of *The Real World* and the two-faced Omarosa on *The Apprentice* (NBC, 2004–present). On *Making the Band II* all the characters were villains at some point. One show would focus on how the lying Dylan was the main force jeopardizing the band. Another show has Chopper's pathologically disrespectful treatment of a bandmate jeopardizing the act's success. On another, the diva attitude of R&B vocalist Sara, the nonrapper of the group, jeopardizes the group's future. Despite being monotonous, this also resulted in a show where the ultimate failure of the protagonists was guaranteed, and everyone watching knew not to become too invested in Da Band because they were certain to break up. Thus, being on TV actually hurt the prospects of this act, as each week's show was an anticommercial for their CD, telling viewers not to buy it. Viewers were discouraged by the dysfunction but also by the music. The feuding rappers were poor collaborators, resulting in awkward tracks with too many rappers hurling incongruous rhymes in too many styles. Despite Fred's declaration that "we the new Beatles, hip-hop version," Da Band's debut CD sold modestly, with no hit singles and not even a popular video (this is remarkable considering that MTV/Viacom was rooting for its success).

Conventional logic suggests that *Making the Band II* should have put some nails in the reality rock 'n' roll TV coffin. Formally it was unable to maintain the quality of other successful reality shows, becoming a redundant loop of dysfunction with no real developments or surprises. As a launching pad for a successful musical act, a rap Monkees, it was a complete bust. The show's ratings were decent enough for a cable channel, but any plusses in that column had to be weighed against the minuses in the music column, where Da Band failed to make money for their label, disappointed a reeling music industry in need of new hit acts, and were an embarrassment to Mr. Combs, one of MTV's biggest stars. Most significantly, *Making the Band II* put the audience in an uncomfortable position. Musical reality TV has thrived when the viewers feel like pundits and judges, but this interactivity always seemed to operate within the context of the producers' master plan. On this show viewers were confounded by the counterintuitive moves that seemed to guarantee Da Band's—and the show's—failure. Everyone who watched knew from the beginning how it would end, so how could anyone investing time, money, and effort into this act *not* know? Surely Viacom would never attempt to cast another band using this same model. If these were the results of TV producers doing their best, then maybe the rock 'n' roll reality train was getting closer to its last stop.

But the combination of inexpensive production and the prospect of big hype has that train chugging along singing "I think I can, I think I can" to the funky beat. As this book goes to press Combs is casting *Making the Band III* and MTV's sister station VH1 has launched a new *Partridge Family*, with the casting process shot as a reality series. As ridiculous as those ideas are, two series proposed for next season seem hell-bent on resulting in groups that will be such commercial failures that they may actually make Da Band look like the Beatles. *Rock Star* (scheduled for CBS, 2005), from reality guru Mark Burnett (*Survivor*, *The Apprentice*), insanely proposes to be a rock version of *American Idol*; the purpose is to find a rock vocalist who will become the new frontman (or frontwoman) of INXS. Putting aside the fact that this implies that the 1980s act INXS would be commercially viable if they were still active (somewhat doubtful), this is a show that will constantly be haunted by the gruesome, depressing suicide (by hanging) of original vocalist Michael Hutchence. Not to be outdone, Fox has announced a deal with the R&B

group TLC to produce an audition show to find a new "L" to replace Lisa "Left Eye" Lopes, the wild rapper of the group who was killed in an auto accident. This is despite prominent promises by surviving members that they would never replace Lopes. This show, with its subtexts of morbidity, disloyalty, and tactless opportunism, dismisses the wholesome vintage vibe of *American Idol*, returning Fox to its earlier reality days of animals attacking and aliens being autopsied. And perhaps that's how it should be. TV rock has always thrived when the big beat of the music basks in the cathode ray glow of TV's crass, commercial dishonesty.

The most successful musical reality shows, just like the rocking performances on *The Ed Sullivan Show* of more than forty years ago, are designed to elicit the maximum response from the hyped-up, hormone-driven teenagers who are the rocket fuel in the gas tank of rock 'n' roll. Perhaps these responses are the result of contrived, manipulative methods designed in boardrooms by businessmen who wouldn't know real rock if it hit them in the noggin. But that's OK. As long as the enthusiastic responses are real (and with twelve-year-olds, all enthusiastic responses are real) it doesn't matter how you elicit them. In the end, no matter how dreadful, unnatural, and doomed the new INXS is, that will be OK, too. To slightly misquote Twisted Sister, you can't stop TV rock 'n' roll.

10

Michael Jackson

Chronicle of a Life on TV

Over the course of his four decades in show business, Michael Jackson has undertaken the ultimate TV rock journey. He caught the tail end of Ed Sullivan's reign, visited *American Bandstand* as it hit middle-age, and helped the *Soul Train* pull out of the station. He was a cartoon rock star and a fixture on 1970s variety shows. When the MTV revolution began he was the key revolutionary. As for reality TV, over the last fifteen years every time he has appeared on TV unscripted, from the Video Music Awards to *60 Minutes* to Court TV, the spectacle has been more surreal and challenging than any fabricated reality show could hope to be.

Jackson's life story is fascinating in part because he grew up on TV. Our cathode ray–damaged eyes watched him go from an adorable child to an awkward but dazzling adolescent to a highly unusual and troubled man pushing fifty. In the meanwhile, there has been a staggering amount of written coverage celebrating, analyzing, denigrating, damning, and defending Michael. But happily for this post-literate era, fans and voyeurs have never really had to do any actual reading to follow Jackson's long, complicated story, which has been rife with triumphs, tragedies, and Terpsichore. The entire drama has played itself out on TV, but for those of you who are not prepared to track down hundreds of hours of footage, the following is a chronicle of Jackson's made-for-TV life.

1969

On August 22, 1969, the Jackson 5ive, a fresh act at Motown, but already chitlin circuit veterans with a half-decade of entertaining behind them, made their national TV debut on the syndicated Miss Black America pageant. Fronted by the bold Michael Jackson (still a week shy of his eleventh birthday) they were certainly excited to perform in front of the cameras, but the challenge didn't phase them. The previous year the Gary, Indiana, family act had appeared on a local Chicago teen show, Swingin' Majority (WCIU, 1967–1968), performing their pre-Motown single "Big Boy." Shortly thereafter they had a chance at a national TV spot, but skipped that trip to New York when they got an opportunity to shoot a program for a far smaller, but profoundly more important, audience. The audition film they shot in Motown's Detroit offices featured little Michael singing James Brown's "I Got the Feeling" in a raw, powerful, voice accompanied by his dynamic dance moves (and his brothers' clumsy funk grooves). The film went immediately to the label's chief, Berry Gordy, in L.A. for viewing. Gordy quickly signed the boys to a recording contract. Soon after recording an excellent debut album for that legendary label the Jackson 5ive found themselves performing in front of an all-black crowd at a televised beauty pageant.

No black woman had ever made it to the finals of the Miss America contest, a fact that suggested to African American entrepreneurs that beauty contests needed their own version of a Negro League. Launched modestly (and untelevised) a year earlier, Miss Black America was an ambitious affair as it entered its sophomore year. Helmed by East Coast DJ/promoter Hal Jackson and featuring black superstars Stevie Wonder, the Impressions, and James Cleveland as guests, the show wasn't looking for more performers. But when Gordy called and suggested the show give a new group a break, Hal Jackson wisely listened. Despite the many beauties that graced the stage that night, it was the Jackson brothers (and nonbrother band members Johnny Jackson on drums and Ronny Rancifer on keyboards) that captured the most attention.

One of Motown's secrets of success was that its artists, primarily from poor, urban black backgrounds, went through training regiments that included charm school and sophisticated choreography lessons. This resulted in a cadre of R&B singers who brought an air of class and sophistication to music that had juke-joint roots. When the Jacksons appeared on this program they had obviously not yet completed their lessons. They were still a raw, imperfect, spare, sloppy unit. Yes, they were super-funky, but their jamming was the antithesis of slick. Johnny pounded a brutal beat, supported by the unornamented bass playing of fourteen-year-old Jermaine Jackson and the sparse guitar work of fifteen-year-old Tito Jackson. Singing harmony was eighteen-year old Jackie Jackson, and doing his best to keep up with the singing and dancing was twelve-year old Marlon Jackson. They performed the Isley Brothers' "It's Your Thing" as if they were rocking a nightclub after hours, and the crowd, an older black audience (parents of the contestants?), responded as if they were in their favorite watering hole. They reacted not with teenybopper squeals but with the kind of applause, smiles, and attention that have to be earned. Although no one in that auditorium had probably ever heard of these boys, they respected the young brothers, and when Michael, commanding the stage with moves reminiscent of James Brown, Al Green, and a teenage go-go dancer, requested, "C'mon now, why don't you give me some of that soul clap," the audience responded with funky, double-time clapping. Despite Michael's unbridled energy, the mid-tempo groove of the song, combined with the rudimentary skills of the instrumentalists, resulted in a mellow, cool vibe, perfect for the church-like call and response Michael initiated with the receptive crowd. The years Joe Jackson had spent making arrangements for his underage brood to play late-night club gigs were paying off, as this nightclub-frequenting crowd (cool dudes were wearing sunglasses and smoking cigars in the audience) understood that these boys were the real thing. The Jackson 5ive would have far more important TV gigs in the near future, but the vibe they created with the crowd at their debut was a vital first step.

Since Miss Black America was aimed at a black audience, hardly anyone cites it as the Jackson 5ive's TV debut. Instead, their official national unveiling was on the October 18 episode of *Hollywood Palace*, titled "Motown at the Hollywood Palace," which also featured excellent performances from Stevie Wonder, the Supremes, and Gladys Knight and the Pips. But it was Motown's littlest, most dynamic star who stole the show (and I don't mean ventriloquist dummy Lester, though he and Willie Tyler did appear as well).

Many people could claim that they "discovered" the Jackson boys. Gordon Keith, who ran the Gary label Steeltown Records, had them under their first recording contract; Pervis Spann, a DJ at black radio powerhouse WVON, was an early champion; the Apollo Theater Amateur Night audience anointed them with applause as winners; Gladys Knight suggested that Motown should take a look at the act; and what finally led to their historic audition was Bobby Taylor's call to Motown after his group the Vancouvers (featuring Tommy Chong, of Cheech and Chong fame) played with the Jackson 5ive at Chicago's High Chaparral nightclub. All these people, and many others I'm sure, had something to do with the Jacksons getting where they got, but one person who had *nothing* to do with it was Diana Ross.

Despite that meddlesome historical fact, Gordy decided that the story of the Jackson 5ive should involve Diana Ross discovering them, which added major star power to their public introduction and was also good exposure for Ross, who was preparing to go solo. On *Hollywood Palace* emcee Ross came out and announced her new discovery, very pointedly speaking only of a single young man who, as a member of a family act, was a dynamic, brilliant young performer. This turned out to be the setup for a joke, as Sammy Davis, Jr., then emerged as if Ross were introducing him. But joke or not, it is notable that during the group's first major media appearance the introduction mentioned only Michael (Ross actually announced the group as "Michael and the Jackson 5ive").

After some joking between Ross and Davis, the boys took the stage in wide-lapelled fluorescent green-and-yellow leisure suits. Unlike the Miss Black America show, here the Jackson 5ive was backed by an orchestra, which made the group's raw instrumental sound undetectable (that gritty vibe was not a part of the group's official sound, as the boys didn't play their own instruments on their recordings, stepping aside for Motown's brilliant session musicians). Also, it was clear that their Motown etiquette lessons had kicked in, as their performance was perfect, with slick moves, confident stage presence, and professional banter. Michael, singing a set of songs culminating in their fantastic hit "I Want You Back," was a marvel. His steps paid tribute to generations of black dance while remaining stylish and original. And despite rejecting the smoky nightclub feel of the group's pre-Motown live performances, Michael's voice kept a soul edge, maintaining the imperfections that denote authenticity in funky black music.

But the *Hollywood Palace* appearance also introduced another element of Michael's performances—the blank, detached look in his eyes that contradicted his emotional singing and masterful moves. The eleven-year-old knew the right way to sing a love song, but not surprisingly, he had no idea what he was singing about.

When Ross and Davis came out to do a brief interview Michael again displayed behavior that called into question his seemingly mature stage magic. He barked banter between songs like a veteran during the set, but in conversation he became as stiff and awkward as any middle-school kid.

Diana then asked Michael to demonstrate his dance steps, noting that "if I do them I'll get arrested," and the band broke into James Brown's "There Was a Time," with Michael's bump-and-grind moves returning him from regular kid to onstage superstar. Sammy Davis, Jr., danced along with Michael, which was as close to an official welcome to big-time showbiz as there ever was. And if anyone had a doubt that the boys had arrived, their next TV appearance would prove it irrevocably.

On December 14 the Jackson 5ive made their debut on *The Ed Sullivan Show*. For any entertainer in the Sullivan era, such an appearance marked a career high point. And for an up-and-coming act, the quality of the performance could determine success or failure in the business. After a brief introduction by the zombie-like Sullivan ("Here are the Jackson 5ive, a sensational singing group . . ."), the boys took the stage.

First they did Sly and the Family Stone's "Stand," appropriate because Motown looked to Stone's act as a new model for crossover success. Earlier in the 1960s the label's plan to make its music cross from the R&B (black) charts to the pop (white) charts involved putting performers in suits and gowns and having them sing show tunes and standards in addition to brilliant Motown originals. But as the flower power era revealed, a new generation of blacks and whites were willing to get together under the peace-and-love banner without prodding, a fact made concrete by the success of Stone's ostentatiously interracial band. Like Stone, the Jackson 5ive featured dense musical production and wore eclectic, wild outfits. And they covered a *lot* of Stone songs.

On *The Ed Sullivan Show* their wardrobe was a remarkable nod to the diverse fashion dos of hippie-chic. Michael was dressed in a fringed purple suede vest and a fuscia pimp hat. Jermaine was dressed like a sensitive French poet, with an oversized brown cravat around his neck. The rest of the group was a flurry of paisley and giant collars. Technically, the show was a triumph. Motown acts had done well on Sullivan's show in the past, particularly the Supremes, with whom Sullivan was clearly enchanted. With Ross's endorsement (Sullivan repeated her Jackson 5ive creation myth when he introduced her in the audience), this act was given the A-list treatment. The carefully blocked shots and perfect editing on the beats made the performance look spectacular. To achieve this, Sullivan's people placed the drummer and keyboard player offstage with the show's orchestra, creating a far stronger visual composition with just the straight line of brothers.

Visually the Jackson's act was distinct. Jackie, a tall man, had little Michael on one side and little Marlon on the other. Flanking that trio were two brothers of medium height: Jermaine, playing his bass, and Tito, playing his guitar. In this symmetrical constellation the brothers would display synchronized moves, with Michael frequently breaking out of the line for dance solos.

When they performed at the Miss Black America show, the Jackson 5ive had played for the same kind of black audience they were familiar with. On the *Hollywood Palace* they played for a white crowd, but from the comfort of an all-black revue, on a show assembled by their new (black) Motown family. But on *The Ed Sullivan Show* they were playing for whites on a white production, and they made the adjustment flawlessly. While the show worked hard to present them as harmless kids as opposed to threatening black men (Michael did some stage banter about meeting a girl at school in the sandbox, and Sullivan wished them "a very merry Christmas, get all the presents you want"), the group didn't pander much to the white crowd. Michael still had a lot to learn.

1970

The Jackson 5ive made several prominent TV appearances in 1970, including a return to Sullivan's stage in the spring and a rendition of the National Anthem at game one of the World Series in the fall. But the one program that defined their year, and cemented their position as pop icons, was the February 21 episode of Dick Clark's *American Bandstand*. Clark introduced the boys in glowing terms, after which they did a dynamic performance of "I Want You Back" in front of a mod set. Despite a younger studio audience than any of their previous TV appearances, the boys in many ways were performing their slick, athletic dance routine in a vacuum, as no crowd was visible or audible during their number (which was shot beautifully, with cinematic angles).

After their first song Clark came out to interview Michael, who (acting as band spokesman) introduced his brothers and then untruthfully presented Johnny and Ronnie as his cousins. He also told Clark that he was nine, although he was actually eleven. Along with the Diana Ross myth, Motown schooled Michael to say these things to enhance the band's appeal. In a way, this was harmless fiction, yet it is notable that an impressionable eleven-year-old's mentors were encouraging him to lie repeatedly. A more interesting exchange between Clark and the boys occurred when the emcee asked what musicians the band admired the most. Michael obviously was profoundly influenced by James Brown—the performer he most directly imitated—and had been intimately inspired by artists like Jackie Wilson and Etta James, for whom he opened during the Jacksons' early career. Yet he told the white host and white audience of this white show that he most dug the Beatles; Blood, Sweat and Tears; and Three Dog Night. Jermaine and Marlon echoed Michael's answer. Only Jackie and Tito cited black artists (the Delfonics and the Chi-Lites).

After the interview the boys performed "ABC" and a short medley ending with a James Brown tribute. But even as he paid homage to the godfather of soul, Michael was molding his performance in a very un–James Brown way for this audience. Forgoing the authentic moves that got him signed to Motown, Jackson opted for a series of Vegas-informed, showbiz hand gestures. The Motown polish was really starting to gleam and though Michael still had the blank eyes of a little boy who didn't understand the words to the ballads, and still spoke in interviews like a kid awkwardly reciting lines in a school play, he was already demonstrating a savvy sophistication for giving each audience what it wanted.

1971

While Clark's audience certainly enjoyed the performance, the boys' true fans— the kids who *breathed* Jackson 5ive—were teen and preteen black girls. "That was pretty profound for those days," Suzanne de Passe, the Motown executive who oversaw the Jackson 5ive's early career, told *Primetime Live* (ABC, 1989–1998) in 1995. "There had not yet been a young black group that created what was tantamount to Beatlemania." Of course Motown was the label that perfected pop crossover, so the majority of the Jackson 5ive's TV appearances and press photos avoided showing an all-black, screaming mob (not exactly a benign image in the early 1970s). However, one TV special not only captured this phenomenon beautifully, but also remains the greatest document of the Jackson 5ive as a live band.

On September 19 the Jackson 5ive's special, *Goin' Back to Indiana*, aired on ABC. The opening half of the show was basic comedy-variety hokum, with Bill Cosby playing Scoop Newsworthy, a reporter who encountered numerous snafus as he attempted to interview the band. Tommy Smothers was on hand as another Cosby foil, and Bobby Darin and a pregnant Diana Ross made cameos. Rounding out the cast were Rosey Grier, Bill Russell, Elvin Hayes, Elgin Baylor, and Ben Davidson portraying the "Dream Team," a massive basketball squad that the Jackson 5ive defeated in a ten-minute musical called "The Day Basketball Was Saved." Because of the Jacksons' youth, the network made a few production concessions to make the show appear hip, most notably Tito's race-car skit done with mod cardboard cutout props and psychedelic rear projection. But for the most part the Jacksons' first TV special was business as usual.

That is, until the special became a documentary about the boys' return to their home state for a concert. On May 29, 1971, the Jackson 5ive had played a concert in Indianapolis to a sold-out arena packed with a nearly all-black crowd.

Courtesy Jake Austen

Unlike the goofy footage that preceded it, this portion of the show was shot in a *cinéma vérité* style, following the boys from their plane to their car to the venue to the stage. As they deplaned the Jacksons met a sea of crying, screaming African American kids, ecstatic about seeing their heartthrobs. The mass of quivering adolescent energy then crowded around the young performers' car, ultimately chasing after the vehicle as it drove off. With these scenes the Jackson 5ive were anointed on TV as genuine instigators and beneficiaries of black Beatlemania.

The live footage that followed was remarkable. It looked more like a theatrical concert movie than a televised music show. On a formal level the concert was shot magnificently, drawing upon the *Monterey Pop* and *Woodstock* films in its use of multiple cameras, dramatic angles, and innovative play between the stage lights and the band. The best thing about the photography was that while it continuously cut from shot to shot to keep things exciting, nearly every shot was wide enough to see the whole visually thrilling band.

Wearing bizarre, eclectic rainbow-pastel superhero costumes (Michael's wardrobe appears to be made out of upholstery fabric) the band looked wild, but their performance was a perfect balance between rough and polished. This was an amazing moment to see the Jackson 5ive as a live act. Their Motown gloss was evident in the tight, joyous choreography. But underneath the slickness was the rawness of the teenage garage band they still were at heart.

In the studio they might have been making funky bubblegum, but as a live instrumental quartet they were *tough*, doing funky versions of rock and soul songs ("Stand," "Feelin' Alright," "Walk On," "I Want to Take You Higher"), not just because their label decided that Sly Stone was a good marketing model but because those were the kinds of songs a teen quartet would want to play in 1971. And they *could* play. Tito's spare blues leads and Jermaine's serious bottom were even more impressive when you consider that they played while performing elaborate, dynamic dance steps. The Jackson 5ive's moves took Cholly Atkins's famous Motown choreography that defined the Temptations and Four Tops and updated it by making the moves more athletic, and at times (especially during the heavy numbers) more aggressive. The highly receptive crowd seemed to be fueling the brothers to give even more than usual, and their steps were downright *badass* during this set. Add to the mix the Jackson brothers' harmonies; Jermaine's rich, deep vocals (unbelievable for a teenager); and Michael's breathtaking magnetism and you had one hell of a concert.

Ending their set with the hit "The Love You Save" followed by the raucous crowd-pleaser "Goin' Back to Indiana," Michael and company had the avid black audience going absolutely insane. When Michael did call and (thunderous) response with the crowd, the camera caught some audience members weeping and others doing some serious dancing. This was really Michael's crowd, and these were definitely his people. As he shouted forceful lyrics about going back to where he started from, it was clear he had already arrived. The next day he would go back to Hollywood, with its Dick Clark Productions, corny jokes, and crossover opportunities, but that night, on that stage, he bellowed the truth when he hollered, "I STILL GOT INDIANA SOUL IN ME!"

1972

In 1972 the Jackson 5ive continued its assault on the mainstream, with the boys returning to *American Bandstand*, appearing in Saturday morning commercials for Alpha-Bits cereal (flying around in a hot-air balloon singing faux Jackson 5ive songs with lyrics like "You're A-B-C-D-licious"), and starring in their own goofy cartoon show. Michael even visited *The Dating Game* (ABC, 1965–1973; syndicated, 1973, 1977–1980, 1986, 1988), where he chose adolescent bachelorette Latanya Simmons.

This also was the year that the Jackson 5ive found their most natural TV home, the studio equivalent of their Indiana concert. Starting that year, and continuing over the next several years, the Jackson 5ive visited the set of Don Cornelius's *Soul Train* and lip-synched in front of the best dancers on TV. No group fit better on *Soul Train* than the Jackson 5ive, and no show suited the Jackson 5ive better than *Soul Train*.

On *Soul Train* the brothers were not only performers in front of a crowd, but also part of an ecosystem where everything around them was an organic part of the performance. *Soul Train* presented the Jackson 5ive with the perfect studio (and home) audience, and during the next few years their performances of "I Want You Back" featuring original 1970 steps, of "Forever Came Today" with dazzling choreography, of Jermaine's fantastic solo hit "That's How Love Goes," of Michael's emotional version of his ballad "Ben," and especially of their robot-dance masterpiece "Dancing Machine" were far better than their performances on other shows.

Soul Train treated the Jackson 5ive like royalty. It assembled tributes and once even devoted an entire show to them. On one episode patriarch Joe Jackson came on the show and played home movies of a family party (Redd Foxx and Eddie Kendricks attended). On numerous episodes Cornelius conducted extensive interviews with the boys (on *Soul Train* we learned that Michael read science fiction and had pet peacocks, that the Jackson 5ive beat the Temptations at basketball, and that Michael loved to take care of Tito's newborn). Cornelius, who could be cold and arrogant at times, showed the Jacksons tremendous respect. He said that Jermaine was destined to become another Marvin Gaye and called the band "the world's most popular group of entertainers."

In one of the Jackson 5ive's best *Soul Train* segments Cornelius let the Soul Train Gang ask the questions. The Jacksons' answers made it obvious that, despite being cool singers and dancers, they were actually just a bunch of nerdy kids. At the same time, the awkward, sincere queries of the dancers made it clear that they too were pretty normal despite being so fly. When asked what it felt like to be superstars Tito responded that it was "the same as being you." And that was the magic of the Jacksons on *Soul Train*; they *were* the same as their audience. The early 1970s *Soul Train* format featured the dancers getting down during performances, so as Michael and his brothers—in their hip, wild outfits—executed their spectacular dance routines onstage, they were surrounded by an ocean of young brothers and sisters in hip, wild outfits doing their own spectacular dances.

The excellent *Soul Train* dancers seemed to inspire the Jacksons to give it their all. Their spins, slides, and steps seemed to have extra pop whenever they performed on the show. Not only did they draw inspiration to do their best, but they also learned moves from the Soul Train Gang. The robot dance, popping and locking moves, and even the moonwalk were black street dances the *Soul Train* regulars honed in the studio that Michael borrowed and tweaked. The show increased the Jackson 5ive's exposure and raised their appearance fees (the perks expected of TV appearances), but it also actually improved the quality of their act.

The entire group or a sibling appeared on *Soul Train* every year from the show's second season (1972) through the seventeenth season (1988). Michael and Janet appeared several times as solo acts until their superstardom made it too difficult. More notably, during the 1980s, when no one else would give them a chance, Cornelius gave brothers Randy and Marlon and sisters LaToya and Rebie opportunities to kick-start their solo careers. But it was during the first few years working together that the Jackson 5ive and *Soul Train* made the most magic. Nowhere else on TV would Michael appear as comfortable and on no other TV stage could he express his funky side any better.

1973–1976

While the Jackson 5ive's *Soul Train* appearances were arguably the soulful apex of Michael's TV career, they didn't herald a TV black power era. By the mid-1970s the TV schedule was a bizarre stew of white-bread talk shows, hokey variety programs, smarmy telethons, silly family specials, and glitzy awards shows. And it seemed like all of them featured the favorite sons of Gary, Indiana. No longer a boy, teenage Michael Jackson was a long, tall, skinny kid with a big natural. But the way he was presented on TV established that this was one black teenager white America didn't have to worry about. The all-American Michael appeared on a Bob Hope special with Ann-Margaret and John Denver; he did "Up a Lazy River" with the Mills Brothers on another special; and on Sandy Duncan's Disneyland special he dressed up in a glittery nautical uniform (a harbinger of couture to come) and sang Gilbert and Sullivan songs. The Jackson 5ive chatted with Johnny Carson on *The Tonight Show*. They also helped "Jerry's Kids" on the *Jerry Lewis MDA Labor Day Telethon*, turning in a surprisingly vital live performance, in which Michael tried to get some call-and-response interaction with the white audience. However, instead of motivating the "soul clap" as he had on Miss Black America, he elicited the "Johnny Carson clap," that odd response of 1970s TV audiences involving polka-friendly clapping on every beat.

The brothers visited Mike Douglas, Merv Griffin, and Dinah Shore. Michael did his brilliant "Dancing Machine" robot dance on Sonny and Cher's silly variety show in 1974, and he did it again the next year (after the couple split) on Cher's solo show, getting robotic *with* Cher (who outclassed the Jacksons' glittering tuxedos with her glittering Bob Mackie dress). They even visited Sonny's solo *Sonny Comedy Revue* (though Bono did not do the robot). Off TV the boys had their own silly, yet extremely popular, Las Vegas act wherein they would ease up on the funk for the older crowd, and would work their sisters into the act, including tiny Janet Jackson doing Mae West impersonations. This corny musical-comedy version of the Jacksons briefly surfaced on their own summer replacement variety show.

Though Michael was maturing into a tall, serious young man by the mid-1970s, he was still being infantilized on TV (either to neutralize his threat as a black male or to preserve the image of the little boy America fell in love with). On 1974's American Music Awards, Dick Clark's answer to the Grammys, Jackson presented an award alongside child actors Ricky Segal and Rodney Allen Rippy. On an excellent episode of *The Carol Burnett Show* (CBS, 1967–1978, 1991; ABC, 1979), Michael and his brothers played elementary school students (who just happened to wear glittering lime-green, open-chested flamenco outfits to school) being led by teacher Burnett in a funky version of the nursery rhyme "This Old Man." On the children's special *Free to Be You and Me*, Michael, looking pretty grown-up already, sang a song called "When I Grow Up." People often argue that Michael's arrested development (as a middle-aged man he lives a life of amusement parks, video games, and cotton candy) is due to his child-star career usurping an actual childhood, but his handlers also forced him to delay adulthood, lied about his age, and refused to acknowledge his post-adolescence. One might even blame Michael's eventual drive toward Caucasian beauty standards on the soul-free roles he constantly played on white variety shows (which far outnumbered his occasional rides on the *Soul Train*). One glaring example of these shows is an excruciating, hokey spoof of *Welcome Back, Kotter* (ABC, 1975–1979) on a 1976 Rich Little special in which the boys narrate the skit with sing-song jingles that would have seemed uncool even on *The Lawrence Welk Show* (ABC, 1955–1971; syndicated, 1971–1982). These absurd, embarrassing TV appearances were emblematic of the fact that Michael and his brothers were not making their own career decisions. A month after suffering through Little's godawful Gabe Kaplan impersonation, they left Motown and signed a contract with Epic, which allowed them more say in their own songwriting, career direction, and promotional appearances. The Jackson 5ive became the Jacksons. They must have found it easy to say good-bye to the type of corny crossover appearances that marked their mid-1970s career.

But even at the heart of that hokey era they (passively) experienced one brief hint of a race revolution. On a late 1974 episode of *The Tonight Show*, guest-hosted by Bill Cosby, the boys did another performance of "Dancing Machine" (a song that, thanks to Michael's amazing dance routine, they performed more than a dozen times on TV, including on three separate appearances on *The Tonight Show* in 1974). The choreographed piece was dynamic, featuring incredible live energy, fantastic sequined three-toned denim outfits, and dancing that hinted at Michael's *Thriller*-era triumphs to come. That said, with Doc Severinsen's *Tonight Show* horn section providing very traditional accompaniment, this was hardly the sound of the revolution. But that didn't stop Cosby from shaking things up in his interview (one of the only Jackson 5ive interviews in which Michael didn't grab the limelight—Bill was fascinated by the act's new conga player, twelve-year-old Randy Jackson). While taking in the mass of young black manhood flooding *The Tonight Show* couch, Cosby briefly pondered the broadcast's impact on Carson's regular viewers.

"When they see this many black people on TV at one time," he said, "they definitely will think there has been a takeover."

Such a revolution would not be televised that night. After the interview Michael and his brothers returned to the stage to sing a medley of toothless ballads—including "Killing Me Softly with His Song" and "Danny Boy."

1977–1981

After the Jacksons said good-bye to Motown (leaving behind Jermaine, who had married Berry Gordy's daughter, Hazel), they began releasing a series of mature, dynamic albums, the best of which (1978's *Destiny* and 1980's *Triumph*) were completely written by the brothers. The days of endless televised vaudeville hokum were over, and Michael only popped up on a handful of weird TV shows during this period (including 1978's *Rock 'n' Roll Sports Classic*, in which Michael professed a love of athletics, and *A Special Sesame Street Christmas* later that year, the only *Sesame Street* show produced without Children's Television Workshop or Henson Studios, a low point in Muppet history).

Michael Jackson was now a more serious artist, sitting down on *20/20* (ABC, 1978–present) in 1978 for an in-depth interview (the last one he would do for fourteen years) and reflecting on his celebrity and inner turmoil. As a group the Jacksons made a few dignified American TV appearances, hosting *Midnight Special* and remaining fixtures at awards shows, but they also began focusing on international TV, visiting England's *Top of the Pops* (BBC-1, 1964–present), Germany's *Musikladen* (ARD, 1972–1980) and doing an interview (in America) for Molly Meldrum's popular Australian show. This kind of transcontinental attention would serve Michael well, as his post-Motown solo career was to be much more ambitious than the light LPs he put out as side projects while in the Jackson 5ive (his biggest Motown solo hits were about animals, a "Rockin' Robin" and a rat named "Ben").

In August 1979 Michael released the spectacular solo album *Off the Wall*, which spent eight months in the top ten and produced two number-one singles. For those songs he produced low-budget music videos, both of which featured Michael grooving in a room. Silly video effects allowed him to dance in front of giant glowing marbles in "Don't Stop 'Til You Get Enough," and Michael merely danced in place in front of a disco laser machine in "Rock With You." Despite their sparseness, these videos were excellent simply because of Michael's joyful dancing. The blank-eyed kid from early Jackson 5ive TV appearances had become a man who looked genuinely happy and satisfied to be expressing himself in music and movement.

However, these videos, along with a clip for the Jacksons song "Can You Feel It," had few TV outlets in the days before MTV. That they were played at all on TV was because the songs were best-sellers, rather than the singles becoming hits because of the videos. That would all change with Michael's thrilling next project.

1982–1983

In December 1982 Michael Jackson released *Thriller*, an incredibly accessible pop/R&B masterpiece that featured deep dance grooves, tough rock riffs (including a notable Eddie Van Halen guitar solo), weepy ballads, and hooks galore. Produced by Quincy Jones with principal songwriting split between Jackson and Heatwave's Rod Temperton (the writer of African American prom perennial "Always and Forever"), "Thriller" was a triumph of studio craftsmanship, and immediately sold briskly. But in 1982 there were only a handful of TV shows that would promote a record like *Thriller*, and if it weren't for the novelty of "The Girl Is Mine," the first single (and the album's weakest track), being a duet with ex-Beatle Paul McCartney, it likely wouldn't have received any TV mention at all.

The problem Jackson faced was that the increasingly influential MTV, launched a year earlier, seemed to be a place for white artists only. After MTV rejected his hilarious "Super Freak," Rick James went on *Nightline* (ABC, 1980–present) to complain about the network's racist policies (his accusation went unchallenged as MTV opted not to send a representative). James's video was no tour de force—it mostly featured the funk singer in an empty studio with *Soul Train* dancer Cheryl Song writhing around as a lot of glitter flew—but it was certainly as good or better than most of the bare-bones, hokey videos that marked the network's inaugural seasons. But it wasn't good enough. To break its own color line, MTV needed an amazing, transcendent Jackie Robinson, not an amusing, controversial Deion Sanders.

Michael Jackson became the face of black music on MTV, but it didn't happen without a fight. MTV reportedly rejected his initial video from *Thriller*, which, as rumor has it, gained entry only after CBS/Epic insisted it be added. This version of the story claims that CBS/Epic threatened to pull their white videos (Rick James reported this scenario on *Nightline*, and without an MTV executive to refute it, it has become an accepted part of music video lore). "Billie Jean" first appeared on MTV on March 2, 1983, and was in heavy rotation by the end of the month. The video's success was inevitable because of the popularity of the album, the success of the hit single, and the superiority of the video.

Not that the video was actually great; it was just a lot better than the other clips on MTV. At the time most artists were making spare videos with little narrative and lots of cheesy effects. In contrast, Jackson made a convoluted video with a confusing narrative and lots of cheesy effects. "Billie Jean" (directed by Steve Barron, who had already done tacky videos for British "new romantic" acts) cast Michael as a Christ-like figure who distributes a redemptive light wherever he walks (if one considers turning a dirty bum into a tuxedoed bum, a cat into a tiger, and a sad billboard into a happy billboard examples of redemption). As he brightens the grim urban landscape, Jackson is pursued by a detective who is continuously flummoxed by Michael's divine nature. In the end Michael climbs into a bed with, but doesn't touch, a woman, causing the linens to light up as Jackson disappears. If one wants to attempt to connect the video's imagery with the song's lyrics (about Michael's denials of a paternity accusation) then perhaps the lit-up bed represents Michael assisting with an immaculate conception, creating yet another baby whose father no private eye will be able to track down for child support.

But the storyline of the video was inconsequential. The reasons this video was successful were its moments that echoed the simple *Off the Wall* clips. Michael Jackson could boogie! Michael's lively dancing, his style of movement, and his command of image synthesized decades of black dance (they referenced tap, jazz, pop locking, and disco). But they also mined decades of dancing on film, in which Fred Astaire, Ray Bolger, Gene Kelly, and Sammy Davis, Jr. utilized Hollywood magic to accentuate their movements. The video's main special effect—a sidewalk that lights up with every step Michael takes—was a gimmick straight out of an MGM dance routine.

The next month MTV viewers saw "Beat It," the video that established Michael Jackson as *the* outstanding artist of this new medium. Yet it too drew from ancient MGM sources. Directed by Bob Giraldi, a successful director of commercials, "Beat It" opens with news of a rumble circulating through a dingy diner. The scene repeats itself in a seedy pool hall and soon gang members are arriving at the war zone by foot, forklift, and sewer grate. Meanwhile, sensitive Michael broods in his dirty SRO room contemplating the senseless violence. He eventually puts on his red leather jacket and dances his way to the crime scene, taking advantage of the abandoned diner and pool hall to bust a few moves.

When Michael arrives at the rumble the motley crew of hooligans is a sight to behold. "Beat It" featured a mix of real gang members and actors/dancers, and it's pretty obvious who belongs to which group. While the actual gangbangers look rough and intimidating, the actors look either too mature (thirty-five-year-old Michael Peters, the genius who choreographed this video with Michael, stars as one of the gang leaders), too pretty (delicate Michael DeLorenzo, later the star of *New York Undercover*, is Peters's lieutenant), or too much like swishy Broadway dancers. Other familiar faces in the video were B-movie actor Stoney Jackson, *Soul Train's* Cheryl Song, and Rick Stone from *Cooley High*.

Regardless of how motley the crews are, all the gangbangers seemed to agree on one thing—Michael Jackson sure can move! Jackson breaks up the fight and then breaks into a dance routine … and that's when the video becomes groundbreaking. While the overall cinematic quality of the entire piece seemed to declare that this clip was raising the bar for music videos, it was the dance number that sealed the deal. As Michael led a group of hoofers in a remarkable routine that combined Peters's Broadway choreography with the unique dance style Jackson developed, it was clear that the medium of videos, in the right hands, was a return to the golden age of Hollywood musicals. The references to *West Side Story* are obvious, yet "Beat It" was not nostalgic. Rather, it used the language of *That's Entertainment* to address a new demographic weaned on *Sesame Street* and addicted to video games, ready for the glitz and spectacle of a movie to be condensed into a few minutes and then repeated relentlessly. The "Beat It" video truly announced Michael Jackson's arrival to the MTV generation. Now it was just all the other generations that needed to get the news.

That would happen on May 16, 1983. Berry Gordy had planned an elaborate network TV special to celebrate Motown's twenty-fifth anniversary, and when a Supremes reunion (predictably) failed to come together he decided to make a

Jackson 5ive reunion the centerpiece of the show. Michael was a rising star and Jermaine had not performed with his brothers in more than half a decade so it seemed like an exciting idea. But Michael was not convinced.

Years of lame TV appearances and months of exploring the completely controllable, easily edited, multiple-take nature of music videos had soured him on the idea of putting his image in someone else's hands. Raised in show business, Jackson had developed into an obsessive perfectionist when it came to his craft, and this offer did not fit into his new plans. He finally came aboard when Gordy made some concessions. After Jackson performed with his brothers he would do a song from his new album, the only non-Motown offering of the night.

Motown 25: Yesterday, Today, Forever was an enjoyable treat, with Diana Ross, the Four Tops, and other Motown greats shining. Other than a few miscues (including an ill-conceived crossover segment in which Adam Ant butchered a Supremes song), the show was fun, and because baby boomers were so crazy about Motown (they dug the "Good Feeling Music of the Big Chill Generation," as one best-selling compilation dubbed it) more than fifty million people were watching. The excitement was palpable as the reunited Jackson 5ive took the stage and performed "I Want You Back," "The Love You Save," and "I'll Be There." The band had their old chemistry, particularly between Jermaine and Michael, and the performance was a celebration appropriate for the anniversary show.

But after the brief set his brothers left the stage and Michael stood alone and declared, "I love those songs . . . those were magic moments with all my brothers, including Jermaine. But you know, those were the good songs, I like those songs a lot. But especially I like . . ." he paused, and with his gentle voice bristling with almost sinister foreboding, added, "the new songs." The teens sprinkled around the crowd were shrieking for Michael to do "Billie Jean," and he obliged. Michael was dressed in a profoundly unique way that night. His outrageous sense of fashion drew from nerd couture (high-water pants with light socks), grandma's closet (a glitter blouse that looked like something an elderly African American church lady would wear), movie gangster style (a fedora, which he flung like a Frisbee to open his number), and outer space (a single, clumsy glove covered in hundreds of glimmering rhinestones). And when he began dancing he proved that his originality went far beyond image.

Blatantly lip-synching to the record, Jackson's performance was about movement, not singing. His command of his body, beloved by all when framed by the kinetic energy of his brothers, suddenly seemed twice as exciting when viewed without distraction. His leg kicks, spins, and frozen poses were familiar to his fans, yet seemed shockingly new. Jackson wasn't going wild—in some ways he was quite subdued. But as he perfectly presented his dance style, it sent most of the audience—in the Pasadena Civic Center and at home—into a frenzy. When Jackson went into his moonwalk—four and a half paces of gravity-challenging pop locking—the crowd erupted. When the routine ended Jackson received a thunderous standing ovation from the exhausted audience.

And it was an interesting audience. With the notable exception of a gaggle of doughy white teens in ugly prom dresses who somehow got V.I.P. seats, the front of the crowd was not only all black, but also was mostly musicians and peers in attendance to celebrate Motown. Michael Jackson was not only convincing laypeople that he had arrived, but he was also lighting up the faces of the most jaded, experienced, and in many cases bitter (many Motown artists left the label under unhappy circumstances) musicians in the world. Although Jackson was mesmerizing, one of the highlights of the performance was in the corner of the screen. The conductor of the orchestra was completely awed by Michael, clapping along with a huge grin on his face until the director apparently reminded him in his headphones to get ready to conduct. The enchantment this wizened professional experienced during that routine was emblematic of the spell Jackson put on America. At that moment he became the biggest star in the world.

As 1983 ended, Michael took MTV to another stratosphere. His popularity had raised the profile of the network, and his videos had set new standards that his followers were quick to mimic. But his new video, which debuted in December, was his masterpiece.

"Thriller" opens in the 1950s with high school kid Jackson and his bobby-soxer girlfriend (played by Ola Ray, one of the few black *Playboy* centerfolds) running out of gas on a scary, deserted road. As they walk and pitch woo Michael tells Ola that he really likes her, but warns "I'm not like other guys." Then, as the full moon shines on them, the movie shifts from a benign *I Was a Teenage Werewolf* to a gruesome *American Werewolf in London*, as Jackson goes through a hideous transformation from man to beast (courtesy of special effects wiz Rick Baker). Just before Wolfman Jackson kills his girlfriend the scene shifts to a movie theater where a delighted Michael and a horrified Ola are watching themselves in the movie. Jackson agrees to take the frightened Ola home and as they walk down *another* scary, deserted road, Jackson (wearing a red and black leather spaceman jacket) sings and dances around his date. Though this portion does not feature the film's most impressive choreography, it is exciting as it demonstrates the magic of movement that marks a true dance genius.

Courtesy Jake Austen

Unlike his previous videos (or his *Motown 25* performance, which wisely used primarily long shots), "Thriller" featured numerous close-ups of Jackson's pretty face. It was pretty clear that part of Jackson's plans for media crossover dominance involved a (relatively) subtle nose job. Though he had always been beautiful to his original fans, the new Jackson was taking no chances; his thinner nose and straightened hair in a Jheri-curl style came closer to the dominant American beauty standard. Of course, most of what made Jackson attractive at this juncture was his youthful, confident energy, and in the "Thriller" video he demonstrated it magnificently, his easygoing, happy acting a real contrast with the blank-eyed, stiff delivery of his childhood TV appearances.

As the young lovers pass a graveyard we hear Vincent Price's evil voice as zombies rise from the earth. One zombie emerges from a manhole cover, a comical reference to "Beat It." The walking dead surround the couple, the song ends, and Ola turns toward her boyfriend, horrified to discover that he too is a zombie! What follows is an amazing zombie dance number, again choreographed by Jackson and Peters. It is definitely the best Michael Jackson video dance routine ever, made better by the outrageous monster costumes. A long instrumental break is inserted into the song so that the magnificent dance sequence can go on uninterrupted.

When the music finally ends Ola escapes to an abandoned house, which is assaulted by zombies (mimicking *Night of the Living Dead*). Just as Michael is going to kill his woman (again) the scene shifts for the last time—cute Michael wakes her up . . . it was just a nightmare caused by the horror movie . . . or *was* it?

The fourteen-minute long "Thriller" was an important video. Its grandness made MTV seem important. That it was directed by John Landis, a feature filmmaker, legitimized the medium, and its budget (over $1 million at a time when videos usually ran under $20,000) marked a new day for music videos. MTV not only treated the "Thriller" debut like a movie opening (building up its world-premiere date like a Hollywood blockbuster's release) but it also, according to MTV executive Robert Pittman, covertly bankrolled it, hiding the payment and recouping the money by producing *The Making of Michael Jackson's Thriller*, which aired on MTV and Showtime and went on to become a best-selling VHS home video.

Thriller the LP sold 600,000 copies in the week after the video first aired and would go on to sell more than fifty million copies worldwide, the most of any album in history. Of course its popularity stemmed from the quality of the music on the record. But unlike the hits of the past, the songs on this record were written with videos in mind. More than Elvis Presley or the Beatles, Jackson had used TV to become a rock 'n' roll superstar. And this time it was the artist himself who was pulling the strings.

1984

In 1984, Michael basked in the success of *Thriller*. He made his most prominent TV appearance in February when he attended the Grammy Awards, for which he was nominated for a record dozen statues and won a whopping eight. His formalwear for the evening, a sequined glitter Naval admiral's uniform, suggested a commander of a unit of Village People. His dates for the evening were the towering former jailbait model (and self-professed virgin) Brooke Shields and twelve-year old Emmanuel Lewis, the tiny star of TV's *Webster* (ABC, 1983–1987; syndicated, 1987–1988). Jackson grinned hugely with each award he won, and though he was shy and quiet during most of his acceptance speeches, he did take one of his many opportunities at the microphone to honor Jackie Wilson, an artist he had observed firsthand and emulated. Wilson had recently died, spending nearly a decade in a semi-comatose state after collapsing on stage during one of his signature dynamic dance routines. If Jackson viewed Wilson's fate

Courtesy Jake Austen

as a cautionary tale, his demeanor didn't betray any sense of worry. As a record fifty-one million home viewers observed, Jackson appeared genuinely happy that night.

Michael would see many of those viewers in person when he set out on a stadium tour with the Jacksons, ostensibly in support of the family's new album *Victory* (which featured a post–*Motown 25* six-man version of the Jacksons, with Jermaine back in the fold), though it was really the *Thriller* tour. The least cohesive of the Jacksons' records, *Victory* was obviously a back-burner project for Michael, who didn't even appear in the music video for the song "Torture," which featured a dancing skeleton as his proxy. Michael was fully invested in the concert, however, and the *Victory* Tour was a huge success, with footage of his screaming, frenzied fans appearing on the local news in every city the tour visited. Notably these fans were a less diverse bunch than in the past, as outrageous ticket prices (shyster/boxing promoter Don King helped organize the promotion) were beyond the budgets of the Jacksons' poorer urban supporters. As Michael looked

out at those crowds he must have savored his victory—he had successfully conquered America's white-girl demographic!

1985–1988

Things cooled down a little for Jackson in 1985. He won only one Grammy, and
didn't attend the ceremony. His most prominent activity was writing and facili-
tating (along with Lionel Ritchie and Quincy Jones) the charity single "We Are
the World," with Bruce Springsteen, Willie Nelson, Stevie Wonder, Bob Dylan,
Ray Charles, Tina Turner, most of the Jacksons (including misfit sister LaToya),
and dozens more crooning for Ethiopian famine relief. The video, which introduced Dylan's unique incoherence to a new generation of kids, became an MTV
fixture.

At the time, there was a lot of talk about Jackson's media dominance and the
possibility of MTV videos leading to a big-screen career. Jackson, an obsessed
movie aficionado, was extremely interested in this. He had a supporting role in
1978's *The Wiz* (the film whose box office failure killed the 1970s black movie
boom) but nothing came after that despite chatter about Jackson possibly remak-
ing *Peter Pan* with Stephen Spielberg. The closest to a real movie Michael made
was 1986's *Captain Eo*, a sci-fi short that showed theatrically at Disney's Epcot
Center. The TV special *The Making of Captain Eo* had to hold Michael fans over
until his next album.

In 1987, five years after *Thriller*, Michael Jackson unveiled *Bad*. MTV marked
the release on *The Magic Returns*, a special that culminated with the debut of the
seventeen-minute *Bad* video, another ambitious "mini-movie" in the tradition of
"Thriller." Directed by Marin Scorsese, it opens with a nonmusical black-and-
white movie in which Jackson plays a meek teenager attending a predominantly
white private boarding school. He returns home to Brooklyn only to find that he
is uncomfortable with his homeboy friends, who are decked out in fresh 1980s
hip-hop gear (ski goggles, puffy winter coats, Cazal glasses). Michael's buddies
(including a relatively unknown Wesley Snipes) tease him and accuse him of
going soft, especially when he is reluctant to assist in their subway mugging
scheme. The narrative, nonmusical portion of this video is pretty impressive, as
it boldly (for a crossover artist) addresses the passive racism of the white boarding school kids (Jackson and a Latino student compare the condescending praise
they've received) and its tough ghetto scenes—particularly one in which a fraz-
zled drug dealer threatens Jackson's posse with a gun—presage the "hood" movies
that would soon revive black cinema.

But the tone of "Bad" changes dramatically when the music kicks in. Upstate prep school has taught Jackson's character that violence is wrong—so in a nod to "Beat It"—he decides to stop the insanity musically. And when he confronts Snipes it is not as the meek, sweatshirted kid in black and white, but as a full color, belt-buckle-adorned super-hero jazz dancer.

Shot in an actual New York subway station, "Bad" features Jackson leading a bunch of Broadway performers dressed as break dancers. The dance moves look great when Jackson does them, but they're pretty effeminate as executed by his backup dancers. While there are some good moves, and some nice cameos by pop lockers and a robotic roller skater, this video can't match its predecessors, as even the dancing is ill-served by too many close-ups and not enough chemistry between Jackson and his crew. Like the video, the album didn't live up to *Thriller*. Eventually *Bad* sold more than twenty-two million copies worldwide, a phenomenal total but a fraction of *Thriller*'s sales.

What is most notable about this video is that Jackson was starting to look different. He'd had more work done following the subtle surgical enhancements that made him prettier for *Thriller*. In *Bad* he looked more streamlined and less natural, and his skin appeared lighter. His hair was still in a Jheri curl but the style was different; it looked more like the long hair metal bands wore at the time. In fact, Michael's new look and attitude was more rock. He designed his first huge solo tour (as seen on the MTV specials *Bad Around the World* and *From Motown to Your Town*) in the style of a wailing rock concert.

Though less omnipresent than he had been in 1983, Jackson still dominated MTV with his new videos and was once again the hottest act in the world. Not bad at all.

1989–1990

As the 1990s approached, Jackson's eccentricities (he seemed to tweak the press by releasing bizarre information about his private life), his man-child act (to compensate for the normal childhood he missed he designed a playful second childhood, complete with a personal petting zoo and carnival rides), and physical modifications became more pronounced (the British dubbed him "Wacko Jacko"). This made it harder for most people to identify with him, and, more significantly, it made him less appealing and attractive to the teen pop audience that usually chooses idols based on looks rather than music quality.

Public opinion positioned Jackson as a performer who gave his all to the business, who was only truly alive when he was on stage or in a recording studio, and who was confused and uncomfortable in the real world. Nineteen-ninety's *Sammy Davis Jr.'s 60th Anniversary Celebration* TV special (in an echo of Jackson's first network TV appearance in 1969) suggested parallels between Jackson and Davis. Davis, like Jackson, was a gifted former child star, divorced from the real world since early childhood, beholden to a family act where his relatives were less gifted than he. Davis was a man who was never really satisfied unless he was "on," so he came alive on stage and led a mess of a life offstage. Jackson frequently honored Sammy publicly (Sammy returned the favor, covering "Bad" in his act). However, to an outside observer, there were many glaring differences between the two. Most prominently, while Davis was sometimes a living caricature and may have been an awful human being on occasion, he always *was* a human being. With Jackson you weren't always sure.

Take for example one of Jackson's more interesting TV appearances. In November 1989 Eddie Murphy was a guest on *The Arsenio Hall Show* (syndicated, 1989–1994), the youthful talk show that reenergized late-night gabfests. Midway through Murphy's segment a surprise guest emerged from the curtain in the back of the set. It was Jackson, the biggest star in the world! Had Elvis Presley popped onto a set in 1950s or the Beatles in the 1960s there would have been electricity and pandemonium in the air, but with Jackson in 1989 it was a little different. Everything seemed to stop for a moment and before any sense of excitement could set in there was a sense of trepidation. Was this really Michael Jackson? If so, *what did he want?*

Jackson had become such an enigma, such an eccentric, indecipherable hermit, that even other celebrities felt distanced from him. Murphy admitted on air that he thought it was an impersonator at first. Jackson joined the comedians, but unlike a loose Sinatra barging in on some crony's show, no easygoing, casual conversation resulted. Jackson's weird, unnatural, quiet behavior made the host, his superstar guest, the studio audience, and the home viewers a little uncomfortable during his time on the set. Jackson may have had millions of loyal fans, but he also seemed to be the rare star whose fans would just as soon not hang out with him.

1991

In 1991 Jackson returned with the bloated *Dangerous* album. While it did not live up to the *Thriller* standard, *Dangerous* eventually sold a hefty seven million copies in the United States and more than twenty million worldwide. The TV event launching the album had MTV, Fox, and BET (the Jackson camp's nod of respect to the superstar's still-loyal African American fan base), as well as international stations, simultaneously premiering "Black or White," the debut video from *Dangerous*. *Rolling Stone* reported the next month that "an estimated half a billion people saw the premiere" of the clip, which soon had the heaviest rotation on MTV of any video in history. *Rolling Stone* also uncovered an MTV memo that implied that the right to premiere the video was conditional upon all the networks agreeing to call Jackson "the king of pop" on the air a minimum of twice weekly.

The video itself was something of a mess. It opened with a mean-spirited skit in which charmless Macaulay Culkin outwits his oppressive father (George Wendt). That transitioned into an expensive video in which Jackson danced with problematic examples of people of color (Jackson presented stereotypical Bushmen straight out of *The Gods Must Be Crazy* and Native Americans as seen in cowboy movies). The video introduced a new digital technology; in a literal interpretation of the song's lyric "it don't matter if you're black or white," it featured a number of people of different ethnicities morphing into one another (all while lip-synching the lyrics). It ended with Jackson morphing into a black panther and exiting the video studio into a ghetto alley. He took human form again and then did a dynamic dance routine that involved a lot of simulated masturbation and the destruction of a car's windows with a crowbar.

The final portion of the video sparked controversy and outrage (*Entertainment Weekly*'s cover story was titled "Michael Jackson's Video Nightmare") that seemed as calculated as Janet Jackson's Super Bowl nipple flashing thirteen years later. Jackson prepared an apology the following day and excised the offensive portion of the video. *In Living Color* and *Saturday Night Live* both ridiculed the "Black or White" video (Chris Rock, as militant talk-show host Nat X, explaining to Jackson why he was outraged: "That was *my* car!"). Ten years later Jackson released the full-length version on DVD, but with a few minor digital adjustments. In the new version, his destruction of property was justified because all the glass he broke was corrupted by racist graffiti declaring "Nigger Go Home," "No More Wetbacks," and the implausible "KKK Rules" painted in hip-hop graffiti style.

On a lighter note, that fall Jackson lent his voice to an episode of Fox's hit cartoon *The Simpsons*. Here Jackson's fantasies about it not mattering if he were black or white were made literal, as he played a white mental patient named Leon Kompowski who believed he was Michael Jackson.

1992

Michael Jackson was all over TV in 1992 as he returned to the stage with his *Dangerous* Tour. But unlike the loose, silly footage of gonzo fans the local news stations showed during the *Victory* Tour, this new hype all came pre-packaged.

Jackson produced footage of himself on tour in Munich, London, Romania (where he was given a unit of Romanian soldiers to use for props), and around the globe, and delivered it all to MTV and its global affiliates (for their *Michael Jackson: Live and Dangerous*, *More Dangerous than Ever* and *MTV Dangerous Diary* specials) and any other network that wanted to cover the event. Each concert special presented Jackson as a man who caused crowds of white European preteen girls to weep with excitement and to faint when he began to sing. The Jackson camp would present those images with increasing frequency over the next decade.

Jackson continued to make expensive, dynamic videos. Yet while there was still a sense of excitement around them (in "Jam" Michael Jackson plays basketball against Michael Jordan; in "Remember the Time" Michael is an ancient Egyptian mystic who woos Pharaoh Eddie Murphy's wife Iman and fights court eunuch Magic Johnson), it could not match his 1983 MTV dominance.

What did mark 1992 as a historical year for Jackson was that despite Hollywood's reluctance to cast him as an actor (*Captain Eo* notwithstanding) it was ready to treat him as a subject. *The Jacksons: An American Dream* was a major, network biographical miniseries about Michael and his brothers. Former Jackson 5ive promoter Suzanne de Passe in association with Jermaine Jackson and his wife Margaret (Jermaine divorced first wife Hazel Gordy in 1988) produced the miniseries. The title refers to the overriding theme of the movie, which follows the Jacksons from poverty to superstardom, representing the opportunities available in America to anyone, regardless of race or class.

But the film's scandal angle was more memorable. It represented Joseph Jackson as a brutal, jealous dictator who beat the success into his children. Lawrence Hilton-Jacobs, an actor best known from the 1970s sitcom *Welcome Back, Kotter* on which he played Washington, played the elder Jackson to wicked perfection. Angela Bassett played Jackson matriarch Katherine. Within the year Bassett would play a similar role (a good-hearted, innocent woman whose life is melodramatically complicated by her marriage to an intense black man) in two other biographical films, as Betty Shabazz in *Malcolm X* and Tina Turner in *What's Love Got to Do with It.*

The best parts of this made-for-TV movie were the performances by the actors playing the Jackson boys at different stages of their career (this series looks at the pre–Jackson 5ive era through the *Victory* Tour). Though the youngest version of Michael was a child actor who couldn't capture little Michael's magic, the other two actors who played him were particularly convincing. The adolescent Michael (played by Jason Weaver, known for sitcom roles and for singing young Simba's songs in Disney's *The Lion King*) was spectacular; his mimicry was so eerily accurate you suspected he might be the mystery child Jackson refers to in "Billie Jean." That was also the case with the actor who played Michael as young adult, Wylie Draper (who died from cancer a year after this movie first aired). Draper's moves were excellent, and he also brought a fine sense of melodrama to his depiction of Michael's inner turmoil. But the real reason these actors were so good was that the movie came just the right number of years after 1983 for the producers to be able to cast actors who had lived and breathed their favorite star during his heyday. Unwittingly the cast had been rehearsing for this movie for almost a decade. The best scene was a dance number, and there was no doubt about where the producers got the reference material to choreograph it so well. In the film, as the Jacksons rehearse "Dancing Machine," we see the robot dance routine as showcased on countless programs in the mid-1970s. However, this time it was not shot by some clumsy TV director, but with close-ups and edits informed by the music-video movement Jackson helped to create. Despite Jackson's not actually being in the scene, this is possibly the best filmed version of this number because it adheres to his principles of perfectionism and final-edit control, elements he had no power over in the days when he was Motown's dancing machine.

The fictionalized movie recalled some of the moments in Jackson's life when he had struggled to control his career and image. The next year would bring media moments that were more out of his control than anything he could have previously imagined.

1993

At its outset, 1993 looked as if it was going to be Jackson's year. First he portrayed himself as all-American boy by performing at Bill Clinton's inauguration. Two weeks later he commanded the largest viewing audience in American TV history when he (and a stuntman impersonator) lip-synched, danced, and flew in a rocket pack during the halftime of Super Bowl XXVII in front of over 133 million sports fans.

Having done something for the guys, Michael did a little TV for the ladies by sitting down with Oprah on February 11 for a live interview on *Michael Jackson Talks . . . to Oprah: 90 Primetime Minutes with the King of Pop*. Winfrey joined Michael at his legendary estate, the Neverland Ranch, famed for its amusement park, animal menagerie, and gaudy decorations (in one shot Jackson stood in front of a huge faux-Renaissance painting depicting the singer as a bullfighter/prophet, wearing a toreador outfit and surrounded by little angels). Winfrey informed the viewers that there were no ground rules and that Jackson had promised to answer everything. However, Winfrey's signature comforting, spiritual-therapist style was guarantee enough that she would not go in for the kill. Other than one segment in which Winfrey (obviously a fan of the miniseries) returned several times to explore his feelings about Joseph abusing him as a child, she took all of Jackson's answers at face value no matter how outlandish they were.

She brought up a list of rumors and scandals. Jackson had not-quite-credible explanations for all of them, and several times he cited horrible tabloid journalism run amok as part of the problem. He said he had never demanded to be called king of pop. His fans and best friend Liz Taylor had dubbed him that, and any media use of the term was of their own volition. He never slept in an oxygen chamber or attempted to buy the Elephant Man's bones (two stories Jackson very likely engineered himself to create attention). He had not read his sister LaToya's scandalous new book so he couldn't comment on its content. And, he also boldly stated that he'd had only had two plastic surgeries (or, to quote more accurately, "you can count on two fingers" the work he'd had done) and that he had done nothing to lighten his skin, but rather was the victim of a pigment-destroying skin disease (vitiligo). He would never bleach his skin because "I'm a black American, I am proud to be a black American."

He made these denials from an alabaster face with a mangled nose, jutting cheekbones that made him look skeletal, and thick bizarre eye makeup that seemed to be compensating for botched cosmetic surgery. When Michael broke into a wide smile or laughed he still looked cute and familiar, but otherwise it is fair (albeit cruel) to say that he looked grotesque.

Jackson then took Winfrey around in a golf cart to show off the amusement park he had built for the terminally ill children that he busses in every three weeks. He even showed her a theater he built where sick kids could watch magic shows and movies. Winfrey heaped praise on Jackson for building little sterile skyboxes into the theater walls so I.V.-dependent kids could watch shows from the relative comfort of their beautiful hospital beds.

While it seems credible that Jackson allowed Winfrey to ask whatever she wanted, Jackson clearly had a hand in deciding the content of the show (for example, the show included yet another screaming Euro-girl montage). Tellingly, when Winfrey asked Jackson to demonstrate the moonwalk he started to direct the cameramen to shoot from certain angles. Though it may not have stood out to most people watching, one of the most profound things Jackson revealed during this interview was that as a child watching James Brown on TV he used to get mad at the directors for going to close-ups when they should have been shooting the dancing. Jackson knew how to direct a production *then*, and he certainly did by the time he did the Winfrey special. His goal for this interview was to look like a holy saint. "I am trying to imitate Jesus," Jackson explained to Winfrey, adding, "I am not saying I *am* Jesus."

He might not have been Jesus, but Jackson's Winfrey interview showed America that, though his scary face and eccentric nature were a bit off-putting, Jackson seemed like a nice person. But any gold he had electroplated to his image with his early 1993 TV appearances rubbed off in the summer.

In August Santa Barbara County police issued search warrants for Neverland Ranch to investigate claims that Jackson had sexually abused one of the children he had befriended. While no one had filed charges—the investigation was at a very early stage—these events unfolded at an interesting time in TV history. A new breed of TV news shows, based upon (and staffed from) the trashy English and Australian tabloid newspapers, had become syndicated hits in the United States, and they were exerting influence upon legitimate TV news. Shows like *Hard Copy* (syndicated, 1989–1999) and *A Current Affair* (syndicated, 1987–1996, 2005–present) practiced "checkbook journalism," paying high prices for inside information. For months after the Neverland search these shows revealed shocking new allegations daily from dubious sources, all well-paid.

Jackson's bodyguards, a French couple that worked at the estate, and his Manila-born housekeepers all had scandalous, often conflicting stories to tell and sell. The fact that they went to tabloids to get paid (various sources were offered between $15,000 and $100,000 for their tales) instead of the police was a problem, and bigger problems emerged when the police dismissed these stories as worthless, and even the editor of the *über*-tabloid *The Daily Mirror* declared that the housekeepers' story was not credible (the same couple had previously sold a completely positive tell-all story).

It's not surprising that tabloid news shows and sleazy daytime talk shows would focus on these unsubstantiated rumors ("Today on *Geraldo*—Michael Jackson, victim or violator . . ."), but their influence on mainstream network news programming was interesting. Network news soon began hiring producers away from the tabloid shows, and suddenly the rules of media engagement shifted dramatically away from journalistic ethics.

Jackson's team (which included lawyer Johnnie Cochran) had detective-to-the-stars Tony Pelicano deliver to CBS News a tape in which the accuser's father seemed to refer to extortion plans (when they were analyzed in context, the tapes turned out to be far less damning, although other evidence emerged that seemed to paint the father as an opportunist/manipulator). At any rate, CBS quickly aired the tape.

Jackson's response to the accusations was one of the most painfully vivid moments in his lifetime of TV appearances. On December 22 he arranged for a network feed from Neverland Ranch. Sitting in a stark room, wearing a relatively normal red shirt, with shockingly pale skin and long straight hair, Jackson declared that the "many disgusting statements . . . are totally false." He spoke in a pained, dire tone, painting himself as the true victim in this situation by describing the "horrifying, horrifying experience which I have been through" as "a nightmare, a horrifying nightmare." While he looked genuinely upset, he also seemed in some ways like a Disney character being set upon by animated witches and villains. In part this was because of the stilted delivery of his prepared statement. But this vibe was mainly due to his makeup. His long, thick eyelashes made him look like Snow White in peril.

However, with the tabloid feeding frenzy, Jackson seemed somewhat justified when he stated, "I am particularly upset by the handling of this matter by the incredible, terrible mass media. At every opportunity the media has dissected and manipulated these allegations to reach their own conclusions." This was an ironic fate for a master of media manipulation, but the more prominent portion of the statement offered no invitation for ironic interpretation. Nearly crying, Jackson described how the police "served a search warrant on me which allowed them to view and photograph my body, including my penis, my buttocks, my lower torso, thighs . . . it was the most humiliating ordeal of my life, one that no person should ever have to suffer. But if this is what I have to endure to prove my innocence, my complete innocence, so be it." Hearing Michael say "penis" was jarring, as his discomfort with the word itself made him seem asexual in a way that would imply his innocence, but also recalled an awkward child in a way that could lend itself for negative interpretation of his odd relationship to adolescence (and adolescents?). He ended his four-minute statement by once again reminding us that, "In no way do I think I am God, but I do try to be godlike in my heart."

Less than a month later, with little TV fanfare from his camp, save a short press statement by Cochran, Michael settled with the boy's family for an undisclosed sum. No civil suit was filed and without the cooperation of the family the criminal case was unable to proceed.

1994–1995

During the next two years Michael worked as a spin doctor. He made a surprise appearance at the NAACP Image Awards to give out an award and declare his innocence. His family launched the ill-conceived *Jackson Family Honors*, an awards show/hall of fame induction meant to mimic the lofty Kennedy Center ceremonies. But with the Jackson parents presiding like monarchs over the ceremony—he with his crazy eyes and processed hair, and she with a tangible sense of disconnect from her husband and the world—this family made the Kennedys look like the Waltons.

Another significant image-mending event occurred on May 26, 1994, when Jackson took a bride. Jackson's secret wedding to Elvis Presley's only acknowledged child, Lisa Marie, caused cynics to hatch a number of conspiracy theories. Some were as simple as Jackson using Lisa Marie as a beard to stave off suspicions of pedophilia; others were as elaborate as a worldwide network of Scientololologists engineering the union so that Lisa Marie (whose mother, Priscilla Presley, raised her with Dianetics) could usurp his riches for their cause.

Whatever the truth, TV viewers got ample time to ponder it during the broadcast and countless rebroadcasts of Jackson and Presley opening the September 8, 1994, MTV Music Video Awards with a huge, histrionic smooch. The ploy to paint Jackson as a stud backfired a bit, as the stiff, jerky embrace and liplock was unconvincing, and even for those inclined to take Jackson at his word, it suggested that perhaps some things are better left unseen. This was also the case with the music video "You Are Not Alone" which featured a scrawny, shirtless Michael and his nearly naked bride acting out an amorous scene from a Maxfield Parrish painting.

America got a more extended opportunity to judge the authenticity of their union when the newlyweds sat down with Diane Sawyer for an interview on *Primetime Live* on June 14, 1995. Like the Winfrey interview two years earlier, this would have no boundaries and in theory, since Sawyer was a journalist rather than a feel-good talk-show host, this would be a more thorough interview.

From the outset, however, it was obvious that his experience with Winfrey had prepared Jackson to manipulate this interview as well. The lighting was extremely favorable and Michael's stylists had done spectacular work so that his skin and face looked robust and beautiful, the best they had in years (Michael seemed to have had collagen injections in his lips to make them appear fuller). He had to answer harder questions this time, but he had excellent answers prepared (he settled the case because his lawyers couldn't guarantee justice in the Southern California court system—a popular concept in the post–Rodney King era). Michael, looking resplendent in a black outfit with gold catcher's shin guards, was in full control. Unfortunately for him, his wife was not as seasoned a performer and apparently had not been sufficiently briefed.

Presley, though brought up as pop culture royalty, revealed herself to be unslick, uncouth, and ill-suited for the role if she was in fact a fake wife. While the chemistry between the couple wasn't particularly convincing, the best argument for this marriage not being an act was that she was such a terrible actress that he never would have made the mistake of casting her. Presley is unsure of interview etiquette and sputters through answers, blurting them out when Sawyer is still talking and ending them incompletely when she realizes Sawyer is trying to speak. She constantly contradicts Jackson with honest, unrehearsed answers, explaining that she'd be willing to have a vacation home overseas when Jackson declares that he would like to move to another country permanently, and adding conflicting details to his story of their courtship. She tells anyone who questions her marriage to "eat it," and bluntly answers (in the affirmative) when asked if the couple has sexual relations.

Presley's most telling moment comes when Sawyer asks about plastic surgeries, to which Jackson begins to give his stock evasive answer. Continuing her unique improvisations, Lisa Marie (acting very proud of her man) then blurts a response that seems to use language that Jackson's camp would never utter, though it is a far more honest and interesting explanation. "He's an artist . . . he is constantly remodifying something, or changing it or reconstructing it . . . if he sees something he doesn't like he changes it, he has resculpted himself!"

Primetime Live also featured the debut of Jackson's very expensive video for "Scream," a duet with his sister Janet. The video was from the *HIStory* album, and its release was perhaps Jackson's biggest PR move in the wake of the 1993 scandal. While he had previously had gaps of a half-decade between albums, his new offering came out a mere two years after *Dangerous*. He packaged it as a multidisc set that not only featured a new album, but also a collection of his greatest solo hits from his post-Motown days. If his marriage didn't dispel the negative impact of the charges against him, perhaps the music would make people forget.

But if *HIStory* was meant to warm people up to Jackson, the special "commercial" he produced for it, which appeared on TV and in movie theaters to announce the album, complicated matters. Modeled after Leni Riefenstahl's Nazi propaganda film *Triumph of the Will*, the short subject opens with troops wearing brown Russian military uniforms marching in lockstep down a cobblestone European street beneath ominous eagle sculptures and banners with what looks like Cyrillic lettering. The film cuts to footage of sweaty, shirtless steelworkers toiling under inhuman conditions in an oppressive factory, working on something of which we see only a giant eye. Then, amidst the marching troops, we begin to see flashes of buckles and baubles, finally revealing that a rosy-cheeked Jackson wearing a black uniform ornately adorned with silver medals is leading this militia. He smiles and waves to the massive crowd of screaming, weeping white contemporary teenagers who inexplicably populate what seems to be a bleak Eastern Europe of the early twentieth-century. The crowd throws confetti with joy, their happiness contrasted with close-ups of goose-stepping jackboots stomping on confetti and rose petals. The army halts at Jackson's command and does elaborate martial maneuvers with their rifles before the gray sky is torn asunder by helicopters and explosions. People scream and run, cars burn, and riots ensue as we see a rappelling SWAT team set explosive charges on a veiled obelisk. Cut to a command center where an evil-looking czar, surrounded by creepy secret police, gives a command and the charges go off, causing the covering to fall revealing a hundred-story tall statue of Jackson, a new Colossus of Rhodes, the sight of which causes

Courtesy Jake Austen

young women to faint in ecstasy. A small blond boy looks to the sky and declares, in heavily accented English, "Michael, I love you!" As the overjoyed mob (which seems to feature no adults save the brutish police in riot gear) hold up candles and turn their hope-filled eyes toward the monolith, a helicopter shoots through Jackson's legs, just missing his crotch. Martial music swells, climaxes, and cuts off just as the fireworks in the sky become an incendiary flash that fades to reveal, engraved in marble, the words "MICHAEL JACKSON—HISTORY."

While impressively making equal references to communism, fascism, and Nazism, this film did little to endear Jackson to any fans he had lost during his trying times. When Sawyer questioned his motives for this piece during her interview Jackson denied it was based on *Triumph of the Will*, but didn't deny he'd seen the film ("I watch everything; I love movies; I love documentaries"). When Sawyer then pushed him to explain, Jackson made a rare admission that he was intentionally courting controversy. "I wanted everyone's attention," he explained.

It didn't quite work. *HIStory* had modest sales compared to his previous chart triumphs, his marriage courted less attention than expected and lasted only twenty months, and America did not opt to erect a monolith in Jackson's honor.

1996–2000

As a concert artist Jackson was an expatriate in the late 1990s, touring for years in Europe and Asia, with Jackson-sanctioned footage of frenzied non-American, nonblack fans occasionally showing up in the United States. He revived the melody and theme of "We Are the World" as "Heal the World," a *HIStory* song, and then launched an ambiguous world-aid effort of the same name. Jackson began visiting Third World countries on photo-op humanitarian missions. He received international honors leading to TV appearances including the Kora All Africa Music Awards (the Grammys of Africa), where he met Nelson Mandela and donated famine relief funds. On India's cheaply produced Bollywood Awards, he received a humanitarian prize, though he deserved recognition as a creative artist since Bollywood musicals were profoundly influenced by his videos (in the 1980s many featured dance numbers with handsome Indian men in "Beat It" jackets doing signature Jackson moves). He also collected televised honors at Monte Carlo's World Music Awards (humbly accepting the award for Artist of the Millennium) and back home as the Jackson 5ive was inducted into the Rock & Roll Hall of Fame. As he had promised Diane Sawyer, Jackson had become a citizen of the world, constantly on the move, emerging on occasion to be feted and honored for his greatness or generosity. He was a long way from where he started and he didn't seem too concerned with getting back.

In 1996 Jackson had an opportunity to return to an old childhood home, but he apparently had lost the house key. Forgoing the independence of syndication, Don Cornelius had arranged for a prime-time network special to celebrate *Soul Train*'s twenty-fifth anniversary. *Soul Train 25* would not be an award show, but rather an induction ceremony to a new Soul Train Hall of Fame, honoring R&B giants who had appeared during *Soul Train*'s first quarter of a century. Nominees, most of who performed, included Curtis Mayfield, Patti LaBelle, Stevie Wonder, and Jackson, who had performed brilliantly on so many excellent *Soul Train* episodes with the Jackson 5ive in the 1970s.

Despite the fact that it was a network production Cornelius managed to put together a pretty authentically soulful event, with a largely black audience, host Arsenio Hall, and a wide array of African American presenters and inductees. It was a perfect opportunity for Jackson to reconnect with his original audience, but he seemed to have no interest in doing so. While other inductees' introductions featured amazing footage of their *Soul Train* guest spots, Jackson opened with his fascist promo video followed by the familiar montage of European and Asian fans. After dramatic, ominous entrance music (hardly celebratory) he performed several recent songs, none of them upbeat and none of them vaguely resembling soul music. He did an interesting nearly a cappella (there was some spare percussion) dance routine that was good, but it was incongruous with the rest of the show. He also did a schmaltzy, relatively soulless version of "You Are Not Alone." His lip-synching was atrocious (at one point, in an obviously prearranged move, he stopped and kissed a fan who gave him a rose, but the singing went on during the

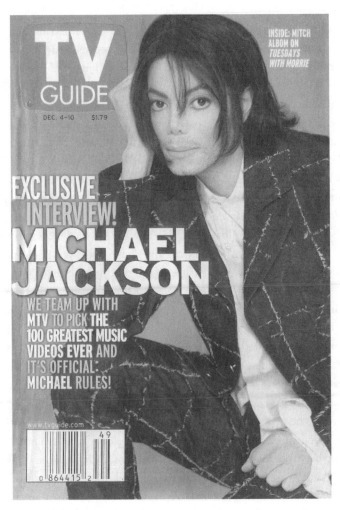

Courtesy Jake Austen.

kiss). Later he found what had to be the only white girl in the audience and brought her on stage to sing to her as she hugged him and screamed.

Jackson did not give an acceptance speech nor acknowledge *Soul Train* in any way. His performance was followed by polite applause. The show, an overall success featuring a number of excellent performances and some remarkable archival footage, ended with Bill Withers leading the inductees and presenters in a joyful version of "Lean On Me." Hopefully no one in the *Soul Train* family had planned on leaning on Jackson. He did not participate in the sing-along, and he was not missed.

2001–2002

In the early days of the twenty-first century, Jackson's disconnection from his original fans and the thinning of his American fan base became issues he was ready to address. He prepared a new album, *Invincible*, and he launched it by celebrating himself in a way that would remind everyone why they should be celebrating him. In September 2001, only days before the World Trade Center attacks, Jackson filmed a spectacular two-day all-star concert at Madison Square Garden, to be edited into a TV special marking Jackson's thirty years as a solo artist. The event featured Usher, Liza Minnelli, Whitney Houston, Destiny's Child, Luther Vandross and others performing their own hits, Jackson's tunes, or (as in the case of Lil' Romeo) their own hits based on samples of Jackson's tunes. The centerpiece of *Michael Jackson: 30th Anniversary Celebration* was the first reunion of the Jacksons since 1984's *Victory* Tour. Following that there was a Michael Jackson solo set.

Due to Jackson's long absence from the charts there was some skepticism about the show, and the event was slow to sell out. Jackson didn't help his buzz when he made a surprise cameo during *NSYNC's performance at the 2001 MTV Video Music Awards on September 6. He briefly danced after emerging from a giant Etch-A-Sketch, but seemed tired and unimpressive compared to the young performers he had inspired.

But despite apprehensions, *Michael Jackson: 30th Anniversary Celebration* was a huge ratings success when it aired on CBS in mid-November, pulling in more than 26 million viewers. The show itself was strong, with its satisfying twenty-minute set by the Jackson 5ive (plus Randy), which had the boys adeptly reprising their dance moves from their 1970 appearance on *The Ed Sullivan Show* and performing hits from their Motown and Epic albums. Of course, they looked quite different than they had when they started. Michael stood out not with his shortness (they are all relatively the same height now) but with his complexion. The chemistry between the brothers seemed excellent; everyone was well-rehearsed and the non-Michael brothers seemed genuinely excited (Randy was jumping around like a jackrabbit) and in good spirits (Jermaine playfully snuck a bass line from his solo-hit "Let's Get Serious" in between songs). Jackson's solo set that followed also was pretty solid, with a good sampling of his hits and a re-creation of his *Motown 25* "Billie Jean" dance routine.

Though it was a good show, the overall package did bear the mark of control freak Jackson. He'd filled the two months between performance and broadcast with endless postproduction (sweetening the music tracks, adding fake crowd noise, and weaving footage from his videos into the performances). Though there didn't seem to be much lip-synching going on at the actual concert, during the Jackson 5ive and Michael's solo portions of the TV broadcast "reverse lip-synching" was abundant, as Jackson and his family seemingly went in and overdubbed vocals throughout their sets. Nevertheless the show proved Jackson was still a vital ratings winner.

One of the more interesting aspects of the *Michael Jackson: 30th Anniversary Celebration* was the audience, which, in contrast to the white teenage crowds that appeared in most Jackson-sanctioned footage, was actually a racially diverse, mixed-age crowd featuring people who had been fans from the 1980s, 1970s, or even 1960s. Acknowledging his original fan base seemed like a wise move, and one of the ways Jackson decided to do this was to position himself not as a messiah/angel/spaceman who was above race, but as a soulful R&B artist drawing from a rich African American tradition. His *Invincible* record wasn't his strongest effort (like the TV special it had layers of overworked, perfectionist postproduction that made it seem clinical), but what was notable about it was that the bulk of the songs were R&B, not pop, due to the influence of producer/writer Rodney "Darkchild" Jerkins and a host of rappers who did cameos (including Biggie Smalls who, in an indication of how long Jackson had spent on this production, had been dead for three years by the time the album came out). While the initial single, "You Rock My World," sounded like a pretty familiar 1990s Jackson dance song, the second single, "Butterflies" (written by the neo-soul group Floetry), and the bulk of the album referred back to Jackson's pre-*Thriller* work. Black radio responded by putting "Butterflies" in heavy rotation.

But the album had disappointing sales and Jackson did not release a video for "Butterflies." Numerous factors contributed to this relative failure (it did debut at number one, go platinum in the United States, and sell six million copies worldwide), including Jackson being an adult artist in a youth market, the CD's R&B edge, and very strong competition. But Jackson placed the blame elsewhere. When he returned to the TV airwaves in July 2002 it was part of the first wave of what cartoonist Aaron McGruder called "the re-negrofication of our most famous racial defector."

"They call me a freak, and it is all just because I am black," Jackson declared, with activist Al Sharpton at his side in a series of New York press conferences. "The minute I surpassed Elvis and the Beatles [in record sales] they called me a freak, a homosexual, a child molester, they said I bleach my skin . . . it is all a big conspiracy. I know my race. I just look in the mirror, I know I'm black." Jackson blamed the failure of *Invincible* on a racist record industry, particularly Sony chairman Tommy Mottola. He said Mottola was "racist and very, very, very devilish," and he accused him of using the word *nigger* to refer to a black artist. Jackson positioned himself as a victim of a long tradition of abuse of black artists by record companies. "If you fight for me," he urged, "you're fighting for all black people, dead and alive. We have to put a stop to this incredible injustice."

Reaction to this appeal was for the most part one of puzzlement. "When is the last time you heard Michael Jackson refer to himself as black?" BET.com asked, and Sony (who continues to keep Jackson under contract) expressed disbelief that an artist for whom they had given huge support would make such statements. Perhaps the most telling sign that either Jackson was no longer relevant or that there actually was a racist media conspiracy was how quickly this disappeared from the airwaves. These were serious charges, yet the press coverage was fleeting. Jackson as an angry black man was obviously not the kind of story that paid the bills. Jackson as a freak of nature was good copy, and in contrast to the low-key coverage of this event, four months later when Jackson awkwardly dangled his new baby from a Berlin balcony to show him off to his fans, the footage was rebroadcast more times than the "Beat It" video.

2003

Twenty years after his fame peaked, 2003 turned out to be (for good and bad) the ultimate TV year for Michael Jackson. The video furor began in February when ITV in England and then ABC in America aired *Living with Michael Jackson*, a documentary that Jackson hoped would paint a more normal, human portrait of him and his family than the public was used to seeing. Martin Bashir, a British journalist who had previously produced a fawning, yet trashy, profile of Princess Di, followed Jackson around for months filming his activities and interviewing him in depth. Much to Jackson's disappointment, the resulting film was far from a fluff job. Instead it was a tabloidesque piece that seemed designed to confirm every scandalous rumor about Jackson.

Much of the negative content in the film is Jackson's fault. It's impossible to blame Bashir for Jackson's tasteless furnishings, his comically overindulgent shopping sprees, and his obsession with toys and games. And it wasn't Bashir who made outrageous, on-camera statements about climbing a magic tree (later parodied on *Saturday Night Live*) or who vehemently defended baby dangling ("I was doing something out of innocence").

Jackson also is less than honest in his interviews. In the film he tells several untruths with a straight face, repeating his claim that he has only had two plastic surgeries and being less than forthright about his children's lineage. After divorcing Presley, Jackson quickly married the unglamorous Debbie Rowe, who worked as a receptionist in his skin doctor's office. Jackson's kids from Rowe both appear to be Caucasian, the boy sporting blond hair (though it is dyed blond, according to *TV Guide*), and don't seem to be of mixed race (Rowe is white), which has led many to speculate that Jackson is not their father. Jackson also offers that his third child has a black mother (Rowe and Jackson divorced in 1999), which makes that child's white looks puzzling. Jackson has custody of all the children and obviously had some sort of prearranged, extremely unusual surrogacy agreements with these women. Whatever the real story is, it is reasonable that he would want to keep these affairs private. However, instead of discreetly avoiding the subject, he willingly offers Bashir several confusing, sometimes conflicting stories. Watching Jackson fib about his face and his kids certainly brings to mind the child instructed to lie about his age, his family, and the identity of the person who discovered him. Though Motown's coaching didn't necessarily damage Jackson's ability to distinguish the truth, it very well may have convinced him that convenient constructions that can help your image are acceptable.

While Jackson certainly earns his "wacko" title in this film, he also comes off as a trusting man who expects Bashir to tell the world that Jackson loves his children and all the children of the world. But as Jackson leads Bashir around his estate and proudly describes his humanitarian efforts to bring hope to terminally ill children, Bashir gushes in agreement, yet overdubs his own ominous narration changing the tone of the piece to one that constantly implies Jackson is a predatory pedophile. This is especially notable when Jackson introduces a young man who was a cancer victim and near death when Jackson befriended him. The young man's miracle recovery, it is implied, has come about in part because of the positive experiences he and other children enjoy when visiting the Neverland Ranch. Jackson then explains that this kid and many others have slept over, some in his bed, and that nothing inappropriate ever occurs. Bashir makes this section of the film a focal point, adding his own comments to ensure that Jackson comes across as a creepy freak to even the most trusting viewers.

Bashir also presents numerous unflattering images of Jackson that may not be as bad as they look. To cloak his children's identities (ostensibly protecting their safety) Jackson has them wear absurd masks in public and on camera, and one of the most horrifying shots in the special is of Jackson awkwardly trying to feed a bottle to an infant through a veil. Though he is portrayed in that scene as an incompetent father, clearly Jackson's nervousness about feeding the baby on camera, and the veil that would not be in place without the camera's presence, are what make him so ham-fisted. In another scene Jackson is mobbed at a European zoo in a scene that demonstrates the obvious fact that superstardom makes life crazy. But according to the narration, Jackson is joyously drinking in the attention while ignoring his own small children who surely would have been killed if Bashir himself hadn't saved their lives.

The show certainly made Jackson look nuts, so in that respect it hurt his image, and it also contributed to police opening an investigation into Jackson's sleepovers, so it may have ruined his life. But it also helped paint Jackson as a victim of the manipulative media, something Jackson had been trying to do for years. Though many who saw the show agreed with Bashir's assessment of Jackson, few who saw it failed to recognize that the journalist had set Jackson up.

And more than a few saw it. Twenty-seven million viewers watched the program, a ratings boom for struggling ABC. Those massive ratings contributed to a tidal wave of Jackson programming, with NBC showing *Dateline: Michael Jackson Unmasked*, a shallow special that revealed little more than the fact that plastic surgeons don't believe Jackson has had only two surgeries. (NBC had promised the Jackson camp that it would shelve this negative special if Jackson would sell the American rights to *Living with Michael Jackson* to NBC instead of ABC.) ABC also aired an hour-long *Primetime Live* Jackson episode and quickly re-aired the original special, while other networks created blocks of Jackson coverage for their newsmagazines.

But the most interesting special that aired in the wake of the Bashir interview was Fox's *Michael Jackson Take 2: The Interview They Wouldn't Let You See*. Produced by the Jackson camp, this took advantage of the fact that one of the conditions to which Bashir had to agree before he could gain access to Jackson was to allow the Jackson organization to videotape the interviews as well, as a safeguard against manipulative editing. This special was Jackson's reaction to Bashir's work, which had made Jackson feel (according to an official press release) "devastated and . . . utterly betrayed by [this] gross distortion of the truth and a tawdry attempt to misrepresent [my] life and [my] abilities as a father."

In *Michael Jackson Take 2* we not only see Jackson give longer, more benign answers to Bashir's questions, but more tellingly we hear Bashir egging Jackson on by telling him what a great father he is and how he admires his work with children. But the reason this alternate version was ultimately more interesting than the documentary it was responding to is that Bashir's work merely provided illustrations and confirmations of rumors we were already familiar with; Jackson's piece, on the other hand, offered some genuinely new information. It featured an interview with Rowe responding to the odd revelations about Jackson's custody arrangement with their children, and while the exact nature of their relationship remains murky, this interview revealed that either Rowe is one of the greatest actresses of our generation or she actually had a genuine, loving relationship with Jackson. They certainly did not have a normal marriage (they were rarely together and they have some financial arrangement in regard to the children), but Rowe passionately defends Jackson, thereby revealing her strong, loyal, and affectionate attachment to him. Clearly, their friendship (presumably forged on his many visits to the doctor she worked for) was real. We also see candid footage of a relaxed Jackson (as he waits to be interviewed by Bashir) laughing and joking with women (his stylists, perhaps) in a manner that also demonstrates warm, normal human relations. In this footage, Jackson comes across as the "gay friend" type who has good, real relationships with women. While this may not be an image Jackson would welcome, it is an example of a more genuine, grounded human being than the freaky alien/messiah persona Jackson and the media have long presented to the public.

My favorite part of this special was footage that Jackson included not to defend himself from Bashir's implications, but merely because he was so proud of it that he couldn't believe it didn't make the original final edit. Describing the fate of his famed 1980s chimpanzee companion Bubbles, Jackson explained how apes become aggressive as they mature and need to live in a more suitable, natural habitat, so he had to move his former sidekick to just such a place. But Jackson made a point to add, beaming with parental pride not unusual for a pet owner, that Bubbles had *excellent* table manners. While describing a pet ape's etiquette may not be exactly normal, the manner in which Jackson boasted about this made him seem extremely human, which, of course, was his original goal when he agreed to the documentary project.

The ratings success of the Fox special led to a follow-up by the same production team in April called *Michael Jackson's Private Home Movies*, which not only served to humanize Jackson, but also reminded America where he came from. The two-hour special compiled a variety of footage, including super-8 films of young Jackson playing in the snow with his brothers in front of their tiny two-bedroom (for nine children) Gary, Indiana, home; video of the Jacksons taking a detour during the *Victory* Tour to visit extended family in rural Alabama, and footage from a 1990s family event Jackson threw honoring his father. The endless footage of Jackson and Macaulay Culkin having water fights at Neverland was a bit disconcerting, as Jackson seemed remarkably adept at acting like a ten-year-old as he approached middle age. But even that seemed humanizing, as he really appeared to be having fun (and he didn't seem concerned with getting his makeup and hair wet). The special even managed to unearth footage of screaming English teenagers outside of Jackson's hotel room . . . and half the crowd was black!

The self-produced Fox specials managed to temper the barrage of negative Jackson coverage resulting from the Bashir documentary, but it wasn't until June that Jackson found a truly welcoming TV home. The third annual *BET Awards* (the highest-rated show in the network's history at the time) honored James Brown with a lifetime achievement award. Though later that year he would receive a Kennedy Center Honor, this recognition had a tangible benefit attached: Mr. Brown would have fifteen minutes of national airtime and a massive, rapt audience of contemporary black music fans. James Brown showed the youngsters how it was done back in the day, powerfully performing several songs with his full revue (including a costumed band, glamorous backup singers and energetic dancers). The hip-hop generation in attendance was enthusiastic for most of the set, but when it came time for the traditional end of a Brown performance, Bobby Byrd's ceremonial draping of a regal cape over Brown's shoulders, the crowd burst into the night's most intense explosion of cheers. Jackson (his participation kept secret from the audience and Mr. Brown) emerged to do the draping. Brown, who traditionally flings off his cape in an unexpected burst of energy, was so delighted to see Jackson that he broke script and insisted Jackson wear the cape. Trying to keep the focus on his idol, Jackson accepted only a brief moment in the spotlight, updating his Motown audition by doing a tribute to Brown's dance moves, this time adding a Jackson flourish with a signature spin. He then, upon Brown's insistence, took the microphone briefly, and with appropriate funk, urged the band to "make it funky" before giving the stage back to Brown.

The most amazing element of this telecast was not Jackson's dynamic performance, the antithesis of the lackluster cameo he had done with *NSYNC two years prior. What was most magical was the audience's reaction. Jackson had rarely faced an all-black crowd since the 1970s. With his porcelain complexion, straight hair, white wives, blond children, and musical crossover ambitions, Jackson logically should have been abandoned by this audience. After a decade of rumors about child molestation, one would expect a Church-influenced black congregation (Gospel star Yolanda Adams received the biggest ovation of the broadcast prior to Jackson's) to disassociate themselves from him.

But instead the audience expressed overwhelming acceptance and excitement. For years Jackson had forced the public to sit through footage of young girls in Europe or Asia breaking into tears of excitement to be in the presence of Jackson, but here, on live TV, we saw a young, American black woman spontaneously shedding tears because her love for Jackson was real, true, and intact. Perhaps that forgiveness and love is part of black America's contract with its celebrities. After centuries of abuse and victimization perhaps black America is so uncomfortable watching white America attack one of their own that they would rather forgive blindly than side with a mainstream that attacks their people. While the O. J. Simpson case is the most polarizing example of this phenomenon, a more fitting analogy to Jackson would be R. Kelly's situation. A popular singer accused of taking underage sex partners, Kelly enjoyed tremendous support among R&B fans despite strong evidence that many of them had seen firsthand (the sex video that sparked the investigation was heavily bootlegged and widely distributed). In fact, later in the same *BET Awards* broadcast Kelly received an award and gratefully acknowledged the cheering crowd, explaining that the unconditional support he received was "what being black is all about."

But obviously the crowd's intense love for Jackson was not just about victimization and forgiveness. This audience had loved Jackson very deeply for a very long time. His music, his performances, his energy, his life since childhood were all things he had given to them. And they treasured these things. After he left the stage with Brown, the electricity of the moment still in the air, actor/singer Tyrese put the mood of the crowd into words.

"Michael Jackson . . . you're still black," he proudly declared. "You're still one of us!"

That fall tested black America's loyalty to Jackson once again. Inspired by tides turning in his favor (and no doubt by the massive success of similar packages by the Beatles and Elvis), Jackson prepared a new greatest hits release titled *Number Ones*. However, on November 18, the day of the CD's release, police raided Neverland investigating new child molestation charges. The next day Santa Barbara

District Attorney Thomas W. Sneddon, Jr., held a televised press conference to announce that there was a warrant out for Jackson's arrest. To many observers Sneddon, who failed to prosecute Jackson's case a decade earlier because of the settlement, seemed to be out for revenge on a man who humiliated him (the HIS- *tory* album featured a funky song accusing Sneddon of conspiring with the CIA and possibly with the Klan to bring Jackson down). When asked at the November 19 press conference if the charges were intentionally meant to coincide with the new CD's release, Sneddon jovially told the TV cameras, "Like the sheriff and I are into that kind of music. . . ."

That is a problematic statement on many levels. Most obviously (and for which Sneddon eventually apologized) it was inappropriate to be cracking jokes when discussing child molestation. But just as disturbing was the suggestion that it would be outrageous for him to listen to Jackson's music. If 50 Cent or a member of Slayer, or even Prince were being prosecuted it would be understandably absurd to expect an uptight older white guy to listen to the defendant's music. But by releasing the best-selling album in pop history, Jackson had literally made some the most accessible music of the past century, and prior to his solo success he was a member of the beloved Jackson 5ive. Few baby boomers (Sneddon was in his twenties at the outset of the 1970s) are aghast at the thought of listening to Motown. To many ears when Sneddon said "*that* kind of music" he meant "black music." Not surprisingly, many African Americans following the story publicly questioned the charges. Black pundits went on cable news channels nightly to declare Jackson's innocence. Many simply charged institutionalized racism, while some offered elaborate conspiracy theories (activist Dick Gregory posited an elaborate situation in which Jackson would be killed and his death made to look like a suicide, all to wrest the crown jewel of white culture, the Beatles song catalog, which Michael had purchased, from his black hands). To many black observers, this came down to Jackson, with his straight hair, tiny nose, and white skin, being as black as the day he was born in the eyes of the racist law enforcement establishment.

As with the charges a decade earlier, both sides were trying their cases in the media long before any indictment. In what legal experts called an unprecedented move, the Santa Barbara County district attorney's office hired a Hollywood public relations firm to handle media inquiries. Strategic leaks revealed everything from the fact that child welfare investigators had declared the charges unwarranted earlier in the year, to the terms of the 1993 settlement, which totaled more than $23 million. TV viewers saw footage of Jackson with the boy, whose face was pixilated to protect his identity. However, it was familiar footage being altered— the footage from the Bashir documentary (which clearly identified the boy) featuring Jackson and the young terminal patient he aided and shared a bed with. This provided ammo for Jackson's detractors (as it put the boy in bed with the singer) and his defenders (who argued that Jackson did not fit the profile of a child molester because molesters try to hide what they do, and Jackson prominently used this boy as an example of a child he slept with but did not violate).

Jackson's televised arrest ("from moonwalk to perp walk" said CBS News) was followed by a bail payment, a passport confiscation, and a month of lying low as his album sales, predictably, faltered. Then on December 28 Jackson returned to TV, granting Ed Bradley an exclusive interview on *60 Minutes* (CBS, 1968–present). Jackson maintained his innocence and blamed the greedy parents for forcing the boy to make the false allegations. He insisted he still would let a child sleep in his bed, explaining, "If you're going to be a pedophile, if you're going to be Jack the Ripper, if you're going to be a murderer, it's not a good idea. That I am not."

Jackson positioned himself as a victim of police brutality, claiming arresting officers manhandled and injured him, supplementing the abuse by locking him in a "doo-doo" smeared bathroom. He also referenced the racist conspiracy against him that he first revealed in 2002, noting that his new record topped the charts "all over the world. America is the only one, because I—I don't wanna say too much . . . it's a conspiracy." Though he seemed somewhat melodramatic and not totally credible during these statements (as if the benign form of lying that Berry Gordy trained him to do early in his career had careened out of control), the content of his interview was less important than its intended audience. By citing police brutality and a racist conspiracy Jackson had purposefully rung two bells sure to resonate with his African American followers, the only Americans who truly rallied behind him in his time of need. He was driving home the message Tyrese had delivered six months earlier: Michael Jackson is still black.

2004

The year 2004 opened with the airing of a Jackson-produced special, which was originally scheduled to run when his CD was released. The molestation charges made CBS pull it from the fall schedule, and this later airing seemed to be part of the compensation the network gave Jackson for the *60 Minutes* interview (in their defense CBS claimed they wanted Jackson to publicly declare, on their airwaves, that he was innocent before they would broadcast the special).

Michael Jackson Number Ones was one of the best-crafted TV specials about Jackson ever produced. Like the album it promoted, *Number Ones* featured Jackson's greatest hits, and it innovatively presented each song in its entirety, blending audio from studio versions and concert performances while showing images from videos, TV appearances, and live shows. As the songs played, contemporary stars Missy Elliot, Beyoncé, Mary J. Blige, Jill Scott, Mya, Savion Glover, Pharrel Williams, and Wyclef Jean shared personal reflections on Jackson's music and dancing, paying tribute to his influence on the generation of R&B and hip-hop artists that followed him. Quincy Jones was also on hand to describe in detail the process of completing *Thriller*. The show made a point of focusing only on black artists, as the new Jackson was in touch with his roots and apparently unconcerned with what Justin and Britney thought of him. The only prominent white voice in the show belonged to Dick Clark who (apparently having not received the memo) pontificated about Jackson transcending race. It was the first Michael Jackson–produced special in almost two decades not to feature an extended montage of screaming pale European fans.

The special was supposed to end with Jackson's new video for the aptly or unfortunately or coincidentally titled "One More Chance," his new single produced by fellow child abuse defendant R. Kelly. However, the real world intervened; as he was working on that video his arrest warrant was issued, forcing him to halt production.

Speaking of the real world, 2004 was a different kind of year for Jackson TV appearances, as he was guaranteed to be the highlight of news broadcasts every time his presence was required or requested at the courthouse. On January 16, TV viewers got a feel for what was in store as Jackson arrived for his arraignment and was greeted by more than 1,500 screaming fans who had traveled from all over the globe to support their hero. Dressed in a black outfit that made him look like a hybrid of Dracula, Harry Potter, and Little Richard, Jackson waved to his supporters, and as he left the court (after being admonished by the judge for being late—his tardiness caused by the adoring throng) he hopped atop his SUV and did some dance moves for the cheering crowd.

As Jackson drove off his people distributed invitations to his fans for a Neverland party that evening to thank them for their support. Party attendees enjoyed free amusement park rides, and were served ice cream sandwiches, cookies, and hot dogs.

And, of course, fried chicken. Because Michael Jackson has soul.

Appendix I

International TV Rock

This book is mostly about American TV, but some amazing video treasures from around the world have added their native flavors to two of the United States' greatest art forms, TV and rock 'n' roll. Here is a random sampling of a dozen notable shows from abroad.

Top of the Pops

I'm sure if I lived in Britain I would be cynical about this show, but as an outsider I have always been impressed by what seems to me to be the most populist music program in the world. If a song is a hit, the performer—whether a big name or an unknown—will turn up on the show to lip-synch or play live. When the California punk garage band Rocket from the Crypt had a minor British hit a few years ago they found themselves sharing the dressing room with a gaggle of performers in Smurf costumes because the Smurfs had scored a novelty hit that week. When a remix of an Elvis Presley song charted a couple of years ago, a jazz-dancing Elvis impersonator appeared in shadow behind a dramatically lit curtain. For more than forty years this weekly live show has featured legendary performances by such giants as David Bowie, the Beatles, and the Spice Girls, but it has also given its stage to the likes of the Four Bucketeers, Man II Man, and Kelly Osbourne. The January 1964 premiere presented the Rolling Stones, Dusty Springfield, and the Dave Clark Five. Since then *Top of the Pops* has showcased thousands of bands. It has been franchised to several countries, and it trumped its American brethren by putting together a Web site featuring brief clips of hundreds of archival performances (www.bbc.co.uk/totp).

Beat Club

From 1965 to 1972 *Beat Club*, featuring sexy Uschi Nerke, was Germany's great rock TV show (the similar *Musikladen*, also hosted by Nerke, replaced it in late 1972 and continued until 1980). What made this show so brilliant was a perfect balance between the vibe of a studio program and the energy of a live concert. The fact that a government-funded show strived to re-create the feel of the German "beat" scene, a genuinely debauched nightclub circuit, was bold and progressive. The show booked challenging bands like the Monks, the Pretty Things, Frank Zappa, and Steppenwolf, which elevated it above its peers. In the mid-1960s the program had the feel of a club, with the well-dressed teens dancing to live music. At the end of the decade and in the early 1970s (especially after it went to color in 1969), it embraced the aesthetics of psychedelic music and metal and began using bizarre camera tricks and video feedback to make it appear that the performers were rocking inside an acid-tripping brain. Visionary director Michael Leckebusch, a music fan who knew how to follow the beat, was an enemy of boring TV; he insisted on moving cameras and frequent cuts. Though acts such as Black Sabbath, Led Zeppelin, and The Who were huge in the United States, there wasn't really a place on American TV for them, but this European stage suited them perfectly (Led Zeppelin's best "music video" is from *Beat Club*). Acts such as the MC5, Small Faces, and predisco Bee Gees, who were never fully appreciated in America, got to shine on the *Beat Club* stage. Perhaps the greatest thing about these shows was that Germany valued them highly enough to preserve them; the footage has showed up regularly on *Night Flight*, HBO, and VH1 over the years. From a contemporary perspective, the 1969 through 1972 episodes are incredible because they herald the visual vibe of MTV. This is some of the greatest rock-on-TV footage ever shot, and to this day music fans love and treasure it.

(Note: *Beat Beat Beat* was another excellent show that many people get confused with *Beat Club*.)

Ronny's Pop Show

I wanted to limit this list to one show per country, but I really can't ignore this gem. I admit that I am easily charmed by monkeys (or apes, to be accurate in this case) dressed as people. As a young man visiting overseas in the early 1980s I was entranced by this German music video show hosted by a chimpanzee named Ronny (in tribute to U.S. president Ronald Reagan, who had costarred with a chimp in the 1951 movie *Bedtime for Bonzo*). Not only was I amused by seeing a banana-eater do comedy bits between Michael Jackson and Paul Young videos, but I also appreciated the implications that the leader of the free world and the MTV VJs were replaceable by lower primates. There were a couple of dozen pop compilation LPs and CDs released under the *Ronny's Pop Show* banner, so Ronny's hairy mug will live on forever in European used-record stores!

Long Way to the Top

In 2001, the Australian Broadcasting Company aired a six-part TV documentary on the nearly fifty-year history of Australian rock 'n' roll. For a number of reasons (including the smaller scale of the industry there) this is a more focused, riveting, successful rock history than any of its American equivalents. Named after an AC/DC song (already a good start), this show not only focuses on acts with international chart success such as the Seekers, Men at Work, the Bee Gees, Kylie Minogue, and INXS, but also on awesome acts like the Saints, the Scientists, the Beasts of Bourbon, the Go Betweens, and the Bad Seeds. The film explains the Aussie commitment to lesser acts by telling the tale of the brief period in 1970 when Australian radio refused to accept payola to play specific major label records. Radio stations were consequently cut off from the hits just long enough to establish a place on Oz radio for local and underground acts. That cracked door has never completely closed. The show celebrates the influence of the blues on Australian rock, and the producers even discuss the influence of indigenous Australian nonwhites. For fans of TV rock, this documentary also celebrated *Countdown*, the 1970s TV show that emerged in the early days of Angus Young's and Bon Scott's pub rock madness (though Molly Meldrum is no Wolfman Jack). Like all such documentaries, the ratio of talking heads to archival music may be too high (though there are some hilarious heads doing the talking, including a hooligan rock fan from the 1970s and a wide-eyed member of a goofy band that toured the

United States with Men at Work), but overall this is a must-see for fans of Aussie rock. The series is available on DVD with bonus jabbering by Nick Cave.

Nardwuar on Much Music

Nardwuar the Human Serviette (*serviette* means "napkin," but don't ask me to try to figure out why or how he is a human one) is an absurdist interviewer from Vancouver, British Columbia, who moved up from cable access and college radio to Much Music, Canada's answer to MTV, and became the best thing on that network. Nardwuar first made a name for himself in the early 1990s by capitalizing on the fact that international media figures and their publicists get confused in Canada and don't know to ignore media credentials from wacky college stations. Asking bizarre questions of Mikhail Gorbachev, Dan Quayle, and Tony Robbins established Nardwuar's legend, but his true forte has always been his in-depth interviews with musical icons. Armed with extensive research about the most obscure trivia concerning his subjects/victims (as well as gifts, visual aids, and props), Nardwuar's grating, nasal voice and odd questions create a precarious balance between annoyingness and sincerity. While the questions and answers are often funny, what really makes a Nardwuar interview worthwhile is that it is a litmus test; seeing how your favorite stars react when presented with this strange pest lets you know if they are genuinely cool or if they are haughty assholes. I can't tell you how disappointed I was to learn that Micky Dolenz of the Monkees is, in fact, a total dick. However, I was pleased to learn that Judas Priest's Rob Halford is a stand-up guy. Though Nardwuar's success has been limited, I've seen some of his distinctive mannerisms in the combative interview comedy of his countrymen Tom Green and Martin Short (in Short's "Jiminy Glick" character). Nardwuar is incredibly knowledgeable about and proud of Canada's rock history. He goes to extremes to find a historical Canadian rock connection to his interview subject, drawing from a massive database of obscure Canuck garage band trivia. While some subjects mistake this for some kind of overcompensating Canadian sense of insecurity (Gene Simmons: "You should be proud of this country, you've got a lot of land, great-looking girls . . . stop whining . . . it's embarrassing"), in fact Nardwuar makes it quite clear that he is a proud son of the North by imploring every interview subject to, in the words of Canadian rock hero Neil Young, "keep on rockin' in the free world!"

A Turma do Balao Magico ("The Magic Balloon Gang")

This program, a kiddie variety show on Brazil's Globo TV network in the 1980s, set the precedent for the more famous (but musically inferior) soft-core porno kiddie extravaganza *Xuxa*. The gang consisted of four remarkable children. Mike was the son of Ronald Biggs, the legendary British train robber (and one-time Sex Pistol) who settled in Rio, impregnated his girlfriend, and was saved because Brazil doesn't extradite expectant fathers. TV viewers fell in love with little Mike when he sang and danced old British music hall numbers for the tabloid press that was hounding his father. Beautiful Simony, the sweetheart of the group, would grow up to become a top-selling ballad singer, a nude model, and the girlfriend of Afro-X, the Tupac of Brazil. Toby, a heartthrob as a kiddie performer, found little media success later in life, but also avoided the child-star curse. And Jairzinho, the only black member of the gang, is the son of Jair Rodrigues, a brilliant Brazilian musician who worked alongside his countrymen Caetano Veloso, Gilberto Gil, Chico Buarque, and other legends. Jairzinho inherited his father's talents, and when he made his way into the Magic Balloons he helped them peak in popularity (to the point where their concerts filled stadiums). What made the show great was that instead of playing condescending children's music or reinforcing to toddlers the most sexist and racist aspects of their culture (as *Xuxa* did), *A Turma do Balao Magico* embraced rich Afro-Cuban musical traditions and actually made excellent music with Brazil's greatest musicians. In a country that regularly embraced poorly crafted novelty entertainment by marginally talented children, this gang raised the bar for children's musical TV.

Kikaida

This Japanese TV show (1972–1973, full name *Jinzo ningen kikaida* or, "Mechanical Man Kikaida") was the most rock 'n' roll of all the monster-fighting robot-hero shows of that glorious era. Ban Daisuke (who recently starred in the horror film *Ringu*, remade in the United States as *The Ring*) played Jiro, a shag-haired, denim-clad drifter who rode around Japan on his custom motorcycle, guitar slung across his back, looking for trouble. Whenever good and righteous people were attacked by an evil Destructoid monster and/or android, a sweet strum of Jiro's guitar heralded salvation. Jiro then transformed into his true identity, Kikaida, a cycle-riding super robot, and saved the day, only to ride off again, a lonely minstrel. In human form Jiro's haircut, clothes, and guitar make him a *rokibiri* (rockabilly) icon, but unfortunately, other than his one mighty guitar strum (not even a power chord, it evokes folk rock), there is little actual rock music in the show. The show's opening theme song, despite launching with a Ramones-like "1-2-3" and ending with a Sunset Strip-evoking "go go go," is more a rousing, 1970s James Bond tune than a rocker. His closing theme sounds like 1970s detective show music (though the song mentions his guitar). But even if the specific music wasn't there, the influence of psychedelic and mod imagery was undeniable, as Kikaida's bizarre costume was the most outrageous and acid trippy of all his robotic peers (which is really saying something). His monster opponents were even more bizarre, and his main villain had an evil flute straight out of *A Clockwork Orange*. Though this was a children's program, like all of the country's superhero/robot shows, in some ways it was geared to an older audience, as evidenced by its prime-time scheduling (unprecedented for a Japanese kiddie show) and its sophisticated exploration of artificial intelligence. Though obscure to most Americans, this show actually was the most popular of all of the era's Japanese imports. Subtitled episodes of *Kikaida* began running in Hawaii in the mid-1970s and were all the rage. The rockin' robot became an enduring figure in that state's pop culture land-scape. It wasn't until the *Power Rangers* import in 1993 that the mainland caught up with the Japanese robot fever that had already infected the fiftieth state.

Kikaida. Courtesy Alex Wald

Escala Musical TV

Many excellent LPs and 45s captured the South American garage rock scene that emerged after the Beatles. But the best way to get the vibe of the movement is to watch the archival episodes of this fantastic Argentine program, the only show in the region to feature obscure local bands, including two of the best. Uruguay's Los Mockers were a bluesy Rolling Stones–influenced group that recorded a number of LPs, including one U.S.-only release. When they appeared on *Escala Musical* ("Music Scale") they played "Paint It Black" in English, and it was as dark and powerful and gritty as the best of the early Stones. Also from Uruguay, Los Shakers modeled their music after the Beatles, and their TV appearances had all the joy and wackiness of the Beatles movies (and maybe even their cartoons!). They sang in English, and it's clear they were trying to do English accents. They were one of the best of the numerous Beatles clones, slightly original even though they were unabashed fans (one of their wacky filmed segments on this show had them genuflecting in front of a Beatles photo). Both of these bands were big in South America with the help of *Escala Musical TV,* a very savvy multimedia outfit. Los Gatos Salvajes, from the Argentine province of Rosario (still a good home of rock 'n' roll, Rosario recently held an Argentine independent music festival), auditioned for the show and received contracts. They played at Saturday parties for their bosses and then did songs on the show on Sunday afternoons. The producers also arranged for their record contracts and compiled footage from the show into a movie. Despite its craftiness, *La Escala Musical* went bankrupt at the end of 1965. The show may have had a brief life but it was in the right place at the right time to capture some of the best garage music ever.

The Villagers

Despite being the motherland of blues, soul, rock 'n' roll, and all points in between, Africa has not been a great place for music TV, due to poverty, government corruption, censorship, and other factors. Fela, the king of African pop, considered Nigerian TV an evil that corrupted his countrymen so he took little part in it. In apartheid South Africa the cultural segregation complicated what could have been a media rich with great music. Though not a music show, *The Villagers* featured a rare soulful mainstream moment in the early days of South African TV. The 1977 soap-drama was one of the country's most beloved programs, an escapist show about Buller Wilmot, a heroic goldmine manager, played by Brian O'Shaughnessy, the Errol Flynn of South Africa. The theme song for the program stands up nicely alongside the great funky American 1970s TV themes. Performed by the Jade Brothers (featuring Mick Jade, an underrated South African musical figure), "The Villagers Theme" is a catchy tune, with a tough harmonica break and a seductive bass line that makes it fall somewhere between a TV jingle and a chewy slab of AM radio bubblegum soul. The reprise was a much deeper, funkier version that utilized a secret weapon. In addition to wild saxophone playing, it also featured Ben Masinga, a black vocalist Jade smuggled into the TV studio, thereby breaking apartheid rules in the name of funk. While this minor blip of collaborative integration did little to free Mandela, it was a baby step toward a new South Africa.

Champs-Elysées

This French late-night show wasn't known to be particularly rocking—in fact it was beloved by older middle-of-the-road viewers. However, on April 5, 1986, it featured one of the great moments in TV rock, if only because it highlighted the profound differences between American and French pop music. That night Paris welcomed rising pop diva Whitney Houston (beautiful, young, and glowing) to its version of *The Tonight Show*. As the perfect mid-1980s pop star Houston was smiling her way through well-sung, but soul-free pop songs, as inoffensive as a bouquet of daisies. Sitting next to her was France's greatest pop icon, the beloved Serge Gainsbourg. This haggard fifty-eight-year-old drunk seemed to be an entirely different species than America's sweetheart. After decades of performing absurdly dirty songs, ranging from breathy orgasm pop ("Je T'aime . . . Moi Non Plus") to a sex song performed with his underage daughter ("Lemon Incest," with Charlotte Gainsbourg, now an international film star) to an upbeat Holocaust rock opera, Gainsbourg could hardly shock France. Shocking Houston, however, was another matter. He kissed her hand and, slurring his words like Foster Brooks, told her she was a genius. Host Michel Drucker, obviously nervous that there was a *tiny* chance that Gainsbourg might say something inappropriate, began furiously translating for Houston, assuring her that he was only saying positive things. This preemptive strike was both ridiculous (because Gainsbourg was speaking English) and fruitless, as it infuriated the French star, who barked at Drucker (in response to the would-be diplomacy), "You are not Reagan, I am not Gorbachev, so don't try it. . . ." Then, enunciating as clearly as a French drunkard can, he exclaimed, "I said *I want to fuck her!*" Houston's appearances on Johnny Carson's couch and as a guest star on *Silver Spoons* had not prepared her for this moment; her eyes opened very wide, and her face froze in the expression of Munch's "The Scream" for about ten seconds. She then settled in and played it somewhere between aston-

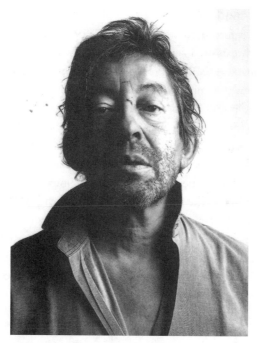

Serge Gainsbourg. Courtesy Jake Austen

ishment and amusement. She diverted Gainsbourg's paws as he attempted to touch her hair and face. Drucker sheepishly explained, "Sometimes he is a little bit drunk." Later on the show Gainsbourg took a microphone and sang *"Visille Canaille"* ("You Rascal, You"), and the program then reverted once again to a cheesy talk show.

Of course, this was much more shocking in 1986 than it would be now because at the time Houston was a pure, sweet *Cosby Show*–era kid. She was years away from her TV rock low point, a 2002 interview with Diane Sawyer. In that interview, a gaunt, manic Houston admitted to "partying" a lot; denied being *addicted* to cocaine, marijuana, and pills (instead offering, "I'd like to think I had a bad habit"); and demanded to see the receipts from the dealer who claimed she bought $730,000 worth of drugs from him. This train wreck was highlighted by Houston declaring, "Crack is *wack!*" But back in 1986, the heart of the Reagan era, she was a fresh-faced diva who appeared on a Nancy Reagan–inspired antidrug record and video called "Stop the Madness," a phrase I'm sure she uttered to whoever booked her on *Champs-Elysées*.

Russian Bandstand

Russian kids were forced to watch this late 1950s show, hosted by Nikita Clarkchev, with threats of violence (disloyalty to the number-one tune, often by Nikita Presleychev, was punishable by death). The program was sponsored by a brand of cigarette with a microphone filter so the secret police could keep track of young people. Oh wait, *Russian Bandstand* wasn't a real show—it was a 1959 comedy record by Spencer and Spencer. Obviously Soviet-era Russia was not interested in Western rock 'n' roll TV programming, and it wasn't until the 1990s that FM radio, touring rock concerts, and a Russian music industry (which includes a great deal of bootlegging) earned the country the honor of having its very own MTV-Russia. In the fall of 1998 Mumy Troll's video "Vladivostok-2000" heralded this bold new era celebrating Russia's embrace of Western decadence. Founded by entrepreneur Boris Zosimov, Russian MTV embraced the similarities between Soviet culture and the American record industry by being cleverly corrupt. MTV-Russia does not accept payola per se, but exacts money from artists who want airplay (a powerful promotional tool) by insisting that the network's own production staff receive healthy fees to make the videos that will get heavy rotation. This unpopular policy left the door open for an alternative music channel, the lower-rated MUZ-TV, which is better with regional programming and with Russian hip-hop. A few years ago MUZ-TV launched its own awards show on which artists like Leningrad, Zemfira, and Splin compete for top prizes. The station looked beyond MTV-Russia as competition as it boasted of plans to "surpass the famous Grammy ceremony."

Eurovision

While *American Idol* is an absolute sensation in the United States, Europe has enjoyed a grander, purer version of it for almost fifty years. Founded in 1956 on the idealistic premise that the medium of TV could be used to foster international brotherhood, the Eurovision songwriting competition features a pop song from each European country (culled from each land's own pageant) competing to be the song of the year. Victory not only guarantees international fame and success for the song, but also a window of opportunity for the pop artist who performs the tune and (most importantly) bragging rights and hosting chores at the next year's *Eurovision* special for the victorious country. The voting (once done electoral college style, now done *American Idol* phone-in style) does not allow voters to vote for their own country, though politics are still involved (certain nations never vote for other nations, regions vote in blocs, and, because of the phone-in system, expatriates and immigrants can vote for their home country from their new base).

One important distinction from talent contests is that this is a *songwriting* competition; it celebrates writing and production. The artist need not be from the designated country (representing Switzerland, Celine Dion, a Canadian singing in French, won in 1988). In fact, at times a song can be completely nonrepresentative of the country. In 1999 Germany's entrant, Surpriz (actually Turkish musicians) sang a song in Hebrew because that year's contest took place in Israel (Dana International, a transsexual diva, had brought the contest back to the Holy Land for the first time since Israel's stunning back-to-back wins in 1978 and 1979). Though a handful of successful acts have won over the years (Lulu, Katrina and the Waves) there is one moment that has defined all subsequent *Eurovisions*: 1974's Swedish victory when ABBA performed "Waterloo." ABBA went on to become the planet's top act. That victory proved (to *Eurovision* fans) that *Eurovision* worked! Each year's actual telecast is a glitzy, loud, tacky spectacle that magnifies the absurdity of Europop and broadcasts that absurdity to 100 million viewers worldwide. The camp value makes it a favorite among gays, the fairytale aspect (an unknown becomes a global sensation overnight) makes it a hit among young girls, and the competitive nature makes it worthwhile for gamblers. But *Eurovision* is worth obsessing over even though it's silly, fluffy, and unimportant. Personally I look to *Eurovision* for a day when we will have a world without wars, a utopia where we can solve all our conflicts through dance music . . . a day when a global dispute can end not with bloodshed, but with such jiggy declarations as "You got served, Baltics!"

> "TV Party tonight . . . we've got
> nothing better to do"
>
> —Black Flag ("TV Party")

Appendix 2

Rock 'n' Roll TV Guide

It seems that over the last few years America has caught a case of list fever. Critical inventories like Modern Library's Top 100 Novels of the 20th Century, AFI's 100 Greatest American Movies, and VH1 and *TV Guide*'s *100 Greatest Moments That Rocked TV* have all sparked debate and begat numerous lists in response. I certainly don't want to disappoint list maniacs, but compiling a list of the hundred best TV rock episodes seems kind of arbitrary and boring. Instead I enlisted the writing staff of *Roctober* magazine to help me program a dream week of the most interesting TV rock episodes. These certainly aren't the most famous shows, and I wouldn't argue that they were the best, but I guarantee that if you glue your eyeballs to our station for seven days, you'll never be satisfied by *TRL* again!

Contributors: GG—Gary Pig Gold, JA—Jake Austen, JB—John Battles, JP—James Porter, KB—Ken Burke

SUNDAY

8:00 P.M.–9:00 P.M. THE ED SULLIVAN SHOW "Episode 939" (originally aired on CBS, 1967)

If it wasn't obvious by his twenty-first (!) season that Ed Sullivan was single-handedly keeping the ragtag, mondo-schizo spirit of vaudeville alive for one hour every Sunday, those who tuned in the night of December 3, 1967, had no remaining doubt whatsoever. Ray Charles and Billy Preston kicked it off with a fiery "Double-O-Soul" duet, a Polish balancing act followed an Israeli music hall troupe, and O. J. Simpson took a polite bow from his seat in the audience. But that's not all! For sandwiched square between Jose Jimenez and a Pepto-Bismol commercial appeared an outlandishly exotic quintet of young Japanese musicians called The Blue Comets who proceeded to introduce the sub-genre known as J-Pop to North America in less than half the time (two songs as opposed to five) it took those Beatles to beat Sullivan's stage into submission three years earlier. *This* particular international incident began with the gentle stroke of a *koto* upon the traditional "Ga Ga Ku" melody, which was then thrown to its knees with a thundering blast from the Comet frontline's matching custom-black Mosrite guitars and Dick Dale-worthy amplification. With scarcely a pause to collect our collective breath the band began its far-out and far-off hit "Blue Chateau" (which had wowed the Budokan the previous year opening for none other than John, Paul, George, and Ringo). After a quick arthritic thumbs-up from Sullivan, the Blue Comets went back to their homeland (where, I'm pleased to report, they continue performing and recording to this very day). As for us vintage 1967 CBS-TV watchers though, it was just a quick cut to Carol Lawrence and Gordon MacRae's "I Do! I Do!" medley, a Dutch Masters cigar spot, and then on to the comparative sanity of the remaining 167 vaudeville-free hours of the week. (GG)

9:00 P.M.–11:00 P.M. COLUMBO "Swan Song" (originally aired on NBC, 1973)

In this amazing movie Johnny Cash played Tommy Brown, a gospel/country/rock star who led the Lost Soul Crusades. When his wife (Ida Lupino!) made it clear that the millions they earned were going to their musical ministry and not into his pocket Tommy threatened to quit. After she played her trump card (evidence that ex-con Brown was guilty of the statutory rape of a backup singer) he decided to take matters into his own murderous hands (decades before his comeback single about spouse-killing, "Delia's Gone"). By the time Columbo got on the case the should-be-grieving widower was throwing an excessive, decadent rock 'n' roll pool party. When the movie climaxed with a wild-eyed Man in Black furiously limping through a dark forest desperately trying to destroy murder evidence, it became very evident that the permed and proper Alan Jacksons and Tim McGraws of the contemporary country world just couldn't measure up. Several things made this episode riveting, but fundamentally the power of the program came from Cash's magnificent, magnetic presence. He combined intensity, coolness, kindness, and cruelty in an intoxicating manner, and his hilarious scenes with the disheveled detective were surpassed only by the stellar live footage of the band playing a rocking, inspiring version of "I Saw the Light." (JA)

MONDAY

8:00 P.M.–8:30 P.M. I'VE GOT A SECRET "Guest: Pete Best" (originally aired on CBS, 1964)

In those bleak, monochrome decades before MTV reared its immaculately coiffed programming, rock 'n' roll was pretty hard to find on the home screen. However, on CBS, the so-called Tiffany Network, rockers who had corrupted the nation's below-the-waist morals were popping up with alarming frequency as novelty guests on none other than that utterly mild-mannered game show *I've Got a Secret*. Guests included the Shangri-Las miming "Leader of the Pack" before a leather-clad Robert Goulet and The Live Wires (Durward Kirby's son's actually quite-good garage combo). And one memorable evening, hot on the Cuban heels of his former mates' debut on *The Ed Sullivan Show*, out slinked a quite understandably somber Pete Best to try in vain to stump the panel with this secret: "I left my job two years ago." "You mean you came all the way from England just to tell us that?" mugged host Garry Moore. Then a huge white title flashed across Pete's mug reading, quite epitaph-like in retrospect, "I was one of THE BEATLES." "Whoa boy!" quipped Moore. "You ever have one of those days?" It was just the latest in a series of embarrassing, humiliating moments for the moody, magnificent drummer. Asked why he would ever leave the hottest property in showbiz, Best mumbled something about starting his own group, to which Moore joined the entire audience in laughter. "He figured it was an act with no future and so he might as well pull out and start an act of his own." As he placed a hand on the by now visibly slumping Liverpudlian's cold shoulder, Moore added, "Well don't

worry. No one's perfect." And with that cruel adieu Pete slinked back to the wings to claim his place then, now, and forevermore at the very tip-top of the Unluckiest People in the World list. You ever have one of those lives? (GG)

8:30 P.M.–9:30 P.M. HULLABALOO "Gary and Jerry Lewis sing (sic!) 'Help!'" (originally aired on NBC, 1965)

When NBC Television suddenly noticed the great big numbers ABC's *Shindig* was pulling in every week, the powers that were immediately ordered up two seasons of "youth programming" of their very own. But while *Shindig* was expertly produced by no other than that highly reputable paragon of British rock TV, Jack Good, NBC's idea of a cutting-edge counterpart was to have Zsa Zsa Gabor croon "High Heel Sneakers" before a sweater-clad swath of *Chorus Line* casualties and deem the whole thing a *"Hullabaloo."* Such casting-calls-from-Hell reached all-new nadir on the evening of September 20, 1965, however, when Gary "This Diamond Ring" Lewis cohosted an entire episode alongside none other than proud papa Jerry. Now, to say that there was little love lost between the so-called King of Comedy and his son is a given (Exhibit A: a painfully anxious eleven-year-old Gary made his NBC-TV debut in 1957, butchering "Sonny Boy" while sitting on his father's resentful lap), but such wholly misdirected family rivalry took on an all-new demeanor that fateful night. Gary at the time was hot on a string of Top Ten hits; Jerry had been a reluctant stranger to the *Billboard* charts since rock 'n' and roll's birth. And while Gary was already smarting under the continued accusations he and his merry band of Playboys were only riding Daddy's coattails up the ladder of success, an oblivious Jerry never lost an opportunity to publicly drag his "big-headed kid" down a rung or four. So when the two faced off on *Hullabaloo*, even special guest star Barry McGuire realized we were *all* on the Eve of Destruction as the tuxedo fur started to fly. In one corner, Gary mimed his current big one "Everybody Loves a Clown" to a set full of *Romper Room* outcasts, while Jerry seized his feature spot to counter with a trumped-up slab of message music called "I'll See Your Light." Let's call that surreal skirmish a draw, shall we? But the star round was the one that pitted father and son squarely at one another's golden throats as they sat uncomfortably side-by-side and butchered the Fab Four's current chart topper "Help!" Granted, Gary tried his best to inject a sliver of sincerity into Lennon's lyrical pleas, but Jerry, unable to follow the song off the cue cards, simply gave up about halfway through and resorted to his trademark idiot act. "Sorry, but it's been so long since I worked with somebody," he smirked as the Hullabaloo Dancers swept around them. Fortunately, Paul Revere and his extremely telegenic Raiders arrived just in time to save the day as end credits rolled. The *next* time Gary showed up to host *Hullabaloo* his dad was conspicuously absent. One concluding word of warning, however: insomniacs such as myself, I'm mortified to admit, still sometimes watch this age-old family feud reignite every Labor Day when, at about five in the morning, Gary and his current Playboys visit the telethon to lip-sync "This Diamond Ring" as dad sweats and mugs up a jealous paternal storm in the background. (GG)

9:30 P.M.–10:00 P.M. THE ANDY GRIFFITH SHOW "Opie's Group" (originally aired on CBS, 1967)

When I turn on *The Andy Griffith Show* and it's in color my first reaction is similar to seeing that Richie has a beard on *Happy Days*. Not that the quality really plummeted when Mayberry spun the color wheel, but something about the particular lurid color of the film stock the show used seemed to add a disconcertingly serious edge to Andy's gang. However, one such episode provides one of the most authentic garage-rock moments in TV history. Little Opie (played by Ron Howard, more than a decade away from being a bearded Richie) has joined a rock band, and it is interfering with his other commitments. Opie is pretty dedicated to this hobby, which becomes obvious once we see his band, the Sound Committee, playing at a house party. Instead of being some outlandish sitcom version of what a wild kiddie rock band should be we see a group of normal-looking, serious boys looking at the frets to make the chords as they play a live lyric-free rock track (a variation on Pacific Northwest instrumental garage rock with a tinge of psychedelia). Not to imply that this was a great song or a great band, but rather that this was a totally *real* teenage band. And the scene with them at this teen party was so authentic and sincere that it seemed completely out of place on a sitcom (and was one of the best uses of that oddly dire color-film stock). One has to assume that this was little Ronnie Howard's real band, and perhaps being in a well-rehearsed, working, humble (it *was* instrumental music) band is what helped ground him, so that he became one of the rare actors to transition from child star to actual adult. Unfortunately, his next band had Potsie as a lead singer. (JA)

10:00 P.M.–11:00 P.M. BEHIND THE MUSIC "Leif Garrett" (originally aired on VH1, 1999)

This was by far the greatest episode ever of this seductive documentary series. Like all *Behind the Music* shows this one told the tale of a meteoric rise to fame, a devastating descent into failure (expedited by drug abuse), and the redemptive light of a bright future. A marginally talented teen pop star who had trouble dealing with life when the applause died, Leif Garrett's was an interesting, if familiar, story. But out of nowhere this tale took a crazy turn when we met Leif's buddy Roland Winkler, a former dancer, a kid defined by the use of his legs. It seems eighteen-year-old Garrett and young Winkler were partying hard one night when a drugged-up Garrett crashed his Porsche, crippling Winkler for life. As modern-day Leif told this sad story VH1 let him know that they had arranged for a reunion with Winkler. Though Winkler was odd-looking, stringy-haired, and wheelchair-bound it quickly became obvious that he was a together, mentally stable dude and that Garrett was the invalid. While this teary, intensely melodramatic reunion made for remarkable TV, what really separates this episode is VH1's shameless dishonesty. At every turn the show let Leif explain how his drug days were behind him and how he had learned from his mistakes, but he made at least half of these statements with slurred words and glassy eyes. For the *Behind the Music* story arc to function he had to be back on his feet and rising as the story ended, but the viewers (and the producers) knew that his new band wasn't going to make it, that he was still partying pretty hard, and that he'd learned little from his past. But the TV audience definitely learned something from this program: if you want to make a riveting documentary all you need to do is find a subject who severely injured his best friend twenty years ago and hasn't seen him since. (JA)

11:00 P.M.–11:30 P.M. NIGHTLY NEWS "Lux and Ivy Go Shopping" (originally aired in 1986)

In 1986 Elvis Presley's back catalog got a major overhaul with excellent compilations like *Rocker* and the six-LP gold box set of early performances. That same year psychobilly greats the Cramps released (by coincidence?) *A Date with Elvis*, their third LP. The Elvis reissues received a short blurb on the local newscast in Los Angeles. Tower Records was the site of this human interest story on the Elvis reissue blitz, and who'd be of more interest to humans than the Cramps' ghoulish front man Lux Interior and his lovely wife (and guitarist) Poison Ivy? The couple were there as fans, eager to buy up the new goodies, and during their brief interview they made no mention of their own celebrity. They played it to the hilt, though, with Ivy (looking splendid in faux leopard and jeweled cat-eye frames) declaring, "I'd buy this (box set) with my last dime! I'd starve myself to get this!" With all the enthusiasm of a couple of kids who'd just discovered rock 'n' roll, Lux and Ivy proudly represented Elvis fans everywhere. (JB)

11:30 P.M.–1:00 A.M. THE TONIGHT SHOW "Guest: Chuck Berry" (originally aired on NBC, 1987)

A jazz drummer wannabe, Johnny Carson did his best to avoid rockers of any stripe during his thirty-year run as the king of late-night TV. Yet when Chuck Berry appeared on the show, the result was pure TV magic. Simultaneously plugging the movie *Hail,*

The Cramps—Lux and Ivy on the left. Courtesy Jake Austen

Hail Rock'n'Roll and his (incomprehensible) autobiography, Berry performed a surprisingly dissonant version of "Memphis." Once at the panel, the rocker proved to be a man after Carson's own heart, confessing that as a youth, " . . . all I wanted to do was comp chords behind a big band." Almost immediately they became soul brothers under the skin. Berry gleefully demonstrated his famed duck walk, talked humorously about a disastrous gig in the South, and explained why he didn't carry a band anymore: "Things got juicy in the sixties. By the late sixties they got smoky too." How strong was their onstage chemistry? Well, Berry, mercurial and mysterious in print interviews, summed up his stylistic evolution more pointedly for Carson than he ever did for *Rolling Stone*. "I wanted to sing like Nat Cole, with lyrics like Louis Jordan, with the swing of Benny Goodman with Charlie Christian on guitar, with Carl Hogan's—who was with Louis Jordan—riff, and with the soul of Muddy Waters." Further, Carson's impeccable ability to set up and time a response allowed Berry to laugh away his three prison stays: "It seems about every seventeen years I make a big mistake." Things were going so well that after a rousing version of "Roll Over Beethoven," Carson actually bumped his two remaining guests and started a third interview segment with Berry before he closed the show with a jam on "Johnny B. Goode." Berry had never seemed so animated and charming on camera and only Carson could've crafted the lovefest that made it so. (KB)

1:00 A.M.–2:00 A.M. TOMORROW "Guests: Little Richard & Wayne Cochran" (originally aired on NBC, 1981)

Tom Snyder's odd, smoke-filled, low-key talk show featured many great TV rock moments (stroke-of-genius department: Iggy Pop and Ricky Schroeder on the same show). This episode was one of the best as the Georgia Peach got together with the white James Brown (a fixture in nightclubs in the 1960s, from Las Vegas to Harlem) to talk about hanging up their rock 'n' soul shoes for the Lord. Though famed for wearing towering pompadours and slick vines in their primes, both men honored Him (the Lord, that is, not Snyder) by wearing conservative hair and threads during this period of their careers. They did not hold back, however, for the climax of the show when they sang an inspiring duet on the gospel standard "One Day at a Time." (JP)

TUESDAY

8:00 P.M.–8:30 P.M. HAPPY DAYS "Fonzie: Rock Entrepreneur" (originally aired on ABC, 1977)

Detroit's Suzi Quatro has had a remarkably interesting musical career. She played bongos in a jazz band as a tot, toured Viet Nam with her sisters in the Pleasure Seekers as a teen (their "What a Way to Die" is one of the best prepunk garage singles ever), and eventually settled in England for a long solo rock 'n' roll career. However, this exceptional expatriate only made one truly successful return stateside, finding brief fame playing an Eisenhower-era version of herself on *Happy Days*. In this two-part episode we met the beautiful Leather Tuscadero (sister of Fonzie's ex-fiancée Pinky). Leather and the Suedes were a hard-rocking act that briefly became the house band at Arnold's Diner. They were of course dis-

covered and offered a tour with Fabian, but when one Suede quit, teenybopper Joanie Cunningham joined the band and defiantly insisted on leaving school to become a touring rock star. I guess it all worked out in the end, but all I really remember is that the band performed Quatro's awesome song "Devil Gate Drive," despite the fact that it was a 1970s glam tune and the show was set in the late 1950s. Quatro appeared sporadically on the show over the next two years. These days she occasionally pops up on British TV (she had a guest role on *Absolutely Fabulous*), she has been a BBC DJ, and she continues to tour Europe playing for thousands. But as far as most of her American fans are concerned she's still off touring with Fabian. (JA)

8:30 P.M.– 8:45P.M. NAT KING COLE SHOW "Guests: The Sparkletones" (originally aired on NBC, 1957)

The suave Cole hosted an excellent variety show that attracted top-notch guests and gained popularity throughout its run. However, it died a fairly quick death because no corporate sponsor was brave enough to have its name associated with a black entertainer (when Max Factor suggested that a black star couldn't sell lipstick Cole responded, "What do they think we use . . . Congo paint?"). Originally only fifteen minutes long (it was underwritten entirely by a network that wasn't generous enough to donate a half-hour) the program was packed with sophisticated entertainment, including classy guests like Ella Fitzgerald, Peggy Lee, Mahalia Jackson, Sammy Davis, Jr., and Eartha Kitt. In fact, Kitt contends that it was sophistication that killed the show because white audiences were much more comfortable with the images of blacks they saw on *Amos and Andy*. Fortunately, the show stepped back from sophistication for several minutes one night and unleashed a quartet of teenagers, aged thirteen to seventeen, who provided (to quote music writer Art Fein) "a tremendous explosion of energy and happiness . . . the greatest Rockabilly thing ever seen on TV." The Sparkletones were kids from Spartanburg, South Carolina, who found themselves in the top twenty with the excellent rocker "Black Slacks." Their fifteen minutes of fame included appearances on *American Bandstand* and *The Ed Sullivan Show*, but this was their best performance captured on film. The show's low budget made it feel as if the boys were squeezed onto a small stage, elevating the voltage of their youthful electricity. The juxtaposition of their wild kinetic energy with the tuxedo-and-gown vibe of the rest of the show also made the Sparkeltones sparkle more intensely. Cole was not a rock 'n' roll activist putting these boys on the same episode as the Nelson Riddle Orchestra to make a point about the validity of the genre. Rather, the kids likely got booked because they seemed like a kiddie act that the youth would dig, much like booking the Chipmunks. The sponsors, whose cowardice would soon keep the likes of Cole, Ella, and Mahalia out of America's living rooms, would have had no problem with these clean-cut teens. Little did they know that fifty years later Cole's easy-listening legacy would have some young folks listening to genteel Celine Dion and Clay Aiken records while it was the Sparkletones and their rock 'n' roll brethren that led suburban white kids to dress, talk, and act like violent black "gangstas." (JA)

8:45 P.M.– 9:00 P.M. COMMERCIALS

Since NBC originally only saw fit to give Nat King Cole fifteen minutes we have some time to kill here. How about we pay some bills by running our favorite TV rock commercials?

THE JACKSON 5IVE FOR ALPHA BITS (1971) You can't beat Papa Joe's boys flying around in a magic Viking sailboat singing an original song and declaring Alpha Bits cereal "A-B-C-Delicious!"

CHUBBY CHECKER'S TV SPOT (1972) We all have our favorite ad starring some superstar (or has-been) selling some two-record compilation LP. Some swear by Slim Whitman and Boxcar Willie's early 1980s epics, but my favorite is this really cheap-looking spot starring Chubby Checker hanging out in a malt shop wearing the thickest damned platform shoes you've ever seen, and pushing "100 of the Greatest Overplayed Golden Oldies of All Time" (or something like that). I especially like the too-cool ending where our man tells us that as soon as we send away for a copy, we'll have it "made in the shade!"

MICKY DOLENZ TV SPOT (1973) After the success of Chubby Checker's commercial the same record label (Adam VIII) got ex-Monkee Dolenz to do a similar spot. Dolenz not only starred but directed as well, and if you remember the high-speed high jinks from the Monkees' TV show, you know what to expect. There were speeded-up clips of Dolenz running through the forest (while "Runaround Sue" by Dion played in the background—get it?), clowning around on a motorcycle (the Shangri Las' "Leader of the Pack"), hanging from a balcony (the McCoys' "Hang On Sloopy"), doing a drag-queen bit (John Fred's "Judy in Disguise (with Glasses)"), and even sitting on the dock of the bay wasting time (Otis Red— . . . aw, if you're reading this book you should know what song this is).

RUFUS THOMAS FOR SCHLITZ MALT LIQUOR (1974) The creator of the Funky Chicken is sipping a can of the stuff backstage when a literal bull (the Schlitz Malt Liquor trademark) charges through the room.

THE BLUBLOCKER HIP-HOPPER (1992) Insomniacs first saw this rapper as part of a thirty-minute infomercial for Blublocker sunglasses that got whittled down to a regular commercial. None of the serious rap fans I know like this ad, but supposedly this guy really counts up the dough on a typical Venice Beach afternoon busting rhymes like, "My name is Geek and I'm a Hip-hopper—yeah, getcha self some Blublockers, unh!" (JP)

9:00 P.M.–10:00 P.M. UPBEAT "Guests: The Box Tops" (originally aired in syndication, 1969)

Let's give it up for *Upbeat*, the incredibly diverse music program from Cleveland, Ohio, hosted by Don Webster. For a syndicated show out of the Midwest, it attracted just about every big-name act of the period that wasn't the Beatles or the Beach Boys. But it couldn't fill an hour's worth of programming with big stars, so common sense dictated it'd have to spotlight some unknowns, and in addition to regional garage bands (like the Sonics and the Rationals) it included utter nobodies like the Velvet Underground, the MC5, and Funkadelic (in their psychedelic phase). The Box Tops weren't has-beens in 1969, but for some reason they were forced to lip-sync their big hit "The Letter," which was already two years old by then. And, man, did they look wasted! The camera kept zooming in on a drugged-out Alex Chilton on lead vocals, while the organ player, hungry for attention, kept mugging at one of the cameras. And toward the end of the song, when the airplane sounds began, that organ player made this motion with his hands as if to suggest that the organ was responsible for the noise. (The Box Tops

and Funkadelic clips still float around; the MC5 and Velvet Underground episodes were reportedly erased). (JP)

10:00 P.M.–11:00 P.M. COP ROCK "Bang the Potts Slowly" (originally aired on ABC, 1990)

Steven Bochco became known as a visionary for creating *Hill Street Blues* (NBC, 1981–1987), which introduced the trend of casting a cop show with a diverse cast of regular-looking people to play characters with complex personalities. A cult hit, he turned it into a commercial success when he revived the idea on *NYPD Blue* (ABC, 1993–2005), which was more stylish but also more mainstream, supplementing the fat, bald protagonist with a cast of sexy models. But in the downtime between these two long-running series Bochco got pretty ambitious, and the bridge linking his *Blue* shows was a little something called *Cop Rock*. The series, once again, showcased a broad cast of characters, it explored familiar themes (crooked cops, illegal interrogations), and it even featured a number of faces that would eventually turn up on *NYPD Blue* (James McDaniel, Gordon Clapp, Jimmy Smits). But it also featured full-scale rock musical numbers with dance choreography. The gritty cops, lawyers, criminals, jurors, and passersby would break into song and bust some moves several times a show. Obviously this was absolutely bizarre, as there was no precedent for a Broadway musical–style TV series, and even if there had been, it was an incongruous format for a complex, realistic urban drama. Many people have cited *Cop Rock* as the worst show in TV history, but that is a failure of vision. This was a surreal experiment that featured original Randy Newman songs and some genuinely jarring transitions between dramatic scenes and songs. The last episode is particularly notable because it features the entire ensemble cast, including cops who had never sung previously, performing a tune about the show being canceled, highlighted by an actual fat lady singing. If the network and Bochco's production company had not lost millions of dollars, one might be inclined to think that the entire show happened just so they could get to this inevitable number. (JA)

11:00 P.M.–11:30 P.M. POP! GOES THE COUNTRY "Guests: Mickey Gilley & Jerry Lee Lewis" (originally aired in syndication, 1978)

Arguably the best country music program of the 1970s, this thirty-minute show mixed brief interviews with Ralph Emery and live performances from the genre's top stars. According to the host, the program that drew the most response was this one, which came as Mickey Gilley's newfound country fame was beginning to crest and Jerry Lee Lewis's was starting to subside. During the interview portion, Lewis eschewed his cornball plaid country suit for a black leather jacket, which provided a startling contrast to Gilley's frilly lavender leisure suit. The two men spoke amiably of growing up in Ferriday, Louisiana; being double first cousins; and learning to play on the same piano. There was no new information, but watching the cousins interact was telling. Gilley, whose Lewis soundalike recordings were controversial with fans, seemed shaky and defensive as he said, "I never really thought about music all that much until Jerry hit with 'Whole Lotta Shakin' Goin' On.'" Meanwhile, the contemptuous look on Lewis's face suggested that he had routinely stolen Gilley's lunch money when they were kids. In between interview segments, the stars performed their current hits (Gilley's "The Song That We Made Love To" and Lewis's

"I'll Find It Where I Can," respectively). During the latter, Lewis crooked his finger at Gilley and mischievously commanded him to play piano. Grinning, Gilley played a lot of tinkling high-octave flourishes and glissandi, but Lewis's suggestive hip thrusts stole the audience's attention. The real show was yet to come. Sitting at two grand pianos for the final segment, Lewis and Gilley, playing together for the first time in twenty-five years, traded verses and hammered out joyous ragtime versions of "Five Foot Two, Eyes of Blue," "Shanty Town," and "Don't Be Ashamed of Your Age." Clearly, both men were having a good time, but Lewis was starting to feel the competitive heat of performance run up his spine. As they performed a duet of the Killer's 1973 hit (the 1949 Sticks McGhee R&B classic) "Drinkin' Wine Spo-Dee-Oh-Dee," he began to catch fire. Gilley's voice worked well with Lewis's, but even though their instruments were miked at the same level, Lewis was playing louder and more flamboyantly than his upstart cousin. At song's end he cried out, "I wanna do a little boogie, OK?" "Let's do it," Gilley answered gleefully. Suddenly, Lewis was doing his own 1958 composition, "Lewis Boogie." Gilley didn't sing on this one, he just muscled the piano for all he was worth, and Lewis was still outplaying him until he could stand the frenzy no longer and he leaped to his feet and kicked back the stool! Suddenly it was a full-scale rock 'n' roll revival show, and an amazed and amused Gilley had the best seat in the house. However, the namesake of the world's largest honky-tonk had some tricks of his own. When the studio audience clambered for more, Gilley introduced the Bill Mack ballad "Drinkin' Champagne," in a key too low for his rockin' cousin. Lewis, who loved the song, clowned the slight away and allowed his very real affection for his cousin to rise to the surface once more. In the years to come, Gilley would abandon his cousin's style on records while going on to bigger and better chart successes. For Lewis, the hits would soon dry up, his health would fall apart, and suspicions surrounding the death of his fifth wife would make him persona non grata in country music. But during one of the final indisputably great moments in his career, Jerry Lee Lewis proved his point: he was the best piano-pumpin' muthah-humper in all creation and now everybody—including Mickey Gilley—knew it too. (KB)

11:30 P.M.–1:00 A.M. THE STEVE ALLEN SHOW "Blue Cheer episode" (originally aired in syndication, 1968)

Steve Allen never made any bones about his disdain for rock 'n' roll, openly mocking it at any opportunity (from dressing Presley down by having him sing to a real hound dog to performing a variation of "Surfin' Bird" in a trash can). To be fair, Allen was not afraid to take a chance. He did give Jerry Lee Lewis his first big break, and Lewis responded with an insane rendition of "Whole Lotta Shakin' Goin' On" that made everyone forget that they'd heard it a million times. Nevertheless, one of the most monumental culture clashes went down in 1968, when Allen had as guests on his show Blue Cheer, the loudest band on the planet. The group actually got to do two songs, *live*, after surviving some silly one-liners (a few without punch lines) their host delivered, intent on cutting them down to size. "Blue Cheer! You wash your underwear in that, your unmentionables, don't you? Well, these guys are stronger than dirt" (no argument there). Allen seemed to tire of trying to put the members of Blue Cheer in their place—though seemingly stoned, the boys were too quick for him—and professed an admi-

ration for the sheer volume of their music, comparing it to a two-mile coastal cannon that exploded near his station in the South Pacific during World War II. Guitarist Leigh Stephens backed that claim by telling Allen the band got their songs from arsenals! Allen asked the band what *Vincebus Eruptum* (the title of their monumental debut LP) meant. When singer/bassist Dickie Peterson answered, "Controlled chaos," in a cool deadpan that was hardly unintelligible, Allen made him repeat himself. Tiring of this routine Peterson said, "Yeah, let us do it," meaning Allen should let the band show him what controlled chaos meant. Allen followed that up with, "Just for that, you're not gonna do it! If there's one thing I can't stand it's a Blue Cheer that has no respect for an old piece of soap." Allen proved to be bluffing as he soon let Blue Cheer go on to control the chaos, with blistering live renditions of "Out of Focus" and their hit version of Eddie Cochran's "Summertime Blues" that were every bit as insane as the studio versions. It's almost unfathomable that this group got to perform live on national TV at all, much less on Allen's show. And even though it may have *sounded* like Viet Nam, the whole thing went off without any casualties, not counting Allen's eardrums, of course. (JB)

WEDNESDAY

8:00 P.M.–9:00 P.M. BEVERLY HILLS 90210 "Castles in the Sand" (originally aired on Fox, 1992)

When TV historians discuss made-for-TV bands (the Monkees, the Partridge Family) and special episodes where favorite characters become rock stars (Greg Brady as Johnny Bravo, Rick Nelson as Ricky Nelson) one mighty figure is tragically missing from the canon. It is time to acknowledge publicly the amazing performances by Brian Austin Green as David Silver on the top teen show of the 1990s. On this episode he made his debut after his manager Steve Sanders bribed the band originally booked to play the beach club to take a hike. Silver wowed the crowd playing two keyboards simultaneously (he was a genius!) and singing in a meek falsetto with Paul Stanley/televangelist extra-syllable pronunciations ("Your sweet caress . . ." becomes "your sweet car-a-ya-esss"). He ended the song by doing a minute of stiff approximations of MC Hammer dance moves. Sadly, his fictional music career never took off on the show (he played briefly in Babyface's band before giving up the stage to become a nightclub owner then the Jewish manager of an anti-Semitic rock band then a shock jock). In real life Brian Green (he dropped the "Austin" for his recording career) also struggled commercially as a musician, releasing one low-selling rap CD (produced by the Pharcyde and Babyface's wife, featuring the debut of Black Eyed Peas). He did get a brief moment of soulful TV rock glory, however, by hosting a 1996 episode of *Soul Train*. (JA)

9:00 P.M.–9:30 P.M. BEVERLY HILLBILLIES "Hoe Down a Go Go" (originally aired on CBS, 1965)
Five words: Jethro in a Beatle wig. (JA)

9:30 P.M.–10:00 P.M. THE DICK VAN DYKE SHOW "I Am My Brother's Keeper" (originally aired on CBS, 1962)
Few sitcoms squeezed as many satirical laughs from rock 'n' roll as *Dick Van Dyke*.

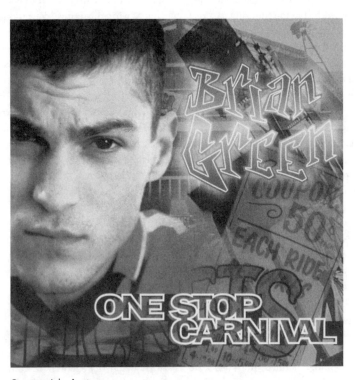

Courtesy Jake Austen

Not only did the show feature Freddie Blassie doing the twist/wrasslin' dance-craze "The Twassle," but we also learned that Van Dyke's character Rob Petrie wrote novelty songs in the Army (notably "Bupkis," which Dick & Dee Dee sang), before becoming a crazed, sleep-deprived rock 'n' roll DJ ("That was 'Mimmedy Mau Mau' by Billy & the Bing Bongs"). One can logically conclude these comic jabs were courtesy of series creator Carl Reiner, whose work with Sid Caesar and Howard Morris as part of the Three Haircuts (a manic take on the Ames Brothers) is still hilarious to behold on kinescope. However, this particular two-part episode (part two was titled "The Sleeping Brother") didn't start out as any type of rock 'n' roll statement. In a star-making turn, Van Dyke's real-life brother Jerry appears as Stacie Petrie, a young soldier so intimidated by his impending discharge that his childhood sleepwalking episodes reemerged and inspired comic high jinks. Awake, Stacie was a shy, rhythm-challenged nerd. Asleep, he was a live-wire banjo-bashing comic, who impressed Mel Cooley enough to elicit an invitation to audition for the vaunted *Alan Brady Show*. The trouble? Stacie had no idea what his more confident somnambulant alter ego was like. Rob taped and played back his brother's sleep-walking act, but Stacie got discouraged and the audition for Alan Brady (in the Petrie living room) seemed all for naught. Suddenly, banjo in hand, sleepwalking Stacie burst from his bedroom and was ready to put on a show. Stacie cracked a few jokes before announcing, "That new rock 'n' roll sensation . . . Skid Row!" (This was thirty years before the metal band of the same name.) Donning a leather jacket and motorcycle cap, Stacie transformed himself into a butt-scratching, illiterate 1950s-style punk. "A lot of you parents say your kids

shouldn't listen to this type of music, and I don't like that," he commented truculently. "You've got your opinion and I've got my opinion. I don't think you ought to listen to Leonard Bernstein!" Cuing a band he had presumably never rehearsed with, Skid Row then launched into a knee-swiveling gibberish rocker that ended up with him quivering spasmodically on the floor before bouncing up and announcing, "For my next number, I'd like to do another ballad." With the walk-away ranting of "I Wish My Heart Would Keep Its Big Mouth Shut," it was clear that Stacie was a hit. But wait! Rob and Laura cornered Stacie in the kitchen and discovered he had actually been awake through the entire audition. "I decided to listen to that tape and be like me," he crowed. As Stacie bashed away at the banjo and sang "Bill Bailey" to a crowd of happy party guests, two lessons became abundantly clear: (1) It's more important to act talented than to truly be talented and (2) rock 'n' roll is a sure cure for emotional illness! (KB)

10:00 P.M.–11:00 P.M. LAW AND ORDER "3 Dawg Night" (originally aired on NBC, 2001)

This episode seemed to reflect the fickle public's secret wishes. In a "ripped from the headlines" re-creation of Puff Daddy's infamous nightclub shooting incident we learned the identity of the *real* killer. It was that bitch, J-Lo! (JA)

11:00 P.M.–12:00 A.M. PLAYBOY AFTER DARK "Guests: Deep Purple" (originally aired in syndication, 1968)

Years before they blew their iconic smoke out on the water, Deep Purple were simply the latest in a long, long line of British hard-pop acts trying to create any dent they could in the U.S. marketplace. Toward that noble end they found themselves somehow signed (alongside Pat Boone and those two nude virgins John and Yoko) to Bill Cosby's grand new Tetra-grammaton Records, and duly headed to American small screens upon finding their debut single at number four on the charts. But there would be no *American Bandstand* or even a visit to Ed Sullivan for *these* guys: after a quick stop to play *The Dating Game*, where Purple patriarch Jon Lord came in third out of three and didn't get the girl ("I was pissed off I wasn't chosen; she was very beautiful"), Cosby immediately pulled some heavier G-strings to plonk the band alongside David Hemmings, his soon-to-be-ex Gayle Hunnicutt, and Don Adams on the October 23, 1968, broadcast of his pal Hugh Hefner's very-late-night *Playboy After Dark* series. Having already hosted the likes of James Brown, Steppenwolf, and the quite-cranky Byrds, Hefner thought it would be equally big fun to invite some bushy-haired foreigners to entertain Barbie Benton, Otto Preminger, and various gyrating *Laugh-In* extras. So onto the $35,000 faux-bachelor soundstage at CBS Hollywood stepped Deep Purple. Following a typically befuddled introduction by a smoking-jacketed Hefner—who then took part in a brief guitar lesson from a less than thrilled Ritchie Blackmore—the amps were fired up for Joe South's "Hush." Barbie began to dance in ways far beyond even the *Laugh-In* contingent, Otto thrust his fingers at his ears before rushing back to the wet bar, and Hefner sucked his pipe in appreciative rhythm as Cosby watched his charges sell a few more records for him. Mission Accomplished! Deep Purple dutifully moved on to *The Merv Griffin Show* before returning to England, recording a spectacular version of Neil Diamond's "Kentucky Woman," before losing the course altogether via Lord's utterly ham-fisted "Concerto for Group and Royal Phil-harmonic Orchestra," which gave birth to Emerson, Lake, Palmer, and generations of severely witless progressive-rock fans the world over. (GG)

12:00 A.M.–12:30 A.M. DON KIRSHNER'S ROCK AWARDS INFOMERCIAL (originally aired 1990)

I remember the 1980s and very early 1990s not so much for the birth of grunge as for the golden age of the infomercial. Yes, I speak of those gloriously insomniac years before TV offered endless reruns of *The Munsters* and *I Dream of Jeannie*—of those delightfully dazed half-hours when newly waxed cars were routinely set ablaze and shiny, happy families hooked up hair-care products to their vacuum cleaners. And if you looked real, *real* closely amid the rash of golden-oldie music pitches, you might spot what has since come to be universally revered as both the *Hard Day's Night* and the *Citizen Kane* of paid public advertisements. "From Philadelphia, the home of rock and roll," booms a distant voice, "and hosted by legendary Monkees star Davy Jones. . . ." We are then treated to a mock-array of "special guest presenters" (Jay Siegel of the Tokens, Johnny Maestro of the Brooklyn Bridge, Ron "Archies" Dante, Felix "I Used to Be a Rascal, But I'm Alright Now" Cavaliere, and a positively troll-like Rick Derringer) pretending to jostle through a welcoming crowd of six or seven senior citizens on a sidewalk. Suddenly stock footage of a stretch limo, license plate for some reason reading "BBC TV" looms up and disgorges "the man who has been at the center of rock and roll for three decades; the man who discovered and developed artists such as Bobby Darin, the Monkees, Neil Sedaka, Carole King, and many others, and who brought rock concerts to network TV. . . ." No, don't touch that dial; it's "Don Kirshner's Rock

Awards," a cleverly disguised thirty-minute hustle for Kirshner's *Sixty Greatest Hits of the Sixties* package, "each song personally selected by Don Kirshner and available for only three easy payments of $19.98 for premium cassette or $23.31 for compact disc" (plus shipping and handling). The legendary Davy Jones gamely proceeds to count down the decade over a montage of public-domain publicity stills and 1960s hits—all primarily Kirshner-controlled of course—and bestows the coveted Don Kirshner Rock Award upon one blessed artist per year. Curiously, almost every lucky winner not only doubles as a special guest presenter, but is also captured amid the bleachered rent-an-audience wildly holding aloft his or her rent-a-trophy. Why, Jones even does a pretty good job of looking surprised as he personally wins not only the DKRA for 1966 ("I'm a Believer"—I guess actual vocalist Micky Dolenz was unable to attend) but for Record of the Decade as well ("I'm a Believer" again—are we seeing a pattern here?). But wait! As the festivities frug to a climax, "the only man who deserves to have his name appear *above* the words *rock and roll* finally appears, bathed in a wash of heavenly white spotlight to multiple standing ovations. "Yes, it's true, I do love rock and roll," the self-proclaimed man with the golden ear admits before the end credits roll over Ron Dante miming "Sugar Sugar" and a concluding graphic with the P.O. box plus a furiously flashing 800 number. You know, I do believe somewhere Ron Popeil is nodding in admiration . . . and I bet those operators are *still* standing by. (GG)

THURSDAY

8:00 P.M.–8:30 P.M. THE COSBY SHOW "Full House" (originally aired on NBC, 1986)

You have to look really hard to catch this one: Bill Cosby, as Cliff Huxtable, spent an entire episode looking for a place in the house to take a nap. Unfortunately for him, he couldn't relax in the kitchen because his daughter Vanessa and her boyfriend Robert were doing homework while "Cosmic Slop" by Funkadelic played in the background! On the surface this was comparable to the time on *Diff'rent Strokes* when Willis tried to teach one of his stepsister's preppie white friends how to dance using Funkadelic's "(Not Just) Knee Deep," but Cosby gets more points for using a decade-old song about prostitution and spousal abuse on the most popular show of the 1980s. (*Diff'rent Strokes* probably used "Knee Deep" because it was a recent hit.) What put the Cosby scene over the top is that it made a point of showing that the kids were listening to the radio, not a tape. Somehow these nerdy, uptight thirteen-year-olds were actually so down that instead of Top Forty radio they tuned in to the freeform station WFMU, the only possible frequency in that area that would have played that song in 1986. Perhaps they gained their hipness during their adventure the week before when they met Stevie Wonder (an important TV rock history moment because Wonder prepared America for electronica *and* Puff Daddy by introducing the Huxtables and the rest of the country to electronic sampling). (JP)

8:30 P.M.–9:00 P.M. THE MUNSTERS "Far Out Munsters" (originally aired on CBS, 1965)

Being from Hollywood, and connected (keyboardist Larry Tamblyn is actor Russ Tamblyn's brother, and singer/drummer

Dick Dodd was a Mouseketeer), the Standells had opportunities to do a good number of movie and TV appearances before their rocking nugget "Dirty Water" raced up the charts. None were more memorable than this sitcom classic. The sweet but monstrous Munster family was delighted with young Eddie Munster's sudden interest in music, but aghast to find that the object of his admiration was none other than (ulp!) the Standells! As it would turn out, the fabled L.A. garage band had a lucrative engagement nearby and had to have lodging for the weekend. Their manager made the Munsters a very generous offer for the use of their house, but wouldn't reveal his clients' identities. The Standells had already trashed several hotel rooms (years before Led Zeppelin made such behavior fashionable), but the manager figured it would be impossible for them to do the Munsters' decrepit, haunted mansion any further damage. The band found they dug the trappings at Chez Munster, and decided to throw a party. What ensued made for one of the most hilarious TV parodies of beatnik culture, which was on life support by then (clueless TV writers didn't quite understand the difference between Kerouac and the Beatles). The friends of the clean-cut Standells were all shaggy, bearded beats with scruffy (though very attractive) girlfriends. The Standells performed two songs, "Do the Ringo," an enjoyable (though hardly "garage punk") organ-led dance number, and a somewhat off-the-cuff rendition of "I Wanna Hold Your Hand." Thus ended the greatest garage rock episode in sitcom history. Some of you might take this as a cue to say, "But the Seeds on *Mothers-In-Law* was cooler because they did their hit, it's in color, and Joe Besser has a cameo." Yeah, but the Standells on *The Munsters* had the Munsters, the most punk-rock family on

TV, and a cameo by a Kellon Garwood as "The Hermit," reciting what's arguably the greatest beat poetry parody of all time: "In a vortex of the future, of that cool tomorrow land . . . we'll all wig there, play a gig there, in that great non-union band! Scooba Doo and Scooba Dabba, life's a gas and life's a grabba! Hip is hip and groove is groovy. Life's a wild Fellini movie. When that hairy fist of silence slugs us, bugs us, puts us down . . . we'll all wing it, we'll all sing it, Guy Lombardo's back in town!" And to prove they weren't posers, when the Munsters crashed the party in their own house and got a load of the Standells up close and personal, they couldn't help but join in on the fun! Soon, Herman was doing an impromptu reading of his own (with the immortal words: "Scooba Doo and Scooba Dye . . . that chicken's not too young to fry!"). Then he turned things over to Lily, who sang a torchy folk ballad. (Yvonne DeCarlo was a torch singer in real life.) When the confusion cleared, the Munsters and the Standells parted the best of friends. "I'll sleep a lot easier knowing the future of America is in the hands of boys like these," sighed Herman Munster. (JB)

9:00 P.M.–9:30 P.M. BEWITCHED
"Hippie, Hippie, Hooray" (originally aired on ABC, 1968)

In this episode the beautiful-witch-becomes-a-middle-class-housewife series entered the age of flower power. Samantha's trendy, look-alike cousin Serena (both played by Elizabeth Montgomery) is arrested at a love-in and her paddy wagon photo makes the front page of the newspapers. Larry Tate mistakes Serena for Samantha. Fearing a conservative client will back out of a lucrative advertising contract, Tate conveys his panic to his number-one employee, Samantha's husband

Darrin Stevens (Dick York). After Darrin insults Serena, the zany cousin purposefully compounds the confusion with Darrin's friends and business associates. Popping in and out of scenes, Serena dons mod minis (in which Montgomery looks absolutely smashing), riddles her conversation with hip argot, and embarrasses everyone with space-violating displays of public affection. Unable to get Serena to confess, Samantha tries to convince the concerned Tates—establishment pigs by any standard—that she is Serena by zapping up a psychedelic guitar and singing the hippie-rock parody "Iff'n," which boasts the following couplet: "Iff'n you wanna leave me weak and weepy, you gotta look wild and weird and creepy." By contrast, Serena sings the Stevens' daughter Tabitha to sleep with the slyly rendered electric lullaby "Rock-a-Bye Baby (With a Rock 'n' Roll Beat)." By show's end, Darrin—the most uptight continuing character in TV history—stumbles into an apology, Serena appears claiming that "love power conquers all," and the business deal is saved. The implied moral of the story? Tolerance, baby, tolerance. No one seemed to be against the cause Serena championed; they were simply worried about how *others* would perceive her actions. This was a surprisingly revolutionary view for such a mainstream sitcom. (KB)

9:30 P.M.–10:00 P.M. WHAT'S MY LINE "Guests: The Supremes" (originally aired on CBS, 1966)

How out of touch were the members of the *What's My Line* panel? Well, the Supremes, then one of the top acts in pop music, inadvertently stumped the panel not just once, but twice as the show's mystery guests. The popular John Daly–hosted parlor game featured clever panelists—columnist Dorothy Kilgallen, actress Arlene

Francis, and publisher-punster Bennett Cerf in particular—who prided themselves on their ability to memorize the entertainment sections of the New York newspapers. As a result, they were seldom caught completely flat-footed by a big-name mystery guest—as long as that guest came from their era of entertainment. Indeed, during its 1950–1967 network run, the venerable game show featured only a few teen idols as mystery guests—Paul Anka, Pat Boone, Fabian, and Ricky Nelson most notably—instead concentrating on Broadway types, aging movie stars, and other game show personnel. In the two years prior to this broadcast, the Supremes had racked up six number-one records and their then current Motown release, "My World Is Empty Without You," was zooming into the national top ten. Moreover, they had played the Copacabana, one of those stuffed-shirt nightclubs the Park Avenue crowd gloried in attending. So, by all rights, the youthful singing trio should have been relatively easy to guess. However, at this point, *What's My Line*'s best-ever panelist Kilgallen had died, and her sharp, analytical mind was sorely missed. Florence Ballard, Diana Ross, and Mary Wilson took turns answering questions, at first using funny voices, but as it became clear the panel didn't have a clue, they eased into their normal voices. It didn't help. Normally, when they were stumped, the panelists removed their blindfolds and uttered something akin to, "Of course, I should have known all along." But this time, when the host asked them to remove their blindfolds and meet the Supremes, their collective puzzlement proved unintentionally hilarious. Their embarrassment was compounded a few weeks later when the group returned as mystery guests, and once again stumped the panel. This time it was the Supremes who seemed shocked at the outcome. This lack of connection with youth culture proved symptomatic of the show's declining fortunes and it was canceled the following year. (KB)

10:00 P.M.–11:00 P.M. PERRY MASON
"The Case of the Final Fade-Out"
(originally aired on CBS, 1966)

There were three things you could pretty much count on during this show's nine-year CBS run.

1. Raymond Burr's girth would increase every year.
2. Some heel would make the viewers wish him dead well before he was actually murdered.
3. Someone would blurt out a confession before any trial actually went to the jury.

This story, while not rock 'n' roll in nature, featured *American Bandstand*'s Dick Clark as a screenwriter hiding ruthless ambitions behind the false demeanor of a pleasant young go-getter. The heel in this case was Barry Conrad (James Stacy), an egomaniacal young actor who messed with everyone around him, especially his TV producer. After pissing everyone off, Conrad did a police shootout scene for his show. Surprise! Somebody slipped live ammunition into one of the prop guns and the actor was shot to death. At first suspicion fell on the prop man (Jackie Coogan), then the old actress Conrad had fired (Estelle Winwood), then finally the show's producer (Denver Pyle). Meanwhile, Clark, playing TV writer Leif Early, drunkenly complained that ideas had been stolen from him in one scene, then in the next rendered a rather insightful witness-stand monologue about showbiz being a "dog-eat-dog racket." The latter, uttered with the sort of matter-of-fact sincerity Clark used in commercials for Clearasil, seemed

to touch home with him. But inevitably Mason tripped him up; he found out that the writer arranged for guns to be used in the scene instead of knives so he could take revenge on the actor for stealing the idea for a new show. "He was an egomaniac," Clark's character blurted. "He stepped on people for the sheer enjoyment of it . . . I'm glad I had the guts to do it." It's a shock to hear perennial nice guy Clark confessing to murder. If he had broken down in this fashion when he testified in front of the House of Representatives Special Committee on Legislative Oversight in 1960 (aka the Payola Hearings), he might've suffered the same ignominious fate as Alan Freed. Instead, he was allowed to divest himself of the thirty-three companies that had a financial interest in providing music to *American Bandstand*. This was the last *Perry Mason* episode. By way of tribute, creator Erle Stanley Gardner took on a bit part as a judge, and several members of the technical crew had roles as witnesses. As for Clark, he eventually forged a lucrative career packaging game shows and award ceremonies. After baring what many believe to be his true essence on *Perry Mason*, he never again attempted a dramatic acting role. (KB)

11:00 P.M.–12:00 A.M. IT'S SHOWTIME
AT THE APOLLO "Shooby Taylor on
Amateur Night" (originally aired in
syndication, 1987)

Shooby Taylor was one of a kind, a visionary who in the early 1980s would bring jazz, country, gospel, and classical records into cheap recording studios and bizarrely scat over them while obviously hearing several other songs in his head. A tape of one of these sessions circulated around the world (and World Wide Web) and became one of the most beloved underground recordings on earth. Irwin Chusid and the gang at New Jersey's freeform radio station WFMU championed him for years, and desperately searched for the elusive "Human Horn." When they finally found him Mr. Taylor was recovering from a stroke and could no longer do his unusual scatting. Though several newspapers and film crews interviewed him, they could not capture his unique gift on video, and he died in 2003 with the visual component of his genius undocumented. But wait! It seems he made a very brief appearance on the televised version of Harlem's Apollo Theater Amateur Night. After moonfaced Apollo emcee Rick Aviles encouraged him, Taylor rubbed the lucky tree stump and hit the stage, playing a mean air saxophone for about ten seconds. Unprepared to see something truly special the notoriously harsh Apollo crowd instantly began booing unmercifully. However, at least one Apollo regular was inspired by the performance. Sandman Sims, the seventy-year-old hoofer who shooed rejected acts off the Apollo stage, seemed to regain the vim and vigor of his 1950s self at the prospect of degrading a Human Horn. His comedic, athletic tap performance made one briefly forget the tragically missed opportunity to capture a true original on film. (JA)

FRIDAY

8:00 P.M.–8:30 P.M. SANFORD AND SON "Fred Sings the Blues" (originally aired on NBC, 1977)

One of the best things about *Sanford and Son* was that once it became a hit Redd Foxx exerted his influence and made the show as genuinely black as was possible at that time. Like all black sitcoms of the 1970s, the production and writing credits read like a B'nai Brith mailing list. However, Foxx cast old colleagues from his 1950s chitlin circuit days in supporting roles, and made sure plenty of improvisation and jokes from his stage act made it into the finished product. This episode is a perfect example of why that could be so successful. After a farcical misadventure (Fred reads in B. B. King's autobiography that he got the blues initially from "E.W." in St. Louis, who Fred assumes was his widow Elizabeth. It turns out that young B. B. was actually heartbroken by Elizabeth's sister, Aunt Esther), Fred, Esther (LaWanda Page, a friend of Foxx's since childhood), and Don "Bubba" Bexley go down to a nightclub and jam with King, who plays an upbeat rendition of "St. Louis Blues" and then lets everyone take a verse. This scene is completely improvised. Both Bexley and Page sing some of their favorite blues lyrics, and then Fred cracks everyone up with, "Hey Mama/Look at Sis/Out in the backyard/[instead of singing the end of this couplet Foxx just makes some rhythmic pelvic thrusts]." This group is really having fun. King would appear on several other sitcoms (*Married . . . with Children, Blossom, Fresh Prince of Bel Air*), but on each he was merely a prop, a personification of a simplistic concept of the blues. In the last two minutes of this episode, though, he commits to videotape something that is truly at the heart of the blues—a genuine, profound mode of communication and commiseration between African Americans. (JA)

8:30 P.M.–9:00 P.M. THE FLINTSTONES "The Girls Night Out" (originally aired on ABC, 1961)

Does there exist a less supportive sitcom wife than Wilma Flintstone? This particular episode highlights all of Wilma's worst tendencies, in the process providing an uncomfortably familiar rock 'n' roll allegory. After Fred whined about his day at work, Wilma countered that he never took her out. This was a fair suburban-style complaint, but Wilma cornered her husband in the argument until all he could do was stomp out of the house with his dinner. Next-door neighbor Barney Rubble met him on the stoop, having endured the same disagreement with his wife. (Since Betty Rubble was an easy-going, good-humored sort, we can only assume that she was following Wilma's lead.) Eventually, the boys realized their wives had a point, so they decided to take them to a local amusement park. The hard-to-please Wilma hated the idea, although she offered no alternatives. Betty was more sanguine about the notion but once there, she allowed Wilma to talk her into a bad mood. Wilma's ill-humored frustration seemed exacerbated by the fact that her gravel pit–working husband was actually having a good time. Fred and Barney stepped into a recording booth in an attempt to provide an irrefutable memento of their night out with the wives. Left to his own devices, Fred began to scat out a rock 'n' roll version of "Listen to the Mocking Bird," titled "Listen to the Rockin' Bird." Through sitcom magic, Flintstone's blend of hipster lounge and novelty rock attitude was automatically supplied with swingin' brass and big-beat percussion. Proud of their work, the boys played the record over and over until their wives tracked them down. Tired and disgruntled, Wilma disparaged Fred's musical achievement and made him leave it in the booth. Later, teenagers discovered the record and turned it into a fluke hit! Hooked up with a Colonel Parker–type manager, Fred was transformed into "Hi Fye: The World's Oldest Teenager." Rather than making Fred look cool, his basic dorkiness was accentuated. He combed his hair down the middle and fitted himself out with geek glasses fifteen years before the advent of Elvis Costello. Surprisingly, Flintstone proved a first-rate rock 'n' roll showman, dancing on tiptoe, leaping into the air, and gesturing manically with his guitar. An instant hit, he took his act out on a whirlwind tour. Initially, Wilma liked the notion, thinking they would travel in luxury, but the realities of life in rock 'n' roll—endless days on bumpy roads, one-nighters, and hearing the same songs over and over—quickly wore on her. Soon she just wanted to go home. Once again, her ire seemed engorged by the notion that Fred was not only good at something, but that he was also enjoying himself. Ignoring the fact that her husband could make more money as an entertainer than he ever could in the gravel pit, Wilma, in a remarkably vindictive act, spread a rumor that Fred was really a square, which instantly ruined his reputation with his fickle teen audience. Before long, Fred and Barney were back at their dead-end jobs, blissfully unaware of the heartless betrayal perpetrated by their short-sighted wives. (KB)

9:00 P.M.–10:00 P.M. ROCKFORD FILES "Just Another Polish Wedding" (originally aired on NBC, 1977)

He may not sing in this episode, but Isaac Hayes (in a recurring role as ex-con Gandolf Fitch . . . that's right, he was Gandolf before Ian McKellen) gets soulful . . . on the skulls of the patrons at a neo-Nazi social club. A well-dressed Lou Gossett, Jr., assists with the ass-whooping. This is perhaps my favorite bar fight in TV history. (JA)

10:00 P.M.–11:00 P.M. HOMICIDE: LIFE ON THE STREETS "Brotherly Love" (originally aired on NBC, 1998)

Homicide was known as an actor's showcase, a gritty, shaky-camera cop show from filmmaker Barry Levinson that allowed thespians like Andre Braugher, Yaphet Kotto, and Kyle Secor to show off their chops. So it was surprising when the show hired an amateur with no dramatic experience to make his acting debut on this episode. Actually, it was more ironic than surprising, as the role of narcotics detective Joe Landrewsky was played by one of the most legendary drug abusers in rock 'n' roll history, Anthony Joseph Perry, better known as Joe Perry of Aerosmith. Drawing more upon decades of posing on stage than decades of eight-balls and shooting up, Perry played Landrewsky as an ultra-cool, modern-day cowboy—Clint Eastwood-meets-Nick Cave. Though his acting was a little stiff, overall this was better than all three Joe Perry Project LPs combined. (JA)

11:00 P.M.–12:00 A.M. THE ARSENIO HALL SHOW "Guests: Rob and Fab" (originally aired in syndication, 1993)

Arsenio Hall may not have been the funniest guy or the best interviewer or particularly easy on the eyes, but in theory his show should have been awesome. A program that was brave enough to put artists too hip for Carson on TV—and successful enough for those artists to want to be on the show—should have yielded amazing performances. Unfortunately, Hall was about five years too late. He had the top rap acts perform on the show, but by 1989 the top rap acts were MC Hammer and Young M.C. He had Prince and his band do a dynamic performance, but in the early 1990s Prince was not producing his best material. Even Madonna seemed to be in a dry spell during that era. The most famous performance on the show was Bill Clinton playing the saxophone poorly, which was a pretty typical example of the quality of the show's musical segments. However, for lip-synch historians like myself, there was one bizarrely important (though still bad) live performance on the show. In 1993, two years after being shamed into returning their Grammy because they had not sung on their album, Milli Vanilli's Rob Pilatus and Fabrice Morvan used Hall's show to prove that they could sing. Being a lame comedian with a mean streak, Hall had been brutal on the boys when the scandal broke, but here he was giving them a chance. The performance was somewhat awkward with the boys displaying only adequate singing ability (Pilatus was less adequate than Morvan). However, the singing and rapping skills of their studio stand-ins hadn't been much better, so while this performance didn't prove that they were talented, it was a dubious triumph because it proved that they actually *could* have recorded "Girl You Know It's True." Hall was polite, though obviously underwhelmed by the performance. By the following year all three of them were show-biz ghosts. Morvan and Pilatus reemerged in 1997 on VH1's then-highest-rated show *Milli Vanilli: Behind the Music,* which sadly had to be reedited in spring 1998 when Pilatus committed suicide. (JA)

12:00–1:00 A.M. ABC IN CONCERT "Keith Richards (Um) 'Interviews' Hunter S. Thompson" (originally aired on ABC, 1993)

A handheld camera wobbles dimly down unlit motel corridors to catch fleeting glimpses of a lone figure approaching in deep, dark secrecy. Around each corner the thoroughly disheveled man lurches with what appears to be an electric cattle prod poised in one hand. With the other, he begins knocking on the wall loudly, repeatedly, to scant reaction at first. Then the image quickly steadies as we hear a strange staccato voice leaking from behind a locked door. As it violently bursts open, said cattle prod is raised in defense as out lunges an equally ravaged creature bleating incomprehensible words of warning through a bullhorn. The camera wisely retreats in horror. Yes, ladies and gentlemen, it's Rolling Stone Keith Richards meeting original gonzo guy Hunter S. Thompson during the dying days of ABC's landmark *In Concert* series. On the night of March 19, 1993, though, Doctor H. lured The Human Guitar into his *true* voodoo lounge, where he served libations of a mysterious nature as the conversation—to use that word *most* loosely—ensues between clips of Keith's band the X-Pensive Winos performing in some far-off EnormoDome. Now, as to the particular gist of this peculiar chat? Uhh, it was something about J. Edgar Hoover and dung beetles, I believe (though, try as I might, despite repeated listenings I simply *cannot* make out what in holy heck these guys are going on about, if anything). Nevertheless, it is sheer delight to witness two certifiable demigods of debauchery interact in such wholly postapocalyptic fashion, especially contrasted with what we saw on most of those ABC Friday late nights: witless Fleetwood Mac and John Fogerty career exhumations. *In Concert*, perhaps realizing that its future now lay in such oddball couplings from hell, tried a couple of months later to reheat this programming soufflé by having Billy Idol hang with Timothy Leary. But, not very surprisingly, no sparks flew there, and ABC put the whole *In Concert* thing to its long overdue rest shortly thereafter. I know, it was only Fear 'n Loathing, but we watched it. (GG)

1:00 A.M.–2:30 A.M. MIDNIGHT SPECIAL "David Bowie—The 1980 Floor Show" (originally aired on NBC, 1973)

In 1973, Bowie was commissioned to host a *Midnight Special* spectacular of his own. Among his guests were Marianne Faithfull, Spanish flamenco-rock outfit Carmen, and rock's most decidedly unexotic, glam-free purveyors of unleaded testosterone, the Troggs. His cohost was Amanda Lear, future disco diva and sometimes nude model. Bowie, for the sake of publicity, implied that she was actually a man. To this day, Bowie fans and detractors alike scratch their heads in unison and say, "What the *hell* was he thinking?" Bowie was an early champion of the aggressive U.S. and U.K. proto-punk sounds that had yet to see a decent revival (*Nuggets* had only been out for about a year), and he had just completed the LP *Pin-Ups*, on which he performed songs by some of his favorite swinging London–era bands (the Kinks, The Who, the Yardbirds, Pink Floyd, Pretty Things, etc.), and it was rumored that he had planned to follow it up with an album consisting entirely of American *Nuggets* covers. Bowie probably thought it sporting to include one still-active band from the era in which he himself had led the underrated Lower Third and Mannish Boys (under his real name, David Jones). Needless to say, bands like The Who and Pink Floyd, both already on the second big wave of their popularity, wouldn't have let anybody get top billing over them, friendships notwithstanding. The Troggs, no doubt, had no such reservations, having not seen a hit in the United States or Britain in years. They weren't in their element, but they were not deterred. Their signature song, "Wild Thing," kicked up a storm, sounding much heavier and more menacing than the original. Singer Reg

Presley, awash in multicolored optical filters, flashed his teeth as his eyes glared at the camera, very much like a modern-day Peter Lorre, who, it has been suggested, influenced Presley's singing style (he often didn't so much sing as *leer* his lyrics). "Wild Thing" sounded for all the world like sex in the mud, but the real dirt was yet to come. "Strange Movies," the Troggs' then-current single, was inspired by Britain's ban of their earlier song, "I Can't Control Myself." (Censors banned the song because it supposedly opened with the sound of Presley reaching an orgasm.) In protest, Presley stated, "They want to ban a nursery rhyme, let 'em. I'll give them something to *really* ban," and proceeded to write a song about a man who sees a porno film and subsequently stages an orgy involving all his friends. The opening line, "Last night, I saw a strange movie," was about all that made it past the TV censors. Presley had to alter the lyrics drastically to stay on the program. This despite the fact that Bowie appeared practically naked in one sequence, singing the line, "Time—he flexes like a whore, falls wanking to the floor," and Marianne Faithfull satirized the church by appearing in a full nun's habit for a duet of "I Got You, Babe." The Troggs went through with the rewrite, still managing to get the message across, despite such embarrassing alterations as "everyone was in bed" becoming "everyone lost their heads" and "gettin' randy" rephrased as "lookin' dandy." The original controversy had been over the grunting chorus of "UH! UH! UH! UH! UHH! UHH! UHHH! WOAH!!!" The new version went "Love! Love! Love! LOVE!!!" Though it was comparable to seeing the *other* Presley from the waist up, you *still* got your sex. (JB)

SATURDAY

10:00 A.M.–11:00 A.M. KIDS ARE PEOPLE TOO "Guest: Patti Smith" (originally aired on ABC, 1978)

At a time when disco was brainwashing the whole universe, somebody booked punk high priestess Patti Smith on ABC's morning talk show for kids to explain this "new wave" thingie to the middle schoolers across the country. After the discussion was over Patti did *not* do a smokin' version of her only Top Forty single "Because the Night." Nor did she do her landmark punk version of "Hey Joe." And she didn't read her poetry either. Nah. She sang her version of "You Light Up My Life!" Some people might have said, "You blew it, Patti!" Others might have thought it was the greatest put-on (putdown?) in the history of rock TV. I'd like to think it was the latter. (JP)

11:00 A.M.–12:00 P.M. AMERICAN BANDSTAND "Episode 2397" (originally aired on ABC, 1980)

Warner Brothers was excited to trot out Prince, their nineteen-year-old androgynous wunderkind who played all the instruments on his recordings and combined the best aspects of black music with keyboard-driven new wave. So the powers that were made arrangements for him to do the TV rounds, and in 1980 and 1981 he made exciting live appearances on *Midnight Special* and *Saturday Night Live*. But his most memorable appearance was on Dick Clark's Saturday afternoon dance show. During his performance of "I Wanna Be Your Lover," Prince, wearing his hair feathered like Farrah Fawcett, a pair of gold lamé pants, and an open shirt revealing his skinny torso, was pretty underwhelming. Perhaps he was still trying to come to terms with being an entertainer as opposed to a creative musician, perhaps he was particularly uncomfortable with lip-synching (the number features the ultra-awkward lip-synch fadeout ending), or perhaps he dabbled in mind-altering substances as a youth. Whatever the case, his dancing was awkward and unimpressive (hard to believe that in two years he would become one of the best dancers in rock 'n' roll), and he seemed unfocused, especially when compared to bassist Andre Cymone and guitarist Dez Dickerson who struck professional rock star poses (despite miming to a record on which they hadn't even played). But the real magic happened during Clark's Q & A (the last interview Prince would do on TV until well into the 1990s). Acting like a coy, disinterested, petulant teenager, Prince was determined to give Clark (who seemed genuinely excited about Prince's talents) one-word answers in a monotone voice without making eye contact with America's oldest teenager. Then the one-word answers were trumped when Clark asked how many years ago Prince's self-produced demos began gaining industry interest. Wordlessly Prince held up four fingers while pursing his lips. The interview wound up with Clark asking Prince how many instruments he could play. After a dramatic pause so long that Clark began to withdraw the microphone, the future Purple One responded in a fey, flat voice, "Thousands. . . ." (JA)

12:00 P.M.–1:00 P.M. SOUL TRAIN "Marvin Gaye Shooting Hoops" (originally aired in syndication, 1977)

Producer and host Don Cornelius devoted this entire episode to Marvin Gaye playing a game of basketball. Just like Shaquille O'Neal, Carl Lewis, and the Super Bowl Shufflers who felt compelled to take their sports fame to the musical stage, Gaye

didn't know his own limitations when crossing over from one realm of showbiz to another. A frustrated athlete, six years earlier a middle-aged Gaye embarrassed himself by trying out for the Detroit Lions. There would be no such humiliation here, however, as *Soul Train* matched Gaye up with a beatable opponent. The outcome: Gaye won, closing the show by doing a victory dance to his hit "Got to Give It Up." (JP)

1:00 P.M.–1:30 P.M. FAT ALBERT AND THE COSBY KIDS "Creativity" (originally aired on CBS, 1972)

Though not the premiere episode, this show revealed the origin of Fat Albert's act, the Junkyard Band. Rudy, the wealthiest of the gang, showed up at the junkyard with his new treasure—a customized white Fender guitar with a big "R" on it and a massive set of amplifiers that transformed into a car at the touch of a button. He told his cohorts that he was going to become a fabulously wealthy rock star, touring around in a star-shaped limo, playing concerts while being pulled on water skis behind a yacht, and making "eleven-million-thousand dollars." Though the boys didn't know how to play anything but the dozens ("There's only two things wrong with your performance . . . your hands!"), they decided the rock 'n' roll lifestyle was for them and furiously tried to raise money to buy instruments. After some zany adventures selling bottles and walking dogs they went to the pawnshop and picked out hundreds of dollars' worth of gear, but they left empty-handed after receiving a derisive reply to their classic inquiry "What can we get for sixty-three cents?" (Boogie Down Productions sampled that line in the 1980s, with Cosby's rotund hero trying to buy less than a dollar's worth of drugs.)

Back in the junkyard the boys got creative. Bill made a drum out of a garbage can, Weird Harold turned a bed frame into a harp, Dumb Donald made a trombone out of steam pipes and a gramophone horn, Russell made chimes out of tin cans, Bucky turned a broken toy piano into a pipe organ, Mushmouth made a guitar out of scrap wood, and Fat Albert turned a radiator and a potato sack into a squeezebox. When Rudy's guitar-car turned out to be a lemon he scaled back his plans and joined the Junkyard Band, an act that instead of rocking the free world seemed content to punctuate the gang's weekly misadventures with didactic tunes. Their first composition, a funky theme song called "We're All Together," was introduced by a live-action Cosby, looking slim, muscular, and cool with his tall afro and skintight "Hey Hey Hey" T-shirt. "Well, there was New Orleans jazz," Bill explained, "progressive jazz, Chicago Dixie, Kansas City blues, Woodstock rock, and now . . . *the North Philadelphia Junkyard Band!*" Though Cosby provided the speaking voices, Fat Albert's singing voice on all his preachy bubble-soul songs was handled by Michael Gray. And while many funk fans may scoff at songs about hygiene, playing hooky, wearing glasses, and being brave at the hospital ("Don't be scared of a hospital . . . you'll be repaired at a hospital, and when you're there—*you'll get ice cream!*"), I can listen to this stuff all day. The Junkyard Band's music is the perfect halfway point between the excellent and responsible Joe Raposo *Sesame Street* music and the crappy but infectious Hanna-Barbera bubblegum tunes. (Note: Like Digable Planets, The Knack, and Guns n' Roses, this group suffered a massive sophomore slump. Avoid their *Rock N Roll Disco with Fat Albert and the Junkyard Band!* LP.) (JA)

1:30 P.M.–2:00 P.M. THE MONKEES "The Monkees at the Movies" (originally aired on NBC, 1967)

This episode is worthwhile because it featured the man who became the Monkees' replacement in the teen idol sweepstakes, Bobby Sherman. A former regular on ABC's *Shindig*, Sherman had been kicking around for a while without much success. On this episode he played Frankie Catalina, the blond pompadour-wearing star of the beach movie *I Married a Creature from Out of Town*. The Monkees, cast as extras, discovered that Catalina was an abusive prick and drove him from the set by messing with his make-up, forcing him to lip-synch at various speeds, and reshuffling his cue cards so his lines didn't make sense. Once the movie was without a star, the group used several ploys to get their own Davy Jones the job. (Micky Dolenz scored some major laughs masquerading as a DJ announcing the song "These Boots Are Made for Kicking!") Once Davy got the job, he became just as big a jerk as Frankie Catalina had been and Peter, Mike, and Micky were forced to teach him a lesson too. Musically, the group also did an inspired job in this episode, cavorting to their hits "A Little Bit Me, A Little Bit You" and "Valleri." Most historical here was the documentary-style tacked-on footage at the end, which captured the Monkees at a significant point in their career. Having just experienced the they-don't-play-their-own-instruments controversy, the group talked quite sincerely about playing their own instruments in concert. These controversies led to their fights with Don Kirshner over creative control, and eventually to the 1968 cancellation of their show. Meanwhile, Sherman became a regular on ABC's *Here Come the Brides*, and enraptured teenaged girls made him their newest icon of cute, buying millions of copies of "Little Woman," "Easy Come, Easy Go," and "Julie Do Ya Love Me" while the Monkees quietly disappeared. (KB)

2:00 P.M.–2:30 P.M. THE NEW SCOOBY DOO MOVIES "The Haunted Candy Factory" (originally aired on CBS,1973)

The incarnation of the long-running Scooby Doo series featured celebrity guest stars, from the hip (Sonny and Cher and the Harlem Globetrotters) to the absurd (Don Knotts and Jonathan Winters) to the dead (Laurel and Hardy and the Three Stooges) to Scooby's fictional Hanna-Barbera brethren (Batman and Josie and the Pussycats). What is most notable about this particular episode is that the gang met one of the most dynamic voices of the 1960s, Mama Cass Elliot, a woman whose powerful singing helped the Mamas and the Papas build an enchanted bridge between Greenwich Village folk music and California flower pop. And all the show's writers can do is make fat jokes. (JA)

2:30 P.M.–3:00 P.M. MISTER ROGERS' NEIGHBORHOOD "Episode 1509" (originally aired on PBS, 1982)

Anyone who grew up with this show remembers Fred Rogers's gentle, honest dialogues with both viewers and his live guests. It's easy to think of him as one of TV's best listeners and most thoughtful speakers, the Oprah Winfrey of kiddie shows. However, it would be a mistake to overlook his role as the Ed Sullivan of the genre. Like Sullivan, the entertainers Rogers welcomed to his show ranged from highbrow classical musicians to common folk artists. Where Rogers and Sullivan diverged was in their interaction with the guests. As opposed to the stiff, distanced Sullivan, Rogers was fascinated with what

his guests did, and he really wanted to hear why they did it. Another important difference was that Rogers's show was not booking acts based on popularity, but rather on how interesting and enriching they might be to young viewers. Thus, some guests who appeared on the program had had little or no TV exposure, and in this case Rogers gave ample airtime to one of the most interesting, important artists of the twentieth century. Otha Turner (who died in his mid-nineties on the same day Rogers passed away) kept alive a tradition of fife-and-drum blues music that was spare, intense, and emotionally powerful. The raw, imperfect notes from his hand-carved fife were chilling and hypnotizing. Based in northern Mississippi, Turner was close enough to Memphis to be on the periphery of the music industry (the annual barbecues he hosted in his later years became legendary among music fans and artists) but far enough removed from modern life that his performances maintained a sincere purity that was rare in our media-saturated age. In this episode neighborhood handyman and music shop owner Joe Negri invited Rogers, Lady Aberlin, and viewers to meet the Mississippi Fife and Drum Corps (Turner and drummers Abe Young and Jessie Mae Hemphill, a legend in her own right), who were rehearsing for a concert. They played fantastic music, then took a break to talk to Rogers and his friends. What made this segment amazing was that, without any prompting or leading questions, every word the interviewees said illustrated how traditional music was passed along through generations, which explained how such a pure sound was possible at the dawn of the MTV age. Turner spoke of "the old man" making him his first fife, Young explained how he had "fourteen children, all of them interested" in music, and Hemphill talked of playing with her granddaddy (a field musician recorded by Alan Lomax). They finished by playing a bare-bones "Glory, Glory, Hallelujah," which Hemphill wanted to do to "show the kids so maybe they'll learn it and bring it on after we're gone." The segment ended with the performers starting a processional; the experience was manifestly African. This eight-minute piece summarized the complicated history of American popular music more clearly than an eight-hour PBS documentary series. My favorite moment of this show, however, was nonmusical. Lady Aberlin listened intently to Turner speaking. She nodded and smiled and sometimes strained to understand his impossibly thick rural Mississippi accent. But eventually his dialect lost her. As the camera cut to a close-up of her lovely face, her eyes were blank with a mixture confusion and defeat, but she still smiled. That smile summarized the inclusiveness of the show: in 1982, Mister Rogers's wonderful neighborhood was one of the few in the country where hearing folks talk like that wasn't going to lower the property values. (JA)

3:00 P.M.–7:00 P.M. COLLEGE FOOTBALL "Miami Hurricanes vs. West Virginia" (originally aired on ABC, 1993)

There are a lot of memorable TV sports rock 'n' roll moments—Marvin Gaye's coked out, soulful rendering of the National Anthem at the 1983 NBA All Star Game (as complete and as weird a reinvention as Hendrix's), KISS standing in for Hank Williams Jr. on *Monday Night Football* in 1993, news coverage of the 1979 "Disco Demolition" riot that caused the White Sox to forfeit a game—but my favorite one was completely sans music. Though I am not a college football fan, in 1993 I became obsessed with watching Rohan Marley, son of reggae king Bob Marley, play football for the Miami Hurricanes. Though handsome, Rohan was not his father's look-alike (as is his older brother

Rogers and Turner (seated with fife). ©Family Communications, Inc.

Ziggy) and he did not have the gentle gaze that his father bequeathed to his numerous other children. Instead he had intense, somewhat crazy eyes, perhaps too intense for a game of soccer his dad might have enjoyed in the pleasant Jamaican air, but perfect for a brutal game of American football. Though far too small (five-foot-eight) to become a pro linebacker, somehow he managed to become a powerful force on the best team in the country, having a tremendous season that peaked in the game against West Virginia, in which he had fifteen tackles. The TV announcers loved to point out the Marley legacy, but the fearless Hurricane would have been singled out no matter what his lineage. The season ended on a sour note when the top-ranked Hurricanes lost the national championship in a game against Alabama in the Sugar Bowl (the Crimson Tide players were inspired by Marley's incessant trash-talking in the media about how he would "kick Alabama's butt"). Though not a musician, he did have a profound impact on the music industry when he married Lauryn Hill. As she bore Bob Marley's grandchildren, Hill became an active part of reggae's royal family, an honor that apparently was more important to her than a recording career. Like all great ex-jocks, Rohan took up acting classes (there was talk of Rohan and Lauryn playing Bob and Rita in a Warner Brothers biopic) and his eyes have softened over the years to take on the relaxed look of his dad. Most importantly, a decade removed from football he has kept the promise he made at the 1993 Sugar Bowl press conference. "The society I live in doesn't let me wear dreads," he expounded, "but if you see me in ten years I'll *definitely* be in dreads." (JA)

7:00 P.M.–8:00 P.M. TOWN HALL PARTY "Guest: Eddie Cochran" (originally aired on KTTV, 1959)

Country music's uneasy alliance with rockabilly and early rock 'n' roll was clear on this obscure but important series. Staged live in Compton, California, and broadcast over KTTV in Los Angeles, the program was seldom seen outside the West Coast during its initial 1952–1961 run. Fortunately, kinescopes survive, and DVDs of some of the greatest performances recently have been released. Although quite short, the Eddie Cochran set is essential viewing because very little live footage exists of the late rocker. Ambivalent to publicity, the Minnesota-born, Oklahoma-bred performer actually blew off an appearance on *The Ed Sullivan Show* by simply not showing up. Fortunately, on February 9, 1959, the young guitar phenom saw fit to do two brief sets for *Town Hall Party*. Looking dapper in a dress suit with baggy pants and sporting a pompadour to die for, Cochran laid down some vibrant versions of his two biggest hits ("C'mon Everybody," "Summertime Blues") as well as pleasingly raw takes of songs associated with Chuck Berry ("School Days"), Fats Domino ("Don't Blame It on Me"), and the Drifters ("Money Honey"). For his slow numbers, Cochran employed his foggy-voiced ballad style on effective—but not sensational—covers of Gene Autry ("Be Honest with Me") and Red Foley ("Have I Told You Lately That I Love You?") standards. Dot recording artists Dick D'Agostin and the Swingers provided spirited backup, though both band and star were hampered by the show's crude single-microphone set up. Triumphing over technical snafus and genuinely enjoying his interplay with D'Agostin, Cochran exhibited loads of natural charm, humor, and intelligence. During a somewhat condescending interview, country singer Johnny Bond asked the twenty-year-old Cochran if rock 'n' roll music would last. "I think rock 'n' roll-will be here for quite some time, Johnny," Cochran replied. "But I don't think it's going to be rock 'n' roll as we know it today." Cochran never lived to see the truth of that prediction. The following year in England he died in a car crash that reinjured Gene Vincent's already game leg. This long-forgotten footage not only provides some joyous moments, but is also a sobering reminder of what rock music lost. (KB)

8:00 P.M.–9:00 P.M. TJ HOOKER "Deadly Ambition" (originally aired on ABC, 1982)

Jerry Lee Lewis made his acting debut in 1968 in a Los Angeles production of *Catch My Soul*, the rock version of Shakespeare's *Othello*, which Jack Good (*Shindig*) produced. Although the play itself got mixed reviews, Lewis received glowing notices (you can hear him rehearsing some of his scenes on the 1995 CD *Private Stash*). Was he a better actor than Elvis? Undeniably, but only as the heavy. Lewis's acting plans were put on hold by his comeback via country music later that year. After signing with the William Morris Agency in 1973, he landed a small part on the "Collision Course" episode of *Police Story* (an anthology series that eventually evolved into the better-known Angie Dickinson vehicle, *Police Woman*). Lewis played the driver of a getaway car whose job was to listen to costar Dean Stockwell rant obsessively about great guns and infamous gunmen. When he got caught at the episode's end, Lewis emerged from the car with his hands

up and barked at the police as if they were rowdy nightclub patrons, "Cool it!"

The *TJ Hooker* appearance provided a meatier role. Playing himself, Lewis wailed through a career-best version of Chuck Willis's "C.C. Rider" at the legendary Palomino Club. Hooker (William Shatner) and Romano (Adrian Zmed) were thrilled to question the rock legend about his former security chief's involvement with diamond thieves. With a straight face and a distracted manner, Lewis explained that the suspect was basically a good ol' boy who went wrong when he started getting involved in cocaine. (Hot stuff coming from one of rock's most conspicuous substance abusers.) Eventually Hooker and crew solved the case—a self-serving detective was to blame—and the cops were treated to a night out at the Palomino Club. "It's identification time," said Lewis before ripping into a lively version of his 1957 hit, "Whole Lotta Shakin' Goin' On." However, Shatner stole the show with some of the hammiest mugging ever. As Lewis rocked the house, T. J. Hooker was on the verge of bursting with rapture out of all proportion to the event, which must have made viewers wonder if he had visited the singer's former security chief before the show. (KB)

9:00 P.M.–11:00 P.M. KISS MEETS THE PHANTOM OF THE PARK (originally aired on NBC, 1978)

This made-for-TV movie is a truly significant moment in TV rock history because it challenged the limits of how much artifice rock fans were willing to endure . . . and it lost! Though it was a ratings success, these two hours of NBC prime time did what the band's previous appearances on TV—including lip-synching with Paul

Lynde and trading jokes with an elderly Jewish comic on *The Mike Douglas Show*—could not. It fundamentally alienated their primary fan base, defeating the once unstoppable KISS Army.

In 1978, KISS was the biggest band in the world. They achieved this status by relentlessly touring, including grueling heartland journeys to obscure towns that rock royalty rarely visited. While it's hard to believe a theatrical band with face paint, fake blood, and exploding guitars had integrity to lose, the fact is that KISS's simple, horny hard rock appealed to the same working-class American teens that dug Zeppelin, Grand Funk, and Ted Nugent. The band's comic book imagery naturally appealed to youngsters, but KISS was by no means considered a kiddie band. This makes it very curious as to why they allowed schlock cartoon kings Hanna-Barbera to produce the KISS movie. "It was sold to us as a cross between *Star Wars* and *A Hard Day's Night*," guitarist Paul Stanley explained, "and it turned out to be nothing like either of them." That's an understatement. Historically, there have been three approaches to making rock magic on celluloid. There's the comedic ironic distance approach (the Beatles, the Spice Girls), the self-important, serious approach (Pink Floyd's *The Wall*, Sting's documentary), or the knockoff teen-exploitation approach (Elvis, Vanilla Ice). KISS took this third option to the extreme, opting for a low-budget live-action version of the worst episodes of *Scooby Doo*. In the film KISS played a rock band made up of cosmic super-powered gods (with Long Island accents). They were playing concerts at an amusement park plagued by a mad scientist who had created evil robots to take over the world. Using their powers, cheap special effects, and some of the worst stunt doubles in history (a husky black man in

KISS makeup does guitarist Ace Frehley's fighting for him), the band foiled the mad scientist's scheme. Fans would have been dissatisfied enough by the poor acting and terrible special effects, but the real bummer was that KISS rarely appeared in the film. When they did materialize, Frehley and drummer Peter Criss hardly spoke. Apparently Ace was supposed to be a spaceman (as opposed to a drug addict) who only uttered the all-purpose monosyllabic exclamation, "Awk!" (In the original shooting script the film ended with the band lamenting the lobotomized mad scientist's lost potential with this poignant bit of dialogue: "ACE: (sadly) *Awk*.") Doing Ace one better, Criss couldn't be bothered to return to the studio for postproduction so all of his dialogue was overdubbed by Norman Alden, a Hanna-Barbera voice actor best known for his work as Aquaman (arguably the Peter Criss of the *Super Friends*). After the film aired, KISS concert audiences consisted of far fewer dazed and confused high school dropouts and more children in makeup; the band's aura of danger was gone forever. But, as in *KISS Meets the Phantom of the Park* itself, the band was victorious in the end. Despite its tremendous shortcomings, ultimately the film's direct appeals to juveniles at the expense of the core KISS audience paid off. The band ended up selling a lot of records in the 1980s to the snot-nosed kids who pushed their bedtimes back to catch the movie. (JA)

11:00 P.M.–11:30 P.M. VH1 CELEBRITY ROCK 'N' ROLL JEOPARDY "George Clinton episode" (originally aired on VH1, 1999)

In theory this was a good idea for a game show—rock musicians answer questions (to be more accurate, since this was *Jeopardy*, they question answers) about rock music. Unfortunately, to make the show interesting they always had a diverse threesome, which instead made the show extremely boring. It seems that white record collector rock guys in their thirties learned all about pop, R&B, easy listening, and all other genres through osmosis while touching those albums as they flipped through record bins. Thus, guys like Scott Ian of Anthrax and Mark McGrath of Sugar Ray would run the board, answering every question correctly while the other two contestants twiddled their buzzers. On this particular episode Dave Mustaine of Megadeth had the honor of humiliating Moon Unit Zappa and Dr. Funkenstein himself, George Clinton of Parliament-Funkadelic. As an acknowledged crack cocaine abuser (a habit that apparently hinders trivia ability more than Mustaine's heroin abuse) it was no surprise that Clin-

ton did not bring the winner's trophy back to the Mothership. But the absolute lowlight, a bizarre TV rock moment, was when Clinton blew a question *about himself!* (JA)

11:30 P.M.–1:00 A.M. SATURDAY NIGHT LIVE "Episode 93" (originally aired on NBC, 1979)

It's not all that unusual to see a white rapper, such as Eminem or Vanilla Ice, surrounding himself with actual African Americans to gain some credibility, but this episode of *Saturday Night Live* offered up a unique variation on that formula. To gain credibility as a futuristic super-gay space freak, David Bowie enjoyed his finest TV rock moment by surrounding himself with *authentic* futuristic super-gay space freaks. The magnificent Klaus Nomi made an underground name for himself by dressing like a robotic porcelain doll and singing

Klaus Nomi. Courtesy Jake Austen

standards in an operatic falsetto (and a heavy German accent) over new-wave disco tracks. History claims his death in 1983 was the passing of the first celebrity from AIDS, though that strains the definition of "celebrity" a bit. Though he deserved worldwide acclaim for his brilliant recordings and performances, the truth is that his uncredited accompaniment of Bowie on *Saturday Night Live* was his only moment in the mainstream. But what a moment! To perform "The Man Who Sold the World" Bowie had himself encased in a legless Dadaist sculpture-costume, which meant his backup singers—Nomi and his equally bizarre collaborator Joey Arias— had to carry him onto the stage. While Bowie magnificently played the role of tortured fey mechanical man, it was his flamboyant android sidemen who made this performance a visual and conceptual coup.

Nomi's distinct soprano didn't hurt either. Though *Saturday Night Live* has not always been the best music venue, there have been a number of memorable performances over the years (including Bowie's second set in this episode where he appeared in drag and he and the boys did "TVC-15" and a butch version of "Boys Keep Swinging"). However, no musical moment in the thirty-year history of the show was as triumphant on artistic and aesthetic levels as this one. With the unlikely help of cross-dressing downtown sodomites, this stands as one of the rare moments when TV gave its audience genuine high culture, delivering a bizarre variation on what the medium's early architects imagined when they programmed shows like *Mantovani, Opera Cameos,* and the *Chicago Symphony Chamber Orchestra* in the 1950s. (JA)

Source Notes

In the following list, I have cited sources on a chapter-by-chapter basis, followed by a list of materials that I used for reference throughout the book. "AI" indicates material from author interviews. "WC" indicates Web citations for information specific to the chapter.

Chapter 1: Rock Around the Box

AI: Edie Adams, Ken Burke, DJ Darryl, Art Fein, Jay McNeely, Domenic Priore, Claude Trenier, Milt Trenier, Skip Trenier

Allen, Steve. *Hi-Ho, Steverino: The Story of My Adventures in the Wacky Wonderful World of Television*. Fort Lee, New Jersey: Barricade Books, 1992.

Allen, Steve. *Reflections*. Amherst, New York: Prometheus, 1994.

Allen, Steve. *Vulgarians at the Gate*. Amherst, New York: Prometheus, 2001.

Baughman, James L. "Television Comes to America, 1947–1957," *Illinois History*, March 1993.

Bowles, Jerry. *A Thousand Sundays*. New York: Putnam, 1980.

Evans, Nancy. "Rock Around the Box," *Crawdaddy*, August 1978.

Faggen, Gil. "Clark Bounces Back in Syndicated Radio," *Billboard*, June 23, 1963.

Faggen, Gil. "'Hullabaloo' Is a Vibrant Vehicle for Pop, Artists," *Billboard*, January 23, 1965.

Fontenot, Robert, Jr. "Backtalk with Bo Diddley," *Offbeat*, June 1999.

Gold, Gary Pig. "To Catch a Falling Star," *Roctober*, Summer 2001.

Goldberg, Marv. "The Ravens," *Orioles Fan Club Bulletin*, January 1965.

Gould, Jack. "TV: The Beatles and Their Audience," *New York Times*, February 10, 1964.

Guralnick, Peter. *Last Train to Memphis*. New York: Back Bay, 1994.

Harrington, Richard. "It was 40 years ago . . . ," *Chicago Tribune*, February 6, 2004.

Harris, Michael David. *Always on Sunday*. New York: Merideth Press, 1968.

Hoeffer, George. "the hot box," *Down Beat*, January 23, 1957.

Hutton, Jack. "Will Bands Last on Television?" *Melody Maker*, January 29, 1955.

Jones, Will. "Radio and TV," *Down Beat*, September 19, 1957.

Knight, Bob. "Sullivan's 'Swinging, Soulful '60s' Does Hop, Skip, Jump on Decade," *Variety*, August 23, 1969.

Leonard, John. "The Ed Sullivan Age," *American Heritage*, May–June 1997.

LIFE Rock & Roll at 50: A History in Pictures. New York: Time-Life Books, 2002.

"Live Local Country & Western TV Shows," *Billboard*, March 23, 1957.

Martindale, Wink. *Winking at Life*. Calabasas, California: Century Hill, 2000.

Mayer, Martin. "Music on TV: A Dim View," *High Fidelity—Musical America*, November 1968.

"Metric Eyes New Vista for Rock," *Billboard*, October 2, 1965.

Morse, Steve. "Can't Get the Date Straight for Rock's Birthday," *Boston Globe*, July 5, 2004.

Strongin, Theodore "Musicologically . . . ," *New York Times*, February 10, 1964.

Sullivan, Ed. "TV Needs Good Music," *Music Journal*, February 1961.

Szatmary, David. *Rockin' in Time: A Social History of Rock-and-Roll*. New York: Prentice-Hall, 1991.

Tosches, Nick. "Ed Sullivan," *Vanity Fair*, July 1997.

"Truck Driver Invents Rock," *Rolling Stone*, June 24, 2004.

TV Guide, September 8–14, 1956.

White, George. *Bo Diddley Living Legend*. Surrey, UK: Castle Communications, 1995.

Wynn, Ron. "Hey Bo Diddley," *Nashville City Paper*, March 27, 2001.

Chapter 2: Lip-Synch Traces

AI: Lou Christie, Elaine Mulqueen, Jack Mulqueen, Jim Peterik, Domenic Priore

WC: www.60sgaragebands.com

Adams, Deanna R. *Rock 'n' Roll and the Cleveland Connection*. Kent, Ohio: Kent State University Press, 2002.

Auslander, Philip. *Liveness*. London: Routledge, 1999.

Boulware, Jack. "Bill Hicks: High Plains Jester," *The Nose Magazine*, 1992.

"Britain's Top Pop TV Show to Be Dropped," *Billboard*, October 10, 1965.

"British TV Nets to Drop Miming Disks in Nod to Musician Union Requests," *Variety*, June 15, 1966.

Clark, Dick. "'Bandstand' Regulars . . . and Irregulars," *Rolling Stone*, February 10, 1977.

Clark, Dick, and Fred Bronson. *Dick Clark's American Bandstand*. New York: Collins, 1997.

Clark, Dick, and Richard Robinson. *Rock, Roll & Remember*. New York: Thomas Y. Crowell, 1976.

Clark Dick, and Michael Shore. *The History of American Bandstand*. New York: Ballantine, 1985.

Coleman, Ray. "Jack Good Shows Yanks How to Pop Television," *Melody Maker*, December 12, 1964.

Dawburn, Bob. "TV Pop: Is It Going to Stop?" *Melody Maker*, January 29, 1960.

"Dick Clark Marks 25th Anni of Show with Rock Classics," *Variety*, December 8, 1976.

Fong-Torres, Ben. "Dick Clark: Twenty Years of Clearasil Rock," *Rolling Stone*, August 16, 1973.

Good, Jack. "The Sound of Sound," *Disc*, 1960.

Jackson, John A. *American Bandstand: Dick Clark and the Making of a Rock 'n' Roll Empire.* Oxford: Oxford University Press, 1997.

Jones, Chris, and John Waters. "Welcome to the '60s," *Chicago Tribune*, January 18, 2004.

"Kiddie A-Go-Go," *Screen*, August 11, 1997.

Kanze, Peter. "Hey Let's Go with Upbeat Show," *Rock Scene*, 1977.

Okuda, Ted, and Jack Mulqueen. *The Golden Age of Chicago Children's Television.* Chicago: Lake Claremont Press, 2004.

Orodenker, Maurie. "Close of Clark Daily Show Marks End of Era," *Billboard*, June 23, 1963.

Passman, Arnold. *The Deejays.* New York: Macmillan, 1971.

Pichaske, David. *A Generation in Motion.* New York, Schirmer, 1979.

"Tele Follow-Up Comment," *Variety*, June 15, 1966.

Thompson, Stephen. "Dick Clark," *The Onion*, November 13–19, 2003.

Chapter 3: Faking the Band

AI: Ken Burke, Anthony Illarde, Rachel Lichtman, James Porter, Alex Wald

WC: www.psycho-jello.com/monkees, www.ricknelson.com

Amory, Cleveland. "Monkees review," *TV Guide*, November 19, 1966.

Baker, Glenn A., Tom Czarnota, and Peter Hogan. *Monkee-Mania.* New York: St. Martin's, 1986.

Cooper, Kim, and David Smay, editors. *Bubblegum Music Is the Naked Truth.* Los Angeles: Feral House, 2001.

Curtis, Jim. *Rock Eras 1954–1984.* Bowling Green, Ohio: Bowling Green State University Popular Press, 1987.

Finn, Ed, and T. Bone. *The Monkees Scrapbook.* San Francisco: Last Gasp, 1986.

Glenn, Brian, and Mark Glenn. *Anthology of Awesomeness.* New York: Pocket Books, 2001.

Green, Joey. *The Partridge Family Album.* New York: HarperCollins, 1994.

Green, Robin. "Naked Lunch Box," *Rolling Stone*, May 11, 1972.

Hayes, Justin Coord. "The Third Degree with . . . David Cassidy," *Las Vegas Weekly*, October 28, 1998.

Javna, John. *Cult TV.* New York: St. Martin's, 1985.

Jones, James. "Out of Sync," *Chicago Reader*, October 25, 1996.

Jones, Shirley, Marty Ingels, and Mickey Herskowitz. *Shirley Jones & Marty Ingels.* New York: Shaplosky Publishers, Inc., 1993.

Lefcowitz, Eric. "Michael Nesmith Interview," *Monkees Business Fanzine*, June 1985.

Porter, James. "Never Mind the Bollocks, Here's the Banana Splits," *Roctober*, Fall 1994.

"RCA, Kirshner Enter New Tie," *Billboard*, August 31, 1968.

T., Mike, editor. *Rockcyclopedia Fakebandica*, www.fakebands.com

Wild, David. "Monkees Redux?" *Rolling Stone*, October 29, 1992.

Chapter 4: The Hippest Trip in Town

AI: Pedro Bell, Oscar Brown Jr., Devorah Heitner, Rob Johnson, Herb Kent, Melissa Harris-Lacewell, Calvin Lincoln, Leah Merrifield, Sergio Mims, Milt Trenier

WC: www.bet.com, www.soultrain.com

"The Apollo: One More Time," *Variety*, May 22, 1985.

"Apollo Theater Foundation, Inc. Seeks to Enjoin 'Best of It's Showtime at the Apollo' Program," *PR Newswire*, June 3, 2003.

Arango, Tim. "Apollo Slugfest: Parsons Backs NBC; Sutton Mounts Challenge," *New York Post*, January 28, 2003.

Berman, Marc. "A Showdown for Showtime: Venerable Series from New York's Apollo," *Media Week*, December 2, 2002.

Bessman, Jim. "Black Cable Network Makes Heavy Commitment to Clips," *Billboard*, March 30, 1985.

"Black Artists Finally Get Television Shows," *Rolling Stone*, September 28, 1968.

Blair, Jayson. "Black Entertainment Television to Open Studio in East Harlem," *New York Times*, July 6, 2000.

Buckman, Adam. "Battle Over Long-Running Apollo Show," *New York Post*, August 15, 2002.

Chapman, Aida. "Soul Train," *Billboard*, September 28, 1974.

Cole, Williams. "Anomaly TV: Inside Bed-Stuy," *The Brooklyn Rail*, April 2003.

Cooper, Daniel. "The !!!! Beat," *Goldmine*, February 5, 1993.

Cooper, Ralph, and Steve Dougherty. *Amateur Night at the Apollo*. New York: Harper-Collins, 1990.

Denisoff, R. Serge. *Inside MTV*. New Brunswick, New Jersey: Transaction Publishers.

Early, Gerald. *One Nation Under a Groove: Motown & American Culture*. Hopewell, New Jersey: Ecco Press, 1995.

Feiwell, Jill. "'Showtime' Won't Be at Apollo," *Daily Variety*, August 14, 2002.

"Fight Slated for Apollo's Name," *Broadcasting & Cable*, June 9, 2003.

Flick, Larry. "'Soul Train' Turns 25 with Box, TV Show," *Billboard*, October 14, 1995.

Fong-Torres, Ben. "'Soul Train' vs. Dick Clark: Battle of the Bandstands," *Rolling Stone*, June 7, 1973.

Fox, Ted. *Showtime at the Apollo*. New York: Holt, 1983.

Foxx, Redd, and Norma Miller. *The Redd Foxx Encyclopedia of Black Humor*. Pasadena, California: Ward Ritchie Press, 1977.

Frutkin, Alan James. "For Two Decades, Gospel Music's Weekly Showcase," *New York Times*, August 19, 2001.

Gardner, Paul. "Nat Cole Praises New TV Attitude," *New York Times*, February 17, 1964.

Gibbs, Vernon. "Soul, Man," *Crawdaddy*, August 1974.

Goldner, Diane. "ICBC swims mainstream," *Variety*, April 14–20, 1997.

Goldner, Diane. "The Star Chamber," *Variety*, April 14–20, 1997.

Greeley, Bill. "Why WNEW: TV 'Black Is' Ain't," *Variety*, December 24, 1969.

Grossman, Jay. "Soul Train Dancers: Doing the Real L.A. Hustle," *Rolling Stone*, November 6, 1975.

Harris-Lacewell, Melissa Victoria. *Barbershops, Bibles and BET.* Princeton, New Jersey: Princeton University Press.

Hill, Lee Alan. "Viewership Splits Along Racial Lines; UPN a Heavy Draw, but Few Shows Cross Boundaries," *Television Week*, February 23, 2004.

Jackson, Hal, and James Haskins. *Hal Jackson: The House that Jack Built.* New York: Amistad, 2001.

"Jackson Hops Aboard 'Soul Train' Dispute," *Variety*, December 13, 1989.

Johnson, Robert L. "For BET, the Picture Is Crystal Clear," *Emerge*, February 2000.

Johnson, Robert L. "The Market Nobody Wanted," *Fortune Small Business*, October 1, 2002.

Jones, Lisa. "Hot Buttered 'Soul'," *Village Voice*, March 12, 1991.

Jones, Tim. "Viacom-BET Deal Erodes Black Media Ownership," *Chicago Tribune*, November 4, 2000.

Liburt, Ellen. "Apollo to Amateurs: 'Come Out and Play,'" *Variety*, April 14–20, 1997.

Littleton, Cynthia. "It's Deal Time at the 'Apollo': De Passe, Heritage Take Over TV Show," *The Hollywood Reporter*, August 21, 2002.

McAdams, Janine. "One to One," *Billboard*, March 17, 1990.

McAdams, Janine. "'Soul Train,' Steams into 20th Season," *Billboard*, March 17, 1990.

McAdams, Janine. "'Soul Train,' Union at Odds over Contract," *Billboard*, October 21, 1989.

McKinney, Jeffrey. "Heritage Networks Wins Showdown: Frank Mercado-Valdes Plans to Build a Bigger Brand after Landing the Rights to 'Showtime at the Apollo'," *Black Enterprise*, October 2003.

McKinney, Jeffrey, and Matthew S. Scott. "Showdown at the Apollo," *Black Enterprise*, January 2003.

Meisler, Andy. "The Beat Goes On for 'Soul Train' Conductor," *New York Times*, August 7, 1995.

Miller, Russell. "Rookies Test City Jest Fest," *Variety*, April 14–20, 1997.

Mitchell, Elvis. "Soul Training," *Village Voice*, August 15, 1999.

"Motown Returns to the Apollo," *Variety*, May 22, 1985.

Neal, Mark Anthony. "Sold Out on Soul: The Corporate Annexation of Black Popular Music," *Popular Music and Society*, Fall 1997.

Nugent, Benjamin. "Train Wreck," *Time*, September 2, 2002.

Page, Clarence. "Signing Off," *Chicago Tribune*, November 8, 2000.

Pinsker, Beth. "Battle of the Networks," *Vibe*, April 2001.

Prestin, Terry. "Percy Sutton's Company Loses 'It's Showtime at the Apollo'," *New York Times*, August 16, 2002.

Pulley, Brett. *The Billion Dollar BET*. Hoboken, New Jersey: John Wiley and Sons, 2004.

Pursell, Chris. "A Tale of 2 'Showtimes'; Battle over Apollo Show Triggers Suit," *Crain's New York Business*, September 2, 2002.

Raines, Johnnie, and Adam Sandler. "Performers Recall Fear of Apollo Auds," *Variety*, April 14–20, 1997.

Reynolds, J. R. "Big draw," *Billboard*, April 29, 1995.

Reynolds, J. R. "Billboard Refutes Soul Train Accusations; April Showers Bring May Conferences," *Billboard*, April 27, 1996.

Reynolds, J. R. "No Stoppin' 'Soul Train' Vet Cornelius," *Billboard*, March 18, 1995.

Riley, Clayton. "A 'Train' on the Soul Track," *New York Times*, February 4, 1973.

Robinson, Leroy. "'Soul Train' & 'Omnibus' Lift Soul TV Hopes," *Billboard*, August 25, 1973.

Ryan, Joal. "'Soul Train' Untracked?" *Eonline.com*, August 20, 2002.

Saunders, Warner. Public interview with Don Cornelius at Museum of Broadcast Communications, Chicago, September 14, 1995.

"'Showtime at the Apollo' Announces New Production Team," *Jet*, September 9, 2002.

Shaw, Sarah-Ann. "The History of *Say Brother*," WGBH.org, 2001.

Shprintz, Janet. "It's Court Time for 'Apollo'," *Daily Variety*, August 27, 2002.

Smith, Danyel. "Changing of Conductors At 'Soul Train'," *Billboard*, October 30, 1993.

"'Soul Train' Plans to Broaden Base," *Billboard*, February, 25, 1984.

Streeter, Leslie Gray. "'Soul Train' Pulls Retro-Maestro Old Navy by the Pants," *Palm Beach Post*, September 7, 2003.

Stewart, Jacqueline. "Negroes Laughing at Themselves? Black Spectatorship and the Performance of Urban Modernity," *Critical Inquiry*, Spring 2003.

Tarlach, Gemma. "Awards Petition Sparks *Soul Train*'s Ire," *Milwaukee Journal Sentinel*, August 22, 2002.

Tate, Greg. "A 20-Year Journey," *Chicago Tribune*, June 19, 1994.

Watson, Jamal. "Apollo at 70," *Amsterdam News*, April 1–7, 2004.

Wicke, Peter. *Rock Music: Culture, Aesthetics and Sociology*. Cambridge, England: Cambridge University Press, 1990.

Wiltz, Teresa, "Ashanti Can't Get Any R-E-S-P-E-C-T," *Alameda Times-Star*, August 20, 2002.

Chapter 5: Never Mind the Bollocks: Here's the Chipmunks!

AI: John Battles, Kim Cooper, Mark Hill, James Porter, Alex Wald

WC: www.chipmunks.com, www.toonarific.com, www.wingnuttoons.com

Bagdasarian, Jr., Ross. *Alvin and the Chipmunks: Forty Years in a Nutshell.* Forthcoming (excerpted on www.chipmunks.com).

Barbera, Joe. *My Life in 'Toons.* Atlanta: Turner Publishing, 1994.

Burke, Timothy, and Kevin Burke. *Saturday Morning Fever: Growing Up with Cartoon Culture.* New York: St. Martin's Griffin, 1999.

Cooper, Kim, and David Smay, editors. *Bubblegum Music Is the Naked Truth.* Los Angeles: Feral House, 2001.

Eaton, Leslie. "Archie Comics and 'Josie' Artist Bare Legal Claws," *New York Times*, February 19, 2001.

Elder, Robert. "Gorillaz Has a Hit Album, but Do They Really Exist?" *Chicago Tribune*, September 7, 2001.

Gifford, Denis. *The Great Cartoon Stars: A Who's Who!* London: Jupiter Books, 1979.

Goldmark, Daniel, and Yuval Taylor, editors. *The Cartoon Music Book.* Chicago: A Capella, 2002.

Maltin, Leonard. *Of Mice and Magic: A History of American Animated Cartoons.* New York: Plume Books, 1987.

Uslan, Michael, and Jeffrey Mendel, editors. *The Best of Archie.* New York: Perigree, 1980.

Waldron, Clarence. "Bill Cosby's Famed Cartoon Character Comes to Life in New Movie, 'Fat Albert,'" *Jet*, December 27, 2004.

Chapter 6: Rock Concert

AI: John Battles, James Porter, Domenic Priore, Randy Young

Alterman, Loraine. "Rock Comes to TV: Well, Sort Of," *New York Times*, April 15, 1973.

Eddy, Chuck. *Stairway to Hell.* New York: Harmony Books, 1991.

Fong-Torres, Ben. "The Decline and Fall of Rock on TV," *Rolling Stone*, October 9, 1975.

Fong-Torres, Ben. "Music Scene," *Rolling Stone*, November 15, 1969.

Gaar, Gillian G. "Love Calls," *Goldmine*, November 6, 1998.

Goodrich, Miles, and Sebastian Goodrich. "The Wonderful World of Sid and Marty Krofft," *Hungry Freaks*, Summer 1997.

Harrison, Ed. "Kirshner Turning a New Direction," *Billboard*, August 20, 1976.

Hecht, Alan. "The Beat Club: Big Daddy of Rock Video," *Record*, March 1984.

Hill, Doug, and Jeff Weingard. *Saturday Night.* New York: Beach Tree, 1986.

Hunter, B. R. *The Midnight Special.* New York: Simon & Schuster, 1997.

Jack, Wolfman, and Byron Laursen. *Have Mercy!* New York: Warner Books, 1995.

"Music Scene," *Rolling Stone*, August 23, 1969.

Ozersky, Josh. "How Come We Overcame and Nobody Told Me," *American Legacy*, Fall 2004.

Rock, Mick. "Bowie Returns: On TV," *Rolling Stone*, December 6, 1973.

Shales, Tom, and James Andrew Miller. *Live From New York.* New York: Little Brown, 2002.

Snyder, Patrick. "R & R Can Be Easy as ABC," *Crawdaddy*, January 1973.

"TV Rock: R&R in Prime Time," *Rolling Stone*, December 6, 1973.

"TV Rock Show," *Rolling Stone*, September 6, 1969.

Werbin, Stuart. "Monkees Man Does 'Fillmore of The Air'," *Rolling Stone*, December 7, 1972.

Werbin, Stuart. "Tubular Rock: The Battle of the Wee Wee Hours," *Rolling Stone*, October 25, 1973.

Yorke, Ritchie. "'Rollin' On The River's' Success Creates TV's First Prime-Time Rock Show," *Billboard*, February 5, 1972.

Chapter 7: Beef Beef Beef Beef Baloney!

AI: Brian Collins, Malcolm T. Danbury, Larry Hardy, Barry Henssler, Anthony Illarde, Andria Lisle, Joe Losurdo, Ian MacKaye, Bloody Mess, Scott Soriano, Barry Stepe, Joey Vindictive, Weasel Walter

Anderson, Mark, and Mark Jenkins. *Dance of Days*. New York: Soft Skull, 2001.

Azerrad, Michael. *Our Band Could Be Your Life*. Boston: Little Brown, 2001,

Battles, John. "The Dickies Dick Around," *Roctober*, Summer 2000.

Blush, Steven. *American Hardcore*. Los Angeles: Feral House, 2001.

Carmody, John. "The TV Column," *Washington Post*, November 3, 1981.

Connolly, Cynthia, Leslie Clague, and Sharon Cheslow. *Banned In DC* (fourth edition). Washington, D.C.: Sun Dog, 1995.

Director, Roger. "Fear and Laughing at 'Saturday Night Live'," *New York Magazine*, November 23, 1981.

Eisenbeis, Hans, editor. "Quincy Punk Rock," *Request Line*, September 1997.

"'Fear' Riot Leaves Saturday Night Glad to Be Alive," *New York Post*, November 2, 1981.

Hanson, Lylee. "Bad Brains Interview," *Damaged Goods*, October 1981.

Hill, Doug, and Jeff Weingard. *Saturday Night*. New York: Beach Tree, 1986.

Holmstrom, John, editor. *Punk: The Original*. New York: Trans-High Publishing, 1996.

James, Darius. *That's Blaxploitation!*. New York: St. Martins, 1995.

Makslan, George. "'Saturday Night' Riot," *Daily News*, November 3, 1981.

Marsh, Dave. "Loony Toons," *Creem*, May 1971.

Nolte, Dan. "Anatomy of an Interview: *Tomorrow* Show 26.6.80," unpublished term paper, 1996.

Novielli, Douglas. "Ian MacKaye," *Verbicide* #5, 2002.

Shales, Tom, and James Andrew Miller. *Live from New York*. New York: Little Brown, 2002.

Vee, Tesco. "VOID," *Touch and Go* #22, 1983.

Yohannon, Tim. "Sab Gray interview," *Maximumrocknroll* 11, 1984.

Chapter 8: Video Vanguard

AI: Chase Adams, Terry LaBan, Phil Milstein, Jacqueline Stewart, Rob Van Winkle

WC: www.fuse.tv, www.mtv.com, www.vh1.com

Altman, Billy. "The Guillotine, Please," *Creem*, January 1985.

Avila, Robert. "Out of Their Heads," *San Francisco Bay Guardian*, June 2, 2004.

Burns, Gary. "Should College Students Study Music Videos?" *Chicago Tribune*, December 14, 1997.

Darling, Cary. "'New Wave Theatre' Cable Show Exposes Rock in Major Markets," *Billboard*, March 21, 1981.

Denisoff, R. Serge. *Inside MTV*, New Brunswick, New Jersey: Transaction Publishers.

"The 50 Greatest Rock Frontmen of All Time," *Spin*, August 2004.

Hay, Carla. "Billboard Salutes Twenty Years of MTV," *Billboard*, July 28, 2001.

Hooper, Joseph. "It's Not All Dazzle: MTV Has a Conscience, Too," *New York Times*, May 14, 2000.

Hoye, Jacob, editor. *MTV Uncensored*. New York: Pocket, 2001.

Jackman, Ian. *Total Request Live*. New York: MTV Books, 2000.

Kaplan, E. Ann. *Rocking Around the Clock: Music Television, Post Modernism and Consumer Culture*. New York: Methuen, 1987.

Kirkeby, Marc. "MTV, 'Night Flight' Lead Cable TV Rock Invasion," *Rolling Stone*, December 10, 1981.

Knopper, Steve. "MTV2: Eclectic Boogaloo," *Spin*, February 2001.

Marcus, Greil. *Ranters & Crowd Pleasers: Punk in Pop Music 1977–1992*. New York: Anchor Books, 1993.

Marsh, Dave, and James Bernard. *The New Book of Rock Lists*. New York: Fireside, 1994.

Roberts, Michael. "Video Obscura: Boulder's Joel Haertling uncovers the roots of MTV," *Denver Westworld*, July 11, 2002.

Schoenfeld, Herm. "TV's New Song Plug Format," *Variety*, November 15, 1967.

Seideman, Tony. "VH-1 Off to Fast Start, Says MTV," *Billboard*, March 30, 1985.

Sheffield, Rob. "MTV: Still Hype-y After All These Years," *Rolling Stone*, September 13, 2001.

Takahashi, Corey. "Getting Back to MTV's Roots, Courtesy of MTV," *New York Times*, December 10, 2000.

Tannenbaum, Rob. "100 Greatest Music Videos Ever Made," *TV Guide*, December 4–10, 1999.

Terenzio, Maurice, Scott MacGillivray, and Ted Okuda. *The Soundies Distributing Corporation of America*. Jefferson, North Carolina: McFarland, 1991.

Wilson, Janelle L. *MTV Ideology: Rocking to a Different Beat*, dissertation, Western Michigan University, 1992.

Wolf, Michael. *The Entertainment Economy*. New York: Random House, 1999.

Chapter 9: Idol Bands Are the Devil's Workshop

AI: Kelly Christiel, Bobby Conn, Jacqueline Goldsby, L. S. Kim, Phil Milstein, Jennifer Peterson, Nikki Stewart

WC: www.idolonfox.com

"Accidental Idol." *Redeye*, April 6, 2004.

Adkins, Greg. "Justin Guarini: Fallen American Idol?" *People Weekly*, December 22, 2003.

Adkins, Greg. "She Bangs, He Sang," *People Weekly*, March 1, 2004.

Berger, Arion. "Orchestrated 'Idols' with Real Live Fans," *Washington Post*, July 30, 2003.

Boehm, Erich. "Striking a Chord," *Variety*, February 26, 2001.

Breznican, Anthony. "Rating of 'Idol' Finale Music to Fox Ears," *Chicago Tribune*, May 23, 2003.

Breznican, Anthony. "'Idol' Minds Give Simon Fuller His Cut," *Red Streak*, January 20, 2004.

Brogan, Elizabeth. "O-joy; 'Making the Band' Apparently Will End Its Run on MTV, and That's Just Fine with the Young Men of O-Town, Who Want to Get on with Making music," *Portland Press Herald*, May 16, 2002.

Brown, Jamie Foster. "The Real Ruben," *Sister 2 Sister,* August 2003.

Christenson, Elise. "Reality TV: A 'Hood Divided,'" *Newsweek*, May 19, 2003.

Chusid, Irwin. *Songs in the Key of* Z. Chicago: A Capella, 2000.

Clover, Joshua. "Jukebox Culture," *Spin*, July 2000.

Elias, Albert J. "The Story of 'The Original Amateur Hour'," *Etude*, September 1956.

"Elton John Decries 'Idol' Voting as 'Incredibly Racist,'" Associated Press, April 29, 2004.

France, Kim. "Sad Stories Say So Much," *Spin*, December 1998.

Gladstone, Valerie. "Reality-Show Pop Stars Need a Choreographer, Too," *New York Times*, April 1, 2001.

Graham, Renee. "Life in the Pop Lane; In Reality, 'Band 2' Is Good for a Laugh," *Boston Globe*, August 12, 2003.

"Hung Butchers 'Take Me Out to the Ball Game,'" Associated Press, May 31, 2004.

Hunter, James. "Video Killed the Radio Star," *Rolling Stone*, April 25, 2000.

Johnson, Steve. "'Idol' Triumphs as Vintage-Era Family Viewing," *Chicago Tribune*, May 22, 2003.

James, Meg. "Cobbling Together This Really Cute Young Band," *New York Times*, March 24, 2000.

James, Meg. "Realizing 'Idol' Dreams," *Chicago Tribune*, January 14, 2004.

Kim, L. S., and Gilberto Moisés Blasini. "The Performance of Multicultural Identity in U.S. Network Television: Shiny, Happy Popstars (Holding Hands)," *Emergences* 11:2, 2001.

Klein, Joshua. "'American Idol' Tour on a Roll," *Chicago Tribune*, July 11, 2003.

Klein, Joshua. "Idle concert," *Redeye*, July 10, 2003.

Marzorati, Gerald. "Rock of Ages," *New York Times*, April 23, 2000.

"MTV's 'I Want a Famous Face' Sets a Dangerous Course Says the American Society for Aesthetic Plastic Surgery," press release, April 1, 2004.

Ogunnaike, Lola. "Strive, Rookie Rappers; Only the Tough Survive; Musical Combat in P. Diddy's Reality Series Competes with the Drama of Troubled Lives," *New York Times*, December 23, 2002.

O-Town and K. M. Squires. *Making the Band.* New York: MTV Books, 2000.

Pappas, Ben. "The Agony & The Ecstasy!" *Us Weekly*, May 26, 2003.

People Extra: The Secrets of American Idol, May 2003.

Petrozzello, Donna. "MTV's 'Making the Band II' features Murder and Drama," *New York Daily News*, October 18, 2002.

Peyser, Marc, and Sean M. Smith. "'Idol' Worship: So Who's It Going to Be: Clay or Ruben? Thirty Million People Can't Stand the Suspense. Inside 'American Idol,' TV's Most Addictive Show," *Newsweek*, May 26, 2003.

Peyser, Marc. "Television: So Bad, It's Good," *Newsweek*, June 24, 2002.

Phillgood, Dr. "Da Band: Too Hot for TV," *Black Beat*, February 2004.

Sandler, Adam. "Cabler markets a new tune," *Variety*, November 2–8, 1998.

Seibel, Deborah Starr. "American Idol's Secrets Revealed," *TV Guide*, March 13–19, 2004.

Seibel, Deborah Starr. "And Now for Their Next Act," *TV Guide*, November 22–28, 2003.

Shaw, Jessica. "American Cheese," *Entertainment Weekly*, March 28, 2003.

Sheffield, Rob. "Enough!" *Rolling Stone*, May 29, 2003.

Showalter, Elaine. "Window on reality: American Idol and the search for identity," *The American Prospect*, July–August 2003.

Smith, Casper Llewellyn. "The Idol Maker," *Blender*, March 2004.

Snierson, Dan. "Joe Mastermind," *Entertainment Weekly*, March 28, 2003.

Tauber, Michael. "Idol Showdown," *People*, May 26, 2003.

Thomas, Harry. "Making the Band," *Rolling Stone*, April 27, 2000.

Thomas, Harry. "Q & A: Gay Rosenthal," *Rolling Stone*, October 12, 2000.

Chapter 10: Michael Jackson

AI: Barbara Holt, Calvin Lincoln, Joe Losurdo, Jim Peterik, Jacqueline Stewart.

WC: www.funkymjsite.co.uk, www.home1.stofanet.dk/Jackson5, www.michaeljackson.com, www.michaelvideos.ro

Akil II, Bakari. "Dick Gregory's Comments on Michael Jackson," *Creativity*, Spring 2004.

Bego, Mark. *Michael!* New York: Pinnacle Books, 1984.

Bego, Mark. *On the Road with Michael!* New York: Pinnacle Books, 1984.

Bernhard, Lisa. "The Once and Future King," *TV Guide*, December 4–10, 1999.

Garr, Gillian G. "It's a Family Affair: The Triumphs and Tribulations of the Jacksons," *Goldmine*, October 13, 1995.

Goldberg, Michael. "The Making of the King of Pop," *Rolling Stone*, January 9, 1992.

Gross, Michael Joseph. "Among the Jackson Faithful," *New York Times*, January 25, 2004.

Jackson, Hal. *The House That Jack Built.* New York: Amistad, 2001.

Jackson, Michael. *Moon Walk.* New York: Doubleday, 1988.

"Jackson Tells CBS He'd Never Hurt Child," Associated Press, December 27, 2003.

Johnson, Steve. "Freak Show," *Chicago Tribune*, January 19, 2004.

Light, Alan. "Michael Jackson: Art and Life as Performance," *Rolling Stone*, January 9, 1992.

McGruder, Aaron. "The Boondocks," Universal Press Syndicate, January 28, 2004.

"Michael & Me," *Vibe*, June–July, 1995.

Motoviloff, Ellen. *The Jackson 5*. New York: Scholastic Books, 1971.

Murphy, Mary, and Jennifer Graham. "The Man in the Mirror," *TV Guide*, November 10–16, 2001.

Powers, Ann. "Just What Does Michael Jackson's Story Add Up To?" *New York Times*, February 13, 1993.

Schodolski, Vincent J. "Jackson Faces Child Molestation Charges," *Chicago Tribune*, November 20, 2003.

Schodolski, Vincent J. "Jackson Lawyer Charges 'Big Lie'," *Chicago Tribune*, November 21, 2003.

Smith, Sid. "Candid Couple," *Chicago Tribune*, June 15, 1995.

Smith, Sid. "Jackson Special Fawning, Ill-Timed," *Chicago Tribune*, January 10, 2004.

Taraborrelli, J. Randy. *Michael Jackson: The Magic and the Madness*. Secaucus, New Jersey: Birch Lane Press, 1991.

Williams, L. Pat. "Media Makes Light of Michael's Plight," *Chicago Defender*, November 20, 2003.

Wilson, Jeff. "Sheriff Denies Jackson Claim of Abuse in Jail," Associated Press, January 1, 2004.

Appendix I: International TV Rock

AI: Thomas Edward Shaw, Speedo, Alex Wald, Paul Zone

WC: www.bbc.uk/TOTP, www.eurovision.tv/english, www.muz-tv.ru

Fowler, Susanne. "Music World Turns Its Eyes to Istanbul," *Chicago Tribune*, May 14, 2004.

Hecht, Alan. "The Beat Club: Big Daddy of Rock Video," *Record*, March 1984.

Hyde, Emil. "Out of (Remote) Control," *Roctober*, Spring 2004.

"Kikaida: An Introduction," Generationkikaida.com, April 2004.

Mier, Brian. "A Turma do Balao Magico," *Roctober*, Summer 2001.

Shaw, Thomas Edward, and Anita Klemke. *Black Monk Time*. Carson City, Nevada: Carson City Press, 1993.

Stevenson, Jack. "Eurovision: The Candy Coated Song Factory," *Bubblegum Music Is The Naked Truth*. Los Angeles: Feral House, 2001.

Appendix 2: Rock 'n' Roll TV Guide

AI: Pedro Bell, Art Fein, Mark Hill, Anthony Illarde, Rachel Lichtman, Calvin Lincoln, Hedda Sharapan, Harry Young

Chusid, Irwin. *Songs in the Key of Z*. Chicago: A Capella, 2000.

Greenfield, Jeff. *Television: Prime Time-News-Sports*. New York: Savings of America, 1980.

Homes, Jr., Venice. *The Beverly Hills 90210 Guide*. East Lansing, Michigan: New King, 1993.

Johnston, Ian. *The Wild Wild World of the Cramps*. London: Omnibus, 1990.

King, Norman. *Arsenio Hall*. New York: William Morrow and Company, 1992.

Paytress, Mark, and Steve Patford. *Bowie Style*. London: Omnibus, 2000.

Ritz, David. *Divided Soul*. New York: Da Capo, 1990.

Travis, Dempsey. *The Life and Times of Redd Foxx*. Chicago: Urban Research Press, 1999.

General Reference

Bego, Mark. *TV Rock*. New York: Paperjacks, 1989.

Brooks, Tim, and Earle Marsh. *The Complete Directory to Prime Time Network and Cable TV Shows 1946–Present*. New York: Ballantine Books, 2003.

McNeil, Alex. *Total Television*. New York: Penguin, 1996.

Newcombe, Horace, editor. *The Museum of Broadcast Communications Encyclopedia of Television*. New York: Fitzroy Dearborn, 1997.

Weingarten, Marc. *Station to Station*. New York: Pocket, 2000.

Whitburn, Joel. *Top Pop Singles 1955–2002*. Menemonee Falls, Wisconsin: Record Research, Inc., 2002.

Whitburn, Joel. *Top Pop Albums 1955–2001*. Menemonee Falls, Wisconsin: Record Research, 2002.

In addition, the following Web sites served as references:

www.epguide.com

www.imdb.com

www.jumptheshark.com

www.mtv.com

www.tvparty.com

www.tvtome.com

www.vh1.com

Index